Liberalism in Illiberal States

Liberalism in Illiberal States

Ideas and Economic Adjustment in Contemporary Europe

MARK I. VAIL

OXFORD
UNIVERSITY PRESS

OXFORD
UNIVERSITY PRESS

Oxford University Press is a department of the University of Oxford. It furthers the University's objective of excellence in research, scholarship, and education by publishing worldwide. Oxford is a registered trade mark of Oxford University Press in the UK and in certain other countries.

Published in the United States of America by Oxford University Press
198 Madison Avenue, New York, NY 10016, United States of America.

Library of Congress Cataloging-in-Publication Data
Names: Vail, Mark I., author.
Title: Liberalism in illiberal states : ideas and economic adjustment
in contemporary Europe / by Mark I. Vail.
Description: New York, NY, United States of America : Oxford University Press, [2018]
Identifiers: LCCN 2017024581 | ISBN 9780190683986 (hardcover) |
ISBN 9780190683993 (pbk.) | ISBN 9780190684006 (updf) | ISBN 9780190684013 (epub)
Subjects: LCSH: Neoliberalism—Europe. | Europe—Economic policy—21st century.
Classification: LCC JC574.2.E85 V35 2018 | DDC 320.51/3094—dc23
LC record available at https://lccn.loc.gov/2017024581

1 3 5 7 9 8 6 4 2

Paperback printed by Webcom, Inc., Canada
Hardback printed by Bridgeport National Bindery, Inc., United States of America

To Charlotte, who keeps the faith

CONTENTS

LIST OF TABLES

PREFACE

While firmly grounded in the tradition of comparative political economy, in some respects this book is also a hybrid, marrying insights and methodologies from other approaches and strands of scholarship. From political theory, it embraces the conviction that grappling with political concepts can change collective ways of thinking and is thus constitutive of political and economic life itself. It shares with intellectual history the notion that the evolution of policy and politics is shaped by ideas and dialogue among their multiple adherents, many of whom do not enjoy canonized status. From political sociology, it accepts the idea that our ways of organizing our collective political and economic lives are deeply socially embedded and that, as Karl Polanyi taught us long ago, the political, social, and economic spheres are inextricably intertwined and mutually constitutive. More generally, the book rests on the conviction that there are advantages to an analytical strategy receptive to these multiple facets of human existence, one that goes beyond a focus on narrowly delimited institutional or policy contexts to seek to understand the broader intellectual currents and traditions that shape our collective lives. Such an approach has costs in terms of parsimony, perhaps, but these limitations, I believe, are outweighed by the richness of the accounts that it enables one to develop and the nuanced attention to intellectual, political, and social context that it affords.

In more specific terms, the book's analytical and evidentiary strategy is informed by elements of two distinct scholarly approaches. The first is what Peter Hall and others have labeled "systematic process analysis" or "process tracing," whereby scholars investigate and explain political and economic outcomes through attention to the (often complex) processes whereby they occur, with a view to seeing "if the multiple actions and statements of the actors at each stage of the causal process are consistent with the image of the world implied by [a] theory."[1] In other respects, it parallels what Skocpol and Somers, in their celebrated analysis of comparative history and historical sociology, have called "comparative history as the contrast of contexts," whereby scholars "make use of comparative history to bring out the unique features of each particular case included in their discussions, and to show how these unique features affect the working-out of putatively general social processes."[2] Unlike practitioners of both of these approaches, however, it explicitly privileges ideas as causal variables in their own right that shape our political and economic universes by informing our individual and collective understandings in politically operative ways. It shares this conviction with the now-burgeoning literature on the power and enduring influence of political ideas.

The book's principal source of primary data is a collection of 136 interviews with a wide array of political and economic elites, including officials in trade unions and employers' associations, members of political parties, and officials in government ministries, as well as members of research institutes and intergovernmental and nongovernmental organizations, scholars, economists, and journalists, who provided both useful perspective on the events under study and indispensable contacts. These interviews were conducted during four discontinuous periods: 2000–2002, 2006–7, 2011, and 2014–16, with the bulk of those used here coming from the most recent three time spans. Anomalous claims unsupported either by other interview data or by publicly available statements and documents were disregarded, and interviews are cited only when they corroborate accounts supported by other data sources, including but not limited to other interviews, some of which are indicated in the notes. The large majority of interviews were conducted in person, usually in the subject's professional office, though a few, particularly in the most recent period, were conducted via phone or electronic correspondence. In most cases, they were conducted in the subjects' native language so as to afford them the greatest possible ability to convey nuance and context.

Finally, a note on language: throughout the book, translations of quotations in French, German, and Italian from both interviews and secondary sources are my own, except for some English translations (from translated editions of works originally written in another language, for example) that I render in the original.

ACKNOWLEDGMENTS

This book has been many years in the writing, and I have accumulated a longer-than-usual list of debts in the process. The list's length is also a function of the book's subject matter. It grapples with a complex topic—liberalism—with complex lineages in a wide range of disciplines—including political science, philosophy, history, and economics. Accordingly, I have sought advice from a wide range of colleagues whose perspectives have greatly enriched the product and prevented me from making a number of significant missteps. Furthermore, because the book grew out of some of the questions explored in my first monograph, my debts extend back many years. I am grateful to all of those who helped me to clarify my ideas, sharpen my arguments, extend my empirical and theoretical reach, and maintain the focus that completing a work of this kind requires. Any shortcomings of the work are of course my own.

I would like first to thank a number of institutions and foundations that have provided both residential and financial support. A formative sabbatical year (2012–13) as a fellow at the Center for Advanced Study in the Behavioral Sciences at Stanford University provided the kind of uninterrupted time and intellectual space necessary for my central arguments to begin to crystallize. Unsurpassed in infrastructure and intellectual resources, the CASBS also provided an intellectual community of unparalleled richness. I am grateful to all of those fellows—in particular K. T. Albiston, Michael Anderson, Cynthia Gordon, Melissa Lane, Jon Levy, Craig Murphy, Anne and Konstantin Pollok, Timothy Schroeder, Kenneth Schultz, Deborah Tannen, JoAnne Yates, and Daniel Ziblatt—with whom long and leisurely conversations about our respective research agendas helped sharpen my ideas. I also spent fruitful periods of research at the Hanse Wissenschaftskolleg (Delmenhorst, Germany), which also contributed financial support (2009–10); the Institut für Politikwissenschaft at the Universität Duisburg-Essen (2014); and the Max Planck / Sciences Po Center on Coping with Instability in Market Societies in Paris (summer 2017), where I put the finishing touches on the manuscript. All of these institutions provided me with intellectual homes away from home and communities from which I drew great support and fellowship.

Though one cannot live by bread alone, it certainly helps, particularly when one is in the field. I am very grateful to a number of institutions, both American and European, for financial support for this project. First, I would like to thank the American Council of Learned Societies for generous support in the form of a Frederick Burkhardt Residential Fellowship for Recently Tenured Scholars, which funded my time at the CASBS (2012–13); the Alexander von Humboldt Stiftung, which financed multiple short-term research trips to Germany and furnished me with my first opportunity for sustained research in the country through a Bundeskanzler Stipendium (2000–2001); Tulane University's School of Liberal Arts, which provided significant financial support through a Young Professor Fellowship, a Georges Lurcy Fellowship, and a subvention grant that helped defray the book's publication costs; and Tulane's Office of the Provost for summer travel funds and a grant from the Committee on Research. Without the support of these institutions, I could never have begun this book, much less completed it.

The list of friends and colleagues who have provided perspective and incisive feedback on my work, as well as helpful suggestions for contacts and scholarly resources, is equally long. Particular acknowledgement is due to three individuals, each of whom has offered his own admixture of invaluable scholarly perspective and friendship. First, I would like to thank Jonah Levy, my dissertation chair at Berkeley, who provided the ideal combination of exacting scholarly standards, generosity with time, and active support and encouragement that only the best advisers can provide. Jonah taught me the craft of comparative political economy, patiently guiding me through graduate school and teaching me to take joy from my successes and to learn from my many mistakes. Since that time, he has acted as an invaluable scholarly mentor and supportive friend. Second, I thank Mark Blyth, whose work has provided this project with important intellectual touchstones and whose support and generous feedback, on both various iterations of parts of this book and my work in general, has been indispensable. A friend and mentor in equal measure, Mark has provided an exemplar of that elusive balance of intellectual ambition, modesty, and painstaking care that is essential to great scholarship. Third, I would like to express my gratitude to Robert Adcock. Since our time as graduate students at Berkeley, Robert, acting as an incisive discussion partner, has helped me to deepen my understanding of my craft, allowed me to benefit from his rare combination of deep knowledge as both a first-rate political theorist and an outstanding methodologist, been an engaged and responsive co-author, and provided patient and insightful feedback on chapters of this book. He has also been a wonderful friend and offered support during difficult times.

In the eight years that I have been working on this book, many other individuals have provided vital intellectual, logistical, and personal support. In particular, Benjamin Bowyer, Robert Fannion, Achim Goerres, Chris Howell, Wade Jacoby, Naomi Levy, Sara Watson, and Sarah Wiliarty have all been crucial sources of perspective on the book's central arguments and close friends besides. I extend particular thanks to Tony and Donna Cook, who have provided a special combination of intellectual companionship and warm friendship that is all too rare. Special thanks are also due to Philippe Popovitch and Edwige Le Brettevillois-Popovitch, who have hosted me in France multiple times and helped me to see their beautiful and complex country through native eyes, as well as offering important logistical support during my time in the field. Achim Goerres and Andrea Diepen-Goerres did much the same in Germany, bringing me into their home on numerous occasions and making me and my family feel very much a part of theirs. Alison Kaufman and Piret Loone both furnished valued friendship and support during my travels. Others who provided valuable feedback on portions of the manuscript or contributed in conversation to the development of its central ideas include Karen Anderson, Jenny Andersson, Klaus Armingeon, Cornel Ban, Sylvain Brouard, Marius Busemeyer, Pepper Culpepper, Michael Freeden, Jane Gingrich, Olivier Godechot, Peter Hall, Gary Herrigel, Jonathan Hopkin, Nicolas Jabko, Paulette Kurzer, Patrick Le Galès, Julia Lynch, Deborah Mabbet, Benjamin Martill, Matthias Matthijs, Linsey McGoey, Kathleen McNamara, Kimberly Morgan, Abraham Newman, Darius Ornston, Craig Parsons, Sidney Rothstein, Waltraud Schelkle, Tobias Schulze-Cleven, Herman Mark Schwartz, Nicolas Véron, and Cornelia Woll. Lipaz Avigal, Katherine Hillman, Michael Jones, Lauren Sobel, and Jake Ward furnished helpful and in some cases indefatigable research assistance, with Michael in particular going above and beyond any reasonable expectations. I extend my apologies in advance to individuals whom I will inevitably have omitted from this list.

At Tulane, a number of colleagues furnished valuable feedback on parts of the work and its core ideas, including Brian Brox, Patrick Egan, John Howard, Gary Remer, Eduardo Silva, and Martyn Thompson. Members of the Political Science Department's "Young [though ever less so] Faculty Seminar," at which parts of this work were presented, also offered helpful suggestions on how to improve the work. I would also like to thank Mary Clark, Christopher Fettweis, Mark Gasiorowski, J. Celeste Lay, and Nancy Maveety for their friendship and support when times were tough. Librarians Eric Wedig and Adam Beauchamp helped me to ferret out essential bibliographic resources and data sources, and Jennifer O'Brien and Gregory LeBlanc furnished outstanding administrative support and made the department run effectively, often against considerable odds.

At Oxford University Press, I am grateful to David McBride, who provided sustained support for the project and shepherded it through the publication process, and to Kathleen Weaver and Emily Mackenzie, both of whom provided outstanding editorial support once the book was under contract. I am also grateful to three anonymous reviewers who provided incisive critiques and helpful suggestions that resulted in a much better final product.

Closer to home, I would like to thank my parents, Dennis and Gwyndolen Vail, who have supported my scholarly career from its inception and helped to instill in me the intellectual curiosity out of which it has grown. My father also proofread an intermediate version of the manuscript with meticulous care, allowing me to benefit from his unmatched sense of language. I owe both of them enormous debts of gratitude that I will never be able fully to repay.

Finally, I would like to thank my wife, Charlotte Maheu Vail. It's hard to know how exactly to thank someone who has been supportive in so many ways. Charlotte has bolstered my confidence when it was at low ebb, patiently read and provided feedback on portions of the manuscript, done well more than her share in caring for our daughter, Claire, when my work on the book was at its most frenzied, and been amazingly patient throughout the entire process. Charlotte epitomizes levels of kindness, warmth, selflessness, and integrity to which I can only aspire. This book is dedicated to her.

ABBREVIATIONS

ACP	Autorité de contrôle prudentiel et de résolution
ANPE	Agence nationale pour l'emploi
BA	Bundesagentur für Arbeit
BaFin	Bundesanstalt für Finanzdienstleistungsaufsicht
BCC	Banche di credito cooperativo
BNP	Banque nationale de Paris
BP	Banche popolari
BPCE	Banque populaire caisse d'épargne
CDU	Christlich Demokratische Union Deutschlands
CGIL	Confederazione generale Italiana del lavoro
CISL	Confederazione Italiana sindacati lavoratori
CGP	Commissariat général du Plan
CSU	Christlich-Soziale Union
DC	Democrazia Cristiana
DDR	Deutsche Demokratische Republik
DM	Deutsche Mark
DPEF	*Documento di programmazione economico-finanziaria*
ECB	European Central Bank
EEC	European Economic Community
EMS	European Monetary System
EMU	European Economic and Monetary Union
ENA	École nationale d'administration
ENI	Ente nazionale idrocarburi
ERM	Exchange-rate mechanism
ETC	Employment and Training Companies
EU	European Union
FAMA	Financial Activity Modernization Act
FDP	Freie Demokratische Partei

FMSA	Federal Agency for Financial Market Stabilization
GDP	Gross domestic product
GNP	Gross national product
HRE	Hypo real estate
IAB	Institut für Arbeitsmarkt und Berufsforschung
IG BCE	Industriegewerkschaft Bergbau, Chemie, Energie
IG Metall	Industriegewerkschaft Metall
IMF	International Monetary Fund
IRI	Istituto per la riconstruzione industriale
MEDEF	Mouvement des entreprises de France
MPS	Banca monte dei paschi di Siena
NPL	Non-performing loans
OECD	Organization for Economic Cooperation and Development
OPEC	Organization of the Petroleum Exporting Countries
PAP	*Projet d'action personalisé*
PARE	*Plan d'aide et de retour à l'emploi*
PCI	Partito comunista Italiano
PD	Partito democratico
PDS	Partito democratico della sinistra
PLI	Partito liberale Italiano
PSI	Partito socialista Italiano
RMA	*Revenu minimum d'activité*
RMI	*Revenu minimum d'insertion*
RPR	Rassemblement pour la République
RSA	*Revenu de solidarité active*
SEA	Single European Act
SFEF	Société de financement de l'économie française
SFSA	Savings and Financial Security Act
SME	Small and medium-sized enterprise
SoFFin	Sonderfonds Finanzmarktstabilisierung
SPD	Sozial Demokratische Partei Deutschlands
SPPE	Société de prise de participation de l'État
TSCG	Treaty on Stability, Coordination and Governance in the Economic and Monetary Union
TVA	*Taxe sur la valeur ajoutée*
UIL	Unione Italiana del lavoro
UNEDIC	Union nationale interprofessionnelle pour l'emploi dans l'industrie et le commerce
VAT	Value-added tax

Liberalism in Illiberal States

Introduction

National Liberalisms in Illiberal States

Competing Conceptions of Economic Order in Contemporary Europe

> Heine told us not to underestimate the quiet philosopher sitting in his study; if Kant had not undone theology, Robespierre might not have cut off the head of the king of France.
>
> —Isaiah Berlin, *"A Message to the Twenty-First Century"*

It is a truism that the postwar era has been one of ascendant liberalism, even if its liberal character has not been uncontested.[1] During the boom of the 1950s and 1960s, political and economic liberalism informed the limits on state power, individual and collective rights to political and economic self-governance, and models of market-based economic growth that became the hallmarks of capitalist democracies across the advanced industrial world. With widespread democratization beginning in the 1970s, the wave of market-based reform, privatization, and deregulation that followed in the 1980s, and the fall of the Berlin Wall and collapse of the former Soviet Empire in the early 1990s, political and economic liberalism came to be viewed as established paradigms, with departures from these norms viewed as either temporary aberrations or authoritarian impositions that lacked long-term viability. Self-satisfied proclamations of the "end of history"[2] and the self-righteous dominance of the so-called Washington Consensus[3] in the 1990s and early 2000s, as well as the continuing political force of many of its core precepts thereafter, were both reflections and reinforcing causes of this sense of liberal hegemony. This putative consensus suggested that the fundamental questions of how political economies were to be organized had been permanently settled in favor of representative democracy and a dominant, if contested, understanding of market-based capitalism, the two of which were presumed to fit hand in glove.

In some respects this is hardly surprising, given the rich history of liberal thought in the West and its central place in the Enlightenment, the early modern repudiation of absolutism and mercantilism, and the conceptions of capitalism and political liberty that were developed and consolidated in the eighteenth and nineteenth centuries. One could indeed argue that liberalism, more than any other set of values, came to constitute the core of Western self-conception, even if the dark legacies of slavery and colonialism significantly tarnished its standing. As early as the nineteenth century, debates about how societies should be organized began to acknowledge the compelling narratives of political self-determination and economic freedom central to liberalism, although, as in the cases of Wilhelmine Germany and Tsarist Russia, this model confronted powerful alternative models. With the defeat of fascism in 1945, the Manichean liberal/anti-liberal dichotomy of the late nineteenth century gave way to a new dualism of liberal capitalism and communism, a contrast which served to consolidate the self-understanding of liberal societies as both morally and ethically superior and more durable. The end of the Cold War and fall of the Berlin Wall seemed to validate these conceptions and suggested that the individual yearning for freedom could be frustrated only temporarily and that those who sought to suppress it did so at their peril, even if more recent events in Europe and the United States have led to justified concern about the resilience of political democracy. With respect to economic matters, this liberal ascendancy has been more unqualified, accompanied and reinforced by an increasingly unquestioning faith in the power of markets as the indispensable and nearly infallible mechanism of humans' economic organization—a modern variant of the "liberal creed" that Karl Polanyi identified with the rise of industrial capitalism in the nineteenth century.[4]

Unfortunately, the generalized use of liberalism as a descriptor of the character of advanced political economies since the 1980s has not been matched with systematic rigor as to its content or its variability, a fact which has undermined our ability to distinguish among variants of liberal societies. In many respects, "liberalism" has become a trope, a moniker invoked equally in Whiggish and self-congratulatory narratives of human progress and in criticism directed at other, ostensibly less free societies, with no ontologically stable notion of its core precepts. In this respect, liberalism has come to be understood more in terms of what it is not (e.g., authoritarian, statist, collectivist) than in terms of what it is, a core value defined by its enemies more than its principles,[5] except in the broadest sense of ill-defined and often self-serving notions of "freedom" and "liberty."[6]

This conceptual vagueness has contributed to liberalism's imprecise application to capitalist democracies, which are generally understood to be related by what they share rather than by how they differ. It has also, somewhat ironically, given rise to an alluring but misleading sense that the United States (as embodying the ostensibly purest form of both political and economic liberalism) represents a point around which, for example, more statist (such as France) and neocorporatist (such as Germany) models should be expected to converge.[7] In this way, liberalism is seen to act as both a leveler of national differences and a Platonic form that will eventually be reflected, with increasing degrees of clarity and purity, in all national manifestations of democratic capitalism, despite periodic challenges to democratic politics and recognition of its vulnerabilities.

Such constraining conceptual homogeneity has been even more characteristic of economic liberalism than of its political variant. To the extent that the content of economic liberalism and the policies and institutions that it underpins have been examined critically, they have tended to be conflated under the rubric of "neoliberalism," a practice that both reflects and reinforces a prevailing tendency to gloss over national differences.[8] This use of "neoliberalism" as a catch-all category for liberalism of all stripes has reduced the term to a more or less pre-established package of essentially negative policy prescriptions, such as privatization, fiscal retrenchment, and deregulation. David Harvey defines neoliberalism as "a theory of political economic practices that proposes that human well-being can best be advanced by liberating individual entrepreneurial freedoms and skills within an institutional framework characterized by strong private property rights, free markets, and free trade." It understands the state's role as "to create and preserve an institutional framework appropriate to such practices," involving "much 'creative destruction' . . . of divisions of labour, social relations, welfare provisions, . . . and ways of life and thought," with a view to creating a social and economic order that "seeks to bring all human action into the domain of the market."[9] By and large, the neoliberal program is seen as varying little with respect to its core precepts across time and place. The reflexive invocation of "neoliberalism" in analyses of political-economic change in continental Europe implies a consensus about limits on state activity and public authority, but one which lacks a substantive and affirmative understanding of how society and the economy should be organized.

As Jamie Peck has eloquently shown, this ambiguity, combined with an essentially negative set of policy and institutional commitments, has allowed neoliberalism to rise to the status of a hegemonic discourse without ever specifying how its core commitments fit with particular domestic political and economic circumstances. Echoing Harvey's assessment, Peck argues that, "for all its doctrinal certainty, the neoliberal project is paradoxically defined by the very *unattainability* of its fundamental goal—frictionless market rule. . . . Pristine definitions of neoliberalization are therefore simply unavailable; instead, concretely grounded accounts of the process must be chiseled out of the interstices of state/market configurations."[10] In this sense, prevailing critiques of neoliberalism as prescribing a highly disembedded social and economic order are unarguable but also tend to miss the point.[11] The transnational, messianic doctrine of neoliberalism, as it has developed since the 1970s, was never intended by its architects to acknowledge and adapt to national political-economic institutions, which are deeply embedded in established fabrics of national life.[12] Instead, as Andrew Gamble reminds us, it was understood as an ideological cudgel with which to "overhaul . . . existing institutions in radical ways," including arrangements such as collective-bargaining institutions and welfare states, which were viewed as impediments to the expansion of market order.[13] In this respect, the central proposition of neoliberalism and the classical liberal tradition from which it drew, that "social relations . . . are a frictional drag that impedes competitive markets,"[14] was a highly ideological position whose aims were essentially negative and reactive rather than affirmative and constructive.

In this context, it is hardly surprising that domestic political traditions bear at best a distant resemblance to such a transnational, quasi-hegemonic paradigm. It follows that attempts to impose such paradigms, whether through the deliberate efforts of policymakers or the reshaped preferences or default assumptions of influential elites, should encounter impediments, resistance, and distortion. This is particularly the case in political economies where the stark, abstract visions of classical liberalism and neoliberalism are marginal to prevailing political discourses. As I detail in Chapter 1, in such states alternative liberal traditions, worked out over more than a century and long before the ascendancy of the conceptually tidy but highly abstract neoliberal visions of a hegemonic market order, have provided nationally distinctive answers to the complex and vexing questions of the desirable extent and character of state intervention in the economy and responsibility for societal welfare, the proper understanding of social structures and relations, and the appropriate scope of market forces as against social, familial, religious, or community ties. The rise of capitalism in the late eighteenth and nineteenth centuries fundamentally transformed the European social and economic orders, transformations perhaps global in their implications but decidedly national in their effects. It also brought in its wake efforts by generations of political and economic thinkers to understand the transformations taking place around them, which represented significant departures from standard templates.[15] In this respect, both classical liberalism in the nineteenth century and neoliberalism since the 1970s—both highly abstract bodies of thought insensitive to variation across time and place—have acted as foils and catalysts for the evolution of national liberal traditions that depart from or even repudiate many of their core premises, even as adherents of these traditions attempt to work out the contours of political and institutional frameworks that socially embedded economic orders inevitably require.[16]

In so doing, political and economic elites in economically illiberal states have developed their own distinctive traditions and, in the process, demonstrated the limitations and impracticability of classical and neoliberalism as hypostasized doctrines of economic order. In this respect, liberal traditions in continental Europe have implicitly called into question the notions, central to neoliberalism and its classical liberal forbear alike, that, in Philip Cerny's formulation, "the future of capitalism lies in enabling 'neoliberal and entrepreneurial man' to act in competitive ways in markets structured around the price mechanism" and that society must be "reinvented along neoliberal lines."[17] Instead, the working out of these traditions over time has been nourished by the twin convictions that neoliberalism is incompatible in important respects with socially embedded capitalism and that markets must be embedded if they are to function either politically or economically.

Of course, the political activation of national alternatives to neoliberalism does not happen in a vacuum; rather, it takes place in dialogue with and against the background of other traditions developed in response to other political and economic dilemmas, all of which have likewise influenced national policy trajectories. French statism, German neocorporatism, and Italian clientelism all emerged in response to distinctive challenges relating to state building, national unification, industrialization, and the consolidation and legitimation of democracy in the nineteenth and twentieth centuries, even if some of these responses were more adaptive than others. As Rogers Smith has reminded us in the American context, however, national traditions are *always* multiple, representing the culminations of a series of parallel but distinct national conversations about the character of social and economic transformations and the proper responses to them.[18] In many cases, as with German liberalism and neocorporatism, these traditions evolve in dialogue with one another.[19] As French, German, and Italian officials have responded to evolving sets of economic challenges since the 1970s, they have sought to synthesize the commitments of their national liberal traditions with the institutional and ideational manifestations of these alternative traditions, sometimes more successfully than others.

Although they have evolved in dialogue with other traditions, national liberalisms, with their distinctive conceptions of the appropriate character of state action in the economic sphere and the proper understanding of its responsibility to society, speak more directly to the kinds of economic uncertainty detailed in this book. When inherited assumptions and institutional arrangements (such as French statist and German neocorporatist frameworks), fashioned under quite different political and economic circumstances, come under pressure, national liberal traditions both frame the ways that elites seek to understand the challenges facing them and help to define the range of politically feasible responses to the questions that they pose.[20] If French, German, and Italian postwar arrangements represented one set of answers to these questions in a particular place and at a particular time, they should not be conflated with national traditions themselves, whose ambit is much broader and whose concepts are older than such limited institutional blueprints represent. The constitutionally based distributions of authority embodied by Europe's postwar models represented but one manifestation of the richer understandings of economic community and political-economic authority inhering in such traditions, which are of much less recent vintage. As authorities sought to fashion adaptive responses to the challenges of austerity and slowed growth after the 1970s, they would again draw on these traditions in important ways, even as they operated within a set of institutionalized incentives and constraints represented by their political-economic models. In the process, they implicitly (and sometimes explicitly) acknowledged the infeasibility of neoliberalism as a recipe for economic adjustment, drawing guidance instead from alternative liberalisms that had grown up alongside the emergence and development of their respective national political, economic, and social orders.

Given the inevitable discrepancies between the prescriptions of the quasi-hegemonic, transnational neoliberal paradigm on the one hand and the realities of complex, socially embedded, and historically derived national social and economic orders on the other, it is inevitable that national liberal traditions offer nationally distinctive answers to the questions of state responsibility and state-society relations. As a result, prevailing approaches in the literature—which might usefully be described as "liberalism as limits" and "neoliberalism as prescription"—are unlikely to provide significant analytical leverage for understanding how and why states respond as they do to episodes of economic stress, particularly (though not exclusively) in continental European countries in which neoliberalism has long remained a marginal economic discourse. These approaches have both denuded the concept's power to advance understanding of how particular national economic and political models evolve and undermined a coherent sense of how, why, and to what extent actually existing societies reject these hegemonic prescriptions and adopt others in their stead. In seeking to advance scholarly understanding of this question, this book analyzes how liberal traditions have operated in economically "illiberal" states, by which I mean states that have long since rejected the abstract and messianic programs of classical liberalism and neoliberalism and in which non-market arrangements—including but not limited to significant state intervention in and regulation of markets, robust collective-bargaining and industrial-relations systems, and expansive welfare states—have always been central to the development and operation of their respective capitalist models.[21] It seeks to assess and analyze how the various economic-cum-political pressures generated by both the climate of economic austerity and the neoliberal paradigm that has helped to generate it are translated in such states into a set of specific, coherent policy responses by national authorities drawing on older, nationally distinctive traditions while seeking to manage the process of economic adjustment within their unique and deeply embedded social and economic orders.

Though this book's case studies are limited to Europe, where neoliberalism has been marginalized within essentially illiberal states, it is important to recognize that, even in Britain and the United States, classical and neoliberalism's respective birthplaces and spiritual homes, liberal programs have long departed in significant ways from these templates, in ways that reflect the infeasibility of imposing highly abstract economic models on concrete and complex social orders. For Americans, "liberalism" connotes a left-of-center, progressive political orientation originating in the Progressive Era and culminating in Franklin Roosevelt's New Deal and Lyndon Johnson's Great Society. In Britain, it reflects a tradition, borne by Gladstone's Liberal Party and the writings of thinkers such as T. H. Green and L. T. Hobhouse, committed to both expanding the suffrage and "recogniz[ing] hindrances [to individual freedom] . . . such as poverty, disease, discrimination, and ignorance, which individuals could overcome only with the positive assistance of government."[22] Both British and American "liberalism," then, departed from classical liberalism's abstract and impracticable vision of a minimalist state and atomized, disembedded social order.[23] Like their continental European counterparts, both British and American liberals concluded that such a vision was insufficient and that government had to act in substantive and sustained ways to "promote as well as protect the freedom of the individual."[24] In their distinctive ways, both British and American liberals argued that meaningful freedom required some degree of social equality that only government could ensure. In so doing, they saw the justice of Hobhouse's claim that "Liberty without equality is a name of noble sound and squalid result,"[25] rejecting classical liberalism's minimalist "nightwatchman state" in favor of a state "obligated to serve the conditions upon which mind and character may develop themselves" and capable of pursuing "the common good to which each man's rights are subordinate [and] . . . in which each man has a share."[26] Far from purely normative, such conceptions of socially embedded markets constructed and constrained by governments reflect the nature of markets themselves, whose operation, as Steven Vogel reminds us, are always inextricably connected with the exercise of public authority.[27] Recognizing in this vein that "neoliberalism . . . has only ever existed in 'impure' form, indeed *can* only exist in messy hybrids,"[28] this book seeks to understand how three national "hybrids"—in France, Germany, and Italy—have, in response to periods of economic uncertainty and upheaval, fashioned trajectories of adjustment far removed from the messianic vision of hegemonic neoliberalism. It argues that France, Germany, and Italy are historically illiberal states, to the extent that they have always rejected the core premises of both classical and neoliberalism, both of which represent highly abstract, decontextualized ideologies ill suited for guiding adjustment of their social and economic orders. Even as they have historically rejected these transnational ideologies' expansive notion of market making in favor of a more embedded conception of the state's responsibility and relationship with nationally specific social structures, these states have fostered distinctive alternative liberalisms that have helped to shape each country's distinctive legacies of state building and social and economic development. Though embracing important elements of market-based adjustment, these traditions have generally rejected the notion, central to both classical liberalism and neoliberalism, that the market should be the central organizing principle of society and that non-market arrangements such as welfare states should be reduced to a minimum. They continued to evolve in the nineteenth and twentieth centuries, as altered circumstances demanded new kinds of responses from political authorities. This evolution continued during the 1970s and 1980s, a period during which the advent of more trying economic times forced elites to rethink many of the assumptions inherited from the postwar boom. In so doing, however, these national liberalisms did not embrace the ascendant neoliberal paradigm, posing instead alternative responses to the economic pressures of the period and questions of how each state should respond.

In invoking the concept of "traditions," I mean clearly identifiable lineages of thought that evolve over time while maintaining a set of core commitments, rather than fixed ideological packages to be deployed or rejected in toto. Borrowing from Duncan Bell, I see traditions as "constructed around a canon of renowned thinkers, which serves simultaneously as a reservoir of arguments, an index of historical continuity, and a powerful source of intellectual authority."[29] Though policymakers usually do not invoke such canonical thinkers explicitly, the analytical perspectives that they help to construct over time, as well as the policy and institutional precedents that they help to inform and justify, influence political elites' understanding of their political and economic context and suggest certain strategies for responding to them, often in subtle but nonetheless powerful, discernible, and surprisingly consistent ways. I argue that these nationally and historically situated traditions act as important *lenses* of elite interpretation and *anchors* of national policy responses to periods of economic uncertainty, when neither past practice nor fixed ideological prescriptions seem to suggest useful or appropriate responses. As such, they help political authorities to interpret the nature of periods of crisis and uncertainty and suggest delimited sets of policy and institutional responses to them that are both historically meaningful and politically feasible. In this way, they act as conceptual reservoirs that authorities turn to in moments of crisis and uncertainty, when existing policy and institutional arrangements, and the analytical frameworks that informed their creation, seem unable to provide needed answers.

In this way, my approach shares some elements with the recent "interpretivist" approach to the study of politics favored by scholars such as Colin Hay, Mark Bevir, and Alan Finlayson. It rejects starkly empiricist and positivistic understandings of political interests and preferences as dictated by objective material interests, as well as strongly rationalist explanations of political behavior.[30] By contrast, the understanding of politics favored here leaves room for varying elite interpretations of the meaning of economic crises and the appropriate responses to them. Accordingly, "it understands politics itself as a kind of interpretive activity. Political movements develop a particular interpretation of the world and attempt to secure the victory of that interpretation over others so that it ceases to appear as an interpretation and looks to be the truth."[31] In like fashion, Bevir argues that political actions and policy choices are driven in part by "a tacit background of assumptions" that make them seem reasonable or appropriate.[32] While fundamentally a work of comparative political economy that views institutions and political and economic interests as powerful determinants of national policy and politics, therefore, this book borrows concepts from other work that helps to explain policy outcomes in ways that neither a mechanistic focus on institutions and the distribution of political power and authority nor a materialist and rationalistic understanding of interests is able to achieve.

I argue that France, Germany, and Italy's liberal traditions, all born of core precepts of the Enlightenment, diverged during the late nineteenth and early twentieth centuries and were then consolidated as governments confronted new challenges in the postwar era. At their core, these national liberalisms each reflected distinctive understandings of the economic role of the state and limitations to it, the nature and structure of society, and the state's resulting responsibilities, in ways that rejected totalizing, atomized understandings of classical and neoliberalism. Central to these traditions were varying conceptions of the appropriate relationship between the public and private spheres, as well as divergent understandings of the relative importance of individuals and groups as components of the social order. As Hobhouse recognized, the tensions between group-based ties such as those of kinship, tribe, and sect have lain in tension with individual claims to personhood and autonomy in conceptions of political and economic communities since ancient Greece. With liberalism's repudiation of absolutism and mercantilism in the late eighteenth century, such communities and lines of authority needed to be redrawn, and different countries drew on different intellectual strands in readdressing this tension between individual- and group-based models of citizenship in a more liberal context.[33] As national political economies confronted the challenges of industrialization, national unification, and political incorporation in the nineteenth century, such questions gained renewed salience as philosophers, economists, and public officials tried to work out how political—and therefore economic—communities should be redefined and how they should be related to the state. In some traditions, such as the German and Italian variants, groups were traditionally viewed as the fundamental building blocks of society, sharing horizontal bonds of mutual obligation that in turn constrained prevailing assumptions of the proper scope of state responsibility. In both Germany and Italy, the existence of prominent social and economic groups (guilds, for example) long preceded, ontologically as well as chronologically, the nineteenth-century emergence of a unified state. This sequencing resulted in well-established patterns of group identity and horizontal obligation, which meant that a central challenge for the state was incorporating, co-opting, or undermining prominent groups.[34] In Germany, decades of successful economic adjustment have stemmed from elites' largely successful efforts to incorporate and establish partnerships with such groups, while in Italy, the enduring illegitimacy of the state and long-standing antagonism between it and core social and economic groups have undermined such partnership and produced a legacy of failed adjustment.

In the French tradition, by contrast, such groups had long been weak and fragmented, partially as a result of a long-established, highly centralized absolutist monarchy under the Ancien Régime and equally centralized forms of governance under its post-revolutionary successors. As Alexis de Tocqueville famously pointed out,[35] the continuity of pre- and post-revolutionary state centralization led to a sustained effort by post-revolutionary elites to undermine the historical influence of the clergy and nobility by suppressing groups, notably with the Le Chapelier Law of 1791, which banned guilds, trade unions (as well as strikes), and other subnational interest groups, such as trading monopolies.[36] This fact was both an effect and a reinforcing cause of a highly individualized conception of society, in which the modal relationship was a vertical one between the state and individual citizens, who were viewed as strictly equal before the law.[37] In this understanding, obligations existed between the state and citizens qua citizens rather than as components of ontologically prior groups, and the state's responsibility for economic welfare was focused on the economy as a whole and on the individual citizens that composed it. Groups were viewed with suspicion and were generally marginalized politically. Much as with Greek city-states, which were distinguished from earlier clan- or group-based identities, nineteenth-century French liberalism (though on a much larger scale) embraced a view of the state as a transcendent community that "suppressed the old clan organization and substituted new divisions, geographical or other. . . . It was based, in fact, not on kinship as such, but on civic right."[38]

In each of these traditions, historically developed conceptions of the structure of society and related patterns of state-society relations informed a distinctive understanding of the appropriate extent, character, and limitations of state action. Each accepted the core premise that the role of the state should be circumscribed and that significant freedom should be granted to non-state actors. To this extent, they were all "liberal." That said, they each rejected the kind of messianic and totalizing market-making agenda at the heart of classical and neoliberalism, protecting and even expanding non-market arrangements, such as social-protection systems, that are among neoliberals' favored targets. At the same time, they varied significantly with respect to the content of those limitations on state power and the character of the economy and society whose welfare its constrained power was meant to serve.[39] In each case, the character of national liberalisms was profoundly shaped through their dialogue with alternative traditions (statism, neocorporatism, and clientelism), which grew out of and reflected deeply embedded (though not always adaptive) conceptions of the social and economic order and legacies of historically based political-economic bargains. In the process, these nationally specific hybrids retained liberal conceptions about limits on state action and, within the context of such limits, the character of the constituencies whom that action was meant to serve. In so doing, they continued to reject disembedded, transnational ideologies such as classical liberalism (in the nineteenth century) and neoliberalism (since the 1970s). Representing elements of both continuity and departure from the older traditions from which they emerged, these national liberalisms were consolidated in postwar institutions and then reactivated in altered variants in response to the ascendancy of neoliberalism in the 1970s. Both historically and contemporaneously, these national variants of liberalism have been activated during periods of economic uncertainty, when established relationships between state and market are destabilized.[40] I provide a comparative overview of each tradition's central characteristics, conceptual structure, and political and policy orientation in Table I.1.

Since the 1970s, the weakness of neoliberalism as a political discourse and enduring political contestation of its core precepts in continental Europe have furnished the conceptual and political space for an older, more substantive, and more complex set of liberal concepts and prescriptions to exert its influence. These liberal traditions recognize important limitations on the power of the state, acknowledge a significant realm of private action beyond state control, and embrace the fundamental market precepts of private ownership of capital, the sanctity of private contracts, and the importance of private decisions about investment and consumption. That said, they reject neoliberalism's totalizing conception of the market and its hostility to non-market arrangements such as social-protection and collective-bargaining institutions, which they view as essential complements to and foundations of a capitalist economic order. In each country, distinctive elite understandings of the appropriate role of the state, the underlying structure of society, and the related character and focus of political responsibility have shaped patterns of social and economic adjustment in the neoliberal era. In France and Germany, national liberalisms have helped to preserve the two countries' socially embedded capitalist models in the face of neoliberalism's sustained ideological challenge, while in Italy, enduring antagonism between state and society has undermined such a synthesis and led to

Table I.1 **French, German, and Italian Liberal Traditions Compared**

	State's Economic Role	*Model of Social Organization*	*Dominant Model of Social/Political Responsibility*	*Prevailing Economic-Policy Orientation*
French Statist Liberalism	Interventionist/ dispositive	Individualistic/ citizenship-based	Vertical (state-citizen)	Macroeconomic
German Corporate Liberalism	Coalitional/ supportive	Group-based	Horizontal (inter- and intragroup)	Mesoeconomic
Italian Clientelist Liberalism	Patrimonial/ protective	Group-based	Vertical (state-group)	Mesoeconomic

a stark division between governing elites and aggressive but politically marginalized neoliberal voices in journalistic and academic circles. Though such traditions, of course, shape policies during times of relative stability, it is during moments of heightened economic uncertainty or crisis that national liberal traditions come to the fore, as prevailing views of the state and market come under sustained challenge and authorities are forced to rethink inherited assumptions and commitments.

This book's discussion of national liberalisms reflects a more affirmative and analytically more productive conception of liberalism than that offered by much contemporary scholarship. It emphasizes the differences between contemporary national liberal traditions and the essentially reactive, negative, and totalizing stances of classical and neoliberalism. From its birth in the late eighteenth century (well before contemporary conceptions of "state" and "market" existed) as a doctrine of middle-class political mobilization, a defense of private property, and a challenge to mercantilism, classical liberalism was generally formulated in negative terms, specifying limits on the power of the mercantilist and absolutist state whose introduction, it was thought, would lead to the unleashing of individual initiative and the expansion of wealth.[41] With some exceptions, such as John Ruggie's influential work on "embedded liberalism," which characterized the postwar order as characterized by a synthesis of constrained market forces embedded within socially and politically responsible institutions,[42] this tradition of "liberalism as limits" carried over into the doctrine of "neoliberalism," which was given new political impetus during the late 1970s and 1980s by politicians like Margaret Thatcher and Ronald Reagan. Echoing Isaiah Berlin's notion of "negative freedom,"[43] this conception has understood liberalism's project as reducing or eliminating obstacles to the (otherwise natural and organic) expansion of market forces, whether in the form of political opponents such as trade unions or of regulations of economic activity. Understood in this way, liberalism entails three central claims: that state power should be constrained, that there should be meaningful separation between the political and economic spheres, and that the interests of societal actors, whether they are construed as groups or as individuals, should take primacy over those of the state.

Such a negative conception of liberalism leaves many important questions unanswered, however. First, it does not define systematic limits on or the character of state power or draw clear distinctions about what sorts of limits are to be favored and how they are to be applied. Second, it does not specify the desired character of the relationship between society and the economy, which, as Polanyi eloquently demonstrated in the 1940s, can never be entirely separate.[44] Third, it does not identify how society should be understood, how and to what extent the interests of individuals should be viewed in relation to those of social and economic groups, or how we should understand society's relationship to the state. In advancing a conception of liberalism that focuses on how each national tradition works to answer these questions in the context of a socially embedded economic order, by contrast, this book identifies concepts that shape authorities' understanding of economic crises and explains how these conceptions inform policy choice.

Analytical Perspective and the Intellectual Terrain

This book focuses on the influence of national liberal traditions during the period of economic austerity and ascendant neoliberalism that began in the early 1990s. During this era, a series of political and economic shocks, both exogenous and endogenous, has destabilized standard assumptions about the dynamics of advanced capitalism and the respective roles of states, markets, and society. The book looks at France, Germany, and Italy—three essentially illiberal states in which neoliberal, free-market ideologies have remained marginal.[45] Yet in all three, it shows that national variants of economic liberalism, all of which were reconfigured in partial opposition to neoliberalism and reinterpreted in the face of the long period of punctuated economic austerity that followed, have shaped policy trajectories and patterns of institutional adjustment in important ways.

The contestation and destabilization of inherited economic models during this period have placed national liberal variants in these countries at the center of policy debates, as venerable understandings of the constitution of society and the appropriate scope of the state and the market have become politically activated and contested. As Peter Gourevitch has shown, periods of economic crisis discredit existing arrangements and lead to searches for new interpretive models.[46] At the same time, as Mark Blyth points out, historical-institutionalist scholars such as Gourevitch fail to bridge the gap between this insight and the "transformative role of ideas," focusing on the adoption of established intellectual paradigms as "autonomic" responses to new economic circumstances in times of crisis and uncertainty rather than treating ideas as agents of interpretation and reinterpretation of the *nature and meaning* of crises themselves.[47] If ideas are always important to politics, they are particularly so when inherited policies and institutions fail and when prevailing understandings of states, markets, and the relationships between the two come under challenge. In its examination of the politics of economic adjustment in illiberal states, this book places ideas in the center of its analytical frame and argues that they are at least as important as ontologically stable interests or institutions in shaping policy outcomes.

Identifying and understanding how liberal traditions have shaped national responses to these economic challenges in illiberal states allows us to fill significant gaps in a number of scholarly literatures. With rare exceptions, contemporary political science has tended to maintain a relatively stark—and unnecessarily limiting—division between political theory and the study of policy and political economy. This fact has constrained our understanding of how ideas shape patterns of economic adjustment and led to an unfortunate tendency to view ideas as a thing apart from, or at least epiphenomenal to, political and economic reality.[48] Furthermore, until quite recently, to the extent that scholars of comparative political economy have been prepared to accept that ideas matter, little systematic work has analyzed the political mechanisms through which their influence is exerted. Finally, scholars who have examined the influence of ideas on policy have for the most part tended to conflate *ideas* with relatively homogeneous *ideologies* or prescriptive *theories* (such as neoliberalism and Keynesianism) borrowed and deployed in parallel fashion by political elites across countries for partisan or instrumental purposes.[49]

As Marion Fourcade has pointed out in her compelling analysis of national traditions of economic analysis, there is "tremendous variability in the national understandings and implementation of such international economic paradigms as 'Keynesianism,' 'monetarism,' or the 'Washington Consensus,'" differences that she attributes to elites' "having been socialized in different economic worlds," which themselves are the products of "differences in the professional backgrounds and institutional location of the experts in charge of . . . policies."[50] In his superb analysis of national variations on "embedded neoliberalism," Cornel Ban extends Fourcade's analysis by explaining how the "translation" of neoliberalism by communities of domestic experts shaped economic policies in Spain and Romania. Whereas scholars such as Fourcade are interested chiefly in *origins* of such differences, I focus on the *effects* of national liberalisms on policy in the face of ideological challenge by transnational neoliberalism, emphasizing how much older traditions inform distinctive conceptions of state, society, and the market and resultant policy departures from neoliberalism's core precepts.[51]

My approach differs in important ways from significant strands of mainstream comparative political economy, which has generally adopted one of two approaches to the study of ideas' influence on policymaking. The first tendency has been to dismiss the influence of ideas outright or to maintain that their influence is so inchoate and vague as to lie outside the proper domain of political science. At a minimum, this perspective views ideas as epiphenomenal to fundamental economic interests or the workings of political institutions. This empiricist privileging of interests and predictable, routinized institutional dynamics effectively reduces ideas to interests or, in a close analog, views them as post-hoc rationalizations of policy outcomes.[52]

For their part, historical-institutionalist approaches have tended to view formal institutional arrangements as the font of diversity among national models of capitalism but to treat ideas as secondary or subordinate. Building on the insights of Andrew Shonfield's seminal *Modern Capitalism*,[53] such prominent scholars as Peter Hall,[54] Suzanne Berger,[55] and John Zysman[56] showed that nationally distinctive state structures and political and institutional relationships between the state and interest groups, themselves the products of national postwar settlements and institutional reconfigurations, tended to yield consistent patterns of policymaking over time. Such work understands interests as highly stable and institutional configurations as both reflections of the array of interests among state actors and producer groups and as avenues for those interests to exert influence. This approach produced a robust and fruitful literature on national models of capitalism, such as French statism, in which a centralized and powerful state yielded a highly insular policymaking process,[57] and German neocorporatism, in which a "semi-sovereign" state generally negotiated solutions with powerful producer groups.[58] More recently, the related "Varieties of Capitalism" literature, inaugurated by Hall and David Soskice, has offered "a firm-centered political economy" that views coordination among firms and stable relationships between firms and public authorities as the sources of stable "institutional complementarities" and "equilibria in many strategic interactions of the political economy."[59]

Though this broad scholarly tradition has been helpful in highlighting national variation among advanced capitalist political economies and in discrediting the popular neoliberal prediction of convergence on an Anglo-American model, its emphasis on stability and its related neglect of the influence of ideas undermines its ability to account for how elites' interpretation of economic challenges informs policy choice. Furthermore, because it emphasizes formal institutions as both the defining characteristics of national political economies and the engines of distinctive patterns of policy, it is also relatively ill equipped to explain departures from such trajectories, outcomes of a kind that politically operative ideational frameworks often generate in moments of heightened uncertainty. In the case of the Varieties of Capitalism perspective, moreover, the centrality of patterns of interfirm coordination leads to an underestimation of the role of the state and, as a result, to the obscuring of how shared sets of assumptions about the extent and character of state responsibility have reshaped national political economies in ways that a focus on narrower sets of economic arrangements and constitutional distributions of political authority fail to capture.[60]

As a result, such approaches offer limited analytical purchase on outcomes that depart from historical policymaking trajectories. Examples include ostensibly statist France's minimal, universalistic economic stimulus in the aftermath of the 2008 financial crisis, the inaction by the historically dominant Italian state during the same period, France's use of labor-market policy as an indirect form of Keynesianism in the late 1990s and early 2000s, and Germany's statist expansion of social protection in the aftermath of reunification. Interest-based approaches, such as those that focus on the relative strength of business and labor and their institutionalized relationships with the state, are likewise unable to explain important elements of these countries' adjustment strategies, such as Germany's strong preference for extensive tax cuts over more efficient direct spending as an instrument of economic stimulus after 2008 and the vast expansion of social protection in the 1980s and 1990s in historically labor-exclusionary France. In such episodes, attention to national liberal traditions, which inform elites' interpretations of economic challenges and help to furnish what Chris Howell has called a "narration of crisis,"[61] provides explanatory leverage over outcomes for which exclusive attention to formal institutions and straightforward economic interests is unable to account.

In partial recognition of these limitations, during the past decade or so, some historical-institutionalist scholars have turned to a study of institutional change as they understand it. Wolfgang Streeck and Kathleen Thelen, for example, explore "*a wide but not infinite variety* of modes of institutional change,"[62] to identify "incremental change with transformative results"[63] and to explore how "institutions can be transformed in subtle but very significant ways through a variety of specific mechanisms."[64] In partial contrast to the Varieties of Capitalism approach, this work sees institutions as undergoing "an evolutionary process that unfolds in an incremental manner and without major disruptions over long periods of time and resulting in profound change."[65] Such work helpfully loosens the connection between formal institutional structures and policy outcomes and recognizes the potential for institutional evolution. That said, its formal understanding of the relationship between institutions and policy and its conception of relatively stable constellations of political-economic interests as the primary sources of policy preferences and outcomes leave relatively little room for understanding how authorities navigate episodes that require departures from established models or in contexts in which new exigencies force them to interpret the political and economic landscape in fundamentally new ways. It also tends to view interests as defined by groups' and individuals' material concerns or quest for power (which becomes both the subject and object of the political process in somewhat circular fashion) rather than as constructed and reinterpreted in reaction to changing circumstances. As a result, it struggles to explain episodes in which prevailing understandings shift and generate outcomes that cannot reasonably be construed as the vector sum of the material interests of competing groups or the operation of institutions that reflect stable distributions of authority.[66] In such instances, one might usefully view ideas themselves as interests, to the extent that dominant elites are invested in a particular, historically rooted understanding of the world and their country's or institutions' place within it.

The other dominant approach to the study of ideas takes them more seriously on their own terms, but it does so by viewing them as packages that catch on during particular historical eras but which have little or no organic relationship to a particular country's intellectual or institutional history. This approach tends therefore to conceptualize ideas as discrete and relatively homogeneous sets of precepts, such as Keynesianism and neoliberalism.[67] In contradistinction to the work on interests and interest groups discussed earlier, which tends to reduce ideas to interests, this work tends to view ideas as influential in their own right but also as exogenously derived sets of prescriptions that policymakers might or might not choose to employ, albeit perhaps in varying ways. Ideas in this approach are thus not so much engines of interpretation of and reaction to economic crises as they are established models to be deployed in their wake.

In the context of this book, the most important work in this vein is the body of scholarship on neoliberalism, to which there are three important limitations. First, neoliberalism, as an essentially negative economic ideology, or one that prescribes *limits* on the scope of state activity and the *removal* of obstacles to market-based economic activity, posits the evolving relationship between states and markets much too narrowly.[68] Second, as I discuss in the context of the French, German, and Italian cases, inasmuch as neoliberalism exerts influence as a global political discourse,[69] it fails to offer much analytical purchase over national variation in policy *outcomes*, despite passing recognition of differences in the prescriptions of neoliberalism across countries. Third and perhaps most importantly, neoliberalism has remained a relatively marginal (and often explicitly repudiated) political narrative in continental Europe; a focus on it therefore provides limited purchase on the influence on state-market relationships of older liberal traditions, which have often shaped and been shaped in turn by illiberal economic frameworks, such as social and Christian democracy.[70]

During this century's first decade, more nuanced and systematic research on the role of ideas began to gain favor among scholars increasingly dissatisfied with the limitations of traditional approaches to the study of political-economic ideas in general and narrow conceptions of liberalism in particular.[71] One of the most influential figures in this body of scholarship was Mark Blyth, whose seminal work helped set the stage for subsequent studies that placed ideas at the center of its analytical strategies. Blyth argues that acknowledging the political power of ideas means resisting the temptation to treat "interests as given and crises as unambiguous," focusing instead on how "economic ideas provide agents with an interpretive framework," which "allow[s] agents to . . . propose a particular solution to a moment of crisis."[72] In like fashion, in work that echoes claims advanced by scholars in the "interpretivist" tradition, John Campbell argues that "crises often trigger institutional shifts in economic governance" and "enabl[e] them to recognize, re-examine, and ultimately reinterpret their previously taken-for-granted assumptions."[73] Campbell and Ove Pederson, echoing Marion Fourcade's insights, argue that distinctive "knowledge regimes," or "sense-making apparatus for elites confronted by unexpected or challenging economic circumstances," develop in particular countries. These regimes, Campbell and Pederson contend, influence policy outcomes by encouraging common analytical assumptions among analysts and research organizations on which policy elites rely.[74] In a similar vein, Daniel Béland argues that "ideational processes can help actors make sense of their perceived interests," thereby introducing important elements of fluidity and interpretation into traditional work on power and interests in politics.[75] Elsewhere, Béland and Robert Cox contend that ideas are "causal beliefs" that shape political action, and the "goals people articulate and the strategies they develop have feedback effects that further shape their original ideas."[76]

As these scholars show, careful attention to the influence of such ideational factors allows us to account for outcomes that neither standard neoinstitutional perspectives, nor standard interest-based explanations, nor standard stories of political partisanship can well explain. Nor can such perspectives account for broad patterns of isomorphism across policy areas or continuity over time and across partisan contexts of the kind described in this book. They would struggle, to pick just a few examples, to explain the growing importance of the state in the ostensibly neocorporatist German model; the surprisingly large size of the post-2008 German stimulus package and the quite limited scope of its French analog, both of which were inconsistent with traditional models of state intervention in the two countries; the expansion of income-support policies by both Left and Right in the historically labor-exclusionary France; the failure of Italian governments after the post-2008 financial crisis to clean up the banks on which SMEs so heavily relied; or the striking similarities between labor-market reforms initiated by the Left and Right in both Germany and France.

Recognizing such limitations, more recent work has focused systemically on how ideas shape policy in periods of economic crisis. For example, Craig Parsons's work on France's role in building the European Union shows that ideas become institutionalized over time and displace alternative frameworks of political understanding.[77] In like fashion, Vivien Schmidt's notion of "discursive institutionalism" "considers the discourse in which actors engaged in the process of generating, deliberating, and/or legitimizing ideas about political action . . . and the interactive processes of discourse that serve to generate those ideas."[78] Recent work by Cornel Ban and Wesley Widmaier significantly extends such scholarship by showing how ideas can coalesce into coherent economic theories in ways that inform the development of distinctive policymaking régimes.[79] In contrast to standard institutionalist or rationalist accounts, such work shows how crises disrupt existing understandings and alliances and how political elites' understanding of the *meaning* of crises derives from a dynamic process of interpretation, which is necessarily informed by the traditions and conceptual tools available to policymakers. This richer conception frames choice, not merely as an option among a set menu of options dictated by institutional frameworks or economic circumstances, but rather as a process which may rewrite and reframe the very menus from which such choice derives.

This book builds on such work but does so in a novel way that marries insights from comparative political economy, political theory, and economic history, extending them to show how evolving ideas and institutional development have interacted to shape nationally distinctive patterns of adjustment to periods of economic uncertainty. I argue that the ideational legacies of national liberal traditions mediate and reshape the influence of both economic interests and institutional effects, helping to define elite understandings of periods of crisis and uncertainty and appropriate ranges of responses to the economic challenges that they pose. In the process, they both provide the impetus for and, in many respects, require the reinterpretation and reconceptualization of transnational paradigms like neoliberalism. In so doing, these national traditions exert powerful influences over the evolution of national capitalisms by helping to define elite conceptions of how the economy works, how state and market should be organized, and how and to what extent the state should intervene in the economy and on whose behalf.

The Argument in Brief

In its analysis of how national liberal traditions have shaped patterns of economic adjustment in the neoliberal era in France, Germany, and Italy, this book focuses on fiscal policy and patterns of state investment, labor-market policy and related social policies, and financial policy and strategies of financial regulation—policy areas that are central and defining elements of the state's role in and relationship to the economy. Analyzing developments in these areas allows us to understand the evolution of three crucial sets of relationships that have shaped how illiberal states have adapted to a neoliberal era: the state's relationships with labor, business, and finance. Though there is significant overlap between these relationships, on the one hand, and policy areas, on the other, each group of policy outcomes sheds light on one or more of these relationships central to each country's political-economic order.

The book explores how national liberal traditions in these three countries have informed national strategies of economic adjustment since the early 1990s. Authorities in each country have worked to synthesize the central precepts and commitments of their liberal traditions with both the exigencies of a more liberal international economic order and the policy and institutional foundations of their respective postwar political economies, even as they have repudiated neoliberalism's messianic and disembedded market-making agenda. In the realm of fiscal policy, confronting the constraints of the Maastricht Treaty on European Economic and Monetary Union (EMU) and growing pressures on state budgets, governments have retooled policies in an effort to support economic growth while managing long-term indebtedness. In labor-market policy, governments of both Left and Right in all three countries have worked to spur labor-market activation and reduce reliance on passive labor-market instruments such as early-retirement programs and unemployment benefits while avoiding neoliberal-style assaults on the welfare state and even expanding income-support policies in some cases. In financial policy, they have undertaken significant, if uneven, liberalization while working to subsidize and bail out what they view as economically strategic segments of their financial sectors. In each of these three policy eras, liberal traditions have shaped prevailing interpretations of economic challenges, favoring certain kinds of policy responses over others by providing distinctive analytical frameworks through which governing elites interpreted prevailing economic challenges and considered the menu of possible solutions, as well as furnishing vocabularies for their legitimation. In this way, liberal traditions acted as both analytical *lenses* through which elites interpreted new economic challenges and *anchors* of certain types of policy trajectories, trajectories that were often at odds with policies and institutional commitments developed in quite different contexts, in ways that conventional institutional or interest-based accounts cannot explain.

In France, a tradition of "statist liberalism"—involving Republican and universalistic emphasis on equality before the law, a Gaullist and neo-Colbertiste privileging of the state as the guardian of aggregate economic welfare, and a vertical model of political responsibility between state and citizen—informed recovery strategies that focused on the macroeconomy and the economic welfare of citizens qua individuals rather than on favored social and economic groups. Emerging from the French Revolution's ambiguous legacies for democracy, the state, and individual autonomy, the French liberal tradition was caught between Constant's notion that "liberty is every man's right to be subject to the law alone" and to "influence the administration of the State" and Saint-Simon's technocratic statism, which posited that liberalism had exhausted its purpose and needed to be replaced by a "collectivism" and the state as the enlightened guardian of collective welfare.[80] This tension among individualism, state responsibility, individual legal equality, and a distrust of groups formed the conceptual core of French liberalism, leading to an oscillation between statism and individualism in both elite conceptions of the state's role and in policy trajectories in the postwar era.[81] From the erection of the dirigiste political economy of the Fifth Republic to its eventual dismantling at the hands of Socialist President François Mitterrand in the 1980s to the period of liberalization that followed in the 1990s and 2000s, policy outcomes continued to bear the hallmarks of this deep and unresolved tension between statist collectivism and a championing of a broader conception of individual economic rights. Since the late 1970s, this tradition has informed policies that sought to adapt France to a more market-based economic order while retaining state responsibility for national economic welfare and subsidizing and protecting individuals left behind by economic development.

In Germany, by contrast, a tradition of "corporate liberalism" (from the Latin *corpus*, "body"),[82] building on but transcending the Ordoliberalism that had emerged from the interwar period, reflects a more pluralist framework that understands groups, rather than individuals, as the fundamental components of social order and has accordingly favored core groups in ways that were often at odds with traditional German skepticism about state intervention. The corporate liberal model grew out of Ordoliberalism's emphasis on groups and its central priority of ensuring competition among them as a means of overcoming the legacies of the powerful state-sponsored cartels of the heyday of German industrialization in the late nineteenth century.[83] After 1945, this tradition evolved further in response to both the social and economic exigencies of the postwar era and Germany's rejection of incipient neoliberalism in the 1970s and 1980s.[84] Whereas the French liberal tradition viewed the state as an essential champion of collective welfare comprising that of individual citizens, the German tradition acknowledged the state as an essential element of the political-economic order but one that constituted a potential threat to freedom as much as an agent of it. In place of the French tradition's macroeconomic orientation, German liberalism informed a "mesoeconomic" focus on groups as the interstices between the macro- and the microeconomy.[85] Developing in reaction to the quasi-religious statism of idealists like Hegel and informed by notions, favored by distinct communities of influential legal scholars and historians, of a group-based organic polity, postwar German liberalism emphasized the importance of a balance between state and group power. This balance shifted over time in response to evolving economic challenges, but that was required if the state was not to become either an obstacle to human diversity or a barrier to humans' natural tendency to form associations.[86] It understood each "class" as both dependent upon the rule of law provided by the *Rechtsstaat* and as making "its own contribution to the common cause"[87] while acknowledging the importance of both state guidance and the welfare state in ways with which early Ordoliberals would have been quite uncomfortable. In the postwar era, this evolving tradition evinced a balanced understanding of state guidance and the power of producer groups, which became privileged interlocutors for state authorities, even as the state's role became more pronounced in response to challenging economic circumstances. During the postwar boom this shifting balance between state and group power informed policy trajectories that relied on state initiative even as they subsidized powerful groups and expanded group-based social protection as a key mechanism of social and economic adjustment. Likewise, since the early 1990s, this tradition has stood apart from neoliberal orthodoxy, deploying constrained state power in the service of strategically important groups and embracing significant fiscal investments that were often masked in Ordoliberal guise.

Finally, in Italy, a tradition of "clientelist liberalism" has time and again resulted in ineffective adjustment and political dysfunction. This tradition grew out of the fraught post-*Risorgimento* context, marked by late industrialization and the slow development of a middle class, a contested state with weak legitimacy, and sharp regional disparities between an industrializing North and an agrarian and impoverished South. Weak and fragmented prior to national unification, Italian liberalism was embraced by northern commercial and political elites in the nineteenth century as a legitimizing ideology for the small-scale and relatively competitive capitalism characteristic of Piedmont and Lombardy.[88] In practice, however, unified Italy fell well short of these ideals, yielding a system that preserved the power of socially prominent groups who colonized the state and diverted its resources to their own ends, alternately blocked and undermined the penetration of state into society, and, most generally, fostered a widely shared distrust of the state. Though Italian liberalism shares with its German counterpart a "mesoeconomic" focus on sectors and groups, the relationship between groups and the state is quite distinct. In Germany, insider groups have been beneficiaries of state largesse and protection and have acted as systemic clients instrumental to a broader strategy of economic adjustment embraced by both Left and Right; in Italy, such groups, including unionized public-sector workers, managers of large state-owned enterprises, independent white-collar professionals, and traditional regional political elites, have played an essentially negative role. They have done so by using their close relationships with particular partisan constellations to block reforms that threaten their economic status, even as their party-political patrons have often led assaults on the vested interests of their opponents. The result has been an enduring pattern of failed adjustment and political and economic sclerosis, with elites evincing a broad distrust of the state even as they have sought to capture it for their own clientelistic purposes.[89] In the postwar period, this tainted legacy helped to sustain the Christian Democratic party state and the system of *Trasformismo*, which degenerated into inertial and corrupt governments aiming to protect vested interests. Since the early 1990s, even as they have repudiated neoliberal economic strategies, Italian authorities have struggled to overcome the resistance of powerful social and economic groups and to reconcile the pressing need for reform with the political realities of a heavily clientelistic system. If the French and German stories have been of successful syntheses of their respective liberal traditions with the institutional bases of their postwar political economies, the Italian story has been one of a broad failure to do so.

In France, Germany, and Italy, these liberal traditions and associated conceptions of society, economy, and state responsibility have shaped the content and scope of policies, which constituencies they benefited, and, ultimately, their effectiveness, as authorities have sought to develop non-neoliberal strategies of economic adjustment in a neoliberal era. Though such conceptions have governed policy and institutional development during the entire postwar period, they have been particularly influential since the late 1970s, when the ascendancy of quasi-hegemonic neoliberalism led national authorities to react to and reject its messianic pretensions even as they worked to foster adjustment to challenging economic circumstances. During this period, political authorities' responses have been informed by conceptual touchstones of their liberal traditions within the parameters of their respective models of capitalism, even as they have been forced to adapt these traditions' central commitments in the face of economic challenges at once substantively different and more intense than those that characterized the postwar boom during which these models were developed. In this way, both the liberal traditions themselves and the operative dynamics of the national models of capitalism whose architecture they helped to inspire have evolved and have continued to shape trajectories of adjustment in mutually constitutive ways.

The Book's Organization

This book privileges ideas analytically as both the progenitors of nationally distinctive policy trajectories and the subjects of a dynamic, evolutionary process.

It shows how liberal traditions operate politically in states that are conventionally viewed as illiberal and that reject the standard prescriptions of transnational neoliberalism—and that indeed have developed their political economies in at least partial opposition to it. While institutionalist or interest-based accounts can shed light on particular components of a country's path of adjustment (the winners and losers from labor-market reform, for example, or the outcomes of battles over fiscal retrenchment), I argue that a focus on each country's liberal tradition and its political effects can provide a more robust understanding of broad national adjustment strategies and the resultant outcomes across a wide range of policy domains.

Chapter 1 provides the intellectual-historical foundations of the book's analysis of contemporary patterns of economic adjustment by analyzing the development of the French, German, and Italian liberal traditions from the nineteenth century to the 1980s, with particular attention to corresponding conceptions of the role and status of the state and its relationship to groups and individual citizens. Using a broad range of historical source material and the works of political philosophers whose thinking has been central to each tradition's development, as well as relevant secondary and critical literature, it outlines the analytical frameworks central to French "statist liberalism," German "corporate liberalism," and Italian "clientelist liberalism." It shows how these traditions shaped the structure of each country's postwar political-economic model and the policy priorities developed during the postwar boom through the early 1970s; the chapter also provides conceptual touchstones for the direction and character of these traditions' evolution in the face of the neoliberal challenge since the 1980s.

Chapters 2, 3, and 4 examine patterns of fiscal, labor-market, and financial policymaking in France, Germany, and Italy in the era of transnational neoliberalism that began in the early 1990s, when authorities were forced by a series of severe economic challenges to cast about for often unconventional solutions that departed from traditional modalities of policymaking. In each chapter, relying on extensive original interviews, publicly available accounts of policy debates, and available economic data, among other sources, I analyze how each country's liberal tradition has shaped elite understandings of these challenges and the range and character of responses to them. In Chapter 2, I focus on France's "statist liberal" tradition and show that, since the early 1990s, French policy responses privileged state responsibility for macroeconomic management while preserving and even expanding policies that supported the incomes of individual citizens rather than subsidize particular social and economic groups. In fiscal policy, this strategy has informed a process of modest fiscal consolidation and constrained Keynesianism, as authorities have sought alternative means for bolstering growth in the wake of the adoption of the Maastricht Treaty and the slowed growth that has been one of the hallmarks of the post-1970s era. In the realm of labor-market policy, French officials have worked to foster labor-market activation and reduce endemic unemployment with measures such as the thirty-five-hour-week laws while subsidizing employers so as to encourage job creation and expanding means-tested income support for the economically vulnerable. Finally, in finance, officials have liberalized financial regulations while supporting and bailing out large banks in an effort to stabilize the French financial system as a source of industrial finance and support for macroeconomically oriented strategies for economic growth.

In Chapter 3, I shift my focus to Germany and its tradition of "corporate liberalism." In contradistinction to the French case, this tradition entails both a circumscribed role for the state and a privileging of politically powerful interest groups, such as unionized industrial workers, large firms and SMEs in strategically important export sectors, and regional banking interests that have played critical roles in providing finance to industry. In fiscal policy, this tradition has informed a strategy of selective expansion and targeted investment designed to manage the challenges of national reunification in 1990 and its aftermath, coupled with a long-term effort to preserve the system's fiscal balance, while also engaging in fairly aggressive, group-focused fiscal stimulus in periods of crisis, notably after the post-2007 economic crisis. In labor-market policy, officials have acted with measures, such as the *Kurzarbeit* program of wage subsidies, to shelter skilled workers in key export sectors from the costs of adjustment, which have been borne disproportionately by a low-wage labor market concentrated in the service sector that expanded after the Hartz IV and Agenda 2010 reforms of the early 2000s. At the same time, governments of both Left and Right have preserved a network of income-support policies that have helped workers adjust while investing in job-creation and -training programs in ways that are starkly different from neoliberal prescriptions. Finally, in the realm of financial policy, officials have worked to shore up key players in the financial system, particularly regional banks that had long acted as crucial sources of finance to the vaunted German *Mittelstand* of small and medium-sized enterprises, often sheltering them in ways that undermined the system's overall capacity to adjust.

In Chapter 4, I turn to Italy, where a tradition of "clientelist liberalism" has long impeded significant reform in fiscal, labor-market, and financial policy. Like German "corporate liberalism," the Italian variant privileges interest groups as central to the social and economic order but does so in a way that undermines effective state action, which is held hostage to clientelistic competition over resources and the selective power of an institutionally fragmented state. If groups are the touchstone of German liberalism, which envisions a robust but constrained state as an essential referee tasked with regulating intergroup competition, then Italian liberalism tends to sacrifice coherent state action in favor of the least common denominator on which divergent and fractious interests can agree and an ineffective political process captured by powerful groups. This tradition has informed an uneven and sluggish trajectory of reform, with a series of frustrated attempts at fiscal reform designed to reduce the massive national debt that was one of the most problematic legacies of the postwar clientelist party state, even as the strictures of Maastricht have sharply limited officials' ability to adopt initiatives that might restore growth. In labor-market policy, likewise, Italian officials have met with limited success in liberalizing work regulations and reducing the costs of unemployment benefits in the face of trenchant resistance by public-sector workers, succeeding only when they could strike isolated bargains between labor and capital sustained by both sustained political initiative and generous side payments or retreat from earlier reforms, as in case of the reforms passed by the center-left Olive Tree coalition under Prime Minister Romano Prodi in 2007. In financial policy, officials have likewise struggled to overcome pressures to subsidize and bail out an increasingly parlous banking sector, which they have struggled to adapt to a more interconnected European financial system. Both the (limited) extent and the character of reform in Italy can best be understood as an outgrowth of the country's liberal tradition and its understanding of interest groups and citizens and their relationship to the state, which has informed a zero-sum conception of politics that has made reform and lasting compromise elusive.

In the book's conclusion, I explore the importance of my empirical findings for understanding national responses to economic crises and for the role of ideas in shaping economic adjustment in illiberal states in a neoliberal era. Though other factors clearly played important roles in shaping each country's adjustment path (the shock of German reunification and the constraints of the Maastricht criteria for European Economic and Monetary Union, for example), I contend that systematic attention to the central analytical frames and related policy priorities in each country's liberal tradition allows for a richer and more coherent understanding of broad patterns of policy and trajectories of adjustment. I also revisit and examine in more detail alternative potential explanations of the outcomes described in this book, including neoinstitutionalist conceptions of national models of capitalism and interest-based approaches, and identify important analytical and empirical limitations within them. Finally, I explore the implications of my research for debates about the importance of ideas in scholarly understanding of the relationship between ideas and interests in advanced capitalist societies and conclude with a brief discussion of the prospects for political democracy in a neoliberal era. I suggest that the experiences of illiberal states in a neoliberal era offer important political-economic lessons, not only for their European counterparts, but also for advanced capitalist economies more broadly in an era in which the certainties and conventional wisdoms of the post–Cold War era have been replaced by deepening uncertainty about the relationship between political and economic freedom and the stability of capitalism and democracy.

1

National Liberalisms in Historical Perspective

Conceptions of State, Society, and Economy in Illiberal States

Liberalism represents one of the central legacies of the Enlightenment in the West. Building on critiques of absolutism in the political sphere and mercantilism in the economic,[1] thinkers such as Tocqueville, Hume, and Smith posited human reason, self-determination and self-ownership, and rule by the consent of the governed as the rationales for a limited state, thereby giving liberalism a relatively coherent doctrinal basis *avant la lettre*. A combination of French rationalism and anti-absolutism and English and Scottish celebrations of individual freedom provided a set of templates for both political liberalism and its economic variant, which sought to limit state power in order to unleash the wealth-creating power represented by the "general disposition to truck, barter, and exchange."[2] Contemporary syllogisms that reduce liberalism to classical liberalism and laissez-faire ignore and distort the subtlety of a multifarious set of doctrines that grappled, often contradictorily and with imperfect clarity, with conceptions of state power and political legitimacy and with the bases of economic rights and privileges in a post-absolutist and post-mercantilist era. Over the course of the nineteenth century, liberalism became a moniker that was applied to a broad range of beliefs that shared an emphasis on limits on state power, meaningful separation between the political and economic spheres (previously tightly intertwined), and the primacy of individual interests over those of the state. Though the seeds of liberalism, as a doctrine of middle-class political mobilization, had been planted as early as the sixteenth century,[3] political and economic upheavals between 1770 and 1850 provided it with a modern doctrinal core, if one that was hardly homogeneous.

For Harold Laski, this core generally involved "a system of fundamental rights which the state is not entitled to invade,"[4] and by the nineteenth century such rights were understood to involve those of the middle class to choose their representatives and accumulate wealth relatively unimpeded. In the economic realm, this involved a rejection of the mercantilist logic of state dominance of economic activity understood as semi-autarkic accumulation and zero-sum competition among great powers. Adam Smith, far from being an advocate of laissez-faire, conceived of his *Wealth of Nations* as a rejection of mercantilism rather than as a celebration of unlimited or unconstrained individual prerogatives in the economic sphere.[5] This essentially negative impetus for liberalism's early formulations has fostered significant confusion among contemporary observers, who tend, often for ideological reasons, to equate a historically situated critique of a mercantilist state with a timeless premise that limits on state economic power must be nearly absolute if they are to be meaningful. Though distortions of early liberal ideas, such reductionist claims are natural outgrowths of an earlier set of doctrines that were always more articulate about the need for *limits* on absolute state power than about the substantive character of the authority that should replace it. This negative conception of liberalism, which might usefully be thought of as "liberalism as limits," tended to elide relatively seamlessly into classical liberalism and associated laissez-faire notions of a minimalist state, much as it has more recently come to be reduced to a fundamentalist neoliberal vision of a "free economy" and a "free society," a "utopian vision" that is "ultimately unrealizable."[6] It has also limited the intellectual reach of much recent work on neoliberalism, which has tended to ignore substantive conceptions of the appropriate scope of state power and state-society relations in favor of a reductionist equation of liberalism and neoliberalism, understood as a relatively homogeneous political project.[7]

As discussed briefly in the introduction, the prevailing tendency to reduce liberalism to neoliberalism yields thin, negative conceptions that fail to capture the central commitments even of Anglo-American liberalisms, ostensibly the domain in which neoliberalism fits most easily. Recognizing the political and social constraints on any attempt to impose an abstractly conceived liberal order and the necessity of socially embedding such an order if it is to endure, early British and American liberals both acknowledged the social nature of wealth and the need for government to sustain the society upon which prosperity ultimately depended.[8]

One of the most eloquent expressions of this conviction is provided by L. T. Hobhouse, whose classic *Liberalism* firmly rejects the classical liberal vision of a minimalist, denuded state and an atomized, disembedded social order. For Hobhouse, individual freedom is meaningfully possible only when the individual exists in a social context of mutual obligation and shared community. Hobhouse embraces an organic conception of society (shared by classical economists from Smith to Marx but dismissed and rejected by both classical and neoliberalism) "conceived as a whole which lives and flourishes by the harmonious growth of its parts, each of which in developing in its own lines and in accordance with its own nature tends on the whole to further the development of others."[9] Believing that "society can safely be founded on [the] self-directing power of personality [and] that it is only on this foundation that a true community can be built," Hobhouse writes, "liberty then becomes not so much a right of the individual as a necessity of society."[10] Because "the common good to which each man's rights are subordinate is a good in which each man has a share," "an individualism which ignores the social factor in wealth will deplete the national resources, deprive the community of its just share in the fruits of industry and so result in a one-sided and inequitable distribution of wealth." [11]

This understanding of the deep connections between individuals and society led Hobhouse and many other Anglo-Americans to recognize the predicates of a mixed economy, including a welfare state and collective-bargaining institutions, as not only permissible but desirable.[12] Even Walter Lippmann—who inspired the Colloque Lippmann that would serve as the wellspring of the Mont Pelerin Society, which would become the institutional home for later neoliberals, such as Milton Friedman[13]—acknowledged as much, even as he and his heirs rejected economic planning and other forms of heavy-handed state intervention.[14] In this way, early Anglo-American liberals acknowledged the necessity of a socially embedded economic order in ways that would find echoes in the Continental liberalisms that would shape postwar Europe.[15] The classical liberal talisman carried by neoliberals after the 1970s had thus long since been abandoned by most European liberals themselves.

Despite this much more subtle and complex lineage of Anglo-American liberalism, the negative conception of "liberalism as limits" has proven quite durable, a fact that brings with it difficulties for those wishing to study cross-national variation in liberalism's manifestations or the policy effects of nationally specific liberal legacies. By reducing liberalism to a set of precepts about the limits on state economic power and equating liberalism and neoliberalism, adherents of this view reproduce Isaiah Berlin's notion of "negative freedom"[16] while abandoning its "positive" counterpart, involving a substantive vision of those patterns of social and economic life in which freedom consists. In so doing they obscure intellectually important and politically significant differences in how national liberal traditions, forged in the post-absolutist crucible of the late eighteenth and early to mid-nineteenth centuries, shape policy and politics in substantively distinct ways. Instead, they treat liberalism as a fixed doctrine, relatively immune to historical challenges and unmoored from dynamic and evolving national institutional frameworks. As Duncan Bell has argued, such an approach is bound to fail, given the diverse and shifting historical uses of the concept of liberalism, which has been invoked by a long line of thinkers, each of which inhabits a distinctive "thought world" that gives the concept meaning. For this reason, Bell argues, only a "contextualist approach," sensitive to the multiple and situationally specific valences of the term, can succeed in providing an analytical frame within which to understand it.[17]

In a similar way, this book emphasizes the nationally specific contexts in which various incarnations of liberalism have evolved, analyzing their intellectual foundations and identifying core conceptions and commitments that have shaped national politics and policy over time. Instead of viewing liberalism as a negative and homogeneous doctrine, it understands the concept as a dynamic, evolving set of ideas with nationally distinctive sources, trajectories, and effects, all of which grew up in rejection of the thin, negative vision of classical liberalism, much as these ideas would continue to evolve in rejection of the decontextualized doctrine of neoliberalism in the twentieth century. Rather than as a stable *doctrine*, the book views liberalism as a *tradition* with essentially national rather than transnational foundations, despite common points of origin in the writings of post- and anti-absolutist thinkers such as Constant, Gierke, and Pareto. In so doing, it shares Bell's view of traditions as "constructed around a canon of renowned thinkers, which serves simultaneously as a reservoir of arguments, an index of historical continuity, and a powerful source of intellectual authority."[18] It also recognizes that within these traditions there exist important tensions—between individual freedom and the claims of society, between individual economic initiative and systemic economic stability, and between the requirements of economic growth and political stability, among others—which national elites have had to devise their own imperfect and historically contingent strategies to resolve.

Conceiving of liberalism in this way affords greater analytical purchase on the kinds of policy developments with which this book is concerned. First, it allows for the evolution of liberal ideas over time in response to shifting economic challenges and crises that are ultimately national in their effects, as well for the interaction between national liberalisms and other intellectual traditions, such as republicanism in France and neocorporatism in Germany. By breaking the hermetic seal on liberal ideas in this way, my approach views liberalism as a set of dynamic national elite conceptions to be studied empirically rather than a fixed ideal to be embraced or abandoned. Second, it sheds light on the interactions over time between liberal ideas and political institutions, which represent at best imperfect manifestations of historically evolving national political and economic commitments. Third, it allows analysis of the effects of liberalism's legacies in countries—like France, Germany, and Italy—in which neoliberalism and related doctrinaire beliefs in the salutary effects of unfettered market forces have remained marginal. Accordingly, it allows for an intertemporal analysis of how national liberalisms have reacted to, and departed from, the quasi-hegemonic phenomenon of transnational neoliberalism since the 1970s. Viewing liberalism as a dynamic tradition with national foundations and national effects, albeit in dialogue with transnational neoliberalism, rather than as an unchanging ideational monolith enables us to understand how the relatively distant origins of classical liberalism refract in states that cannot be usefully described as essentially "liberal."

I focus on how national liberal traditions have shaped responses to the era of neoliberal hegemony and economic austerity since the early 1990s. It is precisely during such periods of economic uncertainty and upheaval that inherited conceptions of state, market, and society are likely to be most in flux. National liberal traditions, which may be politically inert or quiescent during periods of stability and prosperity, are likely to be activated at such times, when conventional wisdoms and arrangements are called into question and elites cast about for solutions to pressing problems. In countries where neoliberalism has remained marginal, such as those in continental Europe, moreover, national liberalisms are likely to evolve in partial opposition to or rejection of neoliberalism's messianic and abstract faith in markets that ignores the socially embedded character of the economic order. At such times, and in ways that a focus on neoliberalism alone fails to capture, national liberal traditions act as both analytical *lenses* through which elites interpret new economic challenges and *anchors* of policy trajectories that are often at odds both with policies and institutions developed in quite different contexts and with conventional models of the operation of each country's political economy that are based upon these arrangements. Whether endogenously or exogenously generated, these periods of economic uncertainty alter prevailing understandings of the relationship between state and market and resulting elite convictions about appropriate policy responses. In the process they create situations in which contemporary "agents are unsure as to what their interests actually are, let alone how to realize them."[19] As a result, an exclusive focus on material interests, putatively stable and straightforward, will not provide the analytical leverage required for understanding such episodes of conceptual and economic fluidity.

In the remainder of this chapter, I trace the development of French, German, and Italian liberalism from the nineteenth century to the 1990s. In so doing, I work to highlight the essential commitments central to each tradition's vision of state, society, and economy, focusing on those elements that are most politically influential during periods of economic upheaval. I do so by selecting key thinkers in each tradition whose ideas are emblematic of key concepts in each tradition and who also helped to shape the views and political commitments of political and economic elites. I argue that one of the central and politically most important differences among these traditions pertains to each one's understanding of the social order—and in particular whether this is constituted by individuals or groups and wherein the role of those entities lies—and in turn to the implications of this paradigm for the role of the state in the economy. This claim flies in the face of much contemporary understanding of liberalism, particularly post-1970s neoliberalism, which is said to have discarded notions of "society" in favor of "individuals." In contrast to this conventional wisdom, I aim to show that the national liberal traditions under examination here not only recognize the existence of a coherent social order but indeed place nationally specific treatments and conceptualizations of society at the core of their worldviews.[20]

I begin with the French case, which I characterize as a tradition of "statist liberalism," involving a republican emphasis on strict individual equality before the law and a profoundly individualistic understanding of social order, balanced by a neo-Colbertiste privileging of the state as the guardian of aggregate economic welfare and significant constraints on economic liberalization.[21] This tradition, I argue, has informed policy strategies that focus on the macroeconomy and workers qua citizens rather than on particular social and economic groups. I then move on to Germany, where a tradition of what I call "corporate liberalism," stemming from the older tradition of Ordoliberalism that grew out of the interwar period and the 1950s,[22] reflects a more pluralist ideational framework that views groups as the fundamental components of social order and has favored targeted subsidies of core groups in the postwar Social Market Economy. I conclude with the Italian case, in which a tradition of "clientelist liberalism," initially forged by nineteenth-century political and social bargains and entrenched after World War II by the Christian Democratic party state, time and again has resulted in ineffective adjustment and political dysfunction. Unlike in Germany, where insider groups have been instrumental to a broader strategy of economic revival, in Italy such groups played a largely negative role, blocking significant reforms that threatened their economic status and informing a shared elite conception of politics as a zero-sum game in which the central task becomes dislodging vested interests in the service of gaining resources for one's own constituents.

French Liberalism between the Individual and the State

French statist liberalism developed during the postwar period from intellectual roots dating from the waning years of the Ancien Régime that were reconfigured in the aftermath of the French Revolution. In the eighteenth century the oppression experienced by the citizenry at the hands of Europe's most centralized and powerful monarchy provided early French liberalism with a decidedly individualist cast, as Enlightenment thinkers sought to establish the intellectual terrain for a defense of individual rights. Because the French state was consolidated long before the Renaissance and the associated emergence of proto-capitalist economic interests (such as guilds), such groups played a limited role in prevailing economic thinking, a fact even more true during the mercantilist era of which France was the purest representative. As a result, the modal economic and social relationships were vertical ones between the state and citizens rather than horizontal ones within and between groups.

Thinkers such as Montesquieu, celebrated in France more for his conception of individual rights than for his support of the separation of powers that defined his reputation in the United States, reflected this historical dynamic. For Montesquieu the emergence of individual liberty was "the incidental result of the self-interested acts of independent individuals" who strive to secure resources by overcoming the system of royal patronage from which they had been excluded.[23] Individual "passions" both give life to the polity and must be channeled in constructive, collaborative directions consistent with a healthy and stable state. Montesquieu's celebration of the separation of powers thus flows from his deeper fears about the destructive potential of both untrammeled state power and unchecked individual passion: "Without respect for individual rights, there is anarchy of the battle of all against all; without political passions, you have despotism, because no one would have any interest in opposing royal power."[24] This understanding was subsequently taken up, first, by the so-called Gournay Circle, which sought to reconcile his ideas with the simultaneous liberalization of English political institutions after the Glorious Revolution; then by Turgot, who built on the Physiocrats' proto-liberal denunciation of mercantilism; and later by Jean-Baptiste Say and the so-called Ideologues, who focused primarily on the economic implications of individual initiative for exchange and production.[25]

Anti-absolutist and anti-mercantilist in equal measure, Montesquieu assigned commerce a central place in his political vision, both as a reflection of human endeavor freed from an absolutist system and as a constitutive force capable of fostering human freedom.[26] At the beginning of his chapter on the subject in *The Spirit of the Laws,* Montesquieu suggests that commerce reflects a way of life that is more constitutive of virtue that its mercantilist alternative:

> The natural effect of commerce is to bring peace. . . . The commercial spirit produces in men a certain precise sense of justice, opposed on the one hand to brigandage, and on the other to those moral virtues that preclude one from adopting a rigid understanding of interests and enable one to sacrifice them at times for those of others.[27]

Montesquieu thus holds up a bourgeois, commercial society as a reflection of a kind of human freedom whose significance extends beyond the economic to the political and social realms. Commerce is for him a necessary if insufficient indicator of a free and meaningful human existence. Equally important, it can emerge only in societies in which state power has been constrained. Thomas Pangle captures this relationship in Montesquieu's thought, emphasizing its capacity to enlarge the scope of the conception of the security essential to freedom: "[With commerce] men cease to seek satisfaction in devotion to the fatherland or king; they think of themselves. And they lose their taste for personal glory, or salvation after death; they look to their material affairs. They become hard-working, tolerant, and peace-loving."[28] At the same time, such societies lack the leadership capable of actively fostering a sense of public virtue, a limitation that subsequent thinkers such as Comte and Saint-Simon would seek to remedy.[29]

This tension between individual rights and state authority would constitute the core motif of post-revolutionary French liberal debates throughout the nineteenth century. This continuity stemmed not only from the intellectual lineage of French liberal thinkers but also from the context furnished by important continuities between pre- and post-revolutionary French political institutions. As Tocqueville famously remarked, for all of the upheaval that it entailed, the French Revolution failed to destroy, and indeed in many ways reinforced, the highly centralized political and economic structures of the Ancien Régime.[30] This meant in practice that post-revolutionary French liberalism was marked by efforts to "tempe[r] its abstract revolutionary attitude by the introduction of an historical point of view" and by a broadly conservative cast.[31] This shift from revolutionary egalitarianism to economic conservatism, inflected with commitments to protectionism, also stemmed from the fact that the beneficiaries of state protection were individual peasants and small producers, who were the great class victors of the revolution, rather than large industrial concerns, which remained underdeveloped at the time.[32] Such tendencies were supported not only by a set of political institutions that had preserved the despotic potential of the old regime but also by the concerns of a nascent middle class concerned with accumulating wealth and seeking political power.[33] France's bourgeoisie was preoccupied with preventing the re-emergence of despotic rule, a fear that would inform a highly individualistic, self-regarding, and defensive notion of freedom that accepted limited public rights in exchange for expansive private ones.[34]

By the mid-nineteenth century, the tension between an expansive notion of individual rights and an enduring elitist conception of exclusive and concentrated political power would become the central leitmotif of French liberalism. For figures such as François Guizot and Benjamin Constant, economic liberalism went hand-in-glove with a distrust of democracy,[35] which for them meant the potential for mob rule and the breakdown of a stable economic order. Guizot, a celebrated historian and perennial public official and intellectual, embodied both the self-satisfaction of the nascent French bourgeoisie and the concomitant emphasis on individual liberties for the commercial classes and distrust of mass democracy central to French liberal thought. He was the central figure among the "Doctrinaires," equal parts philosophers and public figures, who "believed in the possibility of a happy marriage between politics and philosophy" and championed a so-called "*juste milieu* between Revolution and Reaction." This they sought to achieve by building "the institutional framework of representative government in a conflict-ridden society that lacked a proper culture of accommodation and bargaining."[36] For his part, Guizot celebrated moderation as the central political and economic virtue, "a distinctively French tradition" that built on Montesquieu's distrust of concentrated power and celebration of commercial society and his critique of the predations of self-serving and politically favored groups, such as the clergy and aristocracy under the Ancien Régime.[37] Informed by the chaos of post-revolutionary France and the nightmare of the Terror (in which his father was guillotined), Guizot combined a strong distrust of popular sovereignty with his support of "democracy as a *social condition*" and a hatred of "arbitrary and absolute power."[38] His views bespoke an elitist bourgeois notion that limitations on popular sovereignty could be justified by a political order that brought with it economic prosperity, combined with a faith in the state's "tutelary" power and a "Republican spirit [that] was unitary and anti-pluralist."[39] Like other French liberals of his era, Guizot thus sought to reconcile the tension between individual liberty and state power in ways that reflected the central preoccupations of his time and place.

In contrast to Guizot's ambivalence about political democracy and his support for granting strong administrative power to the state, Constant was much readier to champion "the individual," which he "urged state and society to respect . . . and refrain from intruding on [his] life aims and profoundest beliefs." For Constant, "society was changing, [and] old forms of interference with people's interests and beliefs were ceasing to be practical or effective"; individual liberty was thus the only sure means of resisting despotism, in contrast to Guizot's trust in moderation and a paternalistic elite. This resistance, however, would take place, not through the ballot box, but rather through the development of "the commercial spirit of the times."[40] By contrast and thereby building on Jean-Baptiste Say's earlier defense of laissez-faire but giving it wider purchase,[41] Constant declared that *modern* liberty "is every man's right to be subject to the law alone, the right of not being arrested, tried, put to death, or in any way molested, by the caprice of one or more individuals."[42]

This intellectual posture, ambivalent about democracy but preoccupied with limiting the state's authority, provides only half of a portrait of nineteenth-century French liberalism. Accompanying this strand, indeed growing out of the same post-revolutionary context, was a technocratic and interventionist element that celebrated the state as the author and guardian of an economic order responsible for creating the conditions for a prosperity in which all could share in ways that dovetailed with and added economic substance to Guizot's belief in a tutelary state. Providing a distinctly French cast to Berlin's distinction between "negative" and "positive" freedom, this lineage sought to deploy the state in enlightened ways in order to manage the chaos of the industrial era while ensuring that the wealth that it created would redound to the general, as opposed to particularistic, welfare. Jean-Charles Léonard de Sismondi, for example, was inspired, by his direct observation of the destructive effects of English industrialization on the working class, to reject the liberal precept, adhered to by Constant, Say, and others, that "the adaptation of labor to its new conditions [would be] automatically effected by the natural laws of competition," and who as a result "did not realize what desolation these laws leave in their wake." This conviction led Sismondi to reject state economic neutrality and to favor state intervention to support the economic welfare of workers and others dispossessed by the market and industrialization.[43] Dismissing the concerns of Constant and Rousseau about the capture of the state by self-serving, parochial interest groups, [44] which gave rise to the famous Le Chapelier Law in 1791,[45] thinkers like Sismondi viewed the liberal economic order as inherently unjust and unequal and sought to use the power of the state to correct, or at least to attenuate, these outcomes.[46] This vision also reflects a substantive view of equality that differs markedly from the Anglo-American conception, ostensibly neutral with respect to individuals but relatively impoverished in its capacity to intervene.[47]

This affirmative vision of the state's role achieved its greatest scope in the work of Saint-Simon and his followers, who championed a technocratic political-economic order with a powerful and enlightened state endowed with foresight and capable of directing the economy to socially useful ends. This economic application of Rousseau's notion of the General Will would come to define a powerful lineage within French liberalism (as well as influence the conceptions of postwar economic policymakers) that would reject the neutralist vision of thinkers like Constant as naive and maintain that the economic and social dislocation that industrialization had left in its wake required a powerful state capable of allowing society to prosper.[48] For Saint-Simon, this meant placing the economy under the guidance of an enlightened despotism that would organize society for the benefit of labor (a preoccupation that he shared with Sismondi) along scientific industrial principles. He credited liberalism with having destroyed feudalism, but he wanted to move beyond atomistic liberal principles into a sort of state-guided industrial collectivism, retaining liberalism's belief in the primacy of the individual, whom he conceived of as an industrial worker, whose welfare required "the substitution of the organic State for the Liberal or individualistic State."[49] In this way, Saint-Simon foreshadowed the views of Auguste Comte, the father of modern sociology, for whom modern "industrial society," in contrast to its earlier "commercial" variant, required a powerful, technocratic state, and "scientifically informed cooperative coordination among elites," in order to manage and direct an increasingly complex society.[50]

Other nineteenth-century French liberals viewed industrial society in similarly dark terms but drew different conclusions about the possibilities of reconciling the sanctity of the individual with a political-economic order capable of delivering the economic goods that make individual freedom meaningful. On the individualist and anti-statist end of the spectrum were thinkers like Fourier, whose conception of society was based upon free associations of individuals who would be guided into social interaction through an inherent force of attraction.[51] Presaging elements of the thinking of Hayek nearly a century later, Fourier thus proposed an organicist and highly utopian vision that had little use for the kind of coercion that Saint-Simon viewed as essential. Like Saint-Simon, Fourier's goal was to create a more harmonious social and economic structure on the foundation of industrialization, but he placed his faith in the wisdom of the individual rather than in the state in order to accomplish it.[52]

For others who shared the liberal celebration of the individual as an object of policy (though not yet as its subject), the state was the only possible solution to the inhumanity of the industrial era. For example, Charles Brook Dupont-White, a nineteenth-century French economist with socialist leanings, argued that only a strong state could reverse the pauperization of the working class brought about by the process of industrialization. Dupont-White celebrated the rights and dignity of the individual, but he also believed that the state is a moral being—a "person that represents society,"[53] which in almost theological terms has an intimate connection with and responsibility for the welfare of society qua collection of equal individuals. Dupont-White believed that "freedom and the State, life and law, grow simultaneously on parallel lines. Freedom, legally speaking, means that no one is obliged to obey the mere will of his fellow man; obedience is due only to the law, the presumed expression of reason. . . . Authority is created to make liberty possible."[54] This framework undergirded a view that "there can . . . be no permanent antagonism between the rights of the state and those of the individual" and "the state's function is . . . to disband the cases and the forces of particularities, which are the greatest enemies of liberty."[55]

In a series of formulations that captures both the tensions within nineteenth-century French liberalism and its twentieth-century heir, Dupont-White claims:

> The State is authority, existing not on its own account but rather created by or for society: no longer by virtue of inheritance, property, membership in a priesthood, but rather by virtue of magistracy; no longer with the right of oriental despots over souls, bodies, and goods, but with the limitations of moral law of which it is the interpreter, with power

> relegated by all either explicitly or implicitly, with a mission of order and public welfare. . . . There is no contradiction between the State and liberty; because the State is the form of authority that appears as soon as man is subordinated to the power of man, and it is deployed as soon as an abuse of force is foreseeable or needs to be redressed.[56]

De Ruggiero succinctly captures the essence of Dupont-White's thesis about the interrelationship of state power and individual freedom: "[Freedom] only exists for all at the cost of a dependence and discipline imposed upon all: that is the work of authority."[57] Echoing Rousseau's famous notion of the General Will, Dupont-White endows the state with the power to reorder society and ascribes to it the wisdom and insight that this task requires. In so doing, however, he renders individual freedom almost notional; the state, whose moral character is presupposed, becomes the essential and quasi-omnipotent protector of the weak and disenfranchised. Almost Hegelian in his idealistic view of the state, Dupont-White moves his concern for protecting the weak so far that the individuals for whose benefit the state has come into existence are subsumed within it.

This oscillation between statism and liberty, along with the focus on individual welfare that preoccupied Sismondi and, to a lesser extent, Dupont-White, reflected the core commitments of French liberalism at the moment of the long-delayed establishment of a stable democratic regime with the advent of the Third Republic in the 1870s. The new constitution brought with it a mixed legacy for French political and economic development, with the large peasantry finally won over to democracy through a free and explicitly republican public education system[58] and a passive state that aimed above all to preserve the economic status quo and protect (and thereby politically demobilize) vested interests. Even as they sought to inculcate citizens with republican (rather than Bonapartist or monarchical) values, French authorities inhabited a set of political institutions that reflected and reinforced the search for stability at the expense of progress. The constitution had endowed the fractious parliament (known as a Chamber without Windows for its opacity) with extensive powers, while creating a weak executive and a largely ceremonial presidency incapable of mounting meaningful legislative initiative. In the words of Stanley Hoffmann, this system was one with "plenty of brakes and not much of a motor."[59]

The model activated the defensive, "negative" strands in the French tradition: limit the power of the state, expand the scope of individual freedom and autonomy, leave unmolested the agrarian legacy of the revolution and the large peasantry that was one of its biggest winners, and shelter the growing middle class from unwanted competition. By the time of the advent of the Third Republic, the statist and egalitarian strands that had inflected French liberal thought earlier in the century had given way to a notional egalitarianism of a form that countenanced inequality in fact and a tolerance of concentrations of wealth, an imperative strengthened by powerful strands of anti-socialism that emerged in response to perceived threats by the political Left.[60] It is in this context that we must understand the proclamation of Adolphe Thiers, the Third Republic's first president, that "the Republic will be conservative or there will be no republic,"[61] in strong echoes of Guizot's earlier formulation that captured the spirit of the bourgeois July Monarchy. Like the July Monarchy, this was a regime of bourgeois consolidation, economically liberal in its noninterventionist posture and content to allow property owners to govern society.

Statism and Liberal Universalism in Postwar France

By the eve of World War II, the very passivity and complacency that had stabilized the Third Republic had eroded its life force from within, leaving a Malthusian, static economy and a military incapable of mobilizing economic and military resources to confront the Nazi onslaught.[62] France's rapid defeat at the hands of the Germans, and the collaborationist Vichy interregnum to which it gave rise,[63] provided postwar French elites with a powerful countermodel as they worked to refashion the French polity, economy, and society. Under the Fourth Republic, French elites invested great power in the political executive, creating, for example, the powerful Commissariat général du Plan (CGP), which was responsible for devising a series of economic plans that guided economic development in strategic sectors such as coal and steel, and also developing a narrow technocratic elite responsible for modernizing a relatively backward, agrarian economy.[64] Even with the ostensible microeconomic focus of planning in strategic sectors, the central strategy was macroeconomic, driving economic development from the top down and center out, based on the assumption that economic modernization would automatically benefit the citizenry that had been left behind by sluggish and uneven industrialization in the nineteenth and early twentieth centuries. As during the revolution, the modal unit of society was the individual citizen rather than the group, individuals whose legal and political equality was to be reflected in shared prosperity.

This early universalistic orientation found parallels in the designs for the postwar welfare state. Under the direction of Pierre Laroque, named Director of Social Assistance in 1944, the leaders of the Fourth Republic endeavored to construct a universalistic network of social protection, in keeping with the influential Keynesian ethos of the time, and French liberalism's universalistic notions of social and economic citizenship.[65] According to Laroque, the revamped social-protection system "aim[ed] not merely at improving workers' material situation; it also, and especially, [involved] the creation of a new social order in which workers can assume their full responsibilities."[66] Laroque's invocation of "workers" writ large as the welfare state's primary constituency reflected the rapid expansion that the French industrial working class had undergone since the 1920s and the postwar vision of economic growth predicated upon Fordist mass production. Though the Fourth Republic, like the Third, retained a strong and fractious parliament,[67] French officials had clearly learned some of the lessons of the Third Republic's failed recipe of stasis and protection, understanding that economic actors could not be left to their own devices if France were to modernize successfully.

That said, the overarching goals of rapid growth and full employment brought with them enduring tensions in prevailing French conceptions of the state's role and its relationship to society, ultimately frustrating attempts to create a universalistic welfare state. Because citizens were assumed to be the long-term beneficiaries of economic modernization through steadily rising wages and full employment, they had unclear claim to directly provided state largesse. This ambiguity, along with the resistance of powerful groups such as white-collar workers who fought to defend their pre-existing, particularistic schemes, undermined the coherence of Laroque's vision and the singleness of the state's purpose.[68] The result was a fragmented welfare state, which, though much more extensive than its prewar counterpart, fell well short of Laroque's solidaristic vision.

If the Fourth Republic thus marked the beginnings of a shift away from negative conceptions of freedom and anti-statism that prevailed under the Third Republic, the advent of the Fifth Republic in 1958 represented its completion. Charles de Gaulle, recalled from the political wilderness to solve a series of parliamentary crises in the face of an expanding war in Algeria, extended the centralist logic of economic planning to the entire political system, supervising the writing of a new constitution that shifted the center of power sharply from the parliament to the executive. This new, so-called dirigiste system (from the French verb "to direct") restored earlier Bonapartist and Saint-Simonian views that "the state represent[s] an oasis of enlightenment and integrity amidst a desert of selfish, risk-averse societal actors"[69] and that, by uniting "the multitude . . . in a single body," the state's pursuit of the "general will" on behalf of all citizens would, in Rousseau's famous formulation, "forc[e] them to be free."[70] Conceived of as "a search for technical truth," economic planning and dirigiste industrial policy acquired legitimacy through a "claim that the dirigiste state was capable of delivering rates of economic growth high enough to provide widely shared real income gains."[71] In the postwar context, "freedom" would be tightly bound up with economic prosperity, and dirigisme returned an activist state to what many saw as its rightful position as the engineer of the general welfare.[72] The new constitution subordinated parliament to a powerful executive, led by a powerful, democratically elected president with the authority to dissolve it at will, the right to rule by decree in emergencies, and unchallenged authority in foreign affairs.[73] The powerful executive was both a reflection of and a driving force behind a new sense of urgency toward economic policy that informed the preference for powerful policy instruments like selective nationalization of key sectors, indicative planning, selective credit allocation, and sectoral industrial policies, all of which were designed to accelerate French economic growth and generalize prosperity. This state-led process of modernization was predicated on an underlying bargain Andrew Shonfield memorably referred to as a "conspiracy in the public interest" between big business and the state.[74] One irony of this strategy was its political exclusion of organized labor, which was viewed as hostile to the project of economic modernization, even as individual workers were viewed as its potential economic beneficiaries.

Accompanying and informing this transformation of political-economic strategy was a marked shift in the character of French liberal discourse, away from negative conceptions of personal freedom from state interference and towards a more substantive, affirmative one in which the economic goods are themselves an integral component of meaningful freedom.[75] Prominent in this moment of inflection was the sociological conception of liberty held by Raymond Aron and others, "who argued . . . in favor of a combination of negative and positive liberty" and "described modern industrial societies . . . as *democratic* societies at the heart of which lies the concept of equality of conditions."[76] Such "conditions" were both political (involving individuals' substantive ability to influence politics and policy) and, even more importantly, economic, since access to a basic means of subsistence was seen as essential to freedom's meaningful exercise. Both postwar liberal thinkers, such as Aron, and the institutional framework of the postwar dirigiste state thus sought to achieve a synthesis of the themes of individual freedom and equality on the one hand and substantive access to the fruits of economic growth on the other.

The liberalism that informed post-1958 dirigisme not only prioritized an affirmative notion of state economic responsibility; it also connected that framework to a particular conception of society. In sharp contrast to the German liberal tradition, the investiture of a Saint-Simonian, technocratic bureaucracy with the task of economic modernization was accompanied by a strong distrust of interest groups, which, in keeping with long-standing French conceptions, were perceived as parochial and self-serving and thus as potential obstacles to the goal of economic modernization. In practice, this anti-group animus applied to small shopkeepers, family-owned businesses, peasants, and, perhaps above all, to a radicalized and anarcho-syndicalist labor movement. Unlike the situation under the Third Republic, which had worked to protect vested interests in the service of political stability, a highly trained technocratic elite now focused upon developing segments of the economy "on which the increase in all other forms of industrial output was believed to depend."[77] As Jonah Levy describes, this distrust of "Malthusian" economic interests drove authorities to divert state resources to so-called national champions—large multinational firms that were intended to act as the engines and stewards of France's prosperity.[78] It also shaped an elite conception heavily skewed toward macroeconomic considerations, with individuals standing to benefit from economic growth once parochial interest groups had been defeated or circumvented.

Even the microeconomic elements of France's modernization strategy, including planning and industrial policy, were all aimed at achieving the macroeconomic outcomes of rapid growth and low unemployment. Jean Monnet's formulation of the goals of planning was clear in this regard: these were to "increase production, expand trade, raise productivity to the level of the most advanced countries, assure full employment, and raise the standard of living, all of which goals were cast in generalized rather than particularistic terms."[79] By the height of the *trente glorieuses*, or thirty "glorious" years of postwar growth, France had consolidated a highly centralized and macroeconomically oriented political economy of which citizens qua workers were understood to be the modal beneficiaries. While successful in generating economic growth and modernization, this strategy also served to justify the underdevelopment of the welfare state, which left unprotected many vulnerable groups, such as single parents and older unemployed people without histories of contributions.

Just as the postwar boom both reflected the success of the dirigiste state and burnished its prestige, slowing growth and mounting social unrest and political instability of the late 1960s and early 1970s tarnished it, leading to another significant inflection in the statist liberal tradition. The dirigiste strategy of labor exclusion and favoring industrial expansion over consumption proved increasingly ill suited to a darkening economic climate, with unemployment rates that doubled between 1963 and 1973 and generalizing anxiety in the face of slowing growth and rising inflation.[80] The system's ineffectiveness in meeting new economic challenges forced authorities to accept some degree of economic liberalization in the face of a deteriorating balance of payments, even as growing social and political unrest, most notably the near revolution of May–June 1968, placed the need for reform in even starker relief.[81] Thereafter, French policymakers would remain on the defensive, looking for hints of industrial unrest and seeking policies that might dampen it.[82] They worked to reduce the imprint of the state on industrial relations by granting legal protections to trade unions, granting workers greater authority within firm-level works councils, and generally seeking to decentralize and revitalize collective bargaining.[83] They also extended subsidies and protective legislation to potentially troublesome groups, such as restrictions on the size and location of supermarkets demanded by politically volatile shopkeepers.[84] Such defensive measures were undertaken in an ad hoc fashion, however, and the core of authorities' policy strategy continued to rely on centralized and technocratic macroeconomic management.[85] As opposed to the German strategy of group subsidization, the French relied on the projection of state power through a series of broad regulatory measures designed to shelter all workers from an increasingly inhospitable economic environment.[86]

French authorities also began during this time to move to fill gaps in France's employment-based, Bismarckian welfare state in ways that sharply departed from standard neoliberal orthodoxies. This shift involved the creation of anti-poverty and income-support policies designed to buffer the growing number of workers unable to find employment. Such measures included cash assistance to single mothers, the handicapped, and the elderly poor, many of whom lacked a consistent employment history upon which eligibility for Bismarckian welfare benefits depended.[87] By the late 1970s, then, France's political-economic model had evolved significantly, yielding at once a state that was less dominant in the policymaking process and a policy agenda that had shifted in a market-conforming direction. Despite this qualified embrace of markets, however, the state preserved and even expanded non-market arrangements such as social policies that helped to preserve social peace and societal consensus, making liberalization politically and economically feasible.

This qualified and buffered embrace of the market accelerated following Socialist President François Mitterrand's famous "U-turn" in the early 1980s. Elected in 1981 as the head of the first socialist administration in the history of the Fifth Republic and supported by a large leftist majority in parliament, Mitterrand initially enacted a number of ambitious measures that hearkened back to the dirigiste heyday, including extensive nationalizations, massive increases in aid to industry, and ramped-up welfare spending, all aimed at fulfilling campaign promises to undertake a "rupture with capitalism."[88] This policy of "redistributive Keynesianism," it was hoped, would help to reverse the post-1973 economic decline, even as it relieved some of the political pressure on a state that had increasingly come to be seen as failing to fulfill its economic commitments.[89] However, in the face of tightening constraints—including a deteriorating balance of payments, growing tensions between a slumping franc and the strictures of the European Monetary System, concerns about accelerating inflation, and mounting losses by nationalized companies—French authorities after 1982 abandoned dirigisme with the same alacrity with which they had initially embraced it. In the two short years from 1982 to 1984, French officials began to dismantle the entire postwar dirigiste edifice, including selective credit allocation to national champions, state ownership of strategic firms, indicative planning, and sectoral industrial policies. In the ensuing decade, they embarked upon an ambitious agenda of privatization, liberalization, and deregulation of product and labor markets, replacing bank lending with equity financing and introducing competition in the financial-services sector.[90]

The repudiation of dirigisme did not end the state's involvement in the economy, however, nor did it entail an embrace of neoliberalism in the manner of Margaret Thatcher or Ronald Reagan. Instead, it was accompanied by additional expansions of welfare benefits, following a logic of what I have elsewhere called "socialized marketization."[91] Rather than favor particular groups in the German fashion, French authorities embarked upon a wide-ranging expansion of individual social rights, working to buffer French citizens from the vagaries of the market to which they were now much more exposed.[92] This expansion of social protection took two principal forms. The first involved the expansion of early-retirement schemes, in which around 700,000 French workers were participating by 1984.[93] The second was an expansion of income-support policies. As unemployment soared to 10.2 percent in 1985,[94] French authorities sought ways to dampen potential social unrest and shore up their political legitimacy. The signal example of this approach came in 1988 with the introduction by the government of Prime Minister Michel Rocard of the *Revenu minimum d'insertion*, or RMI, which established a state-financed minimum income and offered job-placement services for recipients; it constituted the first generalized anti-poverty benefit in the history of the French welfare state.[95] Any citizen was eligible, subject only to a basic means test. Denied its traditional dirigiste tack, the French state opted for a Keynesian agenda by other means, expanding citizen-based social protection even as it confronted both political and budgetary constraints on the state's role in the economy.[96]

By the late 1980s, then, French statist liberalism had been consolidated as a distinctive alternative to neoliberalism, one that accepted the *liberal* premises that the state's role in the economy should be circumscribed even as it rejected *neoliberalism's* messianic faith in the market, its hostility to social protection, and its commitment to a disembedded vision of the capitalist order. While French authorities liberalized the economy, they also extended a robust network of social protection cast in a highly individualistic vein. After the advent of the Maastricht Treaty in the early 1990s, which enshrined deflationary, monetarist assumptions at the heart of the nascent currency union, French authorities would work to channel market forces in ways that supported growth, even as they preserved the social-protection system and regulated labor market central to their embedded and socialized vision of capitalism.

Social Groups and the State in German Corporate Liberalism

If the French Revolution provided the genesis for French statist liberalism by creating contradictory imperatives for individual freedom and state responsibility, in Germany it acted as an anti-model, fueling a widespread elite rejection of the French model in favor of one that was at once more organic and more decentralized. Given that "Germany" did not yet exist but rather represented an assemblage of widely scattered principalities, it is perhaps somewhat misleading to speak of German liberalism at all. However, the absence of a defined German political order should not distract from the existence of a much more coherent set of ideas formed within the framework through which ethnic and linguistic Germans perceived the revolution and came to define their own incipient nationalism in contrast to it. The conclusion of the Napoleonic Wars and the collapse of the Holy Roman Empire created an impetus for a definition of the German nation state on new terms. As de Ruggiero points out, it was this new nationalism, conjoined with romantic notions of spiritual freedom and awareness, that tied German nationalism to early forms of German liberalism:

> The idea of the Fatherland, of the German nation, was the new bond which replaced the broken fetters of the Empire. . . . It is no mere historical accident that the national claims of the nineteenth century in Europe, especially those of Germany and Italy, had originally a Liberal character. To peoples possessing no tradition of political unity, only freedom could give the idea of a common citizenship capable of overcoming and dominating their political dismemberment.[97]

German liberalism cum nationalism sought to free Germans from statelessness by creating a Leviathan of their own, to be crafted out of disparate, much older political communities.

The nationalist imprint of early German liberalism can be traced through the writings of a number of nineteenth-century thinkers, all of whom furnished key elements of what would become early twentieth-century Ordoliberalism, which would itself evolve into distinct tradition of what I have dubbed "corporate liberalism." Many of these thinkers would focus on social and economic groups, which they saw as organically evolved bearers of the linguistic and cultural traditions that would come to define the German nation. In a nationalist tradition that lacks a state as a symbol and defender, German liberals viewed groups as naturally constituted, organically derived associations whose natural attraction to one another (whether on social, political, or economic grounds) led them to provide mutual assistance, support, and validation. In contrast to the French case, where the establishment of a state long predated the emergence of economic groups during the Renaissance and early commercial era and where social and political bonds therefore tended to be vertical, in Germany such groups (guilds, for example) preceded the creation of the state by several centuries.[98] As a result, social bonds tended to be horizontal—both within and among groups—with the state working to support and co-opt powerful groups in an effort to consolidate its authority.[99] In keeping with this historical pattern, romantic liberals tended to view such groups as "'personalities'—societies, corporations, communities, universities, classes, religious associations, and an entire network of legal and political relations binding this complex manifold into . . . national unity."[100] For Kant and other German Enlightenment thinkers, this emphasis went hand in glove with a jaundiced view of the state, desired as the future bearer of German nationalism but also distrusted as a potential threat to group interests and to the individual's freedom to join and participate in the communities that underlay them.[101]

Few German liberal thinkers provided clearer and more coherent formulations of this intertwined distrust of a potentially predatory state and defense of individuals' group memberships than Wilhelm von Humboldt. In his early twenties when the Revolution broke out, Humboldt rejected it as "ahistorical and inorganic" and believed that the revolutionaries' approach "would never correspond to reality," because it would "block the development in individuals, retard the natural evolution of society, and would only lead to conformity to an imposed order."[102] Humboldt emphasized the importance of *Bildung*, approximately translatable as "education," to the growth of the human soul and saw a despotic state as the most important threat to that process.[103] This process of education, however, would not take place alone or remain the province of atomized individuals; rather, it would take place in "mutual relations with others," since "only the free association of individuals can create anything really organic, while State intervention can realize nothing but an uncreative machine."[104] He argued further that "developing human capacities to the full in their diversity and individuality was an urgent task, but a task for which laws, government, and regulation were generally inept."[105] These convictions grew out of two interrelated premises. First, "the state must abstain from actively providing for citizens' welfare and must not go a step further than their safety from domestic and foreign enemies requires." Second, "natural law, in relation to people's communal lives, marks a very clear boundary. It prohibits all actions, by which the state culpably interferes in the affairs of people's communities."[106] Taken together, such statements reflect a belief in individuals' understanding of their own shared interests, mutual responsibilities for their collective welfare, and limits on the state's rights to interfere in the communities that such interests inform.

In such a vision, moreover, religious, economic, and social groups precede the state both chronologically and ontologically, and their interests should take political precedence over those of the state to the extent consistent with social order. For Humboldt, as for many early German liberals, society and community were to be defined by common priorities and affinities, rather than abstract, atomized raison d'état, epitomized by the French Revolution's betrayal of its early liberal ideals. Humboldt's juxtaposition of organic group identity with the predations of an overmighty state were shared by his younger brother Alexander, the great scientist and naturalist, for whom the rise of the German middle class represented a healthy, if defensive, response to the authoritarianism of the Prussian state, which was part and parcel of the European turn to reaction after the failed promise of 1789.[107] The incipient German nation must draw its strength from such groups, who were understood to be the fundamental components of the social order and represented a healthy, communal counterpoint to the decadence of German-cum-Prussian militarism, arbitrary and oppressive monarchy, and reactionary, quasi-feudal socioeconomic order. Rejecting this institutional order, nineteenth-century German liberals viewed self-organizing groups—notably the *Mittelstand* of small and medium-sized businesses and, as industrialization accelerated, trade unions and "new groups of manufacturers and retailers, officials and teachers, farmers and workers, white-collar employees and shopkeepers"—as "the best defense against social upheaval" and indicative of a salutary process of "lateral differentiation" that strengthened social bonds and "channeled [citizens'] energies towards collective action."[108] This perspective was also echoed in the preference of governing elites for economic cartels, which were viewed as anticompetitive bastions of economic order.[109]

The themes developed by early liberals informed strands of thought among German legal historians, who also privileged groups as central to the social and economic order. Although a wide variety of groups, including religious communities and professional associations, were central to this vision, groups defined by shared economic interests were the most important manifestation of this pattern. Perhaps the most influential such historian was Otto von Gierke, whose *Deutsche Genossenschaftsrecht* constituted a milestone of German legal and social history. For Gierke, the development of Germanic society since the ninth century was defined by the evolution of social and economic groups and their changing relationship to public authority. From its earliest feudal incarnations, German society was defined by group membership, most basically and immediately in the family, which was "the oldest of all human ties" and "can be viewed as the prototype of all contemporary Constitutional categories."[110] This "old Germanic fellowship . . . emerges in a personal community where membership is hereditary and gives rise to a specific type of *peace* and of Right. Membership of this fellowship means *freedom*."[111] Later, as feudalism gave way to the commercializing pattern of the High Middle Ages and the Renaissance, such groups took on a more explicitly economic character, notably in the form of guilds and other such associations. These associations, or "free unions," as Gierke calls them, represented a "new thinking that was more powerful even than the marvellous ideas of feudal monarchy and universal hierarchies."[112] As early as the twelfth century, "the fusion of the old principle of the market community with the new principle of free union" created guilds, which "became the oldest German community and therefore simultaneously the embryo of the German state and the German commune."[113]

Gierke's conception of voluntary associations as the bedrock of the social order was central both to his conception of liberalism and prevailing conceptions of society and its relationship to the state in nineteenth-century Germany. But his was not a static notion of social structure. Rather, it entailed a view of groups' "moral independence from the state" as "the cornerstone of a just constitution and legal system." As a result, "the recognition of real group personality, as well as of individual personality, is essential to human liberty, and . . . the arbitrary treatment of associations is the hallmark of tyranny."[114] For Gierke, then, liberalism entailed the recognition that organically constituted groups, composed of free individuals coming together to pursue common interests, were irreducible components of a free society. In analytical moves that would anticipate both Ordoliberalism's emphasis on equilibrium between state power and social order and the Social Market Economy's architects' prioritization of a socially embedded market, Gierke thus viewed freedom as both defined and protected by the strength of social groups. Far from an early version of the thin conception of "civil society" popularized in the 1990s by writers such as Robert Putnam, which amounted to veiled arguments for society to assume tasks from a state weakened by neoliberal reform,[115] Gierke's framework celebrates state power and group personality (what he called *Gesamtpersönlichkeit*), which he viewed as mutually dependent concomitants of a just and stable social and political order. This conception finds echoes in various strands of nineteenth-century German political thought, from Hegel's view of society as an intermediary that helps to reconcile antagonisms between the state and individuals to the broader conception of the *Rechtsstaat* (imprecisely translated in English as "rule of law"). Together, such strands helped to define the "essence of German liberalism," whose "foundation stone . . . consisted in self-government, understood not as the participation of people in a legislative and governing parliament, but as the possession by local bodies of governmental functions conferred upon them by . . . the state."[116]

From Ordoliberalism to the Social Market Economy: Groups and the State in Postwar Germany

Recognizing these intellectual antecedents allows us to understand the emergence of Ordoliberalism out of the chaos of the Weimar Republic. If thinkers like Gierke celebrate an ideal of balance between group autonomy and state power, the post–World War I context provides a dark anti-model of predatory groups colonizing and eventually destroying the state on which all legal and social order ultimately depends.[117] From the development of economic monopolies in key industrial sectors like coal and steel to the ideological (and increasingly physical) battle between parties of the Far Left and Far Right at the expense of coherent parliamentary politics, the 1920s in Germany can be well understood as a period during which the power of groups of various stripes first eroded and then displaced the *Rechtsstaat* at the center of German democracy. For this reason, Ordoliberals such as Rüstow and Eucken could not accept the championing of laissez-faire and individual spontaneity celebrated by Hayek and other Austrians, still less a minimalist state whose proper role classical liberals reduced to a police function and the enforcement of contracts. By contrast, Rüstow argued that the "rise of powerful special interests" under Weimar made the state "the easy prey of political parties" and thus rendered it "incapable of acting independently for the larger good." The solution, thought Rüstow, Eucken, and Müller-Armack, was to create a new political order based on the politics of order (*Ordnungspolitik*), in which a powerful but not despotic state would "supersede the weak *party and intervention state*" and thus restore the balance between state power and the independence of social groups.[118]

It is in this sense that the Ordoliberals understood the state's role as preserving but never undermining competition among relatively autonomous social groups, which they viewed as the antidote to Weimaresque clientelism, the cartelization arising from nineteenth-century industrialization, related predatory economic practices, and political and social chaos. This "humanist form of market economics" was "rooted in the understanding that the full capacities of markets could only be realized through their embedding in a robust legal and social order, including preemptive, 'market-conforming' interventions on the part of the state."[119] Drawing from early strands of so-called neoliberalism, a term originally coined by Rüstow to refer to the anti-laissez-faire (hence "neo-") liberalisms that grew out of the Mont Pelerin Society in the 1930s and 1940s, Ordoliberalism prioritized a strong state as a cure for the pernicious "democratization of the economy."[120] This outcome led the state, in Rüstow's words, to be "pulled to pieces by avaricious interests," to become a "total state" (a concept he drew from Carl Schmitt) focused on delivering clientelistic goods to rapacious interest groups, which was a giant built on feet of clay, "at the mercy of the interest groups of the plural society."[121] Ordoliberalism distinguished between political democracy, which it championed, and economic democracy, which was a recipe for chaos, stagnation, and corruption. Figures such as Rüstow and Röpke, members of the so-called Freiburg School that rejected Nazi totalitarianism and "ultra-liberal purism" in equal measure, championed instead "a market economy underpinned by a responsible, effective state that policed rules, promoted competition, and provided within limits for social need."[122] They were also responding to a postwar context in which unprecedented physical destruction and penury made the Austrian and classical liberal models of a minimalist state and laissez-faire seem childish fantasies.

In its place, Ordoliberals posited a combination of Rüstow's *Vitalpolitik* (which recognized the need to provide basic economic and social goods) and Röpke's " '*structural policy*' designed to 'no longer assume the social preconditions of the market economy . . . as given' "[123]—a balance between recognizing and responding to group demands and preserving the autonomy of the state that was essential to the survival of the capitalist order. This early concern for the (limited) distribution of economic goods, which the Austrians rejected as pandering welfarism, grew out of the realization that "stability and security for the working class was prerequisite to securing the market economy." But it did so in a way that continued to privilege groups such as small firms and family agriculture that were the building blocks of the social and economic order. Even as they cautioned against the monopolistic tendencies of big business, Ordoliberals celebrated the "independent middle strata" of society, who, "extolled as the 'healthy core' of an ailing society," "were to constitute the 'fertile soil' . . . of the desired order."[124] That order itself was not "a natural phenomenon, but rather a cultural-political product, founded on a constitutional order, which cannot continue to function correctly unless one focuses attentive care on it, much as one 'cultivates a garden' [using Böhm's words]."[125] Thus, the prevailing vision of the structure of society and the economy dovetailed seamlessly with a normative and moral conception of the proper scope and focus of public benefits and state action.

In the 1950s these orthogonal strands were synthesized into a more coherent vision of policy and politics as the chaos of the postwar world gave way to the emergence of the postwar German model. This model bore the stamp of Ordoliberalism's emphasis on the importance of a robust state as an arbiter of market rules and a bulwark against monopolistic market power, but it also evolved in ways that were required by Germany's chaotic and penurious postwar situation. Applying this legacy to the postwar German context required two important shifts. First, it required a richer and more specific notion of the state, which was to be responsible for restoring economic stability and prosperity rather than merely acting as a neutral referee among organically constituted economic actors. Second and relatedly, it would involve a greater emphasis on the equitable distribution of economic goods in ways that would contravene market outcomes in important respects. This second shift reflected both an economic and political logic. Economically Germany was simply too devastated and impoverished for the Ordoliberal model of prosperity and robust competition within a healthy and decentralized market order to be anything but a remote ideal; accordingly, workers and employers would need access to goods that the market was incapable of creating. Politically it reflected the need to legitimize the postwar German order and to secure the support of workers and capital whose active participation and investment would be essential to the country's economic recovery.

The concrete task of working out these modifications to the Ordoliberal ideal was taken up most importantly by Ludwig Erhard, Adenauer's economics minister and future chancellor, and Alfred Müller-Armack, an economist associated with the Freiburg School and later secretary of state in the Economics Ministry. Müller-Armack became the most influential figure in developing a synthesis of Ordoliberalism and Rüstow's *Vitalpolitik* that became the core of what he would call the Social Market Economy, as well as working to gain the support of both the public and policymakers who would be responsible for creating it. Müller-Armack's "aim was to promote the social market economy as a strategy for transferring the principles of the new liberalism into potentially hostile political and societal spheres" and to respond to the question that abstract Ordoliberalism had left unanswered: "[w]hich societal groups and social forces should be charged with the mandate to secure a competitive order committed to Ordoliberal ideals, given the already existing pluralistic structures . . . in parliamentary democracies?"[126]

Inheriting this emphasis on groups from nineteenth-century German liberalism, Müller-Armack borrowed from Marxism a view of capital and labor as the primary constituents of a capitalist economy but replaced Marx's emphasis on class conflict with a more hopeful vision that sought to mute conflict through the creation of an expansive welfare state.[127] For Müller-Armack, social compensation was essential for moving beyond the "framework of rules" posited by Ordoliberals to "a new type of equilibrium informed by the divergent objectives of social security and economic freedom."[128] His "aim was to promote the social market economy as a strategy for transferring the principles of new [Ordo] liberalism into potentially hostile political and societal spheres without neglecting the ultimate . . . objective of creating a new kind of strong state."[129] In practice this meant creating an order in which various social strata had the means and the initiative to become active, informed participants in a market society in which opportunities and responsibilities would be balanced. Without access to employment—a scarce commodity in the early postwar era—and social support for those unable to find it, such a vision would be unrealizable. In Müller-Armack's words, "To disregard [the] process of redistribution, in assessing the social dimension of the market process which sustains it, would be to fail to appreciate the social content of the social market economy."[130] Though it shared with Ordoliberalism a belief in the importance of the state's role, the Social Market Economy as envisioned by Müller-Armack and its other conceptual architects embraced a far more active role for the state than the more passive, organicist view advanced by Ordoliberals could have tolerated.[131]

This vision would provide both the ideational blueprint and the legitimating ideology for an increasingly successful German economy in the 1950s and 1960s. The combination of neocorporatist collective-bargaining institutions, firm-level works councils, powerful industrial banks that provided deep pools of patient capital to firms, and broadly consensual political and economic relationships reinforced the social peace and economic success that the Social Market Economy helped to create.[132] As an extensive literature in the 1970s and 1980s showed, many continental European countries, including Germany, Austria, Switzerland, and Sweden, responded to challenges of the postwar era by similarly dividing authority among states and robust producer groups that enjoyed legally enshrined rights in collective bargaining and economic and social policymaking.[133] Although each country devised institutional variations on this theme, with, for example, various degrees of concentration among producer groups, they all privileged social and economic groups and rejected both statist and neoliberal conceptions of an atomistic and disembedded political-economic order.[134] But what was becoming the German corporate liberal tradition provided specific variations on this common theme that stemmed from a distinctive set of intellectual conceptions of the state's role and its connection to society.

As in the French case, Germany's postwar model and associated state-society relations were thus not sketched on a tabula rasa but rather were outgrowths of older liberal traditions, in the German case ones that placed groups at their conceptual center. The evolution of strands of German liberalism into interwar Ordoliberalism and then into neocorporatism and the Social Market Economy in the 1950s and 1960s reflected continued adherence to principles that endowed groups with a privileged position, albeit in ways that evolved with prevailing economic circumstances.[135] These revised arrangements underpinned a stunning degree of economic growth and dynamism, sustained by generalized social peace and broad consensus, that muted partisan conflict and the class divisions that had been the hallmarks of nineteenth-century industrialization. By 1962 Germany had become the world's largest exporter, specializing in high-quality consumer and industrial goods. With rapid economic growth and declining and eventually trivial levels of unemployment, the country's economic performance could well justify the moniker of *Wirtschaftswunder*, or "economic miracle," that was used to describe its dramatic and improbable recovery.

The emphasis on groups that became central to German liberalism stemmed not only from a reconfigured understanding of Marxist class analysis but also from Social Catholicism, which was influential among Rhenish Catholics, including CDU Chancellor Konrad Adenauer. Also called Christian Socialists, Social Catholics saw full employment and economic redistribution as desirable goals of public policy and emphasized the political and social responsibilities of all social and economic groups.[136] In contradistinction to France, where social and economic groups were marginalized and politically delegitimized, in Germany they were seen not only as legitimate but as essential components of the social, political, and economic order. In this way, prevailing German understandings of liberalism and the relationship between the state and social actors drew on multiple sources, all of which rejected the classical and neoliberal view of society as a collection of atomized individuals.

This understanding enshrined capital and labor with a powerful and prominent position across the postwar German economy. From the welfare funds that were governed by worker and employer representatives, to the system of sectoral wage bargaining, to the works councils responsible for shop-floor governance on the firm level,[137] postwar Germany was governed by groups in relatively harmonious mutual dependence. Thus, combining an Ordoliberal distrust of monopolies and emphasis on competition with a Social Catholic understanding of the social role of groups, the Social Market Economy reflected a "balance between the liberal and the social democratic impulses in postwar Germany."[138]

As in France, the worsening economic climate in the late 1960s and 1970s, involving slowed economic growth, inflationary pressures arising from the 1973 OPEC oil shock, and slackening international demand for exports, forced German elites to re-examine some of the precepts of the Social Market Economy. Although Germany continued to perform better than most of its European neighbors,[139] the apparent durability of the new challenges brought about a shift in focus from legitimizing the Social Market Economy to defending it against new economic pressures. In practice, this meant the end of social-policy expansion, and related efforts to secure wage moderation and dampen inflation, which undermined both workers' purchasing power and the export competitiveness on which the German economy depended. The Social Democratic governments following Chancellor Willy Brandt's victory over the CDU in 1972 had to ponder for the first time significant economic trade-offs among competing interest groups, who were now fighting for increasingly scarce resources.[140]

German authorities' reaction to the economic challenges of the 1970s involved updating many of the assumptions inherited from Ordoliberalism and modifying key institutional aspects of the Social Market Economy, even as they explicitly rejected the expansive neoliberal view of a market society and a denuded state. Just as Ordoliberalism had evolved in the face of the challenges of postwar reconstruction, its ideological heir continued to shift in response to the challenges of the post-1970 era and to the related rise of neoliberalism. This evolutionary process informed the consolidation of an intellectual framework of "corporate liberalism," which would shape Germany's responses to the challenges of an era of slowed growth, economic austerity, rising unemployment, and growing social unrest beginning in the early 1990s. In Germany, unlike Britain or the United States, this new inflection of liberalism maintained an important role for the state and preserved, indeed nurtured, the welfare state and the collaborative relationships among producer groups that had been instrumental to Germany's postwar economic success.[141] It was precisely because Germany, like France and Italy, rejected neoliberal prescriptions that it had to look elsewhere for a template—in this case, to the premises of Ordoliberalism as modified by the consolidation and, later, the challenged legitimacy of the Social Market Economy.

That said, Germany stood out from its neighbors in a number of important respects informed by its distinctive liberal tradition. First, unlike France and Britain, Germany had never opted for a robust Keynesianism model,[142] preferring to focus on wage bargains and social policy as the primary tools of economic management. Second, as in France, classical liberal thought had remained a marginal discourse throughout the postwar period, with the small and ostensibly liberal FDP, the perennial coalition partner with the SPD and the CDU under Foreign Minister Hans-Dietrich Genscher, focused mostly on foreign policy. Whereas elsewhere "[n]eoliberalism achieved [its] (ecologically) dominant position by variously exploiting, reflecting, and intensifying conditions of globalizing economic turbulence since the 1970s,"[143] in Germany what Phillip Cerny has dubbed "embedded neoliberalism"[144] never took root.

This strategic and intellectual stance helped to spur an evolution of a more nuanced and less optimistic model of "corporate liberalism" that would govern German economic adjustment in the post-reunification era. Just as the economic realities of the immediate postwar period had forced a modification of traditional Ordoliberalism, the twin challenges of a global economic slowdown and the rise of neoliberalism spurred the emergence of a new prevailing economic model that worked to adapt the Social Market Economy to new economic circumstances. The "corporate liberal" framework preserved the emphasis on key economic groups, but it left behind the Social Market Economy's optimistic emphasis on economic expansion and focused instead on adapting inherited economic arrangements to less propitious circumstances by prioritizing a robust social-protection system and role for the state, though one that was selective in its favored constituencies, in a context of liberalization and intensifying international competitive pressures.[145] As the dominant policy agenda moved ever more towards liberalization and social and labor-market policy reform in the 1980s and 1990s, governing elites worked to subsidize and protect vested economic interests while often imposing costs on such unincorporated and politically more marginal constituencies as younger workers, single women, and the long-term unemployed. If the Social Market Economy had been designed to provide core groups with policy authority and economic privilege, then the ethos of corporate liberalism involved rejecting broad-based neoliberal adjustment strategies while protecting and subsidizing key groups at the expense of a growing number of economic outsiders.

State Colonization, Anti-statism, and the Politics of Groups in Italian Clientelist Liberalism

Prior to the 1860 *Risorgimento*, economic liberalism played a relatively minor role in Italian political discourse. Historically beset by deep social and economic divisions between north and south, political fragmentation, and profound economic backwardness, Italy industrialized late and then only partially, as northern states like Lombardy and Piedmont increasingly left behind the quasi-feudal and latifundian southern two-thirds of the country. The result of this uneven and sluggish pattern of economic development was a small and regionally concentrated middle class hamstrung in its efforts to industrialize and forced to focus on political and social stability rather than economic development. The underdevelopment of the Italian middle class and the lack of economic development until the eve of the *Risorgimento* meant that liberalism remained a doctrine embraced by a small northern elite and had little bearing on the political or economic development of the country.[146] Equally important, the political and cultural dominance of the Catholic Church meant that even Italian liberals tended to view society through an ecclesiastical lens that "[could] not grant the individualism that is a postulate of capitalism" and instead understood liberalism as intimately bound up with "a corporative organization of society."[147] The group-based conception of social organization that would inflect Italian liberalism's understanding of postwar social and economic challenges was thus embedded within it from the beginning.

Italian unification granted new currency to the liberalism of figures like Count Emilio Cavour (founder of the Italian Liberal Party and premier of Piedmont).[148] As political liberals such as Giuseppe Mazzini celebrated what they saw as the fulfillment of a long-frustrated Italian national destiny, economic liberals such as Cavour and Carolo Cattaneo hoped that unification would provide an opportunity to reform the Italian political economy along the lines of English and French liberalism, which they much admired, thereby transforming a largely backward agrarian nation into an industrializing and commercial one.[149] Such hopes were frustrated, however, by both the absence of a robust indigenous liberal tradition and concerns about the need to "prevent the fragile state constructed by Cavour from succumbing to illiberal forces" took precedence over "substantive elaborations of new institutional solutions inspired by the liberal tradition."[150] The weakness of native Italian liberalism and the lateness of industrialization gave Italian liberalism a character "largely reflected" from France,[151] and for liberal Italian economists of the period, "economic liberty was inseparable from political liberty and was indeed seen as a natural extension of it. . . . [T]hey saw economic and political liberty as two aspects of the same concept,"[152] both informed by a legitimizing, romantic ideal of individualism.[153]

Although the *Risorgimento* thus breathed life into an erstwhile moribund doctrine, it also created a close identification between liberalism and the new Italian state that would leave the doctrine on the defensive against those who stood to lose from the new political and economic order. In the aftermath of the Napoleonic wars, Italian liberals, frustrated in equal measure by the authoritarianism of Italian city-states and the patronage and clientelism that undergirded them, formed "sects," or organizations of like-minded individuals, separate from and hostile to the state.[154] This fragmented pattern would be reinforced after the *Risorgimento*, with alienated liberals unreconciled to a state that quickly sacrificed the principles of economic freedom and competition to political expediency. The original *Blocco storico*—or "historical bloc"—Antonio Gramsci's term for the elite bargain that folded southern Italy into the new nation[155]—had sacrificed social and economic integration on the altar of political unity.[156] The increasingly illiberal and clientelistic character of the new nation left a toxic legacy: the widespread perception of the state as illiberal and corrupt. The political landscape remained fragmented beneath the veneer of national unity, and policies served the economic interests of dominant elites rather than foster a process of national social and economic integration.

The outcome was a state that was viewed as both the embodiment of liberty and the symbol of its betrayal. The elite character of the *Risorgimento*, imposed by "a virtual act of conquest sanctioned by a merely nominal plebiscite,"[157] would undermine both the stability and the liberal character of the Italian state for decades to come. Even as they paid lip service to individualism and freedom, Italian authorities, encouraged by both economic interests that were sharply delimited by region and class and the need to dampen societal resistance to the state's very existence, laid the groundwork for a state surrounded by a hostile society and increasingly hypocritical in its adherence to its early ideals:

> [I]n fact the government . . . was widely separated from this lofty ideal [of the state as the personification of the ethical substance of the individual], and tended not so much to vitalize the state within the consciousness of the individual, as to erect it into an independent principle, isolated from all that spiritual process which justifies it and unifies it with the will of the citizens. Thus, by a slow and imperceptible degradation, two things were in practice dissociated, which in the idea of a Liberal State should have been, and theoretically were, conjoined: authority and liberty, law and autonomy, active citizenship and passive citizenship.[158]

This "slow degradation," stemming from the purchase of national unity by the draining of liberalism's vitality, would have important implications for the emergence of Italian "clientelist liberalism" after World War II. Like its French counterpart, nineteenth-century Italian liberalism venerated the individual and equality before the law but did little to deliver the economic and social goods on which individual dignity relied. Like its German analog, Italian liberalism accepted the existence of particularistic social and economic interest groups but, by contrast, treated them as threats to be placated rather than sources of enduring economic strength and bearers of privilege and responsibility. By the late nineteenth century, this perspective evolved into the tacit doctrine of *Trasformismo*, whereby collusion between elites on the Left and Right was designed to insulate the state from the predations of social groups. Giovanni Giolitti, an Italian liberal and perennial prime minister in the late nineteenth and early twentieth centuries (and the originator of the term *Trasformismo*), in 1901 provided a crystalline and emblematic statement of Italian liberals' fear of what contemporary French elites had come to call *les classes dangereuses*:

> No one should deceive himself into thinking that the lower classes can be prevented from acquiring their share of economic and political influence. The friends of existing institutions have one duty above all: it is persuading these lower classes, with facts, that they have more to hope from existing institutions than from any dreams of the future.[159]

The result was a liberalism that was both particularistic and illegitimate in the eyes of those who viewed the state's very existence as a betrayal of the nation's foundational principles.

Two figures in particular would inform the character of the subsequent development of Italian liberal thought and reinforce its profoundly anti-statist character: Vilfredo Pareto and Luigi Einaudi. Pareto, best known in Anglo-American circles for his postulate of "optimality,"[160] focused his criticism on protectionism, which he viewed as a primary means of "despoilment" that protected a small number of interests at the expense of society as a whole.[161] This critique stemmed from Pareto's view, shared by many of his liberal contemporaries, that the new Italian state was an essentially clientelistic mechanism designed to benefit the favored few, in particular southern agrarian elites and a few strategically important northern industries, notably coal and steel. Such mechanisms were profoundly colored by the character of the *Risorgimento* and Italy's weak industrialization, which led powerful but woefully uncompetitive economic interests to rely heavily on the state for their economic survival.[162]

This understanding of the clientelistic character of the Italian state in turn informed Pareto's notion of political action, which centered on undermining clientelism and promoting a state in which all citizens were substantively equal before the law. The so-called circulation of elites, whereby power shifts cyclically among elites within and out of government, effectively precludes government's acting on behalf of society as a whole. Over time, Pareto believed, such a situation could lead to revolution or at least sustained political instability—a perspective no doubt supported by continual peasant-led unrest in the South that was periodically put down by the state with brutal force.

Increasingly, as Pareto well understood, erstwhile political enemies from Left and Right joined forces in the service of political stability and against the mounting threats from socialism, according to a logic of *Trasformismo*, "the process whereby during the 1880s the old party labels of Left and Right lost their meaning as governments became shapeless amalgams of one-time opponents," which "bur[ied] old differences, and focus[ed] collectively on ad hoc issues" while holding coalitions together through the use of patronage and corruption."[163] By the end of World War I, Pareto had become sufficiently disillusioned by decades of Italian political degeneration that he came to oppose democracy itself,[164] which the Italian Right increasingly viewed as a hopelessly corrupt bargain between dominant elites and a disenfranchised mass public that had traded meager state-derived benefits for meaningful political influence.[165] Writing in the post–World War I era, when the ineffectiveness and growing instability of Italian democracy helped to legitimate and fuel Mussolini's rise, Pareto issued blistering criticism of the regime in language that anticipated criticisms of the clientelist liberal model that consolidated itself after World War II, in particular the dysfunctional role of social and economic groups:

> When central power crumbles the power of some individuals and some collectivities [groups] will grow. These collectivities remain subordinate in theory to the seat of central government. But in practice they gain autonomy. Those who do not belong to such collectivities are weak. No longer protected by the sovereign, they must look elsewhere for protection and adjudication. They can either trust a powerful patron, enter into secret or public partnerships with other weak people, or join associations, communes, or trade unions.[166]

Group Capture and the Failed Synthesis of Postwar Italian Liberalism

Pareto's cynical anti-statism provided something of a model for postwar Italian liberals, who shared his view of the clientelistic state (reinforced by the long interregnum of fascist corporatism) but used it as inspiration for a more substantive and ideologically coherent campaign against its potential predations. The most famous and influential such figure was Luigi Einaudi, who fled Fascist Italy in 1943 and later became influential in the Colloque Walter Lippman and the Mont Pelerin Society while also serving in a number of government posts, notably positions as the governor of the Bank of Italy and minister of finance in the late 1940s. For Einaudi, as for his nineteenth-century forbears, political and economic liberalism were closely aligned, and the market, which he described in Hayekian terms as "a polycentric order that guarantees social and political pluralism," is "the other face of democracy."[167] Einaudi deeply distrusted clientelistic groups and believed that Italy's economic and political revival depended on overcoming their hold on the Italian political economy and on dislodging the political structures that coddled them, notably the prefects that were the Italian state's local representatives. He declared in 1944, "Get rid of the prefect! Abolish every trace of the centralised machine. . . . The unity of the country does not come from prefects. . . . It is made by Italians, who must learn at their own cost and [in] making mistakes to govern themselves."[168] For Einaudi, as for Eucken and Rüstow, economic freedom centrally entailed freedom of association into autonomous, politically independent groups, in contradistinction to an uncoordinated amalgam of atomized individuals. Instead of the groups that had emerged in corrupt symbiosis with the state, Einaudi had in mind organically evolved associations that "do not contradict the principles of competition, but rather are an instrument of its full realization and perfection."[169] This emphasis, an understandable reaction to the highly centralized fascist state, also reflected the hopes of unleashing individual initiative within a socialized and embedded economic order, leading to a civic mindedness that would improve the economic fortunes of the least well-off. In this vision, which reflected a liberal variant that mirrored some elements of its German counterpart, groups would act both as a reflection of human freedom and as bulwarks of a humane capitalist economic order, even as it rejected the atomized vision of Manchesterian liberalism.[170]

Einaudi's initial optimism about the prospects for an Italian renaissance seemed justified by Italy's surprisingly rapid economic recovery and healthy economic performance in the first decade following the war. Although Italy's challenges were distinct from those faced by Germany, since it had neither fully industrialized before the war nor been subject to the same degree of physical devastation, observers described early postwar Italian recovery as "miraculous" with perhaps equal justification. Helped along by Marshall Plan aid, annual economic growth averaged 6 percent between the late 1940s and 1963, prompted by rapid growth in new construction, exports, and investment, which increased by an astonishing annual average of between 9 and 11 percent.[171] Although such aggregate figures masked widespread economic precariousness, which was particularly concentrated in the South, by the late 1950s Italy had become an industrialized country properly so designated, with average annual rates of growth of per capita GDP reaching 5.3 percent by 1963 (nearly ten times the 1951 figure) and the size of the economy roughly doubling.[172] The result was a seemingly overnight transformation of the country "from a land of peasants into a modern industrialised nation."[173]

Whereas Pareto focused his criticism on the state's protectionist and clientelistic practices, Einaudi's enemy was the clientelistic state itself, whether controlled by the Left or the Right, whose self-appointed mission to "realize the final state of the nature of society" he understood to be both futile and unjust. In Einaudi's view, statism tends to foster monopolies and "dangerously corrupts the principle of competition, reducing consumers' power to reward or penalize entrepreneurs' initiatives."[174] As finance minister under the early postwar Christian Democratic governments, he made such goals the centerpieces of the so-called Einaudi Line, a move that alienated many of his more socially oriented and Catholic colleagues and nearly led to a split in the Christian Democrats (DC) in the late 1940s.[175] Informed by his hatred of monopoly and the statism that sustained it, Einaudi aimed to implement his vision of a liberal state, which he argued had several essential tasks to fulfill; this echoed some of the themes of German Ordoliberalism. These tasks included circumventing or dismantling obstacles to economic competition, such as tariffs, quotas, public concessions, and cartel-like economic conspiracies. Fully recognizing that, left unchecked, capitalism tended toward monopoly, Einaudi worked to combat obstacles to competition that either originated in state action or emerged organically from the nature of human intercourse.[176] At the same time, however, he departed from the market fundamentalism of some of his Mont Pelerin colleagues, granting to the state the equally important task of "improving the chances of the most disadvantaged," as opposed to "working to achieve actual equality, which was incompatible with liberal principles."[177]

To the dismay of many Italian liberals, Italy's remarkable record of postwar economic achievement was not matched in the political arena, where this vision of a vibrant group-based civil society underpinning a competitive democratic politics was repeatedly frustrated. From its earliest inception, the Italian state had been designed to placate the interests of powerful groups whose opposition could easily unravel the hastily sewn thread of the fledgling political order. This foundational bargain informed a deeply dysfunctional parliament, which "after 1876 was turned into a forum where interest groups haggled with one another for favours, reflect[ing], and at the same time widen[ing], the gap between what critics now referred to as 'legal' and 'real' Italy."[178] The coalitional politics of *Trasformismo* led to the emergence of a system of "revolving centrism," with the DC at the center of a series of rapidly shifting coalitions held together through patronage, and a related framework of *Sottogoverno*, or "subgovernment," whereby various pieces of government ministries were colonized by the DC and their allies. This cynical strategy, which sacrificed long-term political integration for the sake of short-term expediency, seriously undermined the authority of the state and yielded a political system that critics such as the poet Giosuè Carducci openly deplored as the "sordid feebleness of liberal Italy."[179]

Italy's postwar economic success merely served to highlight the widening discrepancy between the country's economic revival and its political dysfunction. The deep divisions that the *Risorgimento* cemented in place, as well as the legacies of twenty years of fascism and a Catholic Church that only latterly recognized the state's legitimacy with the 1929 Lateran Pacts, yielded an Italian society that deeply distrusted the state "as at best ineffective and at worst an intrusive, hostile power that could do little good and much harm."[180] This public alienation enabled an increasingly dominant DC to use its alliance with the Americans—and its hostility to communism in general and the radical Italian Communist Party (PCI) in particular—to present itself as the only responsible, legitimate party of government. The consolidation of Christian Democratic rule was held together with the same glue that had cemented the First Republic after 1860—patronage and graft. After 1945,

> political patronage seeped into every corner of society while the state industrial enterprises were eventually politicized, mismanaged, and run hopelessly into debt. Public administration, the universities, the postal and telephone systems, health care, and most other public services were turned into marvels of inefficiency. Whatever the state touched, it seemed to debase.[181]

Italian liberals' growing marginalization and alienation was reflected in the struggles of the Italian Liberal Party (the Partito liberale Italiano, or PLI), founded during the wartime resistance by Einaudi and Benedetto Croce, to garner significant electoral support. It would also come to characterize neoliberalism throughout the postwar era, reducing it to an audible but disempowered voice highly critical of an increasingly corrupt and dysfunctional regime.[182] Even as the Italian state became more illiberal, its critics became less so, eventually constituting a small but vocal neoliberal community; they used their trenchant criticism of the predations of the Italian state to launch a more generalized attack on the postwar European Keynesian consensus.

The most important platform for such criticism soon became the school of finance economics at the Bocconi University in Milan, which was founded by Einaudi and attracted a number of renowned neoliberal academics, including Alberto Alesina and Guido Tabellini (as well as the recent technocratic prime minister, Mario Monti).[183] Over the course of the 1960s and 1970s, scholars at the Bocconi School revised Einaudi's relatively humane liberalism into a more doctrinaire neoliberalism that would make common cause with adherents of the Chicago School in the United States. It is no coincidence that the sole meaningful instance of neoliberal economic ideas in the debates detailed in this book should be found in a country whose political class had perverted liberal notions of a limited state and an empowered civil society into a clientelistic and corruption-riddled system captured by insider groups. As one former official in the Italian Treasury and member of the Council of Economic Advisors under Berlusconi stated drily, "liberalism has never had a big reception in Italy."[184] This ideological estrangement extended even to Einaudi's relatively moderate ideas, which were far from what we might today characterize as doctrinaire neoliberalism and analogous to the softer forms of Ordoliberalism that were influential during the inception of the German Social Market Economy.

Over the course of the 1950s and 1960s, as Christian Democratic hegemony was consolidated, state-based clientelism and its vocal neoliberal critics were synthesized in a tradition of "clientelist liberalism," which both reflected and encouraged an almost schizophrenic Italian view of the state. On the one hand, liberal limits on state activity, the repudiation of fascism and the embrace of representative democracy, and the creation of a successful, if problematic, model of market capitalism all represented the fulfillment of long-delayed Italian aspirations to join the ranks of the world's advanced democracies. On the other, the manner of its consolidation and exercise in the decades after the war justified public fears that the Italian state was an enemy rather than ally of individual Italians' capacity to realize their liberal aspirations toward developing their full human and economic potential under its aegis. The result was a highly *negative* liberal tradition held together through clientelistic means, favoring established clients such as large state-owned enterprises and family businesses but excluding industrial labor. This strategy betrayed a more *affirmative* liberalism that, echoing Sismondi in France, Müller-Armack in Germany, and Hobhouse in Britain, championed individuals' capacity for self-realization. This betrayal fostered a widespread sense that freedom could be achieved only in *opposition* to the state rather than in *cooperation* with it. In Maurizio Viroli's view, this dynamic resulted from "centuries of serfdom [that] got the average Italian to oscillate between servile habit and anarchic revolt."[185] Although both state officials and their neoliberal critics embraced liberal limits on the state, for the former such limits served primarily clientelistic ends, whereas for the latter they entailed a vision that aimed to dismantle the state's clientelistic apparatus.

Such divisions and the zero-sum political understanding that informed them led to a series of economic-policy decisions during the 1950s and 1960s that undermined the social and economic renaissance for which Einaudi and other like-minded intellectuals had hoped. Early proposals to construct a Catholic-inspired "Christian socialism," which took seriously Einaudi's plea to improve the plight of the economically disenfranchised and aimed to counter the electoral threat from the Left, foundered on the perceived need to create a "clientelist party machine in the South," a choice which "counteracted any attempts at a comprehensive policy reform on the basis of a Christian Democratic world-view."[186] This choice effectively represented the abandonment of a project of welfare-state expansion, which might have shored up support for the regime on a much broader social and economic base, in favor of prioritizing policies designed both to spur economic growth and industrialization and to protect the vested interests of favored clients, particularly large firms in the energy, metal-working, and engineering sectors.

The instruments of this shift towards planning and state-led industrial policy and away from broadly equitable patterns of economic growth were large state holding companies responsible for both managing state-owned enterprises and financing large infrastructure projects. These included IRI (the Istituto per la Ricostruzione Industriale), founded under Fascism and preserved after the war to bail out and subsidize struggling firms in strategic sectors, and ENI (the Ente Nazionale Idrocarburi), which consolidated several energy and petrochemical firms under one administrative aegis.[187] Though not instruments of planning in the strict sense, these entities offered policymakers powerful administrative and financial instruments to spur Italian reconstruction and development in ways that strongly favored certain interests over others.[188] Emblematic of what Andrew Shonfield called Italy's postwar model of "state capitalism," in the early 1960s, IRI and ENI together directed over 20 percent of all Italian capital investment in manufacturing, transportation, and communications.[189]

This shift away from policies of economic redistribution toward state-led industrial policy left a mixed legacy of significant macroeconomic accomplishment coupled with festering social and economic problems in less favored segments of the political economy. To be sure, Italy enjoyed unprecedented rates of economic growth and, at least in the industrialized North, left behind the historical burdens of economic backwardness. From the immediate postwar period until 1963, annual economic growth averaged 6 percent, with growth in prioritized sectors such as heavy industry, construction, and exports even more robust.[190] The Italian budget was roughly in balance well into the 1960s, debt was manageable, and modest land reforms resulted in some improvements in the plight of the most impoverished southern peasants.[191] These positive developments, however, masked serious economic inequities, particularly among the peasantry and low-skilled industrial workers. The vast majority of peasants remained landless and lived in very primitive conditions, and many moved north in the (often vain) hope of finding a job in Italy's expanding industries. Outside of the relatively prosperous but small worker aristocracy of skilled northern labor, Italian society continued to languish economically, with the deep poverty of the immediate postwar period left unaddressed in the South.[192] Despite widespread calls for the creation of a British- or Scandinavian-style welfare state to remedy these problems, successive postwar governments failed to do so. For his part, de Gasperi was committed to liberal notions of self-reliance and captive to the anti-leftism of the Catholic Church, while his successor Amintore Fanfani worked unsuccessfully to distance the DC from the church and to incorporate voters across social classes.[193]

The failure to incorporate large segments of society economically spurred growing social and political unrest as Italy's postwar boom came to an end in the late 1960s. As the Christian Democrats became increasingly preoccupied with fending off the growing threat from the Socialist and Communist parties, they sacrificed the universalistic aspirations of Social Catholics to more pedestrian and sectarian political calculations. Agencies such as IRI and ENI increasingly became vehicles for dispensing patronage and ensuring electoral support from powerful economic interests, particularly in the South,[194] thereby reflecting and exacerbating "a deformed relationship between citizen and state"[195] that "was in direct contradiction with the values of a liberal economy."[196] Christopher Duggan observes succinctly that this change helped create a state bureaucracy that "came to resemble a medieval kingdom: a patchwork of feudal lordships, each semi-autonomous, and quite ready if the occasion suited to rebel against the centre," with predictable effects on economic performance and efficiency.[197] Unlike Germany, where well-incorporated groups represented economic partners for governments of both Left and Right, in Italy economic groups divided into camps centering on parties of Left and Right, on whom they were increasingly dependent for economic protection. In the area of social policy, this dynamic encouraged the diversion of social-policy funds to clientelistic ends along highly partisan lines, a tack visible in the proliferation of particularistic pension schemes for favored occupational groups and the increasing (and often dubious) reliance on disability pensions, which were treated as the spoils of political victories made possible by these groups' reliable support of the DC.[198]

Italian liberal critics of the postwar order thus had ample justification for their claims that the Italian state represented a case of squandered opportunities. From its remarkable record of economic revitalization after the war, the state increasingly seemed to preside over a pattern, nonlinear but seemingly inexorable, of economic decline after the 1960s. Over the course of that decade, workers began to press for increased wage gains and improvements in social protection outside established channels of collective bargaining. The Italian state increasingly catered to the well-connected and politically important while neglecting the broad goals of economic development and rising living standards that had been the central policy goals of the immediate postwar era. The social and political unrest of the late 1960s—stemming from revolts by students frustrated by an underfunded and antiquated university system, workers angry about stagnant wages despite low unemployment and rapid growth, and the growing ranks of impoverished peasants who had migrated northward to work in miserable and menial factory jobs—culminated in widespread industrial unrest during the so-called Hot Autumn of 1969 and the emergence of Stalinist and Trotskyite groups willing to use violence to press for revolutionary change.[199]

In typical fashion, Italian authorities turned to clientelistic means to solve the problems that clientelism itself had created.[200] In the aftermath of the Hot Autumn, officials agreed to a modification of the so-called *Scala mobile*, a "wage escalator" that had been included in contracts since the late 1940s, so as to provide "100 percent indexing, with quarterly revisions, thereby raising wages nearly as fast as prices."[201] Given Italy's stagnant productivity rates, the result was significant wage-push inflation, which exacerbated a decline in Italian economic performance following the OPEC oil shock of 1973 and the collapse of Bretton Woods.[202] Having obtained wage increases out of line with productivity, Italian workers, particularly those in the public sector and in large state-owned firms, such as Fiat, came to view the state as their protector. Relatedly, many in the private sector, particularly in small, internationally competitive firms in northern Italy, framed arguments for trimming the size and scope of the state in terms of the need to break these clientelistic relationships, for their part seeking mostly to be left alone.[203]

It would not be long before the negative economic effects of these clientelistic bargains would become clear. In contrast to the postwar boom, when real GDP per capita more than tripled and averaged an annual increase of nearly 5 percent,[204] during the 1970s nearly every major indicator of Italian economic performance and competitiveness declined sharply. Real labor costs increased by more than 30 percent between 1970 and 1975, as annual worker productivity increases plummeted from 4.4 percent between 1969 and 1973 to a negligible 1.5 percent between 1973 and 1979.[205] Between 1963 and 1969, average annual GDP growth was an impressive 5.3 percent and inflation rates were a moderate 3.4 percent, whereas the corresponding figures between 1969 and 1979 were 3.3 and 12.2 percent, respectively.[206] Spurred on by rising wages against the backdrop of an oil-related spike in input costs and slowing growth, unemployment rose from 3.8 percent in 1970 to 5.2 percent in 1979, despite the additional labor protections introduced after the Hot Autumn.[207] Public debt exploded from 33 percent of GDP in 1969 to 65 percent in 1979, with annual budget deficits reaching nearly 10 percent of GDP by the late 1970s.[208] This trend continued apace during the 1980s and 1990s, with public debt reaching an alarming 103 percent of GDP in 1987 and unemployment reaching a postwar record of 11.8 percent in the same year.[209]

While the consolidation of "clientelistic liberalism" had successfully preserved the Christian Democratic party state, it had done so in a way that undermined and ultimately suppressed the substantive, affirmative vision of individual and collective self-realization of postwar liberals like Einaudi, thereby ceding the political ground to an increasingly strident, if politically marginalized, group of neoliberal critics of the state. If neoliberalism was absorbed into American and British political DNA in the 1980s and 1990s, in Italy, as in France and Germany, it remained a politically marginal discourse. From their earliest incarnations in the early stages of industrialization up to the postwar period, all three traditions recognized important limits to the separation of the political and economic spheres, a neoliberal article of faith. Far from their rejecting "society" as a normative construct of the well-intentioned but feeble-minded Left, as neoliberals contend, the notion of an organic and socially embedded economic order is central to each of these three Continental liberal traditions, even if each offers a distinctive vision of the character of that society and the state's relationship to it. Unfortunately, in Italy this process of embedding was diverted from productive ends by a dysfunctional series of institutional and historical legacies. But in all three countries, the emphasis on social cohesion and the state's role in fostering economic adjustment represented a repudiation of neoliberal precepts. In this way, all three liberal models echoed the insights of early twentieth-century liberals like Friedrich Hayek, celebrated but rarely examined by many contemporary Anglo-American neoliberals, whose concern for the maintenance of social cohesion informed a vision that "explicitly condoned a vigorous role for the state," including the development of "forms of social insurance . . . that compensated victims of sickness or accidents, and that ensured a basic minimum of food, shelter, and clothing for all."[210] Even liberal paragons like Hayek acknowledged that economic freedom was both impossible and meaningless in the absence of a stable social order, in marked contrast to later neoliberals like Milton Friedman, for whom the acceptable scope of state action was considerably more limited and the prevailing vision of society more individualistic.

The Contemporary Legacies of National Liberalisms in Illiberal States

From their beginnings in the nineteenth century, national liberal traditions in France, Germany, and Italy have evolved in response to changing political, social, and economic circumstances. Far from fixed, each tradition represents a dynamic set of core principles that have been reinterpreted over time, as circumstances have reshaped elites' understanding of the character of the challenges facing each country's political economy. Although each tradition has evolved continually since its earliest incarnations, certain critical junctures have represented important moments of historical inflection in each. Some of these inflection points stemmed from new economic challenges—as in the evolution of German

Ordoliberalism into conceptions of the Social Market Economy in response to postwar realities—while other determining challenges have been ideological—as in the emergence of neoliberalism in the 1970s and each tradition's simultaneous rejection of its precepts. At such moments of social, economic, and ideological challenge, these traditions have fostered certain interpretations of the essential nature of moments of economic uncertainty while also suggesting a defined menu of politically and economically appropriate responses.

One of this book's central contentions is that such menus tend not only to be consistent with prevailing elite understandings of the character of national liberalisms but also to evoke similar themes and points of emphasis across time in ways that traditional explanations of policymaking, such as those that focus on state capacity or partisanship, simply cannot explain. In France, the tradition of statist liberalism has informed policy responses that favor both macroeconomic forms of intervention and measures designed to support individuals' economic welfare. German corporate liberalism, by contrast, has tended to view groups rather than individuals as the building blocks of the social order and as the intended beneficiaries of state action across partisan lines. Whereas the state is viewed as the primary driver of economic policy in France, in Germany the state is more circumscribed and both limited and supported by group prerogatives. While groups constitute favored partners with the state in Germany, in Italy they represent self-serving and clientelistic obstacles to effective state responses. Italian clientelistic liberalism juxtaposes self-serving and politically connected groups with an excluded neoliberal minority that focuses its criticisms on the corruption and inaction that such clientelistic relationships spawn.

The remainder of the book traces out these responses since the early 1990s, exploring how authorities have interpreted episodes of economic upheaval and uncertainty in the context of a sustained neoliberal challenge to their political and economic orders, as well as how their interpretations have informed distinctive patterns of policy responses. In so doing, it focuses on three central issue areas that have defined how national liberalisms have shaped trajectories of adjustment: the state's evolving relationships with business, labor, and the financial industry. Taken together, these three sets of evolving relationships have both informed and been shaped in turn by elite conceptions of the state's role and appropriate menus of policy and institutional responses to periods of heightened economic challenges, when established paradigms have proven limited in their applicability. While rejecting neoliberal prescriptions of expansive market making and attacks on non-market arrangements such as social protection and collective bargaining, these responses have been colored by national liberal traditions that furnish distinctive analytical lenses through which to understand the state, society, and the economy and the proper relationship among them. These traditions have informed responses that often diverge significantly from standard accounts of the dynamics of each country's "national model" or "variety" of capitalism, reminding us that political institutions do not operate in predictable, mechanistic ways but rather respond to human interventions informed by human understandings of periods of uncertainty. To be sure, some traditions have been more conducive to constructive responses than others, as in the stark contrast between the German and Italian responses to the labor-market crisis of the early 2000s and the unexpected differences between the French and German responses to the economic perils of the post-2008 period. Such differences in effectiveness cannot be dismissed as the products of more or less perfect implementations of obvious and rationally derived menus of policy measures suggested by hegemonic ideologies like neoliberalism. Instead, they reflect national authorities' efforts to muddle through periods of economic uncertainty as their national liberal tradition provides them with the light to see.

2

Degrees of Freedom and Constraint

French Statist Liberalism and Economic Citizenship in the Shadow of Maastricht

As described in Chapter 1, one of the hallmarks of nineteenth-century French liberalism was the tension between a strict concern for individual freedom and equality before the law and an affirmative, technocratic concern for ensuring societal welfare. From its earliest inceptions, even in the thinking of classical liberal figures like Jean-Baptiste Say, French liberal thought rejected Manchesterian laissez-faire in favor of a complex, if imperfectly resolved, synthesis between a substantive notion of individual economic freedom and an understanding that such freedom cannot be absolute and must be embedded in a coherent social order if it is to remain meaningful. This idea was intertwined with the prevailing conviction that basic economic resources must be available to all and that the economy as a whole must function in such a way as to make them available, for the sake of both social stability and long-term economic prosperity. Thus caught between Constant's notion that modern liberty "is every man's right to be subject to the law alone"[1] and Saint-Simon's technocratic belief that the social and economic dislocations brought about by industrialization required a state capable of guiding economic development,[2] French liberals over time came to understand substantive individual freedom and state power as both circumscribed and tightly interconnected.

During the nineteenth and early twentieth centuries, French liberal discourse oscillated between an emphasis on individual freedom and equality, on the one hand, and state responsibility for ensuring the general welfare (even at the cost of infringing on individual freedom), on the other. This conflict emerged from earlier tensions among French liberalism's core commitments, which, during the early and mid-nineteenth century, were both reflected in and reinforced by the country's political instability, as it lurched between brief and unstable democracies and various anti-democratic regimes, whether of monarchical or Bonapartist incarnations. In this context, public declarations of liberal principles—for example, in the writings of Jean-Charles Leonard de Sismondi[3] and the technocratic socialism of Saint-Simon—tended to emphasize the state's crucial role in ensuring the provision of economic goods and benefits that were viewed as a necessary, if not sufficient, condition for political stability. This tendency reflected prevailing concerns about the effects of accelerating industrialization during the Second Empire, when France began to catch up economically with the English and the Germans, a process that displaced hundreds of thousands of people from the countryside and began the long process of shifting France from an agrarian to an industrial society.

As was the case in Germany, the French authorities in the postwar era drew on these intellectual antecedents as they worked to revamp their political and economic institutions in ways that represented admixtures of tradition and novelty, with a view to correcting for the failures of previous regimes. France's rapid defeat in 1940 at the hands of the German army, the legacies of the economic and political decline of the Third Republic, and the long national nightmare of collaboration under Vichy had brought home the urgency of political and economic modernization.[4] Still a predominantly agrarian country in 1940, with a large peasantry and a relatively small industrial base, France after the war faced the daunting task of modernizing its economic and political systems in ways that would permit both the rapid economic growth that reconstruction required and the legitimization of democratic politics that elites hoped it would support. In contrast to the "republican synthesis" of the Third Republic, whereby elites bought political stability through protection of vested economic interests,[5] the postwar recipe rejected such a defensive and inertial approach in the context of economic devastation and the necessity of restoring France's international political and economic standing. The stakes were simply too high, the legacies of the war too painful, and the potential cost of failure too great.

Whereas Germany had divided political authority in its new constitution in ways that reflected both its rejection of its authoritarian past and the well-established status of powerful social and economic groups prior to national unification, France responded to the failures of its earlier constitutional avatars by concentrating power in a state established and consolidated centuries earlier. Beginning with the Fourth Republic, the new constitution under which France was governed between 1947 and 1958, French authorities invested greater power in the central state in ways that were designed to modernize France from the top down and center out and to transform an agrarian country into an industrial powerhouse. Fearing the resistance of parochial interest groups such as small businesses and labor, who, officials feared, were not reliable interlocutors in the modernizing project, authorities entrusted this task to a narrow elite trained at a series of newly created and revamped *grandes écoles*, the most important of which were the École nationale d'administration (ENA) and the École polytechnique. The instrument favored by state officials was a series of five-year plans, devised by authorities within the powerful Commissariat général du Plan (CGP), that set indicative targets for production in strategic sectors such as coal and steel that were instrumental to rapid industrialization and economic development.[6] Though technically sectorally focused, the plans' orientation was heavily macroeconomic, emphasizing the "*interrelationships* between different economic activities" and a growing emphasis upon coherence in economic policy.[7] Using such mechanisms and wielding centralized political authority, postwar French policymakers hoped to circumvent the Malthusian shopkeepers and businesses that had resisted modernization in the nineteenth century and the anarcho-syndicalist trade unions that resisted the very premise of a capitalist economic order. The result was an incipient alliance between the state and big business, which Andrew Shonfield famously dubbed a "conspiracy in the public interest,"[8] and the exclusion of interest groups that were presumed to be at best ambivalent about economic modernization.

The transition from the Fourth to the Fifth Republic in 1958 represented a significant additional concentration of power and responsibility in the central state. The new constitution created a powerful executive controlled by a president elected to a seven-year term and with sweeping powers, including the right to rule by decree in national emergencies, the power to dissolve parliament at will, and a functional monopoly over national defense and foreign policy. Though governed by a prime minister and his cabinet, parliament was functionally subordinate to the president, both as a matter of constitutional law and as a result of the hegemony of political Gaullism. In the economic realm the task of administering the process of industrialization fell to a coterie of elite bureaucrats cast in a Saint-Simonian mold, within both the planning commission and, with a growing dominance over economic management, the increasingly powerful Finance Ministry.[9] This new dirigiste model of state-led development used powerful tools such as industrial policies and selective credit allocation to favored firms to foster the emergence of Fordist "national champions" that were to act as France's international economic vanguard and secure its competitive position in the global economy while providing the basis for economic and employment growth.[10] If the state under the Third Republic had been captive to parochial interest groups, this logic under the Fifth Republic was reversed, the state constituting the driving economic force and interest groups being either captive and subordinate to it or politically marginalized and excluded.

This revamped political-economic model was extraordinarily successful, resulting in a period of rapid economic growth that sustained healthy employment and rising incomes. The statist logic of the dirigiste system subsumed individual concerns within the collective, presuming that individual welfare would flow as a natural by-product of economic expansion. In this way the historical tension within French liberalism between state responsibility and individual citizens' welfare oscillated toward a set of arrangements that favored the former, abetted by the generalizing prosperity of the *trente glorieuses*, the "thirty glorious years" of postwar growth. As in the German and Italian cases, the intellectual lineages of the French liberal tradition evolved and shifted in response to the prevailing economic and political climate. During the 1950s and 1960s this climate was dominated by a generalizing prosperity that supported the state's accretion of prestige and of both implicit and explicit authority. Such standing was well earned, with economic growth rates averaging 5.7 percent and unemployment averaging a negligible 1.8 percent between 1959 and 1969.[11] As discussed in detail in Chapter 1, the postwar boom accompanied an inflection of French statist liberalism away from the defensive notion of individual liberty prevalent in the late nineteenth century toward a Saint-Simonian conception of the state as the guardian and progenitor of citizens' economic welfare. This shift was both reflected in and shaped by postwar liberal thinkers such as Raymond Aron, who "described modern industrial societies . . . as *democratic* societies at the heart of which lies the concept of equality of conditions."[12] In the 1950s and 1960s the positive economic climate certainly seemed to justify such optimism, which highlighted the improving fortunes of French citizens, whose shared prosperity constituted the foundation of their political equality.

By the late 1960s, however, the generalizing prosperity of the first two postwar decades began to wane, as France's Fordist economic model confronted a saturation of global demand for mass-produced products and a series of exogenous shocks destabilized the French political economy. The near revolution of May–June 1968, spurred by workers angry about the inequitable distribution of the gains from growth between capital and labor and students resentful of France's highly centralized and opaque political system, coupled with the effects of the OPEC oil shock of 1973, made clear that the traditional labor-exclusionary dirigiste model could no longer sustain the happy marriage of economic growth and political stability.[13] As slowing growth, rising unemployment, and mounting social unrest undermined the legitimacy of the dirigiste model, French authorities increasingly found themselves on the defensive, working to shore up the system's stability through policies of social and economic compensation.[14] Having spent the previous two decades favoring industrial expansion over wages and consumption, French authorities were now forced to confront both the economic and political costs of this strategy.

As detailed in Chapter 1, this shift in political and economic climate led to another inflection of the statist-liberal tradition, as policymakers struggled to deal with a new set of realities. Whereas the postwar boom had both driven and resulted from a strong emphasis on the tradition's statist elements, the post-1960s context informed a shift toward its equally significant but still latent distributive elements and an emphasis on workers' incomes and economic citizenship and equality. At the same time, the growing dysfunctions of the dirigiste system, which was being forced to tackle a growing list of increasingly daunting social and economic tasks even as its capacity to do so declined, led to pressures for economic liberalization.[15] In practice this shift involved a turn toward efforts to expand universalistic social-protection schemes and income-support policies, which had remained underdeveloped during the postwar boom as a result of both the dominance of dirigisme's developmental imperative and the resistance of white-collar professional groups to a universalistic scheme. For example, authorities introduced new benefits for single mothers and the elderly poor, both of which groups lacked the employment histories on which eligibility for benefits in France's largely contributory welfare state were based. If, during the postwar boom, the statist liberal model had informed an assumption that economic equity would be a natural by-product of a macroeconomically oriented strategy of industrial expansion, it now underpinned a renewed emphasis on distributive outcomes as the model's effectiveness at macroeconomic management declined.

Following the election of Socialist François Mitterrand as president in 1981, this renewed emphasis on the distributive implications of policy intensified, as the new administration pursued a "redistributive Keynesian" agenda of intensified state intervention and sharp increases in public spending.[16] In addition to a wave of nationalizations and large increases in aid to favored industries, Mitterrand's administration worked to address the past failures of the dirigiste model to deliver steadily rising incomes for all workers. Such measures included a 15 percent increase in the minimum wage and the creation of a national health insurance scheme for workers without coverage. As Jonah Levy has described, however, a combination of economic pressures, including a worsening balance of payments and repeated runs on the French currency resulting from the government's policies, as well as a political decision not to leave the European Monetary System (EMS), led the government to abandon its "redistributive Keynesian" strategy almost as quickly as it had embraced it. In the "U-turn" of 1983/84, the administration not only reversed its post-1981 policies, but it began to dismantle the entire edifice of dirigiste policymaking.[17] In the ensuing decade, first under a Socialist government after 1984 and then under the center-right administration of Prime Minister Jacques Chirac after 1986, French authorities embarked upon a program of market expansion that in some respects rivaled that of Margaret Thatcher, privatizing state-owned enterprises, slashing aid to industry, reducing regulations, and cutting a wide array of state spending.

In other important respects, however, French authorities rejected a neoliberal strategy of expansive market making, undertaking an unprecedented, sustained expansion of the social-protection system and welfare benefits in order to help workers adjust to a more liberal economic context and to shore up the legitimacy of the government's project of liberalization.[18] Rather than make the market the guiding principle for all social and economic activity, as orthodox neoliberalism prescribed, French officials of both Left and Right worked to synthesize a more liberal economic order with a robust series of measures designed to bolster workers' incomes and promote social and economic solidarity.[19] Far from being neoliberal, this strategy reflected the notions of economic equality and citizenship at the heart of the statist liberal tradition, commitments that the strained economic circumstances arising from post-1970s economic decline had made an increasingly important priority. The emblematic example of this strategy of socialized marketization was the 1988 *Revenu minimum d'insertion* (RMI), which married a guaranteed minimum income with job-search assistance for all citizens, irrespective of contribution histories or professional classification.[20] Even as they sought to expand the scope of market forces, then, French officials worked to bolster workers' social rights and to embed the process of marketization within a more robust model of economic citizenship. No longer able to pursue Keynesian strategies through traditional means, French officials increasingly did so through social and labor-market policy, taking a new approach to bolstering aggregate demand and spurring economic growth.

By the beginning of the 1990s, France had accepted the market as the central driver of economic development, even as it erected a generalized edifice of individual social benefits designed to help workers qua citizens adjust to a less sheltered economic environment. Like Germany and Italy, France rejected the neoliberal formula in favor of a more complex and nuanced strategy of parallel programs of liberalization, marketization, and social-policy expansion. Unlike their German and Italian counterparts, however, French authorities focused their social-protection measures on individuals beset by economic precariousness rather than structurally important or politically connected social and economic groups. In the process they preserved the state's role as a guiding force of the country's path of economic development, even as they learned to live within the fiscal and economic limitations on state intervention posed by the dismantling of dirigisme and the looming limits on fiscal deficits and national debt enshrined in the Maastricht Treaty on European Economic and Monetary Union. This statist liberal framework would come to constitute the central interpretive lens and related menu of policy options with which French policymakers would confront and respond to the economic challenges to come.

In the remainder of this chapter, I investigate how this statist liberal framework evolved in the post-dirigiste era and how this evolution shaped the process of economic adjustment. In working to facilitate the French economy's adaptation to this challenging economic climate, French authorities rejected the prevailing international discourse of neoliberalism and developed policies that reflected the enduring tension between the state's power and its economic responsibilities toward French citizens. As in Germany and Italy, key initiatives in fiscal and labor-market policy and financial regulation have borne the imprint of the interpretive framework furnished by France's national liberal tradition, centering on an effort to adjust to a more market-based economic order while preserving a robust notion of social rights and economic citizenship. This process has informed distinctive patterns of relationships with business, labor, and finance, the particularities of which have shifted with prevailing circumstances but which all reflect broad patterns of continuity that the statist liberal tradition has helped to inform. In fiscal policy, authorities have limited traditional Keynesian strategies while seeking other means for achieving macroeconomic stimulus, relying on reforms of the labor market and a robust network of "automatic stabilizers" and policies of income support to pursue essentially Keynesian goals. In so doing they have adopted a more supportive posture toward a wider array of businesses, both relying on traditional support for large concerns and working to promote the growth of SMEs. With respect to labor, governments of both Left and Right have continued to marginalize labor unions, with which successive administrations have continued to have relatively conflictual relationships, even as they have worked to bolster the incomes of individual workers. Finally, in finance, French officials have worked to support large banks through favorable regulations and an aggressive bank bailout in the aftermath of the post-2007 financial crisis. Such initiatives have continued to bear the stamp of traditional assumptions that large financial concerns must play a central role in broader strategies for fostering economic adjustment and growth. I present an overview of the dimensions of these policy trajectories, highlighting the state's role, favored policy instruments, major constituencies, and prevailing social and economic goals, in Table 2.1.

In each of these areas, policies have reflected an emphasis on macroeconomic measures designed to foster economic growth, a broad-based promotion of business with a growing emphasis on SMEs, and individuals' economic welfare, in contrast to the German preference for subsidization of economically strategic groups and sectors and the Italian patterns of alternating co-optation of and political assaults upon powerful interest groups in the context of a heavily partisan and cynical anti-statism.

Table 2.1 **Orientation of French Statist Liberalism by Policy Area**

	State's Economic Role	*Major Constituencies*	*Favored Instruments*	*Prevailing Social/ Economic Goals*
Fiscal Policy and State Investment	Expansive but constrained	Business (with growing emphasis on SMEs) and workers qua citizens	Broadly based direct spending	Macroeconomic expansion
Labor-Market Policy	Subsidizing	Business and workers qua citizens	Employment subsidies and labor-market regulations	Job creation through demand stimulus
Financial Policy	Protective	Large industrial banks	Targeted subsidies and strategic bailouts	Macroeconomic stability and preserving state-finance linkages

Statist Liberalism and Keynesianism by Other Means: France as Reluctant Austerian

In the early 1990s France confronted two sets of economic challenges, one exogenous and the other a product of political choice. The first was a relatively severe international economic downturn, which, beginning in the late 1980s, confronted all advanced industrial societies with slowing or negative growth, increasing unemployment, and mounting strains on public budgets. French officials watched with alarm as growth slowed to 1.0 percent in 1991 and unemployment spiked to an unprecedented 10.5 percent in 1987 and an even more alarming 12.3 percent by 1994.[21] This downturn both reduced revenue in the form of declining tax receipts and intensified pressure on state budgets in the form of rising expenditures on unemployment insurance and other social benefits. As elsewhere on the European continent, moreover, the fact that many social benefits in France's welfare state were funded by social contributions shared between firms and workers led to high non-wage labor costs and created disincentives for firms to hire new workers, particularly given the poor prospects for economic growth. The worsening economic climate, coupled with the repudiation of dirigisme in the previous decade, forced French authorities to seek new means to spur economic growth, drawing upon elements of the statist liberal tradition to negotiate the shift from dirigisme to a more market-based economic order. Unable to rely upon the dirigiste tools of restrictions on layoffs, sectoral industrial policies, and aggressive Keynesian demand stimulus to restart economic growth and address the rising unemployment levels that were quickly becoming a political liability, French officials were forced to turn to other, less direct means of encouraging firms to create jobs.

The second set of challenges, which stemmed from a series of political choices made by French authorities in the 1980s and 1990s, involved the fiscal-policy strictures laid out in the 1992 Maastricht Treaty (subsequently formalized in the ill-named 1998 Stability and Growth Pact) that constituted the basis of the nascent European Economic and Monetary Union. These bargains, which the French endorsed with some reluctance, made it clear that membership in EMU involved an acceptance of at best a modest and constrained fiscal-policy strategy.[22] Although the Maastricht limits on debts and deficits were often honored in the breach as the 1990s wore on, particularly by large and powerful states such as France and Germany, they nonetheless reflected a broader deflationary policy regime in EMU member states, even as EMU removed traditional instruments such as currency devaluation from national authorities' policy arsenals. Taken together, these two sets of challenges left French officials without the very kinds of fiscal- and monetary-policy discretion that had lain at the core of the dirigiste model, even as they confronted an economic climate that was the most difficult in more than a decade. The underlying bargain of EMU, by which French officials exchanged policy autonomy for an ostensibly influential role in shaping economic policies in the incipient Eurozone, would inaugurate a period in which they sought to achieve the goals of dirigisme—rapid economic modernization, growth, and employment creation—without its means and were forced to turn to other, proximate strategies to sustain demand, notably the expansion of the edifices of universalistic income support and social protection. In so doing, they worked to develop policies that both accounted for the more austere economic environment that prevailed after the early 1990s and avoided the pitfalls of politically infeasible and economically ineffective neoliberal strategies of aggressive market making. I provide an overview of key French economic indicators since the early 1990s in Table 2.2.

Early in the negotiations over the Maastricht Treaty, it became clear that France's vision for the incipient common currency diverged significantly from Germany's and that France would have to face some unpleasant trade-offs in order to preserve its seat at the table of European policymaking. During most of the postwar period France, in an implicit acknowledgment of emerging American hegemony, had sought to achieve on the European level the kind of international political and economic influence that it could not sustain as a nation state. This strategy worked well during the 1960s and 1970s, when rapid economic growth,

Table 2.2 **Economic Indicators for Selected Years, 1991–2013, France**[a]

	1991	*1995*	*1998*	*2003*	*2006*	*2009*	*2013*
GDP Growth (%)	1.04	2.09	3.56	0.82	2.37	−2.94	0.58
Unemployment Rate (harmonized) (%)	9.63	11.95	12.05	8.50	8.84	9.11	10.30
Inflation (CPI) (%)	3.21	1.80	0.65	2.10	1.68	0.09	0.86
Public Budget Deficit (% of GDP)	−2.83	−5.12	−2.41	−3.86	−2.34	−7.16	−4.04
Public Debt (% of GDP)	35.95	66.59	77.02	78.51	76.86	93.16	110.99

[a]OECD data, from data.oecd.org and stats.oecd.org, except:
public debt for 1991, from IMF, Public Finances in Modern History Database (2013), http://www.imf.org/external/np/fad/histdb/.

France's nuclear capability, and Germany's need for international legitimation enabled France to shape the character of the European Economic Community to its liking (most controversially with Charles de Gaulle's de facto exclusion of Britain), even as it used the EEC's institutions to serve its economic interests.[23]

After the end of the postwar boom in the 1970s, however, and particularly after the repudiation of dirigisme in the early 1980s, France was no longer able to use the power of the French state to drive economic growth in the traditional fashion, nor could it count on an international economic environment of growth and expanding demand that had once made France one of the world's largest exporters.[24] Instead, it was forced to accept limits on the scope of state intervention in the economy even as it sought other means whereby to achieve its essentially Keynesian goals. If France's international geopolitical and domestic international economic ambitions had been mutually reinforcing and consistent during the postwar boom, they now increasingly worked at cross purposes as a more secure and prosperous Germany began to punch at its weight in negotiations over the future of the EU. Increasingly, French policymakers faced the unpalatable choice of relinquishing their dominant role in the EU or accepting a regime of economic austerity and fiscal restraint that was anathema to officials long accustomed to using a powerful state to invest in a particular vision of economic development.[25]

In the early 1990s, two developments in particular brought French officials to an important crossroads with respect to this dilemma, forcing them to chart a new strategy for fiscal policy. The first, to be discussed in Chapter 3, was the shock of German reunification, which created a larger and potentially hegemonic Germany at the heart of the continent, despite the daunting challenges of rebuilding the devastated economy of the former DDR and incorporating its citizens into the German Social Market Economy. This unexpected development confronted French authorities with the unpleasant prospect of eventual German economic dominance and their relegation to also-ran status in Europe.[26]

The second set of events that presented French officials with the prospect of undesirable trade-offs were the treaty negotiations themselves, led by Jacques Delors, the French socialist who had been an ardent supporter of France's remaining in EMS while he was French finance minister under Mitterrand (1981–84). As head of the European Commission, Delors made French national economic goals secondary to, or at least dependent upon, those of fostering European integration and providing European unity with a durable foundation of economic institutions, which would ostensibly form the basis of and create pressures for deepening political integration. Having already committed to European monetary institutions while embracing the twin strategies of "competitive disinflation" and a *franc fort* ("strong franc"),[27] Mitterrand had effectively bound France to a set of arrangements that sacrificed authorities' ability to diverge from the German line of austerity and a prioritization of combating inflation above all, for the sake of "tying one's hands to the German currency anchor" so as to be able to ascribe to European constraints often unpopular policies that were central to its domestic policy strategies.[28] The decision to embrace European economic unity, however, reflected not an abject French abandonment of the pursuit of national economic goals but rather a calculated gamble "that [France] can find a new role for itself in a strong united Europe that can both compete with the United States and Japan and control Germany's expanding might."[29] In essence, France chose to accept an EMU that was more deflationary and anti-Keynesian than it would have preferred in the anticipation of using its influence within the bloc to shift, gradually and by degrees, the orientation of European fiscal and monetary policy in a direction more supportive of growth and rising incomes.

Although the austere and deflationary character of EMU was not inevitable, the confluence of German economic interests and France's philosophical subordination to Germany by the late 1980s made it increasingly likely. Germany in general and the Bundesbank in particular, which had long been the fulcrum of the incipient monetary union, undermined France's ability to champion an alternative model to Germany's anti-inflationary and monetarist commitments. Although French officials continued to resist France's transformation into a "de facto deutsche mark zone," their prior embrace of EMS had stacked the deck against their chances of realizing their ambitions of tilting EMU in a more expansionary direction.[30] For their part, German officials managed to convince their citizens to give up their cherished deutsche mark, forged through years of sacrifice during postwar reconstruction and the Economic Miracle that followed, only by emphasizing the importance of deepening the process of European integration that had restored their nation to credibility and by repeated assurances that the euro would be strong and stable rather than weak and inflationary.[31] Given the constraints on fiscal and monetary policy that went along with EMU, however, France's bargain increasingly came to seem like a Faustian one, essentially maintaining the *form* of political parity with Germany and continued geopolitical relevance on a European scale while sacrificing the *substance* of its preferred economic vision on the altar of European unity and for the sake of an influence that remained elusive.[32]

The inconsistencies within France's position on EMU and ambivalence about its sacrifice of national sovereignty and the prospects for national fiscal-policy strategies were not limited to elites, moreover, as widespread negative reaction among the public augured ill for those who might have hoped to establish a national political consensus on these questions. As nationalist and anti-Maastricht politicians like Philippe Séguin, of the opposition center-right Gaullist Rassemblement pour la République (RPR), presciently forecast that the treaty would dilute French sovereignty and cause France to be "ruled by technocrats in Brussels even more remote than their own aloof ministers," French public support for the treaty eroded over the course of 1992.[33] By August, a month before a scheduled national referendum on whether to approve the treaty (on the heels of Denmark's no vote), public support had slipped to 56 percent, down from 65 percent in June, and representatives of Mitterrand's governing Socialist Party launched a somewhat panicked campaign to secure voters' approval.

In the end the referendum passed by the narrowest of margins (51 percent in favor), but the weakness of this approval and the fact that the Socialists had to resort to dire warnings of domestic and international economic chaos in order to secure it reflected enduring deep divisions within French society over both the wisdom of EMU and its monetarist and deflationary character. Apparently persuaded by the arguments of officials like Séguin that the treaty represented an irreversible loss of French sovereignty, nearly half of the French public expressed a willingness to sacrifice France's position within Europe in order to preserve its ability to chart its own economic course. For those who supported the treaty, the calculation was both more cynical and more pedestrian. In the words of Jean-Paul Betbéze, director of economic research at the large French bank Crédit Lyonnais, "We are currently living in a monetary system imposed by Germany. If France votes 'no,' we will lose the opportunity to have a greater role in a common monetary system."[34]

The public's grudging approval of the treaty bore the imprint of the tensions within France's statist liberal model, involving a continuing central role for the state in the domestic sphere, a guarded embrace of market-based liberalism, and frustrated attempts to pursue a robust Keynesian strategy at the European level. Having turned to the market as the central economic principle in the 1980s even as they expanded income-support programs and eschewed neoliberal strategies of dismantling public-sector initiatives, French authorities had now committed themselves, with marginal public support, to a European monetary regime that both ended monetary-policy autonomy and introduced strictures on fiscal policy that would seriously limit their room for maneuver. Over the course of the 1990s, a growing discrepancy emerged between France's continued commitment to spurring growth through macroeconomic means and the character of the policy regime laid out in the Maastricht Treaty. As the decade wore on, consistent difficulty in meeting the treaty's limits on fiscal deficits and debt was encountered by a growing number of countries, including France and, as I discuss in the next chapter, even Germany, whose government had committed to monetarist orthodoxy (strongly and vocally favored by the Bundesbank) as an article of faith in order to obtain parliamentary approval of the treaty.[35]

In response to growing criticism and pressure by members of its governing coalition and concerns that the Maastricht criteria were insufficiently enforceable, the German government, with French acquiescence, insisted on a formal Stability Pact (later modified to the Stability and Growth Pact at French insistence, an almost entirely semantic change), formally adopted in 1998, that would cement in place a more rigid set of constraints.[36] France's decision to bind itself to a regime of monetarism and austerity left it ill equipped to respond to an increasingly unfavorable political-economic environment at home. During the mid-to-late 1990s, as rates of economic growth declined and unemployment continued to rise (reaching a postwar high of 12.6 percent in 1997),[37] French authorities sought ways to use a state with significantly reduced capacity to generate sustained economic growth. The political stakes were high, as growing public clamor for the state to address rising joblessness forced authorities to convey an image of "not being resigned in the face of unemployment," even as unemployment cast the very "political identity" of the establishment into question.[38] Under both the "plural left" administration of Prime Minister Lionel Jospin in the late 1990s and early 2000s and under his center-right successors, the prevailing strategy centered upon efforts to rein in growth in public expenditure while extending tax cuts to business, with an increasing focus on SMEs, which had become the primary drivers of job growth in the post-dirigiste era.[39] Concerns about the tensions between the burdens of public debt and the need to stimulate growth and employment heavily colored French fiscal policy in the early-to-mid-2000s, when authorities continued to seek a feasible recipe for stimulating the economy on the domestic level, as the possibilities of a coordinated European effort to foster growth seemed increasingly remote. As will be seen, this strategy increasingly focused on seeking other ways to promote economic growth and stimulate demand, including labor-market policies of Keynesian inspiration and a reliance upon an expanded ensemble of income-support and social-protection policies (described in Chapter 1). In so doing, French officials sought to achieve the economic growth and expansion of employment that the demise of dirigisme and the strictures of Maastricht would not permit them to accomplish by traditional statist means.

Keynesianism by Default and Universalistic Income Support during the Great Recession

These same tensions remained in place as the country confronted the near meltdown of the international financial system after 2007 and the Great Recession that followed in its wake. Though the crisis did not hit France as hard as it did Germany, the impact was still significant, with GDP declining by 2.94 percent in 2009 and unemployment spiking from 7.43 percent in 2008 to 9.27 percent in 2010.[40] Though Keynesianism had fallen out of favor among mainstream economists elsewhere after the stagflationary 1970s, it had remained an important conceptual touchstone within French economic discourse. The post-2007 crisis, along with the role that transnational neoliberal orthodoxies of deregulation, expansive markets, and denuded states had played in its rise, led to a return of Keynesianism to the center of policy debates across the advanced industrial world, thereby seeming to vindicate the French position. Even ardent devotees of neoclassical economics such as Richard Posner responded to the crisis with apologiae declaring their renewed commitment to Keynesian principles.[41] This shift created a favorable environment for another inflection point in the development of French statist liberalism, whose macroeconomic orientation and emphasis on the demand side of the economy fit well with the new intellectual climate.

That said, France's past political and economic choices left the prospects for a Keynesian revival there uncertain at best. The constraints of EMU and two decades of economic liberalization left French authorities ill equipped to restore a robust Keynesian approach to fiscal policy even as they continued to reject standard neoliberal recipes. As growth rates plummeted and then turned sharply negative, unemployment skyrocketed, and tax revenues dried up, such limitations were particularly acute in countries that had signed on to EMU, as the strictures on fiscal policy and the deflationary biases of the currency union's monetary-policy regime both exacerbated the slowdown and limited the tools with which policymakers could confront it. Perhaps nowhere were these limitations more keenly felt than in France, whose Faustian bargain in the service of EMU had done nothing to obviate a statist worldview even as it had traded away most of the means of carrying out a corresponding strategy. As a result, it was far from clear in 2007 how French authorities might respond or how effective such a response would be. One government official succinctly captured this ambivalence, observing that "French liberalism is always intermeshed with powerful strands of protectionism and economic nationalism."[42]

Even as they struggled to fashion an effective policy response, French officials clearly felt a sense of urgency as the depth of the crisis became clear in 2008 and 2009. The conservative administration of French president Nicolas Sarkozy was among the first in the OECD to turn to Keynesian remedies; it embarked on a strategy to boost economic growth and stabilize the economy, in keeping with the macroeconomic, citizen-focused orientation of the statist liberal tradition, rather than subsidize and shelter favored economic groups in the German fashion.[43] In 2008 the administration quickly proposed a significant, though relatively modest, package amounting to €26 billion, or about 1.3 percent of GDP. The package prioritized public infrastructure projects, including four new high-speed rail lines, a new canal in the Nord-Seine *département*, and significant renovations of public buildings.[44] Like his economic adviser Patrick Devedjian, who stated that "all projects must start in 2009. . . . We want rapid results,"[45] Sarkozy displayed little concern for the short-term fiscal impact of the measure: "What else could we have done? Sit there with our arms crossed and watch the crisis explode the deficit while waiting to see how bad the damage would be?"[46] This sense of urgency was echoed by the former head of Sarkozy's UMP party, who hailed the measure as a "massive demand stimulus" while Budget Director Eric Woerth claimed that the goal was "to spend as quickly as possible."[47] One official explicitly characterized the intellectual climate in the government at the time as "very Keynesian," as authorities were intent on heading off the crisis or at least limiting its negative effects on the French economy even as they were forced to acknowledge fiscal limitations on the potential scope of their response.[48]

Though classically Keynesian in inspiration, the French stimulus effort also reflected statist liberalism's focus on the structural predicates of the macroeconomy rather than on the connected theme of income support. In crafting the package in this way, French authorities hoped to accomplish an efficient translation of spending into growth and employment. Sarkozy's public declarations echoed this strategic orientation: "This crisis is structural, and over the long run it will change the economy, society, and politics." He demanded that public enterprises "accelerate their future investments," since "events command us to move quickly in order to put the brakes on the recession."[49] When asked about the government's response to a massive union-led demonstration in January 2009 for salary increases, Prime Minister François Fillon's reply reflected the assumption that workers' incomes would increase naturally as a result of initiatives focused on stimulating the macroeconomy: "[The unions] should not be deceived about our priorities: today, the absolute priority is employment. Unemployment is continuing to rise. . . . In this context, the totality of our room for manoeuvre must be directed towards employment and *towards the economy as a whole*. This is what we will tell the social partners."[50] Rather than cater to politically volatile interest groups such as the trade unions, the government initially assumed that the generous network of automatic stabilizers, which had been expanded significantly in the 1980s and 1990s, coupled with the economic growth that stepped-up public spending would promote, would accomplish this task. Over the course of the 1990s and early 2000s, this strategy of sustaining demand through social-policy expansion, common to governments of the Left and the Right, had resulted in an increase in public social spending from 25.2 percent of GDP in 1985 (after Mitterrand's U-turn) to 28.7 percent in 2005, before the 2007 financial crisis. Thereafter, it increased to 31.5 percent of GDP in 2013, as the network of automatic stabilizers compensated for the effects of the Great Recession. In this respect, even as French governments worked to bring their overall budgetary numbers into line with the Maastricht criteria during the 2000s, decades of quiet resistance to austerity and a prioritization of citizenship-based income support had baked in the mechanisms of demand stimulus that would prove critically important, if perhaps insufficient, in the aftermath of the 2007 financial crisis.[51] As Finance Minister Christine Lagarde observed at the time, "The French model provides shock absorbers that were already in place. We haven't had to reinvent our unemployment, health, or welfare systems."[52]

While consistent with statist liberalism's emphasis on macroeconomic initiatives and universalistic models of income support, however, the relatively modest scope of the initial post-2007 French stimulus initiative fit less well with the political realities of the period. Faced with mounting union-led protests and following a summit with union leaders, the government agreed to spend an additional €3 billion on supporting consumption in an effort to allay public fears that the package unfairly favored business. This second law's income-support initiatives were designed to support aggregate demand and consumption across the economy rather than target specific groups in the German fashion.[53] For example, it included a €200 bonus for recipients of the *Revenu minimum d'activité* (RMA, France's minimum income benefit), more generous unemployment benefits, and a €150 subsidy for low-income households.[54] Taken together, the two packages reflected statist liberalism's "statist" orientation (through direct spending and a macroeconomic orientation) and "liberal" footprints favoring means-tested income support and support for business. At the same time, the combination also reflected the tradition's universalistic emphasis on the economic welfare of individual citizens, whose incomes would serve as a means of stimulating demand and economic growth.

France's fiscal-stimulus measures were relatively modest, and they focused overwhelmingly on direct spending (the most efficient means of stimulating demand) designed to revitalize the macroeconomy, rather than on tax cuts. To be sure, fiscal constraints and France's high levels of public debt provide part of the explanation for this timidity, leading to what Susan Milner, quoting Christian Noyer, governor of the Bank of France, has labeled "pocket Keynesianism" or "sectoral and partial Keynesianism."[55] At the same time, however, it is clear that the robustness of France's income-support policies provided a much more efficient means of converting public spending into aggregate demand than was the case in Germany, where less efficient tax cuts were the chosen tool (see Chapter 3). By 2010 France had spent a total of €38.8 billon on stimulus measures (1.75 percent of GDP), about the same as the packages adopted in the more liberal United States (1.9 percent) and United Kingdom (1.4 percent). Of that amount, only 6.5 percent was composed of tax cuts (compared to 45.4 percent in Canada and 34.8 percent in the US), with the rest made up of direct spending, a fact that reflects statist liberalism's vertical model of political responsibility and its de-emphasis on the roles of economic groups, to whom an approach that favored tax cuts would have left greater discretion over spending.[56] About €10 billion was spent on public investment, including infrastructure (€1.4 billion), defense (€1.4 billion), publicly funded research (€700 million), monument restoration (€600 million), and subsidies to public enterprises (€4 billion).[57] Officials relied upon the country's generous safety net[58] to sustain demand, even as they introduced measures that modestly expanded income support.[59] The package was also short-term, with 75 percent of the spending in 2009 and the remaining 25 percent (including the time-delimited income-support measures) in 2010.[60]

The statist liberal tradition thus shaped interpretations of and responses to the crisis in two important ways. First, it supported macroeconomic strategies that focused on public spending on infrastructure, investment, and subsidies to business and, eventually, income-support policies as well. Second, it favored a surprisingly small stimulus that relied on existing protections and emphasized efficient translation of spending into demand rather than a more particularistic (and less efficient and certain) strategy of targeted subsidies or tax cuts. But it also reflected the realities of the post-Maastricht context, in which France's statist impulses were checked by powerful constraints on fiscal policy. According to one former official in the *Trésor* in the Ministry of Finance during Sarkozy's presidency, the government agreed that the country required a large stimulus package but felt constrained by fears of the effects of mounting public debt. As a result, they focused on efficient translation of spending into demand and many one-off measures, such as forgiving firms' VAT debits and accelerating infrastructure projects that had already begun. This strategy aimed at stimulating demand across the economy "without indebting the state in the long term."[61] If French elites were willing to deploy the state, in other words, they did so through modest, macroeconomic measures, even as they sold the package as an aggressive act of public responsibility for social and economic welfare, in keeping with

Sarkozy's promise not to "leave anyone behind."[62] This emphasis on macroeconomic outcomes and reliance on existing social-protection arrangements rather than a massive extension of measures to support consumption made French officials extremely reluctant to cut back these measures in the face of very high levels of debt and repeated demands from Germany, the ECB, and their allies that France cut spending in order to stabilize the euro.[63]

This pattern of ambivalence and indecision, informed by the enduring tension between France's statist impulses and the fiscal strictures deriving from EMU, led to a similarly muddled response to the post-2010 crisis in the Eurozone. After the signing of the Maastricht Treaty, under the rubric of *gouvernement économique,* French authorities from the 1990s on thus sought to advance an alternative model to the insistence of Germany and the ECB on economic austerity, balanced budgets, and so-called structural reform, which effectively meant copying Germany's prioritization of export competitiveness over stepped-up investment in domestic industry and infrastructure.[64] As the Eurozone crisis deepened in 2010, with widening yield spreads on European sovereign debt amid bailouts of Greece, Portugal, Ireland, and other Eurozone countries, observers became increasingly concerned that France could be the next European domino to fall. Nonetheless, Sarkozy's administration avoided significant budget cuts and worked instead on convincing Germany to soften its insistence on austerity.[65] According to one highly placed official in the Elysée during Sarkozy's presidency, the French viewed their role as nuancing Germany's dogmatic position that all countries' debts must be treated exactly alike and to keeping such pronouncements by German officials from unsettling international bond markets.[66] At home, however, a reluctance to cut spending for fear of sapping demand and stifling economic growth limited the extent of French budget cuts. Confronting an alarming budget deficit of 7.1 percent of GDP in 2010,[67] Sarkozy proposed €65 billion in budget cuts and tax increases for 2011, with only €7.5 billion scheduled for 2012, most requiring implementation after the 2012 presidential election.

Sarkozy's defeat at the hands of socialist François Hollande in 2012 did little to alter this policy stance or to resolve the underlying tensions of France's statist liberal tradition with respect to fiscal policy. Elected on promises to step up public spending at home and to resist austerity at the EU level, Hollande's administration combined a rhetorical embrace of reflation, aimed at satisfying the leftist constituencies that had elected him, and a substantive, if halting, pursuit of fiscal rectitude. Initially Hollande seemed poised to fulfill his campaign promises to reverse Sarkozy's modest spending cuts and adopt new spending initiatives designed to restore growth and create jobs, committing the government to hiring 60,000 additional teachers and creating 150,000 new youth jobs, as well as rolling back the previous administration's increase of the retirement age from sixty to sixty-two.[68] He promised to finance these measures in part through a controversial 75 percent tax on households with annual incomes over €1 million, coupled with higher taxes on large firms, while also raising the minimum wage to support consumption.

At the European level, Hollande promised to demand the renegotiation of the Eurozone's fiscal compact, negotiated in 2012 under the leadership of Sarkozy and German Chancellor Angela Merkel, which committed signatories to reducing public debt and deficits but in ways that would offer greater support for economic growth. Hollande proclaimed grandly that he intended to give "a new direction to Europe" and that "austerity need not be Europe's fate."[69] He had also been among the most vocal advocates of euro bonds, a greater role for the European Investment Bank, investments in infrastructure, and other measures to stimulate growth. This leftist variant of statist liberalism soon came up against significant limitations both political and economic, however. Economically he faced a situation of continued economic stagnation (GDP growth in 2012 was effectively zero),[70] rising unemployment (which hit 9.9 percent in the same year),[71] and a deficit of 4.8 percent of GDP at the end of 2012 (well above the government's target of 4.5 percent).[72] This dim reality made it clear that Hollande's prior commitments to cut the budget deficit to 3 percent of GDP and to stabilize the national debt as a share of the size of the economy by 2015 were unrealistic.[73] Politically, Hollande faced both unyielding insistence on austerity by Germany and an increasingly restive public, which soon began to notice the inconsistencies between Hollande's rhetoric and the policies that he was working to put in place and to blame Hollande for France's poor economic and labor-market performance.[74]

Despite the pro-growth platform that had propelled him to the French presidency, Hollande gradually but inexorably shifted to a qualified embrace of austerity measures, including budget cuts and tax increases on the wealthy aimed at closing an almost €37 billion budget gap.[75] His vacillation and grudging acceptance of the austerity imperative also fomented growing discontent on the Left of his own party, with a growing number of his ministers (along with a growing number of voters) publicly questioning his leadership and painting him with the same brush as the austerity-minded Germans. In August 2014, tensions within his government spilled dramatically out into public view, as Economy Minister Arnaud Montebourg called for a "major change" away from austerity, a demand echoed by Education Minister Benoît Hamon, a leader of left-wing dissidents within the Socialist Party. Feeling that his hand was forced, Hollande reshuffled his cabinet, firing Montebourg and Hamon and naming Manuel Valls, a young pro-market reformer loathed by the socialist Left, as the new prime minister.[76] While this dramatic move quelled the revolt on the socialist Left and expelled anti-austerity dissidents, however, it did little to reconcile the tensions within the administration's policy approach. Even as he admitted, in an interview in *Le Monde*, that "there is a demand problem all over Europe . . . that is mainly due to the austerity policies of the past several years" and called for renewed stimulus and investment on the European level, Hollande inconsistently claimed that "any measure using the budget to relaunch activity would increase our public debt and worsen our foreign trade [deficit]."[77] Locked in a persistent struggle between the placating of French socialists and budgetary pressure from Germany and the European Central Bank, France maintained its apparent commitment to austerity in 2014/15. As a result, in September 2014, amidst mounting opposition within his party and cabinet, he barely survived a confidence vote in parliament centered on his fiscal policy. By 2015 France had reduced the deficit to 3.5 percent—at the expense of record high unemployment—and delayed its (rather dubious) goal of achieving a balanced budget to 2017.[78] Once again, French authorities found themselves caught between the statist macroeconomic imperative of promoting economic growth and boosting incomes, on the one hand, and constraints, now all the tighter as a result of the entrenched orthodoxy of austerity at the European level, on the scope of state action, on the other. Statist liberalism as it applied to fiscal policy thus represented an awkward compromise that French authorities accepted *faute de mieux*, with individualistic programs of income support providing much of the support for aggregate demand in the absence of aggressive state fiscal policies.

The inconsistencies of Hollande's policy positions thus reflected tensions embedded deep within the statist liberal tradition. Following the break with dirigisme in the mid-1980s, France consolidated a variant of liberalism in which the respective roles of state and market were never really resolved, leading to a series of inconsistent and constrained responses to periods of economic crisis and upheaval. For all the liberalization and marketization that France undertook in the 1980s and 1990s, governing elites never relinquished their attachment to the state as the guiding force behind economic development, thereby continuing to repudiate standard neoliberal orthodoxies. This state-led process of marketization, moreover, was undertaken in the face of two conflicting imperatives—maintaining influence at the European level and following a strategy of demand stimulus and public spending that was inconsistent with both the preferences of dominant European elites and EMU-derived constraints partially of France's own making.

After Maastricht, French authorities had essentially traded away the substance of their vision of potentially reflationary *gouvernement économique* for a European architecture that offered the forum for such economic coordination without the European political will that would be required to accomplish it. As a result, they were limited in their capacity to respond aggressively to economic crises, forced instead to rely upon existing social-protection arrangements and the automatic stabilizers that they entailed. This strategy of constrained stimulus and "Keynesianism by default" seems likely to continue in light of the 2017 election of Emmanuel Macron to the French presidency on promises to constrain overall public expenditure while expanding social benefits for excluded groups such as entrepreneurs and the self-employed.[79] Like his predecessors on both the Left and the Right, Macron seems poised to pursue a macroeconomically oriented strategy that prioritizes the welfare of individual citizens even as it acknowledges the sharp constraints faced by policymakers seeking to support purchasing power and incomes. As historian Lucien Jaume has recently pointed out, Macron's promises to "emancipate" individuals' productive capacity (to be discussed in the context of his proposals for labor-market reform), combined with state-led efforts to support citizens economically, represent merely the most recent inflection of the statist liberal tradition's state-individual dyad. In Jaume's words, from the eighteenth century on, "there was a division among French liberals: on one side were those who favored administrative power and the elites, while on the other were those who championed the individual and his rights as enshrined in the Constitution."[80] For all of the claims of Macron's novelty as a reformer and economic innovator and criticisms of his "neoliberal" orientation by the Far Left, he is thus actually taking a page from a very old playbook, one that long predates the advent of neoliberalism and rejects many of its core precepts. His strategy represents merely the most recent incarnation of a distinctive set of principles and a consistent (if not always entirely coherent or effective) analytical framework that has informed a course of political-economic development that both grants a role to market-based competition and eschews the aggressively neoliberal strategies favored elsewhere.

Subsidizing Employment and Liberal Keynesianism: Statist Liberalism, Economic Citizenship, and French Labor-Market Reform in the Shadow of Maastricht

Since the 1990s, successive French governments have worked to combat rising levels of joblessness and to reform France's labor-market institutions in ways that are supportive of long-term job growth. As unemployment continued to rise in the early-to-mid-1990s, exceeding 10 percent by the middle of the decade, voters increasingly blamed French authorities for failing to address a jobs crisis whose severity would have been unthinkable in France's Fordist heyday. Declining rates of growth in the 1970s and 1980s, coupled with devastating processes of deindustrialization in erstwhile industrial heartlands such as Pas de Calais in the North and Le Creusot in Burgundy, undermined the assumption that full employment would be a natural outgrowth of their developmental strategies. Instead, rising levels of unemployment and generalizing economic precariousness came to be seen as harbingers of France's economic decline and as symptoms of the fecklessness of the political class. If generating economic growth and spurring industrial development had been the central goals during the *trente glorieuses*, addressing unemployment, albeit in ways that would create a virtuous circle between economic and employment growth, had become the central preoccupation of policymakers and the public alike in the age of austerity. In an episode emblematic of the political-economic dynamics of the era, center-right president Jacques Chirac, elected in 1995 on promises to "heal France's social fracture," watched France's jobless rate climb steadily to 12 percent in 1997, seemingly helpless in what many were now viewing as a true employment crisis.[81] In the process, the political power and prestige that had accrued to France's statist model in the prosperous 1950s and 1960s were now converted into recriminations that helped unseat the government of conservative Prime Minister Alain Juppé in 1997, barely two years after it had come to power.

Unlike German authorities, who interpreted declining labor-market performance as a product of structural mismatches between labor demand and supply and restrictions on the development of low-wage labor, French officials have tended to understand rising joblessness as a symptom of weak economic growth and insufficient aggregate demand. As a result, they have adopted a series of policies of quite different inspiration, working to boost labor-market participation rates and incomes and spur economic growth even as they have subsidized employers' labor costs and worked to create jobs directly. If the German strategy has involved folding a demand-side strategy within a broader supply-side approach, in France the converse has been the case, with supply-side measures embedded within and dependent for their success upon a broader strategy of labor reallocation and bolstering economic growth boosting incomes across the labor market rather than within particular segments of it, in the German fashion. The French strategy also involved a distinctive understanding of the relationship between macroeconomic and microeconomic initiatives in ways that differed from its German analog. The German approach involved prioritizing a microeconomic focus on strategic firms and sectors in the hope of shoring up Germany's export-oriented growth model, while in France, microeconomic measures (such as subsidizing firms' labor costs) were understood within a more macroeconomic perspective focused on broadly based job growth as a mechanism for bolstering aggregate demand, outcomes which were to become mutually reinforcing.

In practice this statist-liberal strategy has involved targeted liberalization of labor-market rules (such as limits on overtime and part-time work) combined with efforts to subsidize employers' share of social contributions so as to encourage hiring, along with constrained efforts to sustain public spending as a support for economic growth. In so doing, French policymakers of both Left and Right have eschewed standard neoliberal strategies in favor of a more socially embedded approach that recognized the need for a supportive state to foster the process of labor-market adjustment. These initiatives included Prime Minister Edouard Balladur's 1993 Five-Year Law on Employment (*La loi quinquennale sur l'emploi*), which permitted firms to negotiate work-time adjustments on an annual rather than weekly basis and offered partial contribution exemptions to employers who reduced annual work time in an effort to create jobs. Cast in a similar vein, Prime Minister Alain Juppé's 1996 *Loi Robien* further liberalized the wage-bargaining process, permitting firm- and branch-level negotiations, reduced the mandated work-time reduction from 15 to 10 percent, and provided generous financial incentives to employers, all in an effort to reallocate labor across a broader segment of the workforce.

This strategy of liberalization, subsidization, and labor reallocation intensified under the "plural left" coalition of socialists, Greens, and communists, led by socialist Prime Minister Lionel Jospin, which governed France between 1997 and 2003. Building upon the initiatives of its center-right predecessors, the new administration focused upon the related imperatives of fostering economic growth by bolstering aggregate demand and reducing unemployment by reallocating labor. The fraught circumstances surrounding the election, moreover, provided it with a strong set of incentives to react decisively. In 1995 Jospin's Gaullist predecessor Juppé had launched an initiative to reform France's public-sector pensions, adopting an insular and technocratic approach that led to the largest public-sector strikes since May 1968, crippling the airlines and public-transportation system and effectively shutting the country down for several weeks.[82] In response, President Jacques Chirac called new elections in the hopes of restoring parliament's authority and increasing his center-right majority. Instead, French voters issued a stunning rebuke of the existing government and returned a parliamentary majority of the Left.[83]

In this fraught political and economic context, the new government sought to walk the line between tackling France's labor-market woes and preserving political support, all with a toolbox that the Stability and Growth Pact had limited significantly. The solution upon which the new administration decided was cast in a classically statist liberal mold—extending the efforts of previous administrations to liberalize labor-market rules while using the state's authority to modify firms' behavior and its resources to subsidize job creation across the labor market in the hope of spurring economic growth by bolstering demand. This strategy of liberalization through subsidization represented an implicit recognition of two important but uncomfortable realities for the new government.

First, it indicated an understanding that state resources were limited by both the earlier dismantling of dirigisme and the acceptance of European strictures on fiscal policy. Second, it reflected policymakers' acknowledgement that, given these constraints, the bulk of job creation would have to take place in the private sector; because the government could not force firms to hire new workers, it needed to create new and significant incentives for them to do so. Officials were thus facing the most severe unemployment crisis since the immediate postwar era, in a context of sluggish economic growth, with one hand tied behind their proverbial backs.

Acting within these constraints and in ways that paralleled the "second-best" strategy adopted in the area of fiscal policy, Jospin's government launched a series of initiatives that both reflected an acknowledgment of these uncomfortable realities and sought to satisfy the demands of its constituencies on the Left. The administration's approach involved two broad categories of intervention. The first comprised subsidization of job creation in segments of the labor market that were particularly affected by high rates of joblessness and long-term unemployment, such as older and younger workers and those with outdated or inadequate skills.[84] The goal was to incorporate such excluded groups into the labor market in order to allow them to realize the full benefits of economic citizenship while bolstering economic growth by increasing workers' disposable incomes.[85] One such measure was the *Programme emploi-jeunes*, "Program for Youth Employment," which offered generous subsidies to firms or agencies in the public sector that hired workers between the ages of sixteen and twenty-five, paying 80 percent of the minimum wage.[86] The measure aimed to cut joblessness among young workers, which had risen steadily since the 1980s and by the 1990s was hovering around 25 percent.[87] It was also intended to provide young workers with training and initial successes in the labor market in ways designed to help them compete for jobs more effectively over the longer term. Jobs were subject to approval by the Labor Ministry, which was responsible for ensuring that they represented real opportunities for lasting employment.[88] Although the measure was expensive (costing about €1.5 billion per year), it succeeded in creating significant jobs for young workers (around 350,000 all told) and demonstrated the government's commitment to social equity and its hope of restoring economic growth by revitalizing this important segment of the labor market.[89]

The most politically salient—and controversial—element of Jospin's labor-market strategy involved the so-called Aubry Laws (named after Jospin's Labor Minister Martine Aubry, who led efforts to formulate the measures) that reduced the standard workweek from thirty-nine to thirty-five hours. Reflecting the government's stated goal of acting as "the counter-current of ultra-liberalism,"[90] the measures were designed to appeal to the government's constituencies on the

Left and to foster job creation by both reallocating existing work and subsidizing employers in order to encourage them to create new positions. This orientation reflected the tensions between the imperatives of state responsibility and support for citizens' incomes at the core of the statist-liberal tradition, operating within the constraints of a post-dirigiste economic context. Although Jospin hoped to use the law to revitalize and systematize France's historically fragmented and conflictual system of industrial relations, the statist impulse was too strong, leading to a strategy that imposed change rather than negotiate it.[91] The first law increased social-contribution exemptions to employers but made them conditional upon the negotiation of a thirty-five-hour weekly work-time limit. Employers were offered €1,372-per worker in annual subsidy in exchange for a 10 percent reduction in labor hours and a 6 percent increase in payrolls, and a €2,134 payment for a 15 percent work-time reduction and a 9 percent increase in jobs.[92] Although the measure succeeded in creating some private-sector positions, most of the associated agreements were struck in the public sector.[93] Hoping to boost participation in the private sector, the administration in 2000 passed a second law that exempted social-security contributions up to 1.8 times the minimum wage and established relatively firm (though flexible) annual limits on work time and overtime for firms that negotiated new contracts.[94] Though such measures focused on microeconomic means, the strategy that they served was widely viewed by French policymakers as Keynesian, with one official stating that the measures were conceived of as demand stimulus in disguise.[95] In this way, French authorities used the ostensibly supply-side mechanisms of deregulation and reducing employers' labor costs, combined with significant state expenditures, as a means of pursuing the classically Keynesian end of fostering economic growth, and, it was hoped, further employment expansion, by boosting demand and consumption. The battle between the state and employers displayed the statist-liberal strategy of boosting growth by bolstering employment levels and workers' incomes while also reflecting both the political constraints imposed by the demise of dirigisme in the previous decade and the legacies of three decades of marginalization of interest groups. While the government's supporters celebrated the measures as efforts to push back the boundaries of neoliberal capitalism and to restore France's fraying social contract, employers decried them as authoritarian and economically counterproductive. The main French employers' confederation (the Mouvement des entreprises de France, or MEDEF), which had not been officially consulted prior to the first law's introduction in 1997, launched a sustained campaign against the measures, and Jean Gandois, MEDEF's president, resigned in protest.[96] This so-called *Refondation sociale* campaign proposed a wide array of liberalizing reforms in social and labor-market policies, focusing on unemployment insurance, vocational training, health insurance, and pensions. MEDEF highlighted the contrast with what it saw as the administration's statist impulses, which led it to impose reforms rather than negotiate them.[97]

Having marginalized interest groups for decades, the state was now forced to confront significant pushback from employers, whose aggressive posture reflected an effort to combat what Denis Kessler, then second in command at MEDEF and the architect of the *Refondation sociale* campaign, denounced as the long-standing "atrophy of civil society."[98] Thus MEDEF's outcry against the laws had more to do with the manner of their formulation and their symbolic association with the Left's agenda than with the substance of the measures themselves. In fact, the initiatives offered quite a lot to employers. Not only did they increase their social-contribution exemptions and offer them greater discretion over the allocation of labor (for example, allowing them to calculate overtime on an annual rather than a weekly basis), they also accelerated the shift from national to sectoral and firm-level collective bargaining, a development that characteristically strengthens employers' hands in collective bargaining. Even as they objected to the measures' statist political optics, privately many employers admitted as much, welcoming the combination of liberalization and subsidization that represented the centerpieces of the law's approach.[99] The impetus for this positive sentiment was reflected in the measures' ultimate effects: by the end of 2002 the laws had led to the creation (or preservation, in the case of planned layoffs that were thus avoided) of an estimated 350,000 jobs, most of which were in the private sector.[100]

Following the Aubry Laws, other labor-market measures introduced by Jospin's administration and its center-right successors reflected the same statist-liberal emphasis upon macroeconomic measures and individual economic security in ways that crossed party lines. One set of initiatives involved relatively minor modifications of some of the provisions of the Aubry Laws while leaving the core of the laws in place. For example, the 2002 *Loi Fillon* allowed some employers to return to a thirty-nine-hour week, raised overtime limits, and limited the application of the thirty-five-hour week to SMEs. After 2007 the conservative administration of President Nicolas Sarkozy and Prime Minister François Fillon passed the so-called Law Promoting Work, Employment, and Purchasing Power, which liberalized the rules governing overtime and supplemental work time, exempting all hours worked beyond thirty-five per week from social security contributions and income tax in firms or sectors with Aubry accords.[101] In 2008 the government introduced a reform, Renewal of Social Democracy and Reform of Work Time, which increased the number of allowable working days and permitted companies to negotiate work time directly with worker representatives rather than require negotiation with officially sanctioned trade-union representatives. In the process the state continued to marginalize trade unions, whose members were concentrated in the public sector, even as it continued to pursue measures designed to bolster workers' incomes.

Succeeding administrations also introduced measures that increased pressures on the unemployed to find work and restricted both the duration and generosity of jobless benefits in an effort to increase rates of labor-market participation and reduce long-term joblessness. In 2000 MEDEF and reform-oriented unions agreed on the so-called *Plan d'aide et de retour à l'emploi* (PARE), which required benefit recipients to sign a job-search contract (the *Projet d'action personalisé*, or PAP) with the Agence nationale pour l'emploi (ANPE), or national employment office, and linked benefit eligibility to participation in a supervised and personalized job-search program.[102] In 2005 the center-right administration of Dominique de Villepin introduced the highly controversial *Contrat première embauche*, "Contract for First Hires," which loosened restrictions on firing workers under the age of twenty-six in the hope of cutting youth unemployment. Major unions and many student groups vigorously opposed the law, bringing more than a million people out into the streets and leading to massive demonstrations, many of which turned violent. The widespread social unrest that followed in the proposal's wake ultimately led de Villepin to back down and rescind the law.

In April 2008, at the behest of the Sarkozy administration, which threatened to impose reforms through legislation in the event of failure, unions and employers began negotiating a new convention on unemployment insurance, which was designed to remedy some of the perceived weaknesses of the PARE.[103] Frustrated with the apparent stalemate of the negotiations, the government decided to impose reforms that required a benefit recipient to accept any job that corresponded to the person's qualifications.[104] Once again, state authorities reverted to an impositional strategy in ways that both reflected and exacerbated the weakness of French collective bargaining and the historic distrust of interest groups. The resulting *Loi sur les droits et les devoirs des demandeurs d'emploi*, which took effect in October 2008, made continued receipt of unemployment benefits contingent upon workers' acceptance of "reasonable" job offers by the national employment office. If the person rejected two such offers, benefits could be suspended, initially for a period of two months and then indefinitely.[105] Even as it worked to coerce the unemployed to seek out available work, however, the administration also acted to enhance the social safety net in other areas. For example, Sarkozy's administration introduced the *Revenu de solidarité active* (RSA), which, unlike the RMI, allowed workers to combine state benefits with some income from a low-paying job. Here again, efforts to liberalize the labor market were coupled with concomitant efforts to shore up workers' incomes and help them adjust to an increasingly challenging labor-market context.

Recent labor-market-reform initiatives undertaken by the socialist administration of François Hollande continued to work to balance state-led labor-market reform with efforts to shore up individual workers' incomes in a challenging economic environment. One important example was the so-called *compte personelle d'activité*, which the government sees as fostering a logic of "individual empowerment" by enabling workers to accumulate credits redeemable for job retraining programs. Another such initiative is the *compte individuelle de formation*, which allows workers to accumulate rights to job-training stints that can be used at any time in their careers.[106] Rather than focus on key groups or sectors in the German fashion, such initiatives operate on a highly individualistic basis. At the same time, however, the inherent tensions of the statist-liberal strategy for labor-market reform have been left largely unresolved. For example, following the purge of dissident leftists from the government in 2014, the then-Economics Minister Emmanuel Macron publicly stated that the Aubry Laws conveyed an image of France as "a country which no longer wanted to work" and "should no longer be put on a pedestal," particularly given the myriad exceptions of its applicability, such as for white-collar workers. He was quickly forced to backtrack in the face of widespread public criticism.[107] Even as the state has worked to reform the labor market while preserving and even expanding the social safety net, it has been forced to confront the political and economic limitations of this strategy in a context of high unemployment and generalized economic precariousness.

Since the late 1990s, successive French administrations of both Left and Right have thus pursued a relatively consistent set of policy priorities that have been informed by the statist liberal tradition's focus on macroeconomic management and quasi-Keynesian efforts to spur economic growth in ways that avoid favoring or subsidizing particular social or economic groups and instead focus on individual workers' incomes across the labor market. The logic of reform has been strikingly similar across partisan lines, with both Left and Right imposing reforms involving a combination of constrained liberalization coupled with robust measures to sustain individual incomes.[108] This fact was echoed by Denis Kessler, the former second in command at MEDEF, who declared bluntly that "Left-Right differences don't matter. The French think that the only way to reform is through the state." Beginning with the Aubry Laws, this agenda entailed significant liberalization of labor-market rules combined with the subsidization of job creation and efforts to foster economic growth through workers' incomes and aggregate demand. Although governments worked in good faith to foster negotiations among the social partners in furtherance of this agenda, they also demonstrated a willingness to impose reforms from the top, sometimes relatively quickly. Unlike its German counterpart, this reform agenda has not subsidized particular groups of employers or workers but rather subsidized employers across the economy, from large firms to SMEs, even as policymakers have worked to revamp the labor market's rules and institutional predicates. These priorities remain at the center of the stated policymaking agenda of incoming President Macron, who made liberalizing the tax system and labor-market rules facing firms one of the central planks of his platform even as he has promised to expand social protection in ways designed to buffer workers from market vagaries. Though with quite different context and connotation, Macron's economic program and strategy for labor-market reform, which he has characterized as "neither Left nor Right," both unwittingly echoes Kessler's earlier lament and highlights the shared understanding of labor-market reform across the partisan divide since the 1990s.

The central goals of the statist-liberal strategy for labor-market reform have been boosting economic growth and workers incomes by reducing unemployment while preserving and even expanding France's robust network of citizenship-based income-support programs in a clear repudiation of standard neoliberal recipes. According to an official in the Ministry of Finance, this strategy has been quite similar across partisan lines and has aimed to "find an equilibrium between flexibility and social protection."[109] In a set of responses striking in their substantive consistency over time and across partisan lines, authorities have also engaged in often acrimonious conflict with representatives of both labor and business even as they have sought to support the incomes of individual citizens qua workers and confronted the necessity of securing the cooperation of private-sector employers who have remained quite skeptical about the wisdom of their initiatives. The effectiveness of this strategy has been relatively limited: 43 percent of unemployed workers still suffer from long-term joblessness and youth unemployment hovers around 25 percent, facts which support the view that most French unemployment is structural.[110] At the same time, however, France's unemployment rate has fallen to a five-year low of 9.6% following Macron's election, suggesting both a cyclical upswing and renewed confidence in a labor market long derided for its sclerotic performance.[111] Despite this progress, France's continued struggles with labor-market performance reflect the inherent limitations of a statist-liberal strategy for labor-market renewal in a post-dirigiste era dominated by fiscal austerity and the constraints deriving from France's continued commitment to EMU.

In the Shadow of the State: Statist Liberalism and Financial Regulation in the Post-dirigiste Era

As discussed in Chapter 1, France's postwar dirigiste model relied heavily upon the state's close relationship with the financial sector in devising policies designed to modernize and industrialize the French economy. Initially, French statism relied upon indicative planning, led by the Commissariat général du plan (CGP), diverting resources to critical sectors such as coal, steel, and nuclear power, upon which the broader goal of rapid industrialization was believed to rely. Over time, however, state authorities moved away from planning and toward more direct financial intervention in the economy, relying upon the Ministry of Finance, and in particular the *Trésor*, to shape economic development through instruments such as selective credit allocation to strategic firms and sectors.[112] This shift in strategic means accompanied a concomitant shift in ends, with large so-called "national champions," such as Bull, Elf, and Thomson, intended to act as France's vanguard in the international economy by establishing a strong competitive position, as well as to sustain domestic economic growth. In shifting from a microeconomic to a macroeconomic focus in this way, French authorities sought to use "state intervention to promote industrial competition."[113] By relying heavily upon the *Trésor* to provide industrial finance and guide development, French officials relegated large industrial banks to a secondary role, which John Zysman labeled the "outer circle of government financial influence on the economy."[114] These banks, many of which were state owned, still played an important role in providing resources for investment to firms, but the dominance of the *Trésor* and the proliferation of potential borrowers meant that they could afford to be cautious in their lending practices, requiring significant guarantees and limiting their exposure to risk.[115]

The state thus had two avenues of financial influence over French industrial development during the dirigiste heyday. Through the *Trésor*, it was able to act as a Gerschenkronian agent promoting late development by providing patient capital to strategic industries,[116] and through its influence over large industrial banks, it could help to ensure a broad pool of capital to sustain firms that had established solid competitive positions. Whereas in Germany large industrial banks remained in private hands and bank-firm relationships were therefore crucially important,[117] in France the process of allocating capital was largely driven by the state itself, with the banks serving as mechanisms of economic policy aimed at spurring economic growth and fostering industrial development and employment.[118] The remaining components of the postwar French financial system entailed the *caisses d'épargne*, or savings banks, which were highly fragmented and focused largely on small-scale retail operations. With respect to the politically favored industrial banks, the prevailing assumption was that political control of financial institutions would ensure the availability of credit for households and SMEs, thereby leading to broader growth and employment creation across the political economy and beyond the narrow realm of favored economic elites. This pattern of subordinating the financial sector to state control, employing state intervention in the service of macroeconomic goals, reached its apogee in the early 1980s, when the incoming socialist administration of François Mitterrand nationalized the entire banking sector in the service of its "rupture with capitalism."

Following the demise of dirigisme in the early-to-mid-1980s, the relationship with the financial sector changed dramatically, as the state relinquished direct control over finance and undertook a significant deregulation of the financial marketplace. After privatizing many of the banks that had been nationalized in the early 1980s, successive governments of both Left and Right sold off some of France's largest industrial banks, including Société Générale under the conservative administration of Prime Minister Jacques Chirac between 1986 and 1988 and Crédit Lyonnais under Lionel Jospin's socialist administration in 1999, following the latter's massive bankruptcy and three successive state rescue plans in the 1990s.[119] At the same time, however, the French state did not relinquish its role within the French financial system, instead working to foster the development of German-style relationships between industrial banks and industry. Given post-dirigiste limitations on French state capacity, French officials increasingly sought to create private-sector relationships that could accomplish the same developmental goals, even as they maintained important, if more indirect, levers of financial influence. The so-called *banque-industrie* strategy of the 1980s and 1990s reflected the enduring tension between a statist impetus and a privatized, deregulatory climate, and its ultimate failure stemmed from institutional and financial limitations that precluded authorities' ability to act as effective analogs to their German counterparts.[120]

The changing relationship between the state and finance was not limited to patterns of ownership, however; a series of deregulatory initiatives weakened the state's interventionist hand and provided banks with greater autonomy. This trend began with the 1984 Banking Act, which allowed for "universal banking," the model whereby investment and retail banking and insurance activities are all housed within the same bank. It also centralized financial regulation and ended the Banque de France's automatic refinancing mechanism.[121] This act was modified by two successive measures—the 1996 Financial Activity Modernization Act (FAMA) and the 1999 Savings and Financial Security Act (SFSA), which strengthened state officials' supervisory and regulatory authority within this more liberalized environment.

By the 2000s, in the years leading up to the 2007–8 financial crisis, the result of these developments was a financial sector much more concentrated in private hands and a state with fewer levers of influence over it. Although liberalization had freed many firms from the tight tutelage of state-owned banks characteristic of the *trente glorieuses*, many firms remained quite reliant upon large French banks.[122] Consolidation among large industrial banks during the previous decade had left two institutions—Société Générale and BNP—in dominant positions, with four so-called *mutuels*, or cooperative banks, occupying much of the rest. The result has been one of the most consolidated banking systems in Europe,[123] as well as one in which close relationships between bank officials and public authorities have been preserved, albeit according to a collaborative (not to say collusive) dynamic rather than a despotic one, as under dirigisme. Nicolas Jabko and Elsa Massoc characterize this system as one in which "large privatized banks are in the hands of a narrow elite coming out of the higher echelons of the political service and made up of political friends." Whereas the state's relationship with the financial industry under dirigisme was vertically integrated and intensely hierarchical, the contemporary system "has shifted to a more informal, horizontally integrated, oligarchic form of business-state relations," a pattern equally emblematic of industry and finance.[124] As in the contexts of fiscal and labor-market policy, this patterns shows that French statist liberalism has adjusted to a more market-based economic order while maintaining important institutionalized connections and patterns of coordination between the state and the financial system in ways that reflect a rejection of neoliberal imperatives of a denuded state and arm's-length economic relationships. At the same time, however, France's financial system remains both concentrated and focused on large industrial investment, as opposed to having deep political and social ties to local and regional public-private institutions like Italy's Popolari or Germany's Landesbanken (see Chapters 3 and 4).

The early 2000s were dominated by two broad efforts to modify the French financial sector. The first involved the consolidation of the *caisses*, which were highly decentralized and had long suffered from significant inefficiencies. Unlike Italy and Germany, however, where the reform of politically connected and economically important savings banks generated sharp local and regional political backlash, in France efforts to consolidate the *caisses* were much less politicized.[125] In 1999 the structure of the *caisses* was changed from that of "ownerless" institutions to banks which were jointly owned by customers and different levels of government (rather analogous to American credit unions).[126] The differences between the relatively impositional French treatment of the *caisses* and the more collaborative and collusive relationships with large industrial banks highlight the distinctive character of the French financial sector. In Germany and Italy, both industrial banks and public savings banks have long served as important sources of finance for strategically important firms of varying size, whereas in France the system—both before and after the 1984 act—maintained a sharp differentiation between strategically important large banks and savings banks. This structure also reflected enduring legal and bureaucratic barriers between regulation of institutional financial transactions and those of households. Only after French banks' rush to enter the field of consumer finance following the liberalization of the 1980s and 1990s, which resulted in unsustainable levels of consumer borrowing, coupled with a relatively hands-off approach to consumer lending by the EU, did the French state step in to constrain consumer finance.[127] This revised approach was maintained by governments of both Left and Right and included such measures as the limitation of consumer refinance programs and restrictions on credit cards.

The other series of important developments in French financial regulation in the years leading up to the 2007 financial crisis involved the absorption of a series of EU financial regulations and directives into French law, with particular emphasis upon adjusting the French financial system to the advent of the euro and the related weakening of French monetary-policy authority. As in the case of fiscal policy, French financial authorities continued to seek a way to accomplish reforms at the EU level that they were unable to pursue unilaterally and to shape European policies in directions that were consistent with their strategy of macroeconomic support for economic and employment growth.[128] Although this strategy met with mixed results, French policymakers successfully bolstered their supervisory authority and established mechanisms with which to govern a more liberal and largely private financial landscape. This movement was highlighted by the 2003 Financial and Security Law, which reformed regulatory authorities by establishing the Autorité des marchés financiers, which operates under the aegis of the *Trésor* and is responsible for both regulating French equities markets to prevent abuses such as insider trading and supervising the provision of a wide range of savings and investment products.[129]

By 2006 France had thus significantly reformed its financial sector, resulting in a system that was both much more deregulated than its dirigiste antecedents and in which the state's direct role had been drastically reduced. At the same time, however, the reforms of the 1990s and 2000s had preserved a significant role for the state—both as a regulator and as a party having close relationships with large industrial banks, which continued to play an important strategic role. The macroeconomic orientation of the statist liberal tradition thus continued to color patterns of French financial regulation and the state's relationship with the financial sector even as it evolved in the face of a shift from the public to the private sector as the central engine of financial provision to French industry. One Finance Ministry official aptly characterized the French post-dirigiste financial strategy in ways that captured its macroeconomic orientation, the connection with concerns for workers' incomes, and the importance of state-finance cooperation in a context in which the state's tools of intervention were limited. He argued that the system focused on "macroprudential risk," involving strategic identification and attenuation of broad "risks for firms and workers," and that the logic of state intervention was based upon "harmonizing the state with the entire financial sector."[130]

As in Germany and Italy, the advent of the 2007 financial crisis posed a series of daunting challenges to the French financial system and the authorities responsible for regulating it. The bankruptcy of Lehman Brothers in the United States and the shock waves that rippled through the global financial system in its aftermath forced French officials to confront the system's vulnerabilities and to work to shore up the banks' role as a source of industrial finance. As discussed, the financial crisis did not hit France as hard as it did some other advanced industrial countries, with GDP declines and increases in unemployment modest by international comparison. In much the same way, the French financial sector experienced relatively modest pressures compared to those of many of its European neighbors, where the banking systems were more exposed to toxic mortgage debt and the performance of economically strategic sectors was more intimately bound up with the fate of banks on which they relied for the bulk of their finance. Furthermore, the losses in France were concentrated in a few large banks, an unsurprising outcome given the fact that France already had one of the most consolidated financial sectors in Europe.[131] Unlike Germany, where the Landesbanken spread the scale and scope of financial losses and were intimately connected to a wide range of strategically important SMEs, the centralized nature of French finance both limited economic exposure and allowed for a more targeted state response. Also facilitating an effective response were the historically close connections between the state and large French industrial banks, a relationship that somewhat paradoxically tightened following the repudiation of dirigisme and the resulting demise of the *Trésor* as the central mechanism of state-based financial allocation. These connections had left in place an environment of solidarity among financial institutions and supported a less adversarial relationship between them and the state, yielding a willingness to work to achieve solutions that both sides found reasonable. As several of the main French banks voluntarily abandoned some of their investment arms and risky financial vehicles following the crisis, some of them seemed actually to welcome state intervention and a retreat to traditional retail banking activities, suggesting a lack of enthusiasm for the universal-banking model and program of deregulation introduced in the 1980s and 1990s.

The bank bailout that French authorities devised in the aftermath of the 2007–8 financial crisis was cast in classic statist-liberal fashion and was heavily colored by a macroeconomic orientation and the twin goals of enhancing stability and preserving large industrial banks' prominent role in the post-dirigiste financial system. As had long been the case, both in the financial sector and in the areas of fiscal and labor-market policy, French authorities were caught between two competing impetuses—the prevailing understanding of the state's extensive economic responsibilities and a recognition of the limits on state intervention in a more liberal era. The character and content of the plan reflects this tension between state responsibility and limitations on state authority. In their discussion of the bailout, Jabko and Massoc argue that "the plan cannot be neatly labelled as 'liberal' or 'interventionist,' nor even located on a simple continuum between these two ideal types. Rather, it was an uneasy and apparently contradictory construction that expressed the singularity of France's post-dirigiste model of capitalism in the early twenty-first century."[132] At the same time, the package was designed to protect the incomes of individual citizens across the economy rather than that of favored groups, reflecting both the statist-liberal prioritization of individual citizens as both the primary clients of state actions and the associated understanding that such a policy would serve Keynesian macroeconomic ends in supporting growth by bolstering aggregate demand. This orientation was clear in President Nicolas Sarkozy's initial announcement of the bailout. The package, he said, was designed to "protect French citizens' jobs, their savings, and their tax revenues. . . . By offering the state's protection, we can hope that we will not have to impose on our compatriots the enormous costs that would result from a collapse of the financial system."[133]

Just as French authorities had justified their protection and subsidization of big business under the Fifth Republic with reference to the macroeconomic implications of this sector's welfare, after 2008 they bailed out parts of the financial sector in the hopes of stabilizing the economy and establishing the basis for macroeconomic recovery and future growth. As the banks' actual and projected losses began to mount, the government moved quickly to shore up the financial system. State officials quickly established the Société de financement de l'économie française (SFEF) and the Société de prise de participation de l'Etat (SPPE), designed to raise capital and provide liquidity to ailing banks and to help recapitalize them.[134] The former was an entity of public law, of which the banks collectively owned two-thirds and the state the remaining share, assigned the task of issuing medium- and long-term loans backed by state guarantees to vulnerable financial institutions. The SPPE was a similarly constituted public agency owned exclusively by the state; its task was to channel funds to financial institutions judged to be fundamentally solvent but suffering from liquidity problems in the teeth of the crisis.[135] France pledged €40 billion to recapitalize its banks and an additional €320 billion to guarantee interbank lending through the SFEF and SPPE in October 2008, amounting to a total of about 18 percent of French GDP. The French bailout included all six major French banks and extracted significant concessions from them, including a guarantee to maintain domestic lending at 3 to 4 percent, eliminate executive bonuses for 2008, and limit dividend payments.[136] This strategy stood in marked contrast to the German bank bailout, in which such macroeconomic considerations were absent or secondary and which focused instead on shoring up segments of the financial sector connected to strategic economic sectors. The novelty of the French approach was its emphasis on collaboration between financial institutions and the state, facilitating a greater volume of recapitalization financing.[137] Further, with the SFEF effectively being run as a private entity—the state serving merely as a guarantor—France was able to maintain the fiscal capacity necessary for relatively sizable stimulus efforts in 2009 and 2010 despite the policy shackles of Maastricht. By July 2009 the SPPE had agreed to extend additional recapitalization for BNP Paribas, BPCE, and Société Générale in the amount of €10.25 billion.

In addition to stabilizing and recapitalizing large industrial banks, the French bailout focused on shoring up large public savings banks and *caisses*, which had previously been peripheral to French state financial strategies but suffered disproportionately large losses after 2008 and therefore threatened to create systemic instability. In this sector, the mutual banks Banque Populaire and Caisse d'Epargne, along with the Franco-Belgian Dexia, suffered the worst effects. Natixis, the investment house connected to Banque Populaire and Caisse d'Epargne, was heavily exposed to the subprime markets that had roiled the American financial system. By summer 2009, Sarkozy had brokered a merger between Banque Populaire and Caisse d'Epargne, an urgent task given their shared interest in Natixis (the banks' shared investment arm and the worst-performing French bank) and the systemic risk that the latter's parlous financial condition clearly posed.[138] Dexia's situation was more grave. It required urgent and massive recapitalization, not just to save the bank itself, but, given its size and importance in the French financial system, for the health of the French economy. As part of the agreement to be included in the SPPE scheme, the state mandated that Dexia change its management. Dexia's recapitalization ultimately included €3 billion from France, €3 billion from Belgium, and €376 million from Luxembourg. As one of the first casualties of the European sovereign debt crisis (with heavy exposure to Greek bonds), Dexia secured state support that outlasted the life of the SPPE and was relegated to the status of a "bad bank" in October 2011.

Since 2009 French financial regulation has seen comparatively limited advances, which is evidence of the sophistication of its preexisting structure. Developments in financial regulation have centered primarily on increased supervision and resiliency, as well as the adoption of regional financial standards. The first of these measures occurred with the 2010 creation of the Autorité de contrôle prudentiel (ACP), which was formed as an independent monitoring authority. The ACP (later renamed the Autorité de contrôle prudentiel et de résolution) merged the French Banking Commission, the Mutual Insurance Supervisory Authority, and the Credit Institutions and Investment Firms Committee. In October 2010 the Sarkozy government passed the Law on Banking and Financial Regulation, which empowered the Autorité des marchés financiers (established in the 2003 Financial and Security Law) with expanded supervisory and enforcement powers. Additionally, the law regulated derivative markets, increased monitoring of credit-rating agencies, and saw the establishment of home-finance bonds.[139] More recent efforts have focused on the regional integration of banking supervision. On July 26, 2013, the government passed the Regulation Banking Act, which allowed the continuation of universal banking (to the disdain of many in the Socialist Party) but required buffers (ring fencing) within each financial institution to prevent contagion in future crises.[140]

Since the 1980s, then, the French financial system and the state's relationship with it have evolved in ways that have reflected many of the core commitments of—and tensions within—the statist liberal tradition. Even as it privatized and deregulated the French banking system in the aftermath of dirigisme's demise in the 1980s, the state maintained close relationships with the French banking sector, particularly with large industrial banks. In so doing it hoped to maintain a tool of intervention in the economy but in a more collaborative way than during the heyday of French statism. These connections were maintained in the service of largely macroeconomic strategies of support for economic growth and stability, and the content of deregulatory and liberalizing measures did little to sever these important, if now less mechanical and formal, connections. At times when French financial institutions required the support of the state, most notably in the aftermath of the 2008 financial crisis, this support was granted in ways designed to preserve the large banks' central role in the French financial system and thereby foster stability across the economy as a whole. French authorities have sought to foster collaborative relationships with French finance in the service of broad developmental goals even as they struggled to find the tools to accomplish this task. Perhaps most clearly reflected in the failed *banque-industrie* strategy of the 1980s, this effort has often been frustrated and has left a legacy of ambiguity in the French state's relationship with the financial industry. In much the same way that President François Mitterrand adopted a so-called *ni-ni* strategy in the 1980s—*neither* privatization *nor* nationalization—the French financial sector has found itself somewhat awkwardly situated between the state and the market economy. Just as in fiscal and labor-market policy, then, the evolving tradition of statist liberalism has informed state strategies that reject neoliberalism even as they struggle to define the new financial landscape between state and market.

Conclusion: Statist Liberalism and French Economic Citizenship in a Neoliberal Era

Since the 1990s French authorities have worked to manage the process of adjustment to an era that has confronted them with a series of daunting economic challenges. The end of the postwar boom and the exhaustion of the Fordist model on which it had been based, and the concomitant slowing of economic growth and emergence of high rates of structural unemployment after the 1970s left French authorities casting about for solutions to the twin problems of economic decline and social unrest, a constant specter haunting a country in which the near revolution of 1968 was still a relatively fresh memory. As conventional wisdom posited that France would become ungovernable if unemployment exceeded various thresholds—first one million, then two—that continued to be surpassed, the task of reducing joblessness and fostering an equitable sharing of economic resources became a matter of shoring up the state's legitimacy rather than a mere technocratic exercise. Formidable in the 1970s, these challenges became even more severe following the dismantling of the dirigiste institutional framework in the 1980s, which left French officials with few of their traditional tools for generating economic growth and employment. Limitations on French officials' economic toolbox were exacerbated by the strictures of the 1992 Maastricht Treaty and the so-called Stability and Growth Pact that followed, which placed strict limits on fiscal debts and deficits and, under the aegis of the incipient European Economic and Monetary Union, removed entirely their discretion over monetary policy. With considerable ambivalence but seeing few alternative means whereby to retain their influence over European policy, French officials signed on to a governance regime fundamentally at odds with their traditional Keynesian perspective. They did so in the (ultimately vain) hope of steering European economic policies in directions consistent with their historical priorities and their championing of state intervention as a means whereby to accomplish both economic growth and economic prosperity broadly shared across the citizenry.

Resisting the siren song of an increasingly dominant transnational neoliberal project, French authorities crafted adjustment strategies informed by their alternative tradition of statist liberalism even as they struggled to reconcile many of this tradition's internal tensions and contradictory imperatives. Retaining a central—albeit altered—role for the state in fostering economic adjustment, French authorities sought to confront the challenges of the post-dirigiste era in ways that incorporated statist liberalism's twin emphases on macroeconomic growth strategies (often using microeconomic means, as in the case of the Aubry Laws) and supporting incomes and economic welfare for French citizens, conceived of as individuals whose primary political allegiance was to the state rather than as members of ontologically prior groups, in the German fashion. In all three of the policy areas under examination here—fiscal policy and state investment, labor-market policy, and financial regulation—French officials worked to manage the policy and institutional limitations of the era while maintaining their commitment to broadly based economic growth, though often with mixed results. Although different in their specific content, policies in each of these three areas reflected the core commitments of statist liberalism—a largely macroeconomic policy orientation and frame of reference; an emphasis on demand stimulus as a means of fostering economic and employment growth; a concern for economic welfare for citizens qua individuals; an ambivalence about the relationship between liberalization and individual economic freedom on the one hand, and state responsibility for aggregate economic welfare on the other; and an emphasis upon shared responsibilities between state and citizen—that have been important hallmarks of the broad corpus of French liberal thought since the nineteenth century. Although the statist liberal tradition evolved in reaction to and by rejection of neoliberalism after the 1970s, these core commitments and conceptual touchstones remained strikingly constant across partisan, institutional, and policy contexts.

These core principles stand out even more clearly when compared to the distinctive German liberal tradition, which is the subject of the next chapter.[141] If French anthropologist Louis Dumont could justifiably portray French economic history as "modernization as individualization,"[142] in Germany the parallel story might best be characterized as one in which "each class [group] should make its contribution to the common cause."[143] As described in Chapter 1, from its roots in interwar Ordoliberalism, German liberalism in the postwar period evolved in ways that both built on and departed from the precepts of the Ordoliberal tradition of Eucken and Rüstow, as the Social Market Economy was consolidated in the 1950s and early 1960s. Preserving the Ordoliberal emphasis upon groups as the fundamental basis of society, German "corporate liberalism" nevertheless reflected postwar social and economic realities, including widespread poverty and unemployment and a public infrastructure that had to be rebuilt from scratch, that were deeply inconsistent with the Ordoliberal championing of a neutral and minimalist state whose primary role was limited to fostering intergroup competition and acting as a neutral arbiter rather than setting the national orientation and direction of economic policy.

As neoliberalism emerged in the 1970s and became a dominant international economic doctrine in the 1980s and 1990s, moreover, German corporate liberalism, like its French counterpart, kept its distance, retaining its distinctive understanding of the constitution of society and its relationship with the state and the market while rejecting the aggressive marketizing principles that were the intellectual core of neoliberalism. In so doing it fostered distinctive elite understandings of periods of economic upheaval after the late 1980s and encouraged particular kinds of responses to them. After German reunification in 1990 and the promulgation of the Maastricht Treaty and in the context of the era of slowed growth and rising unemployment that followed in the wake of these developments, German officials adopted policies that reflected growing (if often masked) state intervention in the economy, leaving behind the template of the postwar "semi-sovereign state,"[144] while subsidizing and protecting social and economic groups at the core of the postwar Social Market Economy. These responses were consistent with the precepts of the corporate liberal tradition and stood in sharp contrast to the policies informed and favored by French and Italian liberalism.

3

Economic Adjustment through Group Subsidization

Managing the Social Market Economy under German Corporate Liberalism

The evolution of German corporate liberalism out of interwar Ordoliberalism was driven by a combination of intellectual ferment and challenging postwar political and economic circumstances. As discussed in Chapter 1, early Ordoliberals such as Rüstow and Eucken furnished key conceptual touchstones that would inform central elements of the corporate-liberal tradition, particularly with respect to the role of the state and its relationship to society. For them, one of the state's most important roles was to act as an agent of balance among the claims of powerful interest groups, which were viewed as the basic building blocks of the social and economic orders. The state as early Ordoliberals understood it was a far cry from the minimalist state of a thinker like Hume or, to a more limited extent, Locke.[1] Nor did they envision a state that would permit the "liberal anarchism" championed by acolytes of the Austrian school and the postwar neoliberals that they would come to inspire. Instead, Ordoliberals believed that "the full capacities of markets could only be realized through their embedding in a robust legal and social order, including preemptive, 'market-conforming' interventions on the part of the state."[2]

Adherents of Ordoliberalism sought to establish and enforce a robust legal order and to prevent the accretion of excessive influence by potentially oligopolistic interest groups, both directly and by promoting competition among them. As Ralf Ptak emphasizes, this concern for providing the state with significant authority grew out of the shared desire to avoid a repetition of the trauma of Weimar. The political chaos of that period was fueled in important ways by a weak and fragmented parliament, itself a reflection of deep political and ideological divisions in society and exacerbated by a gulf between parliamentary and executive authority that allowed the state to be colonized and ultimately conquered by antidemocratic forces. With the nightmare of Weimar in mind, Ordoliberals advocated a model of *Ordnungspolitik*, whose central goal "was to secure a socially embedded and well-functioning competitive order."[3] Accordingly, "Ordoliberalism ventured beyond a limited safeguarding and correcting role for the state in an effort to prevent abuse of monopoly power or to promote and stabilize competition."[4]

If the idealized Ordoliberal blueprint was a far cry from the minimalist state envisioned by nineteenth-century advocates of laissez-faire, neither was it a state that directed economic activity or assumed responsibility for macroeconomic performance in the French fashion.[5] Instead, it had to contend with significant limits on its authority and, to the extent possible, was to remain neutral as to the competing claims of interest groups. Concentration of power, whether in the form of a predatory state or avaricious, self-serving firms and interest groups, was viewed as the enemy of a just and stable social and economic order. Given that a self-regulating, neutral state is just as unlikely to emerge spontaneously as are socially minded interest groups, "Ordo-liberals try to attack both state interventionism and the laissez-faire pluralism of private pressure groups."[6] That is, they sought a state that, as a matter of both constitutional design and accepted practice, equally lacked the capacity to displace private economic actors in the market economy and the legitimacy to dominate or reorder social and economic structure. For early Ordoliberals, then, *Ordnungspolitik* "restrains both the state that practices it, and the private sector that grows within it, through the indirect regulation of the economic constitution," whose implementation "must be based upon a reciprocal duty of . . . members [of the community] to act in the terms laid out in" it.[7] Though robust enough to prevent the oligopolistic concentration of economic power and to maintain a just and competitive order, in Böhm's words, "the essential liberal principle is that 'the state must in no case authorize or confer particularistic privileges.'"[8]

This rather abstract vision quickly came up against concrete postwar social and economic circumstances, however, reflecting a tension that constituted an early driving force in the evolution of Ordoliberalism into the institutional foundations of the Social Market Economy. Breezy assertions, such as Böhm's claim that public "coercion derives from the situation, not from political authority" and that "[e]qual freedom of all others imposes an inherent limit upon the freedom of each and everyone"[9] fit awkwardly with a postwar Germany that was physically and economically devastated, with widespread hunger, homelessness, and mounting public-health crises, exacerbated by the millions of destitute refugees streaming in from formerly German territory to the east. In such a dire context, the German state was forced to intervene in the economy and society in ways that were more direct and dispositive than

Ordoliberals would have preferred and that would ultimately involve to some extent the process that they abhorred: picking winners and losers. The grim landscape threatened to undermine the legitimacy of the broad Ordoliberal project, which, "[i]nstead of tackling the current societal, social, and political conditions . . . remained oriented towards an abstract ideal of society that displayed features of enlightened absolutism and preindustrial social structures."[10] This orientation also ignored the important fact of a large and impoverished working class, whose "stability and security was a prerequisite to securing the market economy."[11]

These concerns forced adherents of traditional Ordoliberalism to make a number of concessions, which would inform the creation of a political economy relatively far removed from the Ordoliberal blueprint. Faced with the pressing needs of postwar reconstruction and the urgency of legitimizing the nascent Social Market Economy in a population with pressing economic needs, postwar authorities were compelled to accept what Rüstow had labeled "'liberal interventionism' aimed at improving the concrete situation of individuals—or what he called their *Vitalsituation*."[12] Although the modal citizens in Rüstow's conception were tradesmen and small property owners[13]—core groups in his vision of a stable social order that would constitute part of the backbone of the German economic model—postwar destitution meant that workers, particularly skilled industrial workers, were the primary recipients of public benefits and one of West Germany's most important political constituencies, as well as part of the backbone of Germany's export-oriented economy.[14]

This vision would form both the main blueprint for and the legitimating ideology of an increasingly successful German economy in the 1950s and 1960s. The combination of neocorporatist collective-bargaining institutions, firm-level works councils, powerful industrial banks that provided deep pools of patient capital to firms, and broadly consensual political relationships among both the major political parties and between the state and producer groups reinforced the social peace and economic success that the Social Market Economy helped to create. Between 1950 and 1973 real annual economic growth averaged 5.0 percent, while unemployment rates averaged only 2.7 percent between 1952 and 1964 and a negligible 0.8 percent between 1965 and 1973. Productivity rates skyrocketed, and the average annual growth of 6.0 percent in real GDP per man-hour between 1950 and 1973 was the highest of any major European country.[15] Inflation, held in check by rapid productivity increases and the aggressive stewardship of the Bundesbank, amounted to a mere 2.7 percent, the lowest in Europe.[16] The federal budget enjoyed a healthy surplus, averaging 2.2 percent of GDP between 1952 and 1972.[17] As the engine of this stellar economic performance, the Social Market Economy benefited from seemingly unassailable prestige, thereby legitimizing postwar modifications of Ordoliberalism, including most importantly the numerous concessions to the imperative of supporting the welfare of the working class.

By the late 1960s and early 1970s, slowing growth and rising unemployment began to erode the credibility of the German model.[18] Whereas the postwar boom had enabled German elites to play a positive-sum economic game that bought political consensus through the distribution of expanding wealth, the advent of hard times in the 1970s forced authorities to begin to accept trade-offs that they had previously been able to avoid. The modified Ordoliberalism that both informed and reflected the assumptions of the postwar Social Market Economy no longer provided a guide for responding to the challenges of a new and darker economic climate in which neither full employment nor rapid growth could be assumed. At the same time, the emergence of neoliberalism in the late 1970s,[19] itself a response to the apparent failure of Keynesianism to respond effectively to slowing growth and the 1973 OPEC oil shock, posed a significant ideological challenge to those countries, like Germany and France, that had rejected standard neoliberal prescriptions for economic recovery.[20] With its agenda of privatization and deregulation and "[i]ts central assumption . . . that the state's main legitimate role was to enforce undistorted competition,"[21] neoliberalism seemed to suggest that "middle ways" between classical liberalism and socialism adopted by Germany and other countries were unsustainable and merely put off difficult but inevitable choices.[22] If the postwar Keynesian bargains appeared to have failed, then, neoliberals maintained that the straightforward solution was to dismantle them and replace them with a concerted attempt to achieve "an essentially utopian vision of the minimally regulated free market."[23]

By the 1980s the corporate liberal framework had evolved in ways that would provide a powerful alternative to standard neoliberal orthodoxies and would shape Germany's policy responses to the subsequent period of heightened economic constraint. It would do so in consistent ways that departed from both standard neoliberal prescriptions and past practices informed by the country's postwar national model of capitalism. In all three of the areas of state activity and concern under examination in this book—fiscal policy and patterns of state investment, social and labor-market policy, and financial regulation and subsidization—German authorities fashioned policy and institutional responses that bore the stamp of corporate liberalism's assumptions about a group-based social order and a state whose central political-economic task was to support and protect it. In this respect, the consolidation of corporate liberalism in the 1980s as an alternative to neoliberalism drew on German liberalism's commitment, clear since the nineteenth century, to advance the interests of economic groups forged in the crucible of nascent German capitalism, in particular the *Mittelstand*, "a society of prosperous small enterprises" that were "most vulnerable to uncontrolled [economic] growth," and their trade-union counterparts, once the distinction between artisanal and industrial workers was cemented by the progress of German industrialization.[24]

Since the early 1990s, authorities have developed the state's relationships with business, labor, and finance in ways that preserved and, in some cases, reinforced the political lines between favored core groups and other, less incorporated segments of the polity and society.[25] In the area of state investment and fiscal policy, governments have invested significant resources in infrastructure and development in key industrial and export sectors while imposing limits on fiscal deficits that disproportionately hurt outsiders such as the young, single mothers, less skilled workers, and the long-term unemployed. At the same time, they have been quite willing to extend state largesse to supporting favored groups, such as skilled industrial workers and export-based firms, albeit in ways that reflected corporate liberal assumptions about group autonomy and horizontal lines of responsibility. Likewise, in the area of social and labor-market policy, governments have subsidized job creation and protected employment in key sectors while expanding the welfare state in ways that favored core groups even as they have adopted reforms that reduced benefits for economic outsiders. In so doing, they have reinforced the supportive connections between the state and organized business and labor while imposing costs on those outside these protected domains. Finally, in the area of financial regulation, authorities have worked to shelter politically connected banks from competitive pressures and external demands for reform while helping them to manage the fallout from episodes of global financial instability, most notably after the financial crisis of 2008 and the ensuing crisis of the Eurozone. I present an overview of the dimensions of these policy trajectories, highlighting the state's role, favored policy instruments, principal constituencies, and predominant social and economic goals, in Table 3.1.

In each of these three areas of state activity, authorities' responses were powerfully informed by the corporate-liberal framework, which supported a prevailing understanding of a socially embedded economy, focusing on core groups in the Social Market Economy, notably business and labor in skilled export sectors, core industrial firms and the regionally concentrated *Mittelstand*, and favored financial clients such as the network of smaller, regionally centered Landesbanken that provide critical financial support to SMEs.

Corporate Liberalism in an Era of Austerity: Strategic Investment and Selective Expansion in German Fiscal Policy

By the mid-to-late 1980s, the vaunted German Social Market Economy was showing signs of fatigue. Though it continued to perform better than many of

Table 3.1 **Orientation of German Corporate Liberalism by Policy Area**

	State's Economic Role	*Major Constituencies*	*Favored Instruments*	*Prevailing Social/ Economic Goals*
Fiscal Policy and State Investment	Selectively expansive/ targeted	Large firms in export sectors, skilled industrial workers, export-oriented SMEs	Targeted investments and tax cuts	Supporting export-based growth strategy
Labor-Market Policy	Subsidizing/ protective	Firms and skilled workers in export sectors	Worker and employer subsidies	Job protection in export sectors
Financial Policy	Subsidizing/ protective	Public savings banks and Landesbanken	Targeted subsidies and bailouts	Preserving financial support for export sectors

its European counterparts, with continued dominance of key export markets, modest unemployment, and tame inflation, the heady days of the postwar *Wirtschaftswunder* had given way to a much less auspicious climate. Between 1973 and 1982, annual economic growth averaged 2.4 percent, declining to a sluggish 1.4 percent in 1987, compared to 4.4 percent during the previous decade.[26] Equally alarming for a country with a historical aversion to inflation and preoccupied (not to say obsessed) with combating it, average annual increases in consumer prices had risen from 3.2 percent during the previous period to 5.2 percent in the subsequent one.[27] Unemployment, which reached a postwar high of 8.0 percent in 1985,[28] was particularly problematic for the German model's prestige, given its long period of full employment in the 1960s and the consensual bargain between labor and capital that lay at its core, as well as a Bismarckian welfare state that drew most of its funding from payroll taxes and was thus susceptible to labor-market downturns. In short, though Germany continued to serve as a model of a successful variant of mixed capitalism informed by balanced but healthy market competition, cooperative relationships between labor and capital, and the support of a generous welfare state,[29] it was clear that the post-1970s global economic slowdown had redefined the character of prevailing economic challenges and the playbook from which authorities would have to draw in responding to them.

These negative trends were not merely economic in nature but rather threatened to undermine the German model's legitimacy. During the postwar boom the German model had divided political authority along lines both geographical (in the context of German federalism) and institutional (with respect to the

German system of social partnership), representing the predicates of what Peter Katzenstein memorably called a "semi-sovereign" state.[30] Delegating authority for key political-economic tasks to a wide range of social and economic actors, the German state was able to foster cooperative and collaborative relationships that both improved economic governance and secured broad-based legitimacy through the support of representatives of capital and labor. Though such arrangements worked well during the postwar boom, by the 1980s they were no longer delivering the deepening pool of resources that had helped to foster political consensus during the first two postwar decades. The strains resulting from slowing growth and rising unemployment were reflected in the government's fiscal balance sheet, with annual budget deficits growing from a negligible 1.4 percent of GDP in 1974 to 2.9 percent in 1980 and hovering around 2.0 percent for the remainder of the decade, some years rising above 3 percent.[31]

In this more austere economic climate, the German state, like many of its counterparts across the advanced industrial world, faced important choices about where to devote the more limited financial resources at its disposal. This implicitly meant deciding whether to follow standard neoliberal prescriptions of slashing public spending in the interests of a balanced budget, accepting high unemployment as the cost of low inflation, and reducing the scale of the state's role in the economy, which, neoliberalism and its adherents in international financial institutions such as the IMF promised, would restore confidence and promote private-sector investment to an extent that would more than compensate for the state's limited largesse. Say's law, according to which supply creates its own demand and will always equilibrate in the medium term,[32] promised to legitimize the state's retreat by providing the resources required to make it economically feasible.

Like their French counterparts, however, German authorities rejected neoliberal prescriptions in favor of a socially embedded strategy that preserved a robust role for the state in supporting economic growth and guiding public investment, though within the broad constraints that the post-1970s economic slowdown had yielded. The analytical framework that that would shape patterns of state spending and investment from the 1990s onward was deeply rooted in the corporate-liberal tradition, acknowledging limits on state spending and seeking long-term fiscal balance and sustainability, but always permitting, and even encouraging, greater expenditures in response to moments of crisis as well as strategic investment in critical components of the political economy, particularly when its institutional foundations were perceived to be at risk. At such moments, notably the aftermath of German reunification and the post-2007 financial crisis and ensuing Great Recession, German authorities showed a clear, if sometimes reluctant, willingness to deploy significant financial resources to support the Social Market Economy and to preserve the high-end, export-based model on which its success had been based. The targets and focus of such expenditures varied, from creating new institutions, to subsidizing key economic sectors, to sheltering key groups, as circumstances dictated. In each period of crisis and uncertainty, however, authorities' interpretation of the nature of the crisis and the state's responses to it bore the stamp of the corporate liberal tradition, with core social and economic groups and the segments of the economy that they inhabited the intended beneficiaries. When fiscal initiatives were undertaken, corporate liberalism also shaped the *means* used to advance them; for example, privileging tax cuts that were consistent with notions of horizontal lines of responsibility and groups' responsibility for collective self-support. I provide an overview of key German economic indicators over the past two decades in Table 3.2.

In many respects, the event that would come to define the economic challenges facing Germany since the early 1990s was the unexpected opening of the Berlin Wall on November 9, 1989, and the dizzyingly rapid process of German reunification that followed in its wake. The challenge of reunifying prosperous West Germany with the sclerotic and hopelessly uncompetitive eastern economy could have taken place according to a number of scripts, some of which (like those that would be adopted in other post-Soviet states) were broadly consistent with standard neoliberal prescriptions of a denuded public sector, slashed aid to industry, weak collective-bargaining systems, rapid privatization and financial deregulation, and vastly reduced public expenditures, leaving it to a hoped-for entrepreneurial spirit and renewed business confidence to drive economic recovery.[33] To be sure, the feasibility of such a recipe was limited by the institutional structure of the West German Social Market Economy, with

Table 3.2 **Economic Indicators for Selected Years, 1991–2013, Germany**[a]

	1991	*1995*	*1998*	*2003*	*2006*	*2009*	*2013*
GDP Growth (%)	5.11	1.74	1.98	−0.71	3.70	−5.62	0.49
Unemployment Rate (harmonized) (%)	5.53	8.25	9.45	9.81	10.28	7.64	5.24
Inflation (CPI) (%)	4.05	1.71	0.91	1.03	1.58	0.31	1.50
Public Budget Deficit (% of GDP)	−3.17	−9.43	−2.53	−4.18	−1.72	−3.23	−0.19
Public Debt (% of GDP)	39.54	54.22	60.47	64.43	68.10	75.32	81.62

[a]OECD data, from data.oecd.org and stats.oecd.org, except:
public budget deficit for 1991 from IMF, data.imf.org;
public debt for 1991 from IMF, Public Finances in Modern History Database (2013), http://www.imf.org/external/np/fad/histdb/.

which the former DDR (the Deutsche Demokratische Republik) would have to be integrated. That said, German authorities could easily have chosen the low road, leaving the East to become a German version of the Italian *Mezzogiorno*, as some came to label this vision,[34] with low wages and cheap labor its primary economic asset, with a weak and disorganized labor movement enjoying limited recourse for resisting the strategy of internal devaluation that neoliberal frameworks implied. West German officials roundly rejected such a strategy, opting instead for a wholesale transfer of the institutions of the Social Market Economy—from corporate governance to industrial relations to financial policies and institutions—to the East.[35]

Chancellor Helmut Kohl closely tied his career and status to the reunification project, displaying unbridled optimism about the feasibility of a relatively painless (and affordable) process and about the soon-to-be-unified country's future. Kohl memorably promised a "flowering landscape" in the East within two years with no tax increases in the run-up to the 1990 national elections.[36] This heady optimism soon gave way to a much grimmer vision, however, as German officials realized the enormous cost, political will, and patience that would be required to transfer the entire institutional edifice of the Social Market Economy to the devastated economic landscape of the former DDR.[37] As Gerhard Ritter observes, "The difficulties and the duration of the transformation of the economy of the DDR from a planned to a market economy and closing the gap between the living conditions in the eastern and western halves of Germany had been completely underestimated."[38] German authorities' efforts to create a market economy in the East, along with the supporting social and economic institutions, would require more extensive government intervention and financial support than most observers realized. The effort to privatize hundreds of sclerotic and uncompetitive state-owned industries,[39] extend social benefits to millions of destitute easterners who lacked the skills to compete in a market-based capitalist system, and rebuild a crumbling infrastructure, much of which had not been touched since before the war, created pressures on German fiscal policy not seen since the late 1940s.[40] These enormous fiscal and social strains were sharpened by the stream of ethnic Germans arriving from elsewhere in central and eastern Europe, all of whom had legal claims to German citizenship and social benefits. Despite these daunting challenges, German authorities never seriously considered a neoliberal adjustment strategy for the East, committing themselves instead to an unprecedented project of fiscal expansion and investment designed to integrate the two former states socially and economically as quickly and effectively as possible.

German authorities' determination to accomplish this task seemed even more remarkable in light of the size of the intertwined political and economic challenges facing them. Politically, the sudden emergence of reunification as a realistic prospect after 1989 and the rapid manner in which the surrounding events unfolded, coupled with growing public enthusiasm for it in both East and West, encouraged Kohl's government to embrace reunification and to make a number of critical policy decisions based upon highly optimistic assessments and powerful political imperatives. For example, a central plank of the 1990 Treaty for German Economic, Monetary, and Social Union was a currency union between the Deutsche Mark and the Ostmark on a one-to-one basis for amounts up to DM 4,000 (ca. €2,045) and at a two-to-one rate for higher balances. The decision, largely for political reasons, to establish parity immediately exacerbated the strains on German budgets, destroying thousands of East German firms unable to pay workers and suppliers at a much higher rate than levels of productivity could justify and leading millions to lose their jobs.[41] Instituted against the backdrop of an international economic downturn and the collapse of the Soviet Union, and with it the bulk of the DDR's export markets, the treaty's provisions ensured that the path to recovery would be more painful and difficult than many had assumed.

Despite these unexpected financial, social, and economic strains, however, and the enormous and sustained commitment of resources that creating a market from scratch in the former DDR would require, German authorities remained committed to a strategy of extensive public investment and fiscal expansion designed to narrow and, ultimately, erase the economic discrepancies between East and West and thereby to make the abstract notion of shared economic and social citizenship a concrete reality. Although officials realized that the relationship between available resources and the task before them was much less favorable than they had initially assumed, they chose to deploy massive political and economic resources in ways that cut sharply against the grain of historical (and Ordoliberal) preferences for limited state involvement in the economy and limits on state spending. Departures from past practice were not limited to the scope of resources committed, however, as the mechanisms by which the process of investment was undertaken privileged the role of the state, which operated aggressively (and sometimes even with a hint of authoritarianism) in ways that were far removed from the traditionally gradualist operation of the postwar German model and Katzenstein's "semi-sovereign state." Just as the challenges of postwar recovery had created pressures for a more extensive welfare state than would have been envisioned by standard Ordoliberal perspectives (as discussed in Chapter 1), so, too, did the shock of reunification encourage the adaptation and evolution of the German political-economic model in ways that standard institutionalist accounts cannot explain.

State largesse was not dispensed indiscriminately, however, nor in the French neo-Keynesian fashion but rather in targeted, selective ways that focused on shoring up the key institutional foundations of the Social Market Economy in both East and West and on subsidizing and sheltering the social and economic groups at its core. In practice this meant protecting, training, and integrating skilled labor in key export sectors, as well as subsidizing internationally competitive sectors and firms, which were crucial to both eastern economic recovery and the reunified country's economic prosperity. The fiscal component of this strategy involved ambitious programs of selective investment, even when such measures required significant borrowing and politically unpopular tax increases. Then as later, Germany's commitment to fiscal rectitude was highly selective, and authorities were willing to qualify or even abandon it in the short term for what were perceived as economically strategic objectives.[42]

Very soon after reunification, the fiscal imperative assumed an air of urgency, as German officials confronted a bleak social and economic landscape that threatened to undermine the high-road strategy for reunification that authorities had adopted. Industrial production in the East declined by 40 percent between 1990 and 1992, real rates of unemployment soared to around 37 percent (including both the registered unemployed and those participating in public-employment and training programs), the active labor force collapsed from 10 million in 1989 to 4.4 million in early 1993, and 3,500 Eastern firms had failed by the end of 1994.[43] Ultimately, German authorities could not credibly maintain their erstwhile optimism in the face of such circumstances, as the Unification Treaty had provided only DM 35 billion (€18.7 billion) for the task.[44] In May 1990, the government created the Fund for German Unity, with assets of DM 115 billion (€59 billion), to supplement eastern welfare funds and provide much-needed additional resources for infrastructure investment. In 1993 it introduced a Solidarity Tax of 7.5 percent on all taxpayers in both East and West, while raising the VAT and excise taxes on a variety of consumer goods.[45] The budgetary situation was made even more pressing by the disappointing outcome of the government's privatization program. Initially expected to provide a major source of revenue, the program actually *lost* money. This situation actually forced the German government to subsidize the *Treuhandanstalt,* and by the end of 1994 the process had resulted in a net loss of DM 230 billion (€117 billion).[46]

The economic dilemmas posed by reunification were rendered even more acute by the constraints on German fiscal policy imposed by the Maastricht Treaty, signed in 1991, which created the terms for European Economic and Monetary Union (EMU).[47] Following the insistence of Bundesbank head Karl-Otto Pöhl that the terms of EMU and the policies of the nascent European Central Bank (ECB) "reproduce the Bundesbank's independence and anti-inflation mandate,"[48] German policymakers were forced to confront fiscal constraints that were sharply at odds with the sudden and massive demand for increased government borrowing and spending. Though Germany, then as later, would ignore the Maastricht criteria when that suited its purposes, it nonetheless felt politically compelled to do what it could to limit resulting government debt, a desire that led to the imposition of the politically unpopular Solidarity Tax. As Nicolas Jabko relates, European elites' adoption of monetarist orthodoxy as the architecture for EMU, at German insistence, helped Kohl in his efforts to sell reluctant German voters on the prospect of abandoning their cherished Deutsche Mark in favor of a single European currency.[49]

Even as they confronted these impending constraints, German authorities' high-road strategy for managing the demands of reunification forced them to ramp up public spending. While they demanded a strongly monetarist model for EMU in the interests of both winning over German voters and anchoring the nascent monetary union to German anti-inflationary preferences, German officials were quick to violate those very precepts at home by financing much of the cost of reunification through deficit spending.[50] By March 1991 Germany's fiscal situation had deteriorated from rough balance of the combined Federal, *Land*, and local budgets in 1989 to a deficit of DM 120 billion (€61 billion), amounting to a full 4 percent of GDP, well above the Maastricht ceiling of 3 percent.[51] Unable to fund such a deficit through accumulated balance-of-payments surpluses alone, German officials assented to a combination of hefty tax increases and extensive government borrowing.

This fiscal shock in turn prompted the Bundesbank, ever fearful of inflation, to raise interest rates three times in 1992, requiring other members of the European Monetary System to do likewise in order to respect EMS limits on the fluctuation of the relative value of members' currencies. This series of events ultimately prompted a major crisis that led to Britain's and Italy's withdrawal from EMS.[52] Germany's expansionary fiscal policy effectively led the Bundesbank to export deflation to other EMS members, reflecting a willingness to sacrifice European solidarity on the altar of the economic orthodoxy that would inform the country's response to subsequent episodes, most notably during the post-2007 financial and economic crisis and the ensuing Eurozone crisis. The effective non-negotiability of orthodox monetary policy on both the domestic and European levels, as well as the implicit fiscal-policy constraints imposed by central bankers, therefore, limited the tools at policymakers' disposal for financing reunification. Thus deprived of the option of full-fledged reflation, Germany opted for a series of policy moves that were informed by its corporate liberal tradition while also recognizing the political and economic constraints of the moment. After significant debate over whether to transform eastern Germany into a sort of low-wage *Mezzogiorno*, German authorities rejected this recipe, committing themselves to sustained but targeted investments designed to allow the former communist East to catch up economically and socially with the West or at least, over time, to begin to converge with it in terms of wages, employment, living standards, and quality of life. Having committed to engineering the eventual convergence of eastern and western social and economic circumstances, German authorities had placed significant political capital at risk, forcing them both to deliver economic results and to sustain the legitimacy of and political support for the project in the face of significant economic pain and dislocation.

In light of these conflicting imperatives, German authorities opted for a strategy of targeted, selective expansion and investment in strategic economic sectors while subsidizing the transition of firms and workers within them. This approach entailed the devotion of significant state resources to structural initiatives designed to replicate institutions and arrangements that were central to the economy's success. This effort prioritized promoting the growth and recovery of the manufacturing sector, which was crucial for establishing the international competitiveness of East German industry, fostering the growth of SMEs in the hope of creating an eastern *Mittelstand* and working to establish western German institutions of social partnership. Officials dedicated extensive funds to eastern industrial restructuring and the promotion of private investment, including money to assist eastern firms in export sectors with the modernization of production techniques, investment subsidies, and tax breaks. Many were administered by the Gemeinschaftswerk Aufschwung Ost, or Joint Task Force for Recovery in the East, a regional assistance program created in March 1991.[53] The government initially concentrated upon the eastern manufacturing sector,[54] which had been hardest hit and was most exposed to international competition.[55] In the machine-tool industry, which had been a critical component of the DDR's economy and represented one of the Federal Republic's long-standing competitive niches, for example, Germany's world share of production increased from 18.9 percent in 1990 to 25 percent in 1991 (representing the addition of a large number of East German firms) but declined rapidly to 18.2 percent by 1993, as thousands of East German firms were liquidated.[56] Enabling such sectors to recover was critical, not just for the sectors themselves, but for shoring up the German economy's international competitiveness writ large.

Germany's response to the challenges of reunification against a backdrop of new fiscal strictures imposed by the Maastricht Treaty thus conformed to the corporate liberal model in a number of important ways. First, it eschewed the kind of top-down, global, and macroeconomically oriented response repeatedly favored by French policymakers (see Chapter 2). Instead, facing limited resources and a financial burden imposed by reunification that was far greater than anyone had expected, German policymakers made a series of choices about how to target their resources and which elements of the political economy to support and, likewise, on which segments to impose costs. This "mesoeconomic" approach meant supporting and subsidizing key sectors of the economy—particularly export-intensive manufacturing—and groups within those sectors that were considered key elements of Germany's political-economic model, notably skilled industrial workers.

The latter half of the 1990s and the early 2000s—the long decade between reunification and the 2008 financial crisis—were marked by Germany's struggles to reduce its budget deficits and sharp debates over how to balance revenues and expenditures. Fueled by slow growth after the global recession beginning in 2001 and by stubbornly high unemployment and associated social expenditures, German budget deficits and debt proved difficult to reduce, with public debt growing from 36.7 to 39.7 percent of GDP between 2001 and 2003.[57] At several points during the late 1990s and early 2000s, Germany breached the Maastricht limits on deficits and debts and was threatened with official censure by the EU (a censure that never came, reflecting a different set of rules for core EU member states than for peripheral ones, who received no such quarter in the post-2007 crisis). In 2006, soon after Schröder's Red-Green coalition was replaced with the first of two so-called Grand Coalitions between the CDU and SPD, the new government enacted a very unpopular increase in VAT from 16 to 19 percent, effective January 1, 2007, designed to address Germany's repeated budgetary shortfalls and bringing Germany close to the EU average rate for VAT.[58] By 2006 the combination of tax increases and accelerating economic growth in the post-recession global recovery brought Germany's deficits once again under control, as they fell to a modest 1.2 percent of GDP in 2006.

German Corporate Liberalism and Keynesianism by Stealth in the Great Recession

As elsewhere across the advanced industrial world, the financial crisis that broke in late 2007 and early 2008, with the collapse of Lehman Brothers in the United States and the meltdown of the subprime mortgage market, took German observers by surprise. It resulted in a sharply deteriorating fiscal situation and renewed debate about the state's proper fiscal-policy position and strategy. After painful labor-market reforms in the late 1990s and early 2000s, Germany had seemed to leave behind the long-standing employment crisis of the previous decade, posting an economic performance between 2003 and 2007 that outstripped that of most of its neighbors. Unemployment fell from 11.1 percent in 2005 to 7.5 percent in 2008, the lowest level since 1993.[59] Recovering from economic growth rates that were zero or negative in the recession of the early 2000s, Germany posted growth rates of between 3 and 3.5 percent in 2006 and 2007, the highest rates in the post-reunification era and significantly higher than those of many of its European neighbors.[60] In some respects the crisis represented a sharper reversal of fortunes for Germany than for most other advanced industrial countries, whose recovery from the recession of the early 2000s had been less robust. Germany's growth rate plummeted from an annual 1.08 percent in 2008 to a shocking –5.15 percent in 2009, stoking fears that the crisis had shaken the German model to its foundations, undermining the high-end export strategy and patterns of successful coordination among firms and economic interests that had fueled the postwar *Wirtschaftswunder* and enabled the country to recover from the shock of reunification.[61]

However worrying Germany's collapse in economic performance was in political and economic terms, the crisis engendered a more fundamental, even existential, crisis of faith among German observers. The deepest economic downturn since the Great Depression led to a generalized re-examination of the nature and dynamics of advanced capitalism and the respective roles of state and market across the entire advanced industrial world. In more neoliberal countries such as the United States and Britain, whose market orders had been shaken if not shattered by the economic chaos, such a re-examination was to be expected, with even neoclassical economists such as Richard Posner issuing public apologia about their belated conversion to Keynesianism[62] and critics like Paul Krugman blaming economists' failure to foresee the crisis on the institutional and intellectual blind spots of their profession.[63] In Germany, however, such a process of introspection was, on the surface at least, surprising, particularly given the fact that the crisis seemed to have vindicated many of the precepts of non-neoliberal economies such as France and Germany's, which had largely eschewed the excesses of American-style finance capitalism and rejected the messianic neoliberalism that had become a quasi-hegemonic doctrine both in Britain and the United States and among global financial institutions. In so doing, many countries in continental Europe had preserved and even expanded their generous welfare states and maintained a robust role for public authority in regulating the economy. But the startling collapse in growth led to increasing concern among German officials, many of whom predicted exploding unemployment, fueled by a collapse in demand for German exports across the EU and United States, which together account for around two-thirds of German export markets (69 percent in 2013).[64] According to a high-ranking official in a key German employers' association, the prospective collapse of German export markets, particularly within EU countries, led German officials not only to fear for the health of the economy but to dread the political fallout and loss of credibility that was likely to follow from a collapse in employment.[65]

Unlike in France, where statist liberal perspectives led authorities to view the crisis as a macroeconomic crisis of demand, in Germany the corporate liberal tradition provided a distinctive analytical lens that informed a "mesoeconomic" understanding of the crisis as a threat to export competitiveness and labor-market performance in key export-intensive sectors. In sharp contrast to neoliberal perspectives, which tend to adopt a view of labor as a cost to be minimized, German authorities viewed skilled labor and the export-competitive firms where they worked as assets to protect and in which to invest. Fears of a shattered labor market carried with them structural implications about the prospects for the economy as a whole. These concerns spurred German policymakers to undertake an aggressive response to support domestic employment while shielding sensitive export markets from the contagion of the international economic crisis.[66] If the challenge of the post-reunification period was to recreate the foundations of the Social Market Economy in the East while preserving its core features, those of the post-2007 crisis were shoring up German employment, sustaining domestic demand as a correlate (rather than as a leading imperative, as in France) and protecting employers and workers in the export sectors that had long been the engines of German economic prominence.[67]

At first, policymakers, suffering from a sense of "helplessness," were initially reluctant to devote significant resources to demand stimulus, due in large part to fears of a resulting "straw fire" of runaway inflation.[68] Even when the government did turn to Keynesianism, it did so with significant reluctance and all the while working to avoid the impression that it was embracing traditionally spendthrift demand stimulus in the postwar British or French fashion.[69] On the contrary, Germany's initial response seemed to conform to conventional images of German frugality and caution, and its stimulus was indeed adopted much later than those of many other countries and only after a good deal of vacillation. In January 2008 Finance Minister Peer Steinbrück proclaimed that there was "absolutely no occasion" for "excessive pessimism,"[70] despite Germany's alarming collapse in GDP. Even in November 2008, when the government finally unveiled the first, modest package, Chancellor Angela Merkel suggested that this was as far as the government was willing to go and that Germany would not engage "in a senseless race to spend billions."[71] Steinbrück, protesting perhaps a bit too much, hastened to add that the package was "not a stimulus package of the old style."[72] The law, dubbed the *Konjunkturpaket I* (Economic Conditions Package I), provided a mere €12 billion (0.25 percent of GDP), which Merkel hoped would trigger about €50 billion in investment. This reluctance was certainly not dictated by the fiscal situation in Germany, which was among the few advanced countries with a balanced budget in 2008.[73] Nor was it consistent with prevailing economic conditions in the country, which experienced one of the most precipitous collapses in GDP in the advanced industrial world.[74] As one business association official observed, the government wanted "to maintain distance from [an impression of] demand management," leading to a certain "helplessness" and a hesitation to tackle the crisis directly.[75]

Such hesitation was short lived, however, as the full measure of Germany's response became clear. As the global economic crisis worsened, German authorities felt that they had little choice but to turn to a sustained stimulus effort, which they focused on core groups, however, rather than frame it in terms of a generalized Keynesian strategy in the French fashion. Authorities were squarely focused on the labor-market implications of the crisis and particularly its effects on Germany's exports; as a result, they would focus their efforts on subsidizing workers and employers in highly skilled, export-intensive sectors.[76] In response to widespread criticism of the first package's limited scope, including a surprising push by the country's normally conservative five economic "wise men" for further spending, the government began to reconsider its relatively modest approach.

After much internal debate, particularly between the Finance and Labor Ministries, with the former largely skeptical and the latter strongly in favor,[77] the government announced a second package (*Konjunkturpaket II*) in February 2009. This more ambitious legislation involved €50 billion in spending and tax cuts, totaling about 1.4 percent of GDP. The measure surprised many, with one SPD official calling it "an incredible change in direction"[78] and a leading trade-union official characterizing it "an unusual response to an unusual situation."[79] The choice was far from easy, with Merkel herself calling the measure the "most difficult domestic policy decision of my time as chancellor." She emphasized the package's focus on SMEs and on boosting the performance of core export firms rather than compensating for failing ones: "We are creating a fund in order to extend support to essentially healthy firms in their hour of need."[80] The president of the Bundesverband der mittelständischen Wirtschaft, a peak organization of SMEs, likewise praised the government's assisting basically competitive SMEs that were having trouble obtaining credit as a result of the global credit crunch rather than bailing out uncompetitive companies, which was anathema.[81] Despite long-standing skepticism about public spending, German officials felt compelled to depart from past timidity, in part as a result of the risks of erosion of export competitiveness. Rather than adopt a global, macroeconomically focused approach in the French fashion, however, they deployed resources in ways that aimed to subsidize political and economic insiders, shore up German international competitiveness, and protect jobs in key economic sectors.

Historical fears of inflation and debt notwithstanding, Germany ultimately adopted quite ambitious economic stimulus initiatives, which, between 2008 and 2010, amounted to €82.37 billion (or about 4.0 percent of GDP, more than twice the French figure),[82] despite lower baseline jobless rates, deficits, and levels of debt. Such enthusiasm for a Keynesian initiative makes sense when we analyze it through the lens of German corporate liberalism. The bulk of the package reflected this focus on core groups, including families, large firms in competitive export markets, and the *Mittelstand*, long considered the backbone of the postwar Economic Miracle. The measures consisted of tax cuts for firms designed to spur investment, as well as a small cut in personal income tax for modest earners and increases in tax thresholds, reflecting horizontal and group-based notions of responsibility for determining how resources were spent.[83] While the first package had focused almost exclusively on tax cuts, however, the second involved somewhat more direct spending, though aimed mostly at core groups in the Social Market Economy (particularly internationally competitive SMEs and skilled industrial workers in export sectors) rather than channeled through aggregate measures.[84] The package's reliance on tax cuts and emphasis on selective subsidization were reflected in the words of Steffen Kampeter, a leading CDU budget official, who warned that the state cannot "prevent a recession" and called for "a protective umbrella for the people against the state, which overtaxes itself."[85] Though the government aimed to convey the impression of "maintain[ing] its distance" from demand-management strategies,[86] it realized that it needed to embrace a strategy that "eased pressures" on key social groups,[87] including core industrial firms and workers, and families with children.[88] If the second package was surprisingly large given historical biases (one Labor Ministry official invoked the German ideal of the "slim state" to explain the strong preference for tax cuts over direct spending),[89] it was also structured in ways that conformed to the German liberal tradition.

In September 2009 the incoming coalition of the CDU-CSU and the liberal FDP enacted a third measure, dubbed the Economic Growth Acceleration Act, which entailed further tax cuts, child benefits, and labor-market spending. The tax cuts amounted to €2.4 billion annually for companies and €945 million in VAT for hospitality services (an important constituency of the CSU, the sister party of the CDU that fields candidates only in Bavaria), while boosting child benefits by €4.6 billion annually.[90] Widely criticized as a "sop to the CSU and FDP" that was both fiscally irresponsible and unlikely to stimulate economic growth,[91] the €7 billion package was defended by the government overwhelmingly in terms of group responsibilities and prerogatives, in line with the corporate-liberal paradigm. According to Economics Minister Rainer Brüderle, it aimed in particular to reduce the tax burden faced by the *Mittelstand,* or Germany's powerful small and medium-sized firms.[92] Aside from tax subsidies, the majority of the reductions (about 54 percent of the total) involved an increase in the standard per-child tax exemption coupled, with a €20 increase in the monthly child allowance.[93] The German strategy of reinforcing existing strengths rather than boosting incomes and demand throughout the economy was also consistent with Germany's at first relatively hands-off approach to shoring up its banking system, although German banks were initially hit quite hard by the crisis.[94]

Germany's surprisingly extensive stimulus measures in 2009/10 deliberately built on preexisting policies and arrangements whose creation the German liberal tradition had informed. Ultimately, Germany adopted the largest fiscal stimulus of all major European countries and the fifth largest (tied with Korea) among G-20 nations.[95] In 2009 its total stimulus to date amounted to about $130.4 billion, or 3.4 percent of GDP, almost six times as large as France's ($20.5 billion) in monetary terms and nearly five times as large as a share of GDP.[96] Taken together, German stimulus spending between 2008 and 2010 amounted to roughly 4.0 percent of GDP.[97] While France's more modest stimulus measures and job-creation efforts were composed almost entirely of direct spending rather than tax cuts, centered on business investment and broad efforts to stimulate demand across the economy, they were also seen as a complement to the existing network of increasingly universalistic social protection, which France had spent more than two decades expanding. Germany's measures, by contrast, were composed mostly of tax reductions (68 percent) and viewed as a crisis-driven effort to defend competitiveness based upon skilled labor while subsidizing and protecting the groups that had long been central to German economic success.[98] Neither Germany's division of political authority and ostensible penchant for political consensus nor an account centered on the strength and preferences of interest groups (both families and export firms were favored despite the latter's greater resources and better organization, for example) nor a narrative that emphasizes partisanship can explain either why German officials adopted such an extensive package in the first place or the patterns of expenditures and investment on which it relied.[99]

In 2010, the mounting European debt crisis led Germany to undertake a partial reversal of its Keynesian policies. Forceful (if rather implausible) domestic criticism about the country's debt led the government to adopt a program to achieve €80 billion in budget cuts by 2014 and designed to move toward the elimination of "structural" debt by 2016, as required by a recent constitutional amendment. Merkel and CDU Finance Minister Wolfgang Schäuble proposed cuts in contributions for the poor to the state pension system and in heating subsidies and child benefits for some welfare recipients, coupled with stepped-up contributions from the financial and nuclear industries. At the same time, the so-called *Sparpaket* avoided cuts to education, infrastructure investment, and research, all critical for long-term economic growth.[100] It also avoided tax increases and sheltered many of the same core groups that had benefited from the stimulus—for example, leaving unemployment benefits untouched and maintaining funding for the *Kurzarbeit* program, as will be discussed. For all of their demonstrative symbolism—in part a response to voters' criticism of the Greek bailouts that had become the controversial centerpiece of the EU's response to the mounting Eurozone crisis—the cuts were relatively modest, amounting to less than 1 percent of GDP over four years. To the extent that they were significant, they placed a disproportionate burden on outsiders, particularly the unincorporated poor. Michael Sommer, head of Germany's leading union federation, agreed: "They want to hit the poor and protect the big fish."[101] Just as Germany's stimulus was more extensive than it appeared, the subsequent reversal was less dramatic and less universalistic than the surrounding rhetoric would suggest.

The years since the advent of the Eurozone crisis have been marked by a continuation of the pattern of subsidization of favored interest groups that has characterized German state spending and investment since reunification, albeit with a shift toward greater fiscal rectitude. As the effects of the crisis have faded and as existing labor-market instruments have helped to sustain steady declines in unemployment rates,[102] German authorities have turned their attention to rectifying earlier fiscal imbalances. Largely as a response to the increase in deficits following the post-2007 economic crisis and stimulus measures fashioned in its wake, in 2009 Merkel's government secured an amendment to the German Basic Law, the so-called debt brake (*Schuldenbremse*), which restricted structural deficits to 0.35 percent of GDP beginning in 2016 and outlawed deficits in the Länder.[103] In the run-up to the 2013 Bundestag elections, Merkel renewed her public commitment to meeting the debt brake's targets of a balanced structural budget by 2016, which she in fact achieved in 2014. Criticized by some (and with some justification) as a "fetish,"[104] the strengthened public commitment to a balanced budget seems in effect to return to Germany's historical baseline of fiscal rectitude while obscuring the deeply embedded fiscal commitments to the core of the Social Market Economy that have informed the corporate-liberal vision since the 1980s. Existing programs that favor political and economic insiders have been left in place, as have labor-market arrangements and differential benefit structures that deepened divisions between protected and exposed groups, beginning with the Agenda 2010 reforms of Schröder's Red-Green coalition in the late 1990s and early 2000s.

Moreover, Germany's renewed commitment to fiscal balance must be interpreted within the context of broader political and economic developments in Germany and across the Eurozone. With continued trade and balance-of-payment surpluses with the rest of the Eurozone and low unemployment, Germany can afford a posture of fiscal propriety that would have been politically and economically unfeasible in times of crisis. This commitment should also be interpreted within the context of the Eurozone crisis, during which Germany used its own commitment to fiscal balance as a cudgel with which to beat countries on the Eurozone's periphery for their ostensible fiscal profligacy. After the height of the Eurozone crisis passed in 2010/11, Germany helped to solidify the dominant but misleading narrative of the Eurozone crisis as stemming from irresponsible borrowing and spending by countries in southern Europe rather than one of global contagion exacerbated by regional economic imbalances from which Germany has profited.[105] In this vein Germany led the charge in passing the Treaty on Stability, Coordination and Governance in the Economic and Monetary Union (TSCG) in March 2012; it closely resembled the German debt brake and saddled Eurozone members with a more strenuous fiscal mandate.[106] This German-led move to regional fiscal contraction has been accompanied by calls from the IMF, France, and Italy for increases in German public investment due to Germany's large balance-of-payments and fiscal surplus, as well as criticisms by the Green Party, IMF, and others for Germany's allowing its infrastructure to crumble.[107] Such criticisms, however, should not obscure the differential effects of Germany's spending reductions, which have left in place arrangements and policies that protect core groups, even as they have imposed costs on economic outsiders and led to underinvestment in public goods. In keeping with the corporate liberal tradition, recent German fiscal policy and patterns of state investment have thus reinforced the prevailing characterization of the German political and economic community as one dominated by favored groups.

Picking Winners, Marginalizing Losers: Group Subsidization and Contemporary German Labor-Market Reform

Just as the corporate liberal tradition has shaped Germany's trajectories of fiscal policy and patterns of state investment in an age of austerity, so too has it governed its strategies for social-policy and labor-market reform. Perhaps even more clearly than in the realm of fiscal policy, social- and labor-market policymaking has eschewed neoliberal prescriptions of slashing spending, disembedding labor by dismantling collective-bargaining systems, and cutting the scope of benefits to bare, residualist minima. Instead, it has involved the preservation of inherited social-policy arrangements (and even their expansion in some cases), along with the investment of significant public resources in efforts to protect employment in key export sectors and shelter workers from the costs of adjustment. As they have preserved a highly embedded social and economic order, however, authorities have significantly liberalized the low-wage and service sectors of the labor market, reducing the generosity of benefits and introducing job-search and other requirements, which, though hardly onerous in comparison to analogs in the United States, represent sharp departures from inherited understandings of the welfare state. Even as they have invested in and sheltered core groups and preserved collaborative and supportive relationships with labor and business in core segments of the Social Market Economy, German officials across party lines have imposed costs on less skilled, often unincorporated, labor-market outsiders, with respect to whom they have developed a much looser and more arms-length conception of economic citizenship.

The first important episode in this broad trajectory of policymaking came in the aftermath of reunification, when German officials matched their project of fiscal expansion with the introduction and extension of a number of instruments designed to accomplish parallel goals in social and labor-market policy. This strategy involved an expansion of the social-protection system aimed at protecting and fostering the social and economic integration (as well as the long-term political support) of key social and economic groups, in particular highly skilled workers in metalworking and other crucial export-intensive sectors, families with children, workers and employers in the *Mittelstand*, and members of the professional middle classes. This effort was not heavily redistributive but rather, in classic Christian Democratic fashion, was aimed at preserving or restoring the economic status of key groups.[108] It was nonetheless critical to the success of the reunification project: "The transfer of the relatively generous social-insurance system from the Federal Republic was intended to combat the impoverishment of the [eastern] population and to ensure the acceptance of the new order."[109]

This strategy involved three central pillars that would help to define the state's relationship with the social partners in the post-reunification context. The first was institutionally focused, involving efforts to create institutions of social partnership that mirrored their West German analogs, including both the system of collective bargaining and that of firm-level works councils. These initiatives would help to define the relationships between the state and social partners in both East and West, working to incorporate eastern business and organized labor into the Social Market Economy in ways that were politically and economically sustainable. At first, many feared that eastern liberalization and privatization and the soaring unemployment to which they contributed would provide employers with a major strategic advantage over workers, resulting in a hollowing out of collective-bargaining institutions nationally.[110] Largely as a result of sustained efforts by western German unions to recruit eastern workers, however, and supported by a range of state initiatives, the West German industrial-relations system was successfully implanted in the East, with few essential modifications and without seriously undermining the integrity of national collective-bargaining institutions.[111] This campaign began in 1990 and 1991, when German unions and employers' associations succeeded in building collective-bargaining frameworks and firm-level works councils in critical industries such as machine tools, chemicals, and automobiles. Driven by a desire to stabilize the German industrial-relations landscape, the social partners were also eager to undermine the residual appeal of former East German communists, who could have profited politically from a generalized sense that workers were being systematically excluded from the economic fruits of reunification.[112] By the mid-1990s the basic framework was in place, allowing eastern industrial workers to participate alongside their western counterparts in firm-level works councils and sectorally based collective bargaining.

The second initiative involved the expansion of social and labor-market policy instruments to the East, a broadly based initiative that reflected both a political and an economic logic. Politically, it was designed to secure the support of economically besieged easterners and to convince westerners that such a protracted and expensive process was worth the cost. This effort was able to capitalize on a shared consensus in East and West that "social protection was largely seen as an essential component of democracy."[113] This meant extending a wide array of labor-market instruments designed to preserve the status of labor-market insiders, including unemployment insurance (paid at a rate of between 60 and 70 percent of a worker's previous wage, according to the number of dependents), unemployment assistance (a less generous flat-rate benefit paid after eighteen months of joblessness), and disability and other pensions designed to provide incomes to older or disabled workers unable to return to the labor force.[114] Economically, the effort was designed to support the reactivation of a large segment of the uncompetitive eastern workforce, which had been decimated by overnight exposure to global markets and, by 1993, counted 1.3 million unemployed (out of 4 million total) in a region that accounted for about a fifth of the reunified country's population, with another 1.3 million relying on wage subsidies or government retraining programs.[115]

The expansion of social- and labor-market policies to the East focused on programs aimed at reintegrating and retraining the segments of the workforce that were critical to the unified country's economic success, notably metalworking, machine tools, and other export-intensive sectors. One such measure involved early-retirement schemes, which were designed to absorb workers unable to compete for reasons of age or skill profile. The Unification Treaty provided for a "transition allowance" (*Altersübergangsgeld*), financed through social contributions equally shared by employers and workers and administered by the Federal Labor Office (the Bundesanstalt, later Bundesagentur, für Arbeit, hereinafter BA). This measure provided benefits equal to 65 percent of previous wages to around 600,000 workers aged fifty-five and older. Eastern workers enjoyed access to this provision until 1992, by which time there were more than a million participants.[116] In 1996 an additional measure permitted workers aged at least fifty-five to work part-time while receiving pension benefits.[117] After a sharp increase, the number of recipients declined as eastern workers were absorbed into the pension system.[118]

The third pillar of Germany's post-reunification social- and labor-market policy strategy involved new active labor-market policies, including a broad array of job-training and employment-creation schemes and the expansion of others. The centerpiece of this strategy involved so-called Employment and Training

Companies (ETCs) throughout eastern Germany, administered and largely financed by the BA. The ETCs acted as temporary employers for workers in key sectors and organized support for those looking for work,[119] whether in the private or public sector. ETCs became one of the government's most important instruments for reintegrating workers into the labor market in the 1990s, with a large share of these workers in the East. At the end of 1993 around four hundred were operating in the new Länder and employing around 90,000 people, or about 40 percent of state-sponsored jobs in the former DDR. Because workers in these schemes were officially employed, trade unions could count them among their members while demonstrating their commitment to their rank and file, and struggling eastern firms could lay off redundant workers at the expense of the state. In this way ETCs provided a means of ensuring social peace while reducing the number of registered unemployed and facilitating the integration of the German labor market.[120]

A related policy initiative, which would be reinstituted and expanded in the post-2007 economic crisis, was the use of short-time work benefits, or *Kurzarbeitergeld*. These schemes, which were funded jointly by the federal government and the BA, allowed at-risk workers to work reduced hours while receiving up to 90 percent of their previous pay.[121] This program, which was aimed specifically at workers in key export sectors, was intended to subsidize the economically displaced until they were eligible for retirement, could be placed in an ETC, or found a new job in the private sector. Other similar policies were also introduced, including numerous schemes which placed people in social-service or infrastructure projects. At the end of 1992, nearly 400,000 easterners were employed in these programs, a level that remained stable through the 1990s.[122]

Although these programs clearly helped facilitate both the economic and political processes associated with reunification, they did so at enormous costs, which were beyond the short-term fiscal capacity of the German government.[123] The share of German GDP spent on labor-market programs grew from 2.26 percent in 1989 to 4.1 percent in 1993, with the proportion devoted to active labor-market policies increasing by more than half, from 1.03 percent to 1.58 percent of GDP.[124] Between 1990 and 1995, total German social expenditures grew from 24.8 to 29.6 percent of GDP, reflecting both the shocks of reunification and the deterioration of labor-market conditions in the early-to-mid-1990s.[125] As early expectations of "flowering landscapes" yielded to a more sober reality, the costs of federal transfers to the East soared, increasing to a level of about DM 150 billion (€76.7 billion) in 1991, representing about 70 percent of the size of the entire eastern economy in 1989.[126] However, as discussed in the previous section, authorities remained committed to fiscal expansion, though they continued to target critical economic sectors and to prioritize support of firms and workers within them.

As the 1990s wore on, rising levels of unemployment made it clear that what had initially been viewed as a reunification-related labor-market shock had given way to a more general pattern of labor-market stagnation. With rates of economic growth that remained below 2 percent between 1995 and 1999 and unemployment rising steadily to nearly 10 percent by 1997,[127] observers began to fear that the vaunted German model itself was under threat and that it could no longer avoid the kinds of trade-offs between growth and equity that neoliberals elsewhere had embraced.[128] Rising budget deficits, which had grown from about 5 percent of total federal spending to more than 15 percent in 1996, resulted in growing public debt, which in the late 1990s was hovering just under the 60 percent of GDP allowed by the Maastricht Treaty. This deteriorating fiscal trend exacerbated concerns about the model's long-term health and survival, as well as about the credibility of Germany's commitment to fiscal rectitude.[129]

Rights, Obligations, and Labor-Market Liberalization under the Red-Green Coalition

If the mid-1990s were a period of stagnation and rising concerns about the country's long-term economic prospects, the end of the decade witnessed a number of exogenous shocks that created a renewed sense of urgency, including the bursting of the dot-com stock-market bubble in the US in 1999–2000, the attacks on the World Trade Center in September 2001, and the ensuing global economic downturn. With the crash of technology stocks and broader declines in global equities markets, exacerbated by the US Federal Reserve's ultimately futile attempt to stave off stock-market speculation by boosting interest rates, global growth declined to its slowest pace since the early 1990s. Moreover, the formal implementation of EMU in January 1999, when euro coins and banknotes were put into circulation, spurred concerns about Germany's economic strength at the core of the new currency, whose deflationary and monetarist rules formally removed from national policymakers' hands many important fiscal and monetary tools that might have enabled them to adjust to such shocks. As German growth collapsed in 2002 and then turned negative in 2003 and as unemployment rose steadily to 10.5 percent in 2004,[130] policymakers began to consider significant changes to German labor-market policy in the hope of saving the core of the Social Market Economy and its export-centered model.

With the election of Gerhard Schröder's SPD-Green coalition government in 1998, German policymakers turned away from their strategy of reducing labor supply to a more aggressive focus on active labor-market policies designed to stimulate the creation of jobs and to encourage job seekers to accept available positions. Traditionally, the principle of *Tarifautonomie*, or "wage independence," reserved to employers and unions the authority to bargain collectively over wages, labor allocation, and other aspects of the employer-worker relationship, and governments of both Left and Right had long been reluctant to call this principle into serious question. Powerful firm-level works councils, composed of employer and worker representatives, controlled shop-floor decisions over the organization of production.[131] Tripartite labor-market institutions, in particular the BA, dominated labor-market policymaking, limiting the state's ability to modify programs such as unemployment insurance. Throughout the postwar era, particularly after the economic slowdown of the 1970s, these limitations on state authority forced successive governments to confront the social partners' substantial de jure control over significant aspects of the policymaking process.

Responding to what was widely understood as a labor-market crisis, Schröder's government shifted both its strategy for labor-market reform and the substantive focus of its policy initiatives, though in ways that conformed to the corporate-liberal understanding of state-society relations. With respect to strategy, the state pushed back against the limitations on its authority stemming from both the principle of *Tarifautonomie* and the informal but long-standing assumption of deference to the social partners in this policy domain. This strategic shift, predicated upon the use of both underexploited avenues of legislative influence and a more aggressive rhetorical style, embodied a logic of what I have elsewhere called "conflictual corporatism," involving increasingly aggressive reform attempts by the state.[132] Though it represented a challenge to the principle of *Tarifautonomie*, this shift in policymaking strategy was consistent with the corporate-liberal emphasis on protecting and subsidizing established producer groups, which were largely sheltered from the costs of adjustment, even as it undermined the political prerogatives of their organized representatives.

As unemployment climbed to a postwar record of 11.4 percent in 1998, Schröder embarked upon a campaign to fulfill his electoral promise to reduce the number of jobless to fewer than 3.5 million by the end of 2003. Initially, the government hoped to address the labor-market crisis in traditional neo-corporatist fashion, working to revive the Bündnis für Arbeit, or Alliance for Jobs, a forum of union and employer representatives tasked with negotiating wage agreements and other initiatives that would reduce unemployment while shoring up Germany's international economic competitiveness.[133] After several meetings degenerated fruitlessly into conflicts among members over their respective jurisdictional prerogatives, the government disbanded the Bündnis and altered its reform strategy.[134] Under the leadership of Labor Minister Walter Riester, the administration henceforth made reforming the labor market its central policy priority, circumventing the social partners, who had repeatedly insisting on clinging to the failed strategy of reducing labor supply. At the same time, however, the government's initiatives subsidized and sheltered both firms and workers in critical export sectors, imposing costs on unincorporated outsiders such as less-skilled workers and the long-term unemployed.[135]

This strategic shift was marked by (and in some ways politically relied upon) a sharp change in tone and rhetoric that challenged prevailing understandings of unemployment, jobless benefits, and the nature of the labor relationship. In contrast to the traditional view of unemployment as a structural problem for which the jobless bore little responsibility and of benefits as entitlements paid for by years of social contributions, the SPD-Green coalition placed new emphasis upon what officials termed the "rights and obligations" of the unemployed. This change was reinforced by a declared strategy of *Fordern und Fördern*, or "demanding and supporting" workers' labor-market reactivation. Schröder declared that "there is no right to laziness in our society!"[136] He demonstrated that he would be much less reluctant than his predecessors to hold jobless workers accountable for their circumstances. More importantly, however, this strategy deepened the already significant cleavage between skilled industrial workers and the long-term unemployed, now portrayed as ontologically distinctive factions rather than as fluid groups whose membership significantly overlapped. In essence, Schröder was working to reduce unemployment by reducing labor-market protections afforded to those outside the export-intensive sectors critical to Germany's international economic success. In those sectors highly skilled workforces enjoyed stable employment and generous wages that had remained more or less unaffected by the prevailing climate of high unemployment and slow growth.

Far from representing an embrace of neoliberalism, however, as some of his most vocal critics on the Left maintained,[137] this more contractual model of the labor market actually reflected many of the core principles of corporate liberalism and showed how far the tradition had evolved from its Ordoliberal roots. Even as Schröder pushed back against the social partners' institutionalized authority, he pursued reforms whose substance favored the economic interests of groups that they represented. Rather than exact costs on established interests such as skilled industrial workers and SMEs, Schröder imposed obligations on unincorporated workers, single women with children, younger workers with lower skill levels, those unemployed for more than a year, and other outsider groups. This pattern provides powerful evidence for the force of the ideas at the core of the corporate-liberal tradition and against conventional interest-group-based accounts of power politics. The administration's conception of the structural character of the political economy, with insider groups at its core, informed a response that worked to sustain and support these sectors and to preserve the benefits available to them, even as it challenged the institutional prerogatives of organized interest groups. Understanding the logic of these reforms thus requires a clear distinction between the political means whereby reform was accomplished and the economic substance of the measures themselves.

The government's policy initiatives fell into two categories. The first, focusing on the supply side of the labor market, emphasized active labor-market policy, using state resources to foster job creation in ways that reversed decades of underdevelopment in this area. It did so by fostering the creation of relatively low-paid jobs, primarily in the service sector, the same segment of the economy in which workers would be disproportionately subject to benefit cuts. This would allow the government to achieve the politically important task of reducing unemployment by creating a second tier of lower-skilled, more precarious workers while preserving the privileged position of labor-market insiders. One important such initiative was the so-called *JOB-AQTIV Gesetz,* or law for Job Activation, Qualification, Training, Investment, and Placement (*Vermitteln*), which restructured the BA's job-placement services in an effort to coerce the long-term unemployed to accept available work, often at significantly reduced wage levels relative to their previous positions. Local branches of the BA were to provide tailored advice and counseling services to job seekers, who in turn were required to accept job offers that the BA deemed "reasonable."[138] The law also introduced new vocational-training programs for new entrants to the job market, reduced non-wage labor costs in the hope of encouraging firms to create new positions, and instituted public-sector job-creation schemes designed to improve public infrastructure.[139] A related initiative was the so-called *Sofortprogramm zum Abbau der Jugendarbeitslosigkeit,* or Immediate Program for the Reduction of Youth Unemployment (referred to as JUMP), which devoted DM 2 billion (€1.02 billion) per year to creating 100,000 new jobs for workers under age twenty-five.[140] This measure created new training and apprenticeship programs (focused particularly on highly skilled, export-intensive sectors), introduced wage subsidies for firms that hired young unemployed workers, and created new job-counseling services.

Such efforts to foster job creation and reduce unemployment were accompanied by a series of more controversial demand-side initiatives that aimed to make joblessness less comfortable and to encourage (not to say coerce) the unemployed to seek out and accept available positions, particularly at the lower end of the wage scale. Following a 2002 scandal at the BA,[141] the government established the Hartz Commission to make further recommendations on labor-market reforms, thereby partially shifting responsibility for labor-market policy from the BA to a small group of experts from government ministries, employers' associations, and unions.[142] As part of a broader set of initiatives dubbed Agenda 2010,[143] the Hartz reforms reduced the length of eligibility for primary unemployment insurance (*Arbeitslosengeld*) from eighteen to twelve months for all workers under the age of fifty-five. The most controversial measure was the Hartz IV reform, which reduced unemployment-assistance benefits (*Arbeitslosenhilfe*), paid to workers whose eligibility for the more generous unemployment insurance has expired, to the level of *Sozialhilfe*, the basic anti-poverty program.[144] But because the long-term unemployed tended to have lower skill levels and to be outside of export-intensive sectors such as metalworking, this reform represented a shift of the burden of labor-market adjustment from highly skilled industrial workers with collectively negotiated contracts to less skilled and more vulnerable workers, largely in the service sector.

Although he was never part of the SPD's left wing and indeed had strong ties to the country's business elite, Schröder's departure from decades of interparty consensus and gradual, incremental policymaking and rejection of both traditional approaches to labor-market governance and decades-old understandings of the relationship between social and labor-market policy still came as a surprise.[145] The German Left, both within the SPD and to its left, as well as the unions, viewed his reforms, and Hartz IV in particular, as a betrayal of the German social contract and an attack on workers' social and economic rights. Although the unions railed against Schröder's reforms, this reaction was more "emotional" than substantive,[146] representing a fear on the part of the mainstream Left of a more generalized rightward shift rather than anger at cuts that hit their membership. Clearly, the sluggish labor market and high jobless rates presented Schröder with a political problem of the first order. It was also clear that he wished to restore the SPD's long-term electoral viability after more than a decade and a half in opposition to the CDU-CSU, and moving to the center, taking a page from the playbook of Tony Blair's New Labour and its "Third Way," offered one way to do this. But none of these factors alone provides a sufficient explanation of either why Schröder decided to depart from long-established traditions of political incrementalism and strategies of labor-supply reduction in favor of an emphasis on active labor-market policy or why he adopted a more coercive posture vis-à-vis the long-term unemployed, thereby rejecting elements of the contributory logic of workers' benefits.

Viewing them through the lens of the corporate-liberal tradition helps to explain these outcomes. For Schröder, Riester, and other members of the chancellor's cabinet, Germany's labor-market stagnation was not a problem of excess labor supply but rather the result of a combination of an ineffective system of labor-market governance (for which the BA was largely responsible) and the failure of labor-market outsiders—the young and low-skilled workers in particular—to adhere to the patterns set by the highly skilled industrial sectors. These included both large concerns such as Siemens and the vaunted *Mittelstand*, which together had been the engine of Germany's postwar success. Schröder's reforms were a far cry from an embrace of Anglo-American neoliberalism, criticism from the German Left notwithstanding. Indeed, much of Schröder's electoral strategy had involved packaging himself as an alternative to both traditional leftist trade unionism and the laissez-faire economics that has little currency in German politics. Rather, his reforms represented a conceptual differentiation between core insider groups of highly skilled industrial workers, who saw little change in their employment status, wage structures, or access to social protection, and individuals outside of these core groups, who would bear most of the costs of adjustment.

Often these twin imperatives were embedded within the same policy initiative. The *JOB-AQTIV Gesetz*, for example, increased the obligations of job seekers and adopted a more contractual model of benefit eligibility even as it devoted state funds to defraying employers' non-wage labor costs and to expanding the scope of the very vocational-training schemes that had long been skilled workers' point of access to the labor market. Likewise, the JUMP reform allocated significant state resources to expanding job and training opportunities for young workers in key sectors, thus in effect working to transform members of one of Germany's long-standing outsider groups—the unskilled young—into skilled members of the country's labor aristocracy.[147] Even Hartz IV, arguably the most liberal of the Agenda 2010 reforms, left unchanged the unemployment benefits (quite generous by international standards) for workers with long employment and contribution histories who were jobless for less than twelve months. Here again, the reform operated by shifting the line between insiders and outsiders rather than by imposing costs on all workers.

Schröder's reinterpretation of the Social Market Economy along corporate-liberal lines diverged in important respects from traditional policymaking patterns while preserving the system's commitment to the welfare of core social and economic groups. As in the early 1990s, when Kohl's response to reunification was predicated upon group subsidization and protection, the late 1990s and early 2000s witnessed a managed process of liberalization that protected established insider groups, invested in opportunities for erstwhile outsiders to gain access to them, and imposed the costs of adjustment on those who remained outside, such as temporary workers, women (who had low levels of labor-market participation), and workers with lower skill levels.[148] Although Schröder felt compelled to respond to Germany's employment status and the widespread perception that it had become the new "sick man of Europe," he firmly rejected a neoliberal course. Instead, he and Riester fashioned a socially embedded strategy that coupled targeted liberalization with limited expansion of market forces and subsidization and protection of economically prominent groups.

This approach should be understood as the product of a corporate liberal tradition that views established economic interests as key constituents not only of the political system but of the very structure of society and the economy. At the same time, it reflects a willingness to use the power of the state to shape economic outcomes in a way that Ordoliberals would never have accepted. As in both the post-reunification and post-2007 contexts, moreover, such efforts to preserve the existing skilled labor force, through stepped-up investment in worker training and the use of policies such as *Kurzarbeitergeld* and the *JOB-AQTIV Gesetz*, also served the interests of firms, particularly those in export-intensive sectors, that relied upon highly skilled labor forces for their international competitiveness.[149] Just as, in the words of an SPD official, "organized labor grew out of liberalism" in the nineteenth century,[150] modern German liberalism continues to serve the interests of organized labor and capital (though in ways that often distinguish between their members and leadership) at the expense of those outside of their ambit.

Subsidizing Insiders and the Politics of Groups: Labor-Market Policy after the Financial Crisis

The legacies of Schröder's administration, which came to an end with a vote of no confidence in 2005 and the ceding of power to a CDU-SPD Grand Coalition under the leadership of CDU Chancellor Angela Merkel, were mixed. On the one hand, many observers credit the Agenda 2010 initiatives with reducing unemployment and laying the foundations for wage moderation that would subsequently fuel Germany's economic success.[151] Others, by contrast, blame the bifurcation of the German labor market for unprecedented increases in economic inequality and precariousness for labor-market outsiders. The latter view was particularly pronounced on the SPD's left wing, part of which would break off in 2007 to form a new party, Die Linke, which now enjoys a stable position in the German party system.[152] Whichever view one favors, it is clear that Schröder's initiatives changed prevailing understandings of the German labor market in ways that reflected both the continued power of the corporate liberal tradition and significant evolutions within it. As the source of a certain understanding of the political economy and as the driver of policy responses to changed economic realities, corporate liberalism had developed from a set of principles that elliptically equated the broad social and economic order with the interests and groups that constituted its core into a framework that continued to champion these interests even as it reflected a stark contrast between them and the growing ranks of economic outsiders. As in the 1940s and 1950s, when the abstract vision of Ordoliberalism evolved as German authorities confronted postwar economic devastation, and in the 1980s, when it developed as a national response to and rejection of neoliberalism, the labor-market crisis and austere economic climate of the late 1990s and early 2000s created the impetus for corporate liberalism to evolve in a less inclusive vein that increasingly mediated trade-offs between insiders and outsiders, effectively redrawing the contours of the German economic community and redefining notions of economic citizenship.

This inflection of corporate liberalism, as it relates to social and labor-market policy and the state's relationship with business and labor, would provide the analytical lens through which German elites would confront and seek to understand the post-2007 financial and economic crises. In contrast to their French counterparts, who viewed the situation in overwhelmingly macroeconomic terms, German authorities interpreted this period of economic upheaval first and foremost as a labor-market crisis threatening the foundations of their export-based model of growth. Accordingly, the crisis drove a series of policy initiatives, including the fiscal stimulus already discussed, which represented both departures from established practice and the revival of traditional instruments in keeping with the understandings that made up the corporate liberal tradition. In the context of social and labor-market policy, this analytical frame informed policy responses that aimed to shelter core business and labor interests even as they worked to address the generalized economic precariousness that the Great Recession was leaving in its wake.

Successive CDU-SPD Grand Coalitions (the first governed until 2009 and the second came to power in 2013) undertook two key initiatives in labor-market policy, each of which aimed to remedy a distinctive set of challenges arising from the post-2007 aftermath.[153] The first was an extension of the *Kurzarbeit* program, which was used liberally in the post-reunification context and had been quickly revived as the depth of the impending recession became clear. As in the early 1990s, the program compensated employers, particularly in key sectors such as automobiles and machine tools, for the bulk of at-risk workers' wages in an effort to obviate the need for firms to lay them off and undertake the expensive and uncertain process of recruiting and retraining workers when the economy and demand started to recover. According to the BA, the measure saved 400,000 jobs and covered 1.4 million workers in 2008 and 2009,[154] allocating about $272 million in 2008 and $2.85 billion in 2009.[155] At the end of the first quarter of 2009, more than 700,000 workers (20 percent of the workforce) were participating in the export-reliant metalworking sector alone.[156] A contemporary report by the Institut für Arbeitsmarkt und Berufsforschung (IAB), the research arm of the BA, makes clear the program's purpose of supporting employment in export-intensive sectors: "Since the end of 2008, predominantly export-oriented firms have increased their use of the [*Kurzarbeit*] program, in order to adjust their labor forces to the decline in international demand stemming from the international crisis, in order to preserve jobs."[157] Relatedly, the program has been used far more in the former western Länder, where manufacturing in export-intensive sectors is more extensive, than in the East, despite much higher rates of unemployment there.[158]

By subsidizing employers in key sectors in an effort to preserve the jobs of highly skilled workers whose vocational training was time-consuming and expensive, the scheme subsidized existing relationships between capital and labor rather than attempt to create employment directly through aggregate demand, in the French fashion. With an unemployment rate of only 7.6 percent in July 2010, compared to 10.0 percent in France and 9.6 percent in the United States, Germany had clearly adopted a strategy that was effective in limiting job losses.[159] At the program's peak in early 2010, about 1.5 million workers were enrolled, and it saved about 220,000 jobs in 2008 and 2009, resulting in a 0.75 percent decline in the national unemployment rate.[160] One union official called the program an "optimal instrument," given the discretion that it allowed for targeting key groups of workers.[161] If the reluctance to embrace aggressive stimulus was filtered through the lens of German corporate liberalism, so, too, was the reliance on *Kurzarbeit*, which was anchored in the fundamental assumptions of the German liberal tradition.

The second key initiative was the introduction, for the first time in postwar Germany, of a statutory minimum-wage law in 2014. If the extension of the *Kurzarbeit* program was designed to shelter workers in highly skilled export-intensive sectors, this legislation was designed to extend some protection to the lower-wage service sector that had expanded significantly as a result of Schröder's Agenda 2010 program. Such concerns were validated by economic realities, as the number of workers earning less than two-thirds of the median monthly income had grown from 24.6 percent in 1998 to 27.6 percent in 2003, as well as by public opinion, with two-thirds supporting some form of national minimum wage.[162] The 2014 measure represented the culmination of years of often acrimonious debate over the issue, starting early in the first post-Schröder Grand Coalition in 2006/7. Supporters of a universalistic, statutory minimum wage included the left wing of the SPD and Die Linke, both of which believed that this was the only way to serve the interests of Germany's expanding low-wage sector. The initiative was opposed by many unions and employers' associations, who sought to protect the cherished principle of *Tarifautonomie* and the politically privileged position that it reflected. For their part, unions had been particularly conflicted about the issue, wishing to preserve the independence of the wage-setting process while also hoping to use state support to establish a wage floor that would push up wages across the economy.[163] Union ambivalence was politically important, given the skepticism of IG Metall and IG BCE, the two unions that represented the strategic, internationally competitive metalworking and chemical sectors. Eventually, in 2007, a compromise was reached that reconciled the competing imperatives of preserving core groups' economic power and addressing growing concerns about workers' economic precariousness and inequality. Supported by the SPD and CDU as well as most unions and employers' associations, the 2007 law modified the relevant prevailing labor legislation (the 1996 *Arbeitnehmerentsendegesetz*) to allow sectorally specific minimum wages to be negotiated by unions and employers' associations, with an allowable 30 percent departure from the agreed minimum in specific contracts.[164] The CDU-FDP coalition that governed from 2009 to 2013 continued to apply the revised legislation, though in a relatively limited way, with negotiated minima established in only five sectors during this period.[165]

Though ostensibly broader in scope and application, the 2014 measure likewise maintained the principle of *Tarifautonomie*, protecting the wage-setting role of the social partners while shoring up wages in the low-wage service sector. Passed by a large majority in the Bundestag, the law established a national minimum-wage standard of €8.50 per hour. On its face, the law could be viewed as a universalistic measure in the French fashion, as it promised to lift incomes for an estimated 3.7 million workers. Such a conclusion would be consistent with the rhetoric surrounding the law, which was celebrated by SPD Labor Minister Andrea Nahles, who proclaimed, "The minimum wage applies now, Germany-wide, in East and West—it applies to all workers. It finally brings decent wages for millions of people that have been working diligently but have been fobbed off."[166] The proposal had been strongly opposed by both Merkel and important segments of the business community, which feared rising wage costs, and Jens Weidemann, head of the Bundesbank, who rather vaguely claimed that the law threatened to "pollute employment dynamics."[167] Merkel's failure to win an outright Bundestag majority in the 2013 elections forced her to accept the SPD demand for a minimum wage as part of the negotiations over forming the Grand Coalition. Objections to the measure by the social partners were more formal than substantive, however, as the high-wage, export-intensive sectors were unaffected. The law's primary political purpose was to bolster the SPD's shaky credentials as a champion of the economically marginalized and thereby to shore up its left flank against potential attacks by Die Linke. At the same time it did not threaten the economic and political power of core economic interests, doing little to narrow the divisions between economic insiders and outsiders that Agenda 2010 had done so much to exacerbate.

Corporate Liberalism and Financial Regulation: Sheltering Insiders and Financing the Social Market Economy

Though novel in many respects, the postwar German economic model built on many of the institutional legacies of late German industrialization in the nineteenth century, in which the banking system played a central role in enabling German firms to compete in the capital-intensive leading sectors of coal, steel, and railroads.[168] Like its nineteenth-century forbear, the postwar German model relied heavily on bank-derived finance for corporate investment and expansion, as opposed to equity markets, as in the United States, or the state itself, as in France. Large industrial banks, such as Deutsche Bank and Commerzbank, would typically issue large, often long-term loans to industrial firms, investing in firms' long-term financial success rather than focusing on short-term returns. In exchange for providing the bulk of firms' investment funds, banks would often be granted positions on firms' boards of directors and act as custodians for individual investors' equity shares, enabling them to vote as proxies.[169] This "credit-based system of corporate finance,"[170] in which large industrial banks, serving mostly large, export-based firms, furnished Germany with a deep pool of patient capital essential to the process of postwar reconstruction and the restoration of German economic might that enabled it to become one of the world's largest exporters by the early 1960s, thereby providing an important engine of the postwar *Wirtschaftswunder*.

While perhaps emblematic of the character of postwar German industrial finance and financial regulation, the cozy relationships between large banks and major industrial concerns represent only one of several tiers in the complex German financial system. In particular, two other tiers make up the heart of local and regional economies and account for the bulk of German lending, each with its own distinctive clientele. The second tier entails private, cooperative banks, the Volks- und Raiffeisenbanken, which are owned by their members and amount to a German analog for credit unions in the United States. The third and economically more significant tier is composed of the public savings banks, divided between the Sparkassen (nationally organized banks with local and regional branches) and the Landesbanken (regional banks owned and administered by the Länder). Regional political officials sit on the banks' supervisory boards, enabling them to funnel loans on advantageous terms to support favored firms and development projects.[171] Whereas the large industrial banks focused on providing large, long-term loans to major industrial firms, the public savings banks centered their activities on retail banking and loans to firms in the German *Mittelstand*. This latter network of banks represented a core element of the German financial system and was intimately bound up in the success of the SMEs that would constitute part of the "backbone of the German political economy."[172]

Their strategic importance made the public savings banks, like the major industrial banks, a key interest group in the postwar German economy; it was both a symptom and a reinforcing cause of well-established patterns of cooperation and protection between them and the federal and Länder governments. Essentially, the Landesbanken and public savings banks acted as financial analogs to the favored firms and skilled workers in Germany's thriving export sector. Until 2005, for example, they were protected by a public guarantee against bankruptcy, a notable departure from German authorities' historical fears of centers of oligopolistic power in the German economy and moral hazard that might encourage reckless behavior at potentially significant public expense. Ensconced in their stable relationships with their respective industrial clients, neither the large industrial banks nor the public savings banks were much interested in innovation well into the 1990s. Nor did they push for any significant regulatory changes that might have enabled them to compete with the rise of investment banking in the Anglo-Saxon world.[173] This deeply conservative attitude was consistent with a traditionally hands-off regulatory posture on the part of state officials, who worked to preserve a framework that was "characterized by a lack of transparency and accountability, low protection of minority shareholders and no binding rules against insider trading."[174] As one journalist aptly put it, "there is little appetite for change in Germany because the banking system is so deeply intertwined with its politics, serving as a rich source of patronage and financing for local projects."[175] Moreover, political polarization has been largely absent with regard to financial reform, with major parties of Left and Right agreed on the structural importance of the banking system to Germany's strategy for growth and international competitiveness.[176] Much as the corporate liberal tradition had helped to inform close and supportive relationships between the state and core groups in business and labor in the realms of fiscal and labor-market policy, so too did it inform and sustain close connections between government at all levels and the financial system.

Beginning in the 1990s, however, the growing internationalization of financial markets, with the American and British financial sectors leading the way, put growing pressure on Germany's three-pillared universal banking system, particularly with respect to financial innovation and the perceived need to begin to compete in markets for riskier financial products traditionally offered by investment banks.[177] The resulting shift represented an important, if grudging, departure from the banks' past practice, reflecting an erosion of the traditional dichotomy between banks and markets, with financial institutions increasingly engaged in market-making activities themselves.[178] Initially opposed by the Bundesbank, which feared the erosion of its control over monetary policy,[179] gradual liberalization was eventually accepted by both the central bank and a growing segment of Germany's financial community, including the powerful Landesbanken, which hoped to profit from the growing trend towards securitization and other investment-bank activities. Such developments reinforced parallel trends, beginning in the 1970s, toward the growing independence of large industrial concerns from their erstwhile banking patrons, as they began to establish in-house financial-management authorities, and toward an increasingly competitive domestic financial industry, with the Landesbanken working to compete with large industrial banks for providing a share of financial services to large, export-oriented firms. In response, the large banks focused increasingly on intermediation with fee-generating investment-bank activities, leaving the Landesbanken to provide the bulk of financial services to both SMEs and a growing number of large firms.[180] At the same time, the latter found an increasing appetite for risk, "rush[ing] into investment activities in foreign markets,"[181] a fact that would assume a central significance during the post-2007 financial crisis.

The erosion of Germany's traditional three-pillared universal-banking system was accelerated by regulatory changes on both the European and national levels that helped to accelerate the deregulation and fragmentation of the German financial system. With respect to the former, the 2001 Brussels Accord ended public guarantees of public savings banks. In the same year, in an effort to establish a coherent regulatory framework for an increasingly complex financial system, the Red-Green administration of Gerhard Schröder established the so-called BaFin, or Bundesanstalt für Finanzdienstleistungsaufsicht (the Federal Financial Supervisory Authority). This move was strongly supported by the Bundesbank, which had lost its leading position in monetary policy to the European Central Bank after the advent of EMU in 1999 and hoped to shore up and consolidate national regulatory structures and shift power away from the Finance Ministry, which had previously managed several separate bodies responsible for financial regulation. Also in the domestic arena, in 2004 the government passed the fourth *Finanzmarktföderungsgesetz*, or Financial Market Promotion Act, which allowed new financial investors like hedge funds to become active in Germany.

Even as the government acted to consolidate regulatory authorities and liberalize significant portions of the German financial system, however, it also continued to shelter the country's industrial and public savings banks—for example, negotiating a four-year transitional period for the implementation of the 2001 Brussels Accord to the strategically important Landesbanken—and eased capital reserve requirements for financial institutions under a provision of the 2004 act, even as European Commission officials increasingly pressed for *tighter* regulations, fearing systemic risks within the increasingly leveraged German banking system.[182] Such fears would turn out to be well founded, as the transitional period of continued state guarantees of the Landesbanken coincided with the explosion of subprime lending in the United States. During this period the Landesbanken exploited their sheltered position to amass enormous debts, composed largely of toxic American collateralized debt obligations and mortgage-backed securities, as well as extensive loans to borrowers in the European periphery, including those that helped fuel the housing bubble in Spain that would burst in the aftermath of the post-2007 financial crisis.[183]

Given such highly leveraged positions in both the Landesbanken and the increasingly investment-bank oriented industrial banks, it came as no surprise that the post-2007 crisis hit the German banking system very hard. The

Landesbanken were particularly vulnerable, having "operated with explicit and implicit public guarantees," leading to "excessive risk-taking [that] went unchecked by regulators," in particular in the American subprime lending market.[184] The post-2007 losses for both industrial and public savings banks were staggering, leading to initial write-downs of $7.7 billion for Deutsche Bank, $3.9 billion for HypoBank, and a combined $16 billion for the Landesbanken and public savings banks. The losses led to significant layoffs for both public and private banks, as well as some consolidations, such as the merger of Sachsen LB with LB Baden-Württemberg.[185] Such defensive moves, however, were far from adequate to deal with the scale of the effects of the crisis in Germany, a scale that quickly surpassed the capacity of Germany's regulatory structure. The previous system, under the authority of BaFin, had focused mostly on *preventing* insolvency proceedings and had few coherent mechanisms for dealing with them once they occurred, particularly on a national scale.[186]

Policymakers' growing realization that individual bailouts of favored financial institutions and relatively weak regulation would be inadequate for dealing with the growing crisis led to the passage of the Financial Market Stabilization Act on October 17, 2008. The act established the Federal Agency for Financial Market Stabilization (FMSA), which was appointed to oversee the Sonderfonds Finanzmarktstabilisierung (SoFFin) fund to support troubled banks.[187] In an effort to prevent bank runs, the measure also guaranteed all private bank accounts.[188] Several Landesbanken, as well as the commercial bank Commerzbank, sought recapitalization support from the SoFFin in late 2008. The goals of the measure were quickly to rescue banks threatened with insolvency, which were to be provided with "help to help themselves," in the hope of reintegrating these institutions into the German financial system, and to restore market confidence.[189] This approach, with its emphasis on subsidizing core institutions and economic interests and on group self-responsibility (even at the expense of the moral hazard of which German authorities were ostensibly so wary), was very much consistent with the corporate-liberal understanding of the crisis.

These early efforts to bail out troubled German financial institutions, however, were modest compared with the 2008 bailout of Hypo Real Estate (HRE), which was one of Germany's largest commercial property lenders. In 2007 HRE had acquired Depfa Bank, which was originally a German bank but had relocated to Dublin in the early 1990s. Under relatively lax Irish financial regulations, Depfa Bank overextended itself through a series of ill-advised investments in large-scale infrastructure projects and in US mortgage-backed securities. With Depfa facing a growing liquidity crisis in 2007, HRE acquired Depfa for €5.7 billion in October 2007, less than a month after the bankruptcy of Lehman Brothers in the United States. By March 2008, a Bundesbank report on HRE warned that the financial burden from Depfa, coupled with HRE's "nonexistent" compliance with banking regulations, spelled a dangerous combination. Further complicating the matter was the fact that German law allowed holding companies (which HRE was) to be beyond the reach of regulation by the Federal Financial Supervisory Authority (Bundesanstalt für Finanzdienstleistungsaufsicht). As the depth of the financial crisis became apparent in fall 2008, the bailout of HRE came to assume systemic significance for German authorities, who feared the collapse of Germany's already shaky three-pillared financial system with its critical strategic connects to the German economic model. After two rounds of negotiations between HRE's board and the FMSA, Hypo was offered €102 billion in rescue funds. As the bank's losses continued to mount, reaching a record €5 billion in 2008, the government decided to nationalize HRE and begin managing a complex restructuring process.[190] With the HRE debacle squarely in mind, in July 2009 the government passed the Financial Market Stabilization Continuation Act, which allowed the FMSA to create "bad banks" to absorb toxic assets up to €200 billion. Though not the only bank to be bailed out, HRE was the largest and most controversial, and the means whereby its bailout was undertaken was emblematic of the German government's corporate-liberal approach to financial regulation and the connections among the state and key groups in the business and financial communities that it informed.

Since 2008 the popularity of the three-pillared financial system, along with the deeply political nature of the regional and local banks, has made financial reform in Germany a challenging political task that has borne strong corporate-liberal imprints. Given that SMEs, long viewed as the backbone of the German economic model, continue to rely heavily on lending from Landesbanken and public savings banks, several attempts at consolidation and additional regulatory reform of these institutions have been met with widespread opposition from both the financial and business communities. Although some Landesbanken mergers have occurred, several of these highly political institutions survived and instead have agreed to cooperate and share resources and expertise rather than merge.[191] Efforts to consolidate the public savings banks and calls to increase reserve requirements have been met with similarly stiff opposition, and policymakers have lost the appetite for pushing for such changes. Instead, they have focused on reforming the large industrial banks, which arguably pose greater systemic risks and have increasingly been peripheral to the core of the German economic model, particularly since large industrial concerns have weaned themselves off reliance on them since the 1990s.

Following the Liikanen Report, written by a group of experts appointed by the European Commission to propose regulatory changes in the EU financial system in the aftermath of the financial crisis, German authorities turned their attention to "ring-fencing" systemically important financial institutions, an approach designed to separate traditional banking activities, such as taking deposits and issuing loans, from riskier trading activities that are traditionally the province of investment banks.[192] In May 2013 the government passed the so-called *Gesetz zur Abschirmung von Risken und zur Planung der Sanierung und Abwicklung von Kreditinstituten und Finanzgruppen*, or Law on Protecting from Risk and Reforming and Unwinding Financial Institutions, which left the task of separating these spheres of activity to the banks themselves rather than mandate changes by law. The law was designed to shelter key financial institutions from more robust European regulations, such as those outlined in the Liikanen Report, in favor of "weaker national-level regulations that would in reality have minimal impact on market-based banking in [Germany's] large banks."[193] Here again, German authorities acted in a classically corporate-liberal fashion, sheltering key insider groups from aggressive regulatory changes and working to preserve existing relationships between key interest groups in the financial sector, much as they had done with respect to business and labor in the case of fiscal and labor-market policy. At the time of this book's writing (2017), growing fears about the potential insolvency of Deutsche Bank (as well as its at-best murky relationship with US president Trump) and indications that the Merkel government is surreptitiously planning for the eventuality of a massive bailout of the bank show clearly that this strategy has been inadequate to address the structural vulnerabilities of the German banking system.[194]

Conclusion: German Corporate Liberalism and Economic Adjustment in the Age of Neoliberalism

As in the French case, then, understanding Germany's response to the economic crisis requires situating it within the country's liberal tradition. Expressed in the Ordoliberal emphasis on an organically constituted, quasi-pluralistic social order, German corporate liberalism as it evolved after the 1960s encourages a state that is nurturing, reluctant to intervene as a matter of course, and respectful of traditional group prerogatives. At the same time, German corporate liberalism has legitimated and reflected a commitment to a state that is much more active and willing to intervene in times of crisis and uncertainty than even the most interventionist Ordoliberals would have countenanced. In like fashion, beginning with the emergence of the postwar Social Market Economy, Germany's liberal tradition informed the development of an array of social-policy and labor-market instruments that were much more expansive and generous than early Ordoliberals envisioned, representing both an acknowledgement of the socially embedded character of Germany's political economy and a rejection of the abstract and atomized vision of political and economic order offered by neoliberals beginning in the 1970s.

That said, Germany's liberal tradition has informed responses that were, not global or indiscriminate, but rather characterized by strong commitments to subsidizing and sheltering and subsidizing core groups and connected financial institutions, increasingly favoring those groups at the expense of unincorporated outsiders. Across all three areas of policymaking explored in this chapter—fiscal policy and public investment, social and labor-market policy, and financial regulation—German authorities have managed the post-1990 period of fiscal austerity and transnational neoliberalism by fostering collaborative relationships with core political and economic interests, including skilled industrial workers, export-intensive firms and sectors, and the network of connected financial institutions that serve them.[195] These collaborative relationships have stood in stark contrast to policymakers' growing willingness to impose costs on individuals beyond these favored domains, as the fiscal constraints of the contemporary era have encouraged economic trade-offs between winners and losers that were perhaps unnecessary during the postwar boom. This pattern is unsurprising given the understandings of state, economy, and society at the heart of the corporate liberal tradition, which, in the words of one Finance Ministry official, stems from and reflects the strength of "groups that represent particular interests" and "develop their goals collectively."[196]

In the next chapter I turn to the Italian case and Italy's tradition of "clientelist liberalism." Italian liberalism shares some elements with its German counterpart, notably the emphasis on protecting insider groups and rejection of Thatcherite neoliberalism. It differs from German liberalism in key ways, however, notably with respect to the role that groups play in shaping policy trajectories, both as participants in the policymaking process and as constituents of policy outcomes. Unlike in Germany, where insider groups have been instrumental to a broader strategy of economic revival, in Italy such groups played a largely negative role, blocking significant reforms that threatened their economic status, a posture that has resulted in enduring political and economic sclerosis. Since the early 1990s this zero-sum vision of politics has made clientelistic links between interest groups and political parties very important, as ideological battles between Left and Right have subsumed and fostered sharp competition between groups for available political and economic resources. This dynamic has led to a pattern of sclerosis and dysfunction, leading to the emergence of an indigenous neoliberal elite that has been strongly critical of these arrangements but has remained politically marginalized. The result has been a sustained and ultimately unresolved battle of ideas between neoliberals and a state in the service of groups who colonized it, a weak penetration of state authority into society, broad distrust of the state across the political spectrum, and a policymaking system unable to respond effectively to economic upheaval. As in France and Germany, neither the long-term trajectories of policy nor the outcomes of specific policy episodes can be explained through a focus on economic interests or institutional structure alone. Such an explanation requires instead careful attention to the character of the Italian liberal tradition, the analytical frameworks that it provides to elites, and the menu of policy options that it presents to them in moments of upheaval and heightened uncertainty.

4

Group Capture and Political Sclerosis

The Failed Synthesis of Italian Clientelist Liberalism

Whereas postwar German liberalism fostered successful collaboration between the state and powerful social and economic groups in confronting the country's daunting social and economic challenges, in Italy a dysfunctional state proved increasingly incapable of doing so. As detailed in Chapter 1, Italian clientelist liberalism reflected deep social and economic divisions that stemmed from the bargains underlying the *Risorgimento*. After the long interregnum of fascism and war in the 1920s and 1930s, this tradition generated policies and institutional commitments that exacerbated these problems rather than act to resolve them. As in the German case, prominent social and economic groups featured prominently in Italian elites' understanding of the social and political landscape and related notions of state responsibility. In contrast to Germany, where core groups in the Social Market Economy acted in cooperation with a supportive state as both engineers and beneficiaries of a successful postwar reinvention across partisan lines, however, in Italy such groups, including unionized workers in public-sector manufacturing and firms, managers of large state-owned enterprises, and regional political elites, fostered a cynical view of the state that led to its colonization and to a prioritization of establishing cozy relationships with dominant parties, often using partisan connections to gain access to sources of political and economic patronage.[1]

Such group colonization both reflected and reinforced Italians' deep distrust of the state, which the legacies of the *Risorgimento* had left illegitimate in the eyes of broad segments of Italian society and which many viewed as structurally incapable of fostering positive and inclusive economic change. Instead, the Italian state was viewed as a set of political and economic resources to be captured rather than as an arena of compromise and consensus. It also informed an understanding whereby the limits on state power—a hallmark of any liberal tradition—were defined in terms of the privileges and vested interests of key social and economic groups. During the postwar period, the result was an enduring pattern of alternating attempts by dominant parties and political coalitions to defend the interests of allied interest groups and to shelter them from the costs of economic adjustment or to block such adjustment altogether. Since the *Mani Pulite* scandal in the early 1990s and the resultant collapse of the dominant Christian Democratic Party (DC), this trajectory has combined with alternating attempts by Left and Right to defend the interests of privileged constituencies even as they work to undermine those of their political opponents. In the rare cases where reform has succeeded and costs have been imposed on economic groups, this has often been undertaken by the very parties for which those groups constitute core constituencies, according to a sort of "Nixon-goes-to-China" logic. More generally, this pattern of frustrated liberalism and a dovetailing of limits on the state's authority with intergroup competition has informed a zero-sum conception of reform, generalized policy stagnation, and widespread cynicism about the capacity of elites to govern.

The contrast between the political and economic role of groups and their relationship to the state in the German and Italian cases is instructive. If groups served as allies and beneficiaries of the German state's project of economic modernization and democratic consolidation, in Italy they acted as impediments to processes of economic adjustment. As Andrea Boltho points out, these differences, which had long existed in the German and Italian liberal traditions, were reinforced by the character of the respective postwar bargains that they helped to inform. The German Social Market Economy was predicated upon a pattern of liberal interventionism designed to "moderate the social costs of unfettered markets. The outcome was a gradual adoption of measures . . . [that fostered] social consensus." Despite difference between the priorities of German parties of Left and Right, moreover, such partnership generally extended across party lines, both parties' relationship with capital and labor being more cooperative than antagonistic. In Italy, by contrast, "a polarization between a conservative business class and an antagonistic, left-wing trade-union movement (polarization that in milder form had already existed before World War I) became entrenched" in the postwar era.[2] As a result, while in Germany groups viewed both themselves and each other as potential partners in a state-supported process of economic renewal, in Italy, each viewed others as antagonists with designs on its resources, potentially with the support of a state captured by competing groups.

In such a context it is hardly surprising that the Italian political system that emerged after the war would reflect profound ambivalence about its liberal predicates. The Christian Democratic "party state" that consolidated its rule during the 1950s and 1960s was indeed liberal in important respects—including its commitment to private property and a market economy, its deep hostility to communism, and its recognition of limits to the state's interventionist capacity.

It was, however, profoundly illiberal in others, including its casual relationship with the rule of law, its heavy-handed dominance of key industries, and the prevalence of corruption and clientelism as mechanisms with which to perpetuate its rule. In short, the postwar Italian political economy was never fully reconciled to the very liberal tradition that helped to shape it, leaving the country ill prepared to confront the challenges of postwar reconstruction and an increasingly competitive international economy. Liberalism in the Italian tradition was both antistatist and supportive of individual freedom and autonomy, though in ways that grew out of deep distrust of the state and a cynical understanding of the political process that tended to foster an acceptance of clientelism and a highly personalistic understanding of politics. In many senses, then, Italian clientelist liberalism was the dark obverse of German corporate liberalism and its Ordoliberal antecedents, which viewed groups as partners in a shared political-economic project rather than as self-interested parties engaged in a sort of Hobbesian war of all against all.

This historical pattern of incomplete political modernization, characterized by mutually reinforcing distrust of the state and clientelist attempts to turn it to clientelistic ends, fostered a tolerance of corruption and a view of politics as a zero-sum game in the postwar era.[3] The *Risorgimento* created a unified Italian state, though only at the cost of preserving and even deepening preexisting social divisions—cleavages that set groups of Italians apart from one another by class, region, religiosity, profession, and worldview. The challenges posed by this legacy were not lost on postwar liberals such as Benedetto Croce and Luigi Einaudi, the latter of whom acted as both president of the republic and head of the Bank of Italy in the first postwar decade. Somewhat paradoxically, Einaudi viewed the Italian state as both a corrupting force that historically served particularistic ends and a potentially transformative agent that could act to break up monopolies and ensure the basis for healthy patterns of political and economic competition. Understanding that dominant currents on both Left and Right deeply distrusted the state, Einaudi and other postwar liberals, picking up a theme that Montesquieu had advanced in France, viewed economic liberalization as a powerful force capable of undermining monopolies and blocking clientelistic claims on political and economic resources. It is in this sense that Einaudi's view of the market as the "other face of democracy" should be understood.[4] By decoupling or at least loosening the ties between political and economic power, Einaudi believed, Italy could deepen and strengthen its democratic institutions in ways that would support economic reconstruction and growth over the long term.

Though justified by Italy's relatively rapid reconstruction and positive economic performance in the first postwar decade, such optimism was driven by largely illiberal domestic institutional innovations that would lay the foundation for the subsequent clientelistic perversion of the economic order. As Andrew

Shonfield relates, the most important such innovation involved the repurposing of the Istituto per la Ricostruzione Industriale, or IRI, which had been created under Mussolini in the 1930s as a holding pen for bankrupt industrial enterprises and in the postwar era remained a state-managed consortium of major industrial firms in which the state invested vast resources in order to return them to profitability. By the 1960s, with 120 separate enterprises and employing nearly 300,000 people, the IRI had become the most powerful agent of postwar industrialization and of Italy's effort to catch up with its neighbors through a process of state-driven economic development. Aided by the reliable provision of finance by the Bank of Italy and such other large public financial institutions as the state-owned Banca nazionale del lavoro, the IRI helped to direct investment to strategic sectors and foster rapid (though regionally uneven) development that would underpin a stunning process of recovery.[5] In sharp contrast to the stagnation and agrarian character of much of the country prior to the war, during the long 1950s annual rates of economic growth averaged 6 percent, and both the size of the economy and per-capita GNP roughly doubled, though there remained major regional discrepancies between northern and southern levels of development.[6] Although "the proliferation of nationalized and semi-public enterprise [was] more the result of historical accident than of deliberate political decision,"[7] this pattern of economic and institutional development suggested that postwar Italian economic progress would not be driven by the dynamics that liberals such as Einaudi had envisioned.

The increasingly illiberal character of postwar economic development in Italy did not merely represent the failure of Einaudi's vision, however. It would also lay the ground for the clientelistic capture of the Italian state and inform a prevailing elite understanding of politics, economics, and society that would ultimately undermine the tradition's liberal components. In the process, liberal ideas about desirable limits on state power became conflated with parochial and often partisan agendas designed to preserve state resources for certain groups while denying them to others. As the intensification of the Cold War converted the anticommunism of the Italian Christian Democrats (DC) into valuable political currency, the postwar party state was consolidated in ways that would synthesize a cynical and zero-sum conception of politics with a reflexive anti-statism that paradoxically viewed state capture as the sole means of establishing secure claims to political and economic resources.

The state's dominance of the postwar Italian economy provided ample economic justification for this perspective. As the state stepped in to fill the gap left by weak Italian industry, it represented an increasingly rich target for politicians, who increasingly viewed their parties as patronage machines reliant for their success upon their ties with and access to the public sector.[8] The postwar doctrine of *Trasformismo,* whereby "the old party labels of Left and Right lost their meaning as governments became shapeless amalgams of one-time opponents,"[9] was nurtured by both political and economic forces acting in concert. The resulting strategy, which sustained coalitions through patronage and sacrificed long-term political integration for the sake of short-term expediency, in turn seriously undermined the legitimacy of the Italian state even as it increased the importance of state capture. As a result, Italian elites would increasingly abandon the pursuit of the general interests of society as a whole in favor of those of powerful groups whose agents and champions were increasingly divided along partisan lines.

With the end of the postwar boom, the toxic legacies of the *Risorgimento* informed a variant of Italian liberalism that would prove ill suited to the managing of Italy's declining economic fortunes. As decreasing growth rates in the 1960s undermined the economic basis of the postwar bargain among the state, capital, and workers, Italian authorities sought to dampen social unrest and purchase political support in ways that compromised the political economy's long-term capacity to adjust. Even before the OPEC oil shocks and the social unrest of the late 1960s and 1970s, the Italian economy experienced mounting difficulties. Beginning in the early 1960s, climbing food and housing prices, along with double-digit annual wage increases in key sectors, led to rising inflation, which reached 7.5 percent in 1963. This development in turn undermined Italian competitiveness and led to a growing balance-of-payments problem, resulting in a trade deficit that tripled between 1961 and 1963. As the capital stock matured, the challenge became satisfying workers' wage demands in a climate of declining international competitiveness, worker productivity, and economic growth.[10]

The industrial unrest of the so-called Hot Autumn of 1969 merely accelerated the shift from a productivist growth strategy to one centering on maintaining social peace, an important inflection point in the evolution of Italian clientelist liberalism. Along with the OPEC oil shock and the collapse of Bretton Woods in 1973, the inflationary wage bargains struck in the Hot Autumn's aftermath would undermine Italy's competitive position and its ability to sustain non-inflationary economic growth. Increasingly, the Italian party state worked to co-opt insider groups, including workers in state-owned enterprises, white-collar professionals, and managers of large state-owned industrial concerns, often administered through consortia such as the IRI and Ente Nazionale Idrocarburi (ENI), the state-owned petrochemical conglomerate. Political elites enmeshed these groups in a web of clientelism that protected their economic interests in exchange for their political support. Since the state was an owner and manager of large segments of the industrial economy, winning elections meant gaining access to the most important distributional mechanisms in the economy. This development resulted in a conflicted view of the state as both the source of economic security and a threat to individual economic freedom and prosperity, represented by its dominance of the productive power of the economy and its enforcement of a set of rules designed to shelter favored groups from the costs of adjustment. In such a context, economic freedom and security became inseparable from access to political power, as Italians increasingly believed that they could live neither with nor without the state.

Economic developments after the troubled 1970s did little to resolve this deep ambivalence while concomitant political developments exacerbated it. Although Christian Democratic hegemony ended in the 1980s with the rise of an electorally viable Italian Socialist Party (PSI) under the leadership of Bettino Craxi, interparty competition did nothing to attenuate the system's clientelistic character, as the Socialists proved even more adept at corruption than their Christian Democratic forbears. Instead of a single-party state, Italy now had two major parties fighting over the spoils of political victory and control of a state that retained a major presence in Italian capitalism. In Tony Judt's characterization, "The Christian Democrats and Socialists in particular used the state sector and public holding companies [like the IRI] to reward colleagues and bribe supporters, often favoring them with public contracts and absorbing them into the . . . submerged power structure that underpinned their dominion."[11] As the DC and PSI alternated in power, the price of cobbling together majority coalitions in parliament increased, as smaller parties were able to play the two dominant ones off in a quest for commitments of public-sector jobs and other clientelistic benefits. Though Craxi ended the inflationary *Scala mobile* system of wage indexation introduced after the Hot Autumn, his spending policies and an increasingly stagnant economy led to a ballooning budget deficit and public debt, which reached 103 percent of GDP in 1987 as unemployment reached a postwar record of 11.8 percent.[12]

As the state became ever more fiscally encumbered and as cobbling together governing coalitions took precedence over meaningful reform, dominant political elites increasingly abandoned any pretense of a commitment to liberalism, whose mantle was donned by vocal neoliberal critics outside governing circles. While the French and German liberal traditions had succeeded in achieving a synthesis (albeit a sometimes awkward one) between national liberal lineages and competing traditions such as statism (in the French case) and neocorporatism and Ordoliberalism (in the German), in Italy, liberalism's intellectual and moral force was eventually exhausted to such an extent that it became difficult to describe the system as liberal at all. This failed synthesis mirrored and reinforced the failure of Italian economic adjustment to an era of economic austerity and neoliberal hegemony, challenges to which Italian elites struggled to find a constructive answer. Nor did the eruption of the *Mani Pulite* scandal in the early 1990s do much to rectify this situation. In a classic example of Pareto's "circulation of elites," the scandal merely converted one framework of clientelistic co-optation into another, dominated by different parties but with significant continuity of leading political figures and colored by the same pattern of political stalemate and mutual distrust between state and society. The result was the failure of distributional coalitions among interest groups and public officials of the kind that had long since become the hallmarks of the more successful German political-economic model.

In this chapter I analyze how this clientelistic liberal tradition and the legacies of failed liberalism that resulted from it have shaped policy trajectories in the areas of fiscal policy, labor-market policy, and financial regulation in an era of transnational neoliberalism. As in the French and German cases, I argue that analytical frameworks informed by domestic liberal traditions have shaped elites' assumptions and priorities and have tended to favor certain patterns of policy over others. In fiscal policy, governments of both Left and Right have struggled to manage Italy's massive debt load and have been reluctant to challenge the vested interests of powerful groups, even as the hegemony of fiscal austerity within the Eurozone has undermined the possibilities for public investment and fiscal support for renewed economic growth. In employment policy, governments of Left and Right have struggled to reform Italy's sclerotic labor market and to rationalize job protections and support for the unemployed without undermining the political legitimacy upon which successful reform depends, all in a context in which skepticism about state power makes such a task all the more difficult. Finally, in financial regulation, authorities have been forced to shore up Italy's bloated financial sector and have worked to prevent contagion in the face of the growing share of toxic debt on institutions' balance sheets. I present an overview of these policy trajectories, highlighting the state's role, favored policy instruments, major constituencies, and dominant social and economic goals, in Table 4.1.

In all three areas, clientelist liberal ideas have led to prevailing understandings of policy change as involving zero-sum trade-offs and of successful reform as predicated upon dislodging sheltered clients from privileged positions. These frames of reference have both undermined public support for reform and diluted and diverted those relatively few substantive measures whose passage governments have been able to secure.

Irresistible Forces and Immovable Objects: Fiscal Policy and the Reconstitution of the Italian Party State

As European officials drafted the Maastricht Treaty, Italy found itself ill prepared to meet the challenges posed by monetary union. As discussed in Chapters 2 and 3, negotiations over the character and provisions of EMU largely followed the

Table 4.1 **Orientation of Italian Clientelist Liberalism by Policy Area**

	State's Economic Role	*Major Constituencies*	*Favored Instruments*	*Prevailing Social/ Economic Goals*
Fiscal Policy and State Investment	Compensatory/ defensive	Politically connected business elites, SMEs, and independents	Limited spending cuts	Debt management
Labor-Market Policy	Defensive/ antagonistic	Unionized public-sector workers	Modest deregulation	Political and social stability
Financial Policy	Sheltering/ compensatory	Public savings banks	Targeted bailouts	Crisis management and protecting financial clients

German model of an anti-inflationary hard-currency regime that left domestic officials with little room for maneuver to stimulate growth and employment, both of which had become central concerns. The prevailing assumption shared by German (and, more reluctantly, French) officials and those in the business community who followed their line was that EMU would foster international competitiveness by keeping export prices low, a sort of European version of the French strategy of "competitive disinflation" from the 1980s. From the Italians' perspective, however, the problem was that domestic inflation, rapidly rising real wages spurred by the tenuous labor settlement following the unrest of the late 1960s and 1970s, and declining productivity rates left the country ill prepared to capitalize on the benefits of this German-inspired model, despite continued (though slowing) increases in Italian exports.[13] In addition, decades of clientelistic politics had resulted in a pattern of "fiscal incontinence" resulting from officials' "aim to buy social peace. Frenetic activism was the defining characteristic of a policy that was used to raise pensions, improve health provisions, boost public payrolls, subsidize industry, etc. Political expedience rather than economic rationality ruled decision-making."[14] As Charles Maier puts it, this dynamic showed that "the struggle for income shares [between workers and employers had been] shifted from the factory floor to the state budget."[15] This dynamic would result in two decades of sluggish growth, stubbornly high unemployment, consistently high fiscal deficits, and levels of public debt that were among the highest in Europe. I provide an overview of key Italian economic indicators over the past two decades in Table 4.2.

Table 4.2 **Economic Indicators for Selected Years, 1991–2013, Italy**[a]

	1991	*1995*	*1998*	*2003*	*2006*	*2009*	*2013*
GDP Growth (%)	1.54	2.89	1.62	0.15	2.01	–5.48	–1.73
Unemployment Rate (harmonized) (%)	8.52	11.18	11.30	8.43	6.79	7.75	12.13
Inflation (CPI) (%)	6.25	5.24	1.96	2.67	2.09	0.77	1.22
Public Budget Deficit (% of GDP)	–10.96	–7.25	–3.02	–3.41	–3.59	–5.27	–2.69
Public Debt (% of GDP)	98.04	121.23	130.67	114.29	115.01	125.96	143.66

[a]Author's calculations and OECD data, available at data.oecd.org and stats.oecd.org, except: public debt for 1991 obtained from IMF, Public Finances in Modern History Database (2013), available at http://www.imf.org/external/np/fad/histdb/.

From its disadvantaged position as a highly indebted country with slowing growth and declining competitiveness, Italy in the early 1990s faced a series of economic and political crises that, along with the fiscal-policy restrictions that underlay Europe's incipient monetary regime, sharply limited the country's room for maneuver. The signature of the Maastricht Treaty in February 1992 was followed less than a year later by turmoil in international currency markets that led to Italy's ejection (along with the UK) from the European Monetary System. The EMS had been established in the late 1970s as a prototype of the currency coordination that would eventually evolve into EMU, with the central aim of limiting intercurrency exchange-rate fluctuation and the kinds of beggar-thy-neighbor unilateral devaluations that had been common in the 1960s.[16] Though a meaningful step toward a single currency, the system failed to adjust to deepening integration of European financial and capital markets following the 1986 Single European Act (SEA) and to growing discrepancies in macroeconomic performance and competitiveness among member states. By the early 1990s this system left weaker economies like Italy open to speculative currency attacks, as the Bundesbank refused to accept an open-ended commitment to defend the Exchange Rate Mechanism (ERM) that limited intercurrency variation and diverging interests between core and periphery frustrated attempts to realign it.[17] In September 1992 a "massive speculative attack" on the lira and the pound led to the ejection of both currencies from the EMS and to 10 percent devaluation of the Italian lira.[18]

In response, the government of Prime Minister Giuliano Amato of the Italian Social Party, elected in June 1992, undertook the first of a series of ultimately futile moves designed to rectify the fiscal and current-account imbalances that had precipitated the crisis and to prepare the country to rejoin European monetary institutions. His $76 billion austerity package proposed significant reductions in health subsidies and pension benefits, cuts in the workforces of state-owned enterprises and outright privatization of others, and tax increases. Amato justified the reforms as the only possible means of stabilizing Italy's dire fiscal situation and restoring its credibility in European economic institutions. In what would become a constant refrain of Italian policymakers, he cited Italian debt as a central factor motivating the cuts and went so far as to call the devaluation a "healthy shock" that would teach Italians that German economic power needed to be curtailed within arrangements at the European level: "If people do not want to be dominated by the Bundesbank, we have to build a more democratic Community so that all European citizens can feel they are sharing in the power to make these decisions."[19] In language redolent of French explanations of their decision to support the currency union and presaging that employed by later caretaker governments, Amato thus accepted harsh austerity for the sake of the relatively remote prospect of influencing the character of the future currency regime.[20] The pension reforms, which proposed raising the standard retirement age from fifty-five or sixty (depending on the category of worker) to sixty-five and increasing the required contribution period from fifteen to twenty years, proved particularly controversial and led to demonstrations by hundreds of thousands of Italian workers in Rome and "almost daily" protests by labor unions (dominated by the public sector), some of which were quashed by police using tear gas.[21] In what would become a recurring theme, the protests that resulted from Amato's attempt to force Italian unions and their dominant public-sector constituency to relinquish their acquired benefits led the government to dilute several of the package's health and pension proposals, leading the business daily *Il Mondo* to editorialize that "suddenly the climate has gone back to that of the early 70s. Throughout the country, the labor union grass roots seems to have chosen confrontation of the hardest kind on the streets."[22]

Following the backlash created by Amato's austerity proposals and the controversy over a government decree that increased government oversight of police investigations of charges of corruption, the prime minister was dismissed by the president and succeeded by a technocratic caretaker government led by Carlo Ciampi, former head of the Bank of Italy, in April 1993.[23] Following in Amato's footsteps on the path towards fiscal consolidation, in September Ciampi released a budget proposal that sought to cut spending and raise taxes while privatizing additional state-owned enterprises in an effort to bring Italian public debt (at $69 billion and growing in 1993) back below the 60-percent-of-GDP threshold set by the Maastricht Treaty. Led by unions and the PCI, workers organized a series of strikes and protests against the proposals, including a violent seizure of a state-owned chemical plant slated for closure. The protests (though presumably not the plant seizure itself) were supported not only by workers but also by Catholic clergy and, in a rare example of public policy advocacy, by President Luigi Scalfaro himself, who argued that job security was of paramount importance. Following some side payments, including an agreement to preserve the jobs of 333 of the chemical workers and to relent on some planned school closures, the government eventually rescinded the entire package in the face of continued protests led by the PCI and public-sector unions.[24] By the eve of the 1994 elections, Italy was thus caught between the proverbial rock of European strictures and the hard place of a legacy of clientelism and patronage.

Severe though it was, this economic upheaval was soon overshadowed (and ultimately exacerbated) by even more dramatic political turmoil, as decades of patronage and the predations of the Christian Democratic party state led to a reckoning. The so-called *Mani Pulite,* or "clean hands" scandal, which broke in 1992, resulted in the arrest and trial of a large segment of the Italian political elite, concentrated in but by no means limited to the leadership of the DC. Also called the *Tangentopoli* ("Bribesville") scandal, alluding to the city of Milan where it first broke, this disgrace shook and eventually destroyed the foundation of the postwar Italian party system. Charges varied but most involved accusations that the relevant figures had been involved in furnishing or accepting kickbacks or bribes in exchange for public contracts for favored insiders or members of powerful political or economic constituencies.[25] More than 1,500 people were arrested, including some of the most powerful figures in the Italian political and economic establishments. In the business world the scandal took down both Carlo di Benedetti, the CEO of Olivetti, and Cesare Romiti, the CFO of Fiat. Within the political elite, arrests included such fixtures as Giulio Andreotti, a seven-time DC prime minister suspected of protecting the Mafia, and Bettino Craxi, the powerful head of the Socialist Party (PSI) and former prime minister, who fled to Tunisia and was convicted in absentia of arranging a large loan to ENI in exchange for a bribe. More than three hundred members of parliament, including four former prime ministers, were arrested and tried. Suddenly, practices that had been taken for granted as standard pieces of the Italian clientelist system were being brought to light and prosecuted with zeal, as many judges (some at considerable physical risk) sought to purge the old clientelism from the system in root-and-branch fashion.

The scandal led to a thoroughgoing restructuring of the Italian party system. As its scale became clear, many established parties, most importantly the DC and the PSI, disintegrated or reorganized into smaller, splinter parties or changed their names and ideologies as an "anticipated reaction" to the scandal's aftermath.[26] The so-called Pentapartito, the Five Parties that had collectively ruled Italy in nearly unbroken fashion since the war, together received 53 percent of the vote in 1992. After *Mani Pulite,* in the 1994 elections they received less than 20 percent, reflecting a growing "crisis of moral authority" in the political system.[27] This scandal would lead to the replacement of the DC on the center-right by a series of parties "far less sympathetic to worker protections," including the Northern League of Umberto Bossi—whose platform advocated secession of the rich, industrialized northern half of the country from the supposedly more corrupt and Mafia-ridden south (or at least much greater autonomy on its part)—the post-fascist National Alliance, and Silvio Berlusconi's Forza Italia.[28] On the left, the PCI worked to fill the vacuum left by the disintegration of the PSI by abandoning its hard-core Marxist agenda and rebranding itself as a moderate social democratic party, now renamed the Partito Democratico della Sinistra, or Party of Democratic Socialism (PDS). In short, both the characters and the plot of the decades-old Italian political drama were transformed, essentially overnight.

The scandal, however, did little to undermine the foundations of Italy's clientelist model and the weakening influence of liberal ideas and indeed helped to cement rather than upend the legacies of the clientelist-liberal tradition.[29] The biggest winner from the scandal, the one who was most successful at filling the political vacuum on the center-right, was Silvio Berlusconi, whose Forza Italia won a surprising 21 percent of the vote in 1994. In that year he became prime minister as head of a coalition comprising his party, the Northern League, and the National Alliance of Gianfranco Fini. Hailing from Milan, Berlusconi was a media tycoon who owned three television stations as well as the celebrated AC Milan football club.[30] He portrayed himself as a newcomer free from the vested interests of the old system, juxtaposing "his role as a successful entrepreneur and a charismatic leader to the corrupt political system that the *Tangentopoli* scandals had exposed."[31] His platform involved a combination of promises to root out corruption and to enact neoliberal policies that would move market forces to the center of the Italian political economy, in the process "creating a second economic miracle by freeing Italy's entrepreneurs from the shackles of the state bureaucracy."[32] It quickly became clear, however, that Berlusconi, who organized his campaign around commitments to use his independence and business acumen to revitalize the Italian economy, with promises that strained credulity, had little intention of implementing significant cuts in Italy's budgets. He had promised to create a million new jobs, reduce taxes, and improve the country's fiscal situation. Contradictory on their face, these promises nonetheless appealed to a significant number of voters weary of scandal and concerned about Italy's decades-long process of economic decline, which had produced stagnant growth, rising unemployment, and declining productivity, all against a backdrop of rapidly growing public indebtedness.[33] Equally important, in Stefano Fella and Carlo Ruzza's formulation, Berlusconi and the center-right were able to present themselves "as a modernising force able to inject the necessary market dynamism required to awaken Italy from its slumbers, in contrast to a centre-left portrayed as wedded to old-fashioned statist solutions and an over-protection of workers that was stifling the Italian economy."[34] In a country in which clientelism had undermined the impetus of liberal ideas and national economic fortunes, Berlusconi promised to loosen the grip of public-sector workers on benefits that were increasingly unaffordable and inconsistent with the task of economic renewal.

It would not be long before the hopes of center-right voters for a period of political and economic rebirth would be dashed, however. Berlusconi proved to be a classic example of old wine in a new bottle, reinforcing rather than addressing the dysfunctions of the clientelist liberal model. As a former member of the Council of Economic Advisors in Berlusconi's second administration explained, Berlusconi was a combination of the consummate political insider and a politically connected state business client. He had always concentrated his business activities in protected sectors and from his first days in power sought to protect business interests in such sectors, notably real estate and insurance.[35] It was not long before the thin veneer of Berlusconi's reformist posture started to tarnish, as he abandoned many of his key campaign promises with surprising alacrity. In a characteristic posture, Berlusconi focused his energies primarily on consolidating his political position and protecting his business interests and those of his core constituencies among small business and the self-employed while undermining those of his rivals (in particular managers of state-owned enterprises and unionized workers in the public sector).[36] His favored tool for carrying out this strategy was the somewhat tired but still effective trope, borrowed from the postwar Christian Democrats, of declared support for Catholic values and vocal (if increasingly anachronistic) anti-communism to create a negative coalition of fear and resentment of the privileges of Italy's economic and political insiders.[37] Using his holding company Fininvest (which would become the center of one of many scandals surrounding his governments) as the "nerve center" of his new party, Berlusconi used his dominance of the media to craft his image as a maverick outsider even as he turned to the venerable mechanisms of patronage and clientelism.[38] He exploited the fact that his two coalition partners had concentrated regional constituencies (the supporters of the National Alliance were concentrated in the South) to distribute political resources to them, portraying himself as the national, trans-regional "glue" that held the coalition together.[39] While focusing his energy on politics, Berlusconi allowed the problems of the Italian economy to fester: the budget deficit continued to grow, the country's debts mounted, and the prospect of rejoining European monetary institutions seemed ever more remote while the promised tax cuts and jobs never materialized.[40]

In both political and economic respects, then, Berlusconi's ascent had the flavor of a traditional restoration of the center-right rather than an advent of a genuinely new direction. Berlusconi deftly exploited Italy's clientelist legacy in burnishing his image as a reformer, even as he used the same system to protect his favored constituencies and solidify his hold on power. His first administration was undone by two ill-considered moves, one political and one economic, both of which represented harbingers of his future political tactics and challenges. In the political arena Berlusconi openly undermined the work of Italian judges investigating corruption charges, claiming (as he would do time and again) that the work of magistrates such as Antonio di Pietro, who had helped to break the *Mani Pulite* scandal, was politically inspired. Such "gauche attempts to derail the anti-corruption campaign contributed to a fast-growing mood of disenchantment with his government"[41] and recalled the adage that Rome was "the cradle of law and the grave of justice." The other move, in the economic arena, was his decision to revisit and extend the Amato pension reforms, which he decided had not gone far enough, seeking to use additional cuts to improve Italy's fiscal profile in the hope of rejoining the EMS while targeting the social benefits cherished by Italy's public-sector workers. In so doing he ignored the trade unions, which he had publicly designated as his primary political opponents and which organized large-scale protests against these measures throughout the autumn. These protests, along with the generally souring public mood, the disclosure that Berlusconi himself was under investigation for corruption, and public disputes between Bossi and Berlusconi, led to Bossi's withdrawal from the coalition and its collapse in December 1994.

Zero-Sum Games and Negative Coalitions: Italian Fiscal Policy during the Advent of EMU

Although Berlusconi's government fell after less than a year, the issues that it left unresolved cast a pall over the actions of subsequent governments. In January 1995 a caretaker, technocratic administration under Lamberto Dini, a former official with the Bank of Italy, assumed power with the stated goal of pushing through reforms in fiscal and labor-market policy that the previous administration had been unable to accomplish. Once again, a neoliberal technocrat was called upon to manage a political system in which neoliberalism was anathema. This agenda involved reducing public debt in the hope of allowing Italy to rejoin EMS, whereafter the government would resign and new elections would be held. Dini's political independence, coupled with qualified support for his administration by a public hungry for stability, indeed helped him accomplish some modest reforms that had proven elusive to his predecessors. In the realm of fiscal policy he cut public spending and raised some taxes, a move which he touted as "a major improvement in public finances," resulting in the stabilization of public debt at just over 120 percent of GDP. The public-sector deficit fell from around 9 percent of GDP in 1994 to 7.3 percent in 1995, and inflation was also brought under control, peaking at around 6 percent.[42] Although these reforms were among the more significant efforts since *Mani Pulite* to stabilize Italy's fiscal situation, their relatively modest scope and the fact that they were undertaken by a caretaker government lent them the feel of being exceptions to the rule.

Following the victory of the left-of-center Olive Tree coalition under Romano Prodi in the April 1996 elections, Italian authorities continued to struggle to manage the country's massive debt against the resistance of entrenched groups. Prodi was an academic economist widely perceived as competent and honest. Despite being on the Left, or perhaps as a result of it, Prodi was able to push ahead with an agenda of fiscal consolidation and reform begun under Dini, with a view to Italy's rejoining EMS and the nascent monetary union, which he made a central goal.[43] In June, Prodi presented the so-called *Documento di Programmazione Economico-Finanziaria* (DPEF), an ambitious budget proposal designed to satisfy the Maastricht limits on public debt by 1998, focusing on a one-time, $3.7 billion "euro tax." This measure was supported by labor unions but resisted by industrialists and shopkeepers, who saw the measure "as a gimmick unjustly aimed at the well off" and feared that it would undermine domestic demand.[44] Others dismissed it as a case of fiscal whistling past the graveyard, resorting to misleading accounting practices designed to secure Italy's readmission to EMS without really tackling the country's deep fiscal imbalances.[45] By the end of 1996, although the reforms had been diluted in response to the concerns of labor unions and Prodi's ex-communist coalition partners, European finance ministers and central bankers agreed to grant Italy readmission to the EMS on the promise of progress and the hopeful direction of reforms already undertaken.[46]

Although Italy's fiscal situation was still quite weak, with government budgets overshooting targets by $30 billion per year and protected deficits of around 5 percent for 1997, such optimism seemed warranted by a decline in the budget deficit to 2.6 percent of GDP by 1998, with public debt, though still at 126 percent of GDP, on a steadily downward trajectory (it would decline to 113.9 percent of GDP by 2001), against a backdrop of modest growth.[47] By the late 1990s there was some reason for optimism that Italy might become a solvent member of the incipient EMU, continuing to occupy the role of a political and economic anchor that it had played since the signature of the Treaty of Rome in 1957. For the most part, organized labor accepted the necessity of wage restraint and restrictions on public spending in the hope that membership in the Eurozone would spur growth and employment, while voters showed a willingness to be patient for the "prospect of continued reform and successful integration into the monetary union."[48] But this hope would ultimately be disappointed, with respect not to Italy's EMU membership, which was secured, but rather to the looked-for liberalization of the Italian political economy and state efforts to boost growth and employment.

Two problems in particular continued to plague Italy, ones that would undermine its economic performance and end up making membership in EMU more of a liability than an asset. The first, to be discussed in greater detail, was (at best) halting progress toward freeing up Italy's notoriously hidebound labor market, which undermined job creation even as EMU removed much-needed economic stimulus and monetary-policy flexibility from policymakers' toolbox. The second was the re-emergence of Berlusconi, whose re-election in 2001 began a decade of almost uninterrupted dominance that highlighted and reinforced the worst dysfunctions of the clientelist-liberal model and undermined Italy's ability to confront mounting economic challenges. If France's membership in EMU represented the acceptance of austerity for the sake of hoped-for influence, Italy's decision to join reflected a similar, if more defensive, desire to preserve its sovereignty from German economic dominance. Given Italy's weaker economic position, its bargain was even less realistic, reflecting a case of unrealized potential frustrated by a parochial but durable elite.[49] While France was disappointed by the character of its bargain, in other words, Italy's negative circumstances could be attributed to failures of leadership and submission to a model that operated at cross-purposes with its stated economic goals.

Berlusconi's return to power in 2001 came amidst a deteriorating global economic context that would exacerbate the dangers of his failure of leadership. Berlusconi's coalition, consisting of his erstwhile partners the Northern League and the post-fascist National Alliance, worked to capitalize on widespread hopes for a more decisive and effective government and a more "presidential" governing style capable of bold action to revitalize Italy's economy and tackle the country's crushing debt.[50] Berlusconi was able to exploit political divisions on the Left, which many Italians associated with the coddling of public-sector workers that had become one of the defining features of the clientelist-liberal model, even as he made "anti-communism" one of his key rhetorical strategies. As Michael Shin and John Agnew point out, the seeming anachronism of this approach made a certain sense in an Italian political context in which "communism" was a code word for left-wing clientelism. "The project of basing society on disinterested cooperation—the possibility of dissociating social contribution from individual rewards"—and the promise of governing by rules and laws rather than personal or institutional connections resonated with a large number of center-right voters, who blamed the Left's constituencies, particularly public-sector workers, for Italy's decline.[51] The appeal of such promises was reinforced by Italy's still moribund labor market (unemployment was 9.6 percent in 2001) and rates of growth (1.8 percent in 2001) that were far too sluggish to make a significant dent in the jobless rate or boost sorely needed tax revenue.[52]

Such hopes would soon be disappointed, however, as Berlusconi proved to be cut from the same clientelist cloth, if perhaps of a different hue, as were the corrupt leaders of the pre-1992 party state, as his brief stint in power in 1994 had suggested. Having established a wide network of political allies, some of whom were widely suspected of Mafia involvement, Berlusconi pursued a populist strategy that consisted of demonizing those who accused him of corruption as venal and self-serving even as he traded favors with powerful elites to protect his business interests and his hold on power, which were two sides of the same coin. Berlusconi's cozy relationship with Italian business was characterized by clientelistic protection rather than using business as a cudgel with which to promote market-based reforms, as he had initially promised. As one former Treasury official observed, Berlusconi had always made protecting business one of the central planks of his political strategy, with the insurance and real estate industries as particularly favored interlocutors.[53] His other favored constituencies were small businesses and the self-employed, whose widespread tax evasion Berlusconi refused to confront even as he focused his tax cuts on helping these groups adjust to the advent of EMU, undermining Italy's fiscal situation still further.[54] Despite investigations of his business dealings dating back to the 1970s and his membership in a number of secretive patronage networks, Berlusconi's lack of explicit political allegiances enabled him plausibly to claim the status of an outsider, even as "he was a protector of the status quo" who worked to shelter his core constituencies from the costs of adjustment.[55] He used his media dominance to curate his anti-establishment image in a country in which surveys showed that nearly half of the population derived their information exclusively from television and "two-thirds claimed never to read either a book or a newspaper."[56] This reliance on media both reflected and reinforced what Sergio Fabbrini has aptly labeled the "personalization of politics" in Italy since the 1990s.[57]

Within a couple of years, as it became clear that Berlusconi would do little to right the fiscal ship, Italy's earlier claims to have made meaningful progress toward meeting the Maastricht criteria came to seem exaggerated, if not entirely fabricated. In the early 2000s the Italian budget deficit had once again risen to 3.1 percent of GDP, though public debt had ostensibly declined to the slightly less alarming level of 106.9 percent of GDP.[58] Even these rather dismal figures came under criticism by observers who questioned the accuracy of official government statistics, leading to public conflicts between Italian officials and members of the European Commission over large differences between the figures released by the Bank of Italy and those from the Italian Treasury.[59] Such disputes hearkened back to the bickering between Italian and EU officials in the run-up to EMU in the late 1990s.[60] Italy having "finessed" its fiscal figures in an effort to qualify for EMU, its economic stagnation and the government's inability to enact meaningful reforms in the face of resistance by entrenched interest groups led to a growing perception of Italy as a country prone to distort statistics for political reasons.

Although the unceasing, trenchant opposition of insider groups was one source of Italian economic stagnation and continuing fiscal imbalances in the early years of EMU, the fecklessness of the political class in general and Berlusconi's governing coalition in particular were equally if not more responsible. The government did little to bolster a stagnant economy or to address the country's fiscal situation, with Berlusconi focusing increasingly on his own myriad judicial and legal problems, as well as those of many members of his coalition.[61] Although too numerous to count or chronicle here, Berlusconi's mounting charges of extortion, tax evasion, fraud, and embezzlement moved from the periphery of the Italian political arena (where they had remained for most of the 1990s), to its very center, creating an almost perpetual distraction from the process of responsible governance and diverting political authorities' attention from the country's festering economic problems and the crying need for reform. The most celebrated such episode, and the one that would eventually result in Berlusconi's expulsion from the Italian senate and his being barred in 2013 from holding public office, was the Mediaset trial, which began in 2005 and involved the indictment of Berlusconi and thirteen others for tax evasion, embezzlement, and fraud.[62] The charges were not limited to Berlusconi; dozens of members of his coalition confronted a wide array of charges, some dating back to *Mani Pulite* and even before.[63] Fiddling (and litigating) while Rome burned, the Italian governing class was ill equipped to confront Italy's mounting economic challenges.

Berlusconi thus represented a "missed liberal opportunity" as both an instrument and a beneficiary of the very system that he claimed to oppose.[64] In effect, his nearly exclusive focus on preserving his own power, protecting his political and economic clients, and frustrating the mounting legal investigations consumed all available political oxygen and displaced badly needed reforms from the government's agenda. Italy's economic growth, spurred in part by a global economic recovery and reawakened demand for Italian exports, recovered slightly to 2.0 percent in 2006. While unemployment declined to 6.8 percent in the same year, such halting progress occurred despite rather than because of governmental initiatives.[65]

Despite the hopeful sign of Berlusconi's 2006 defeat at the hands of Prodi's resuscitated Olive Tree coalition, the perverse dynamics of the clientelist-liberal model of self-serving elites, entrenched interests, and self-reinforcing cynicism about the state left the country very poorly situated to confront the post-2007 financial and economic crisis. By 2006 the global economic recovery from the recession of the early 2000s (helped along by what few observers yet realized were housing bubbles in many advanced industrial countries) had improved

Italian economic growth and helped reduce unemployment. At the same time, a decade after Italy's readmission to European monetary institutions on the promise of positive trajectories in fiscal policy, Italian debt was still a crushing 105.1 percent of GDP.[66] Worker productivity continued to decline, with the result that levels were lower than they had been in both 1973 and 1993.[67] Labor-market rigidities and wage levels misaligned with productivity continued to undermine Italian competitiveness, with the declines particularly sharp (and alarming, given their central role in the country's position in the international economy) among the celebrated industrial districts of the "Third Italy" in the center and north of the country.[68] A decade of political neglect and stagnation had exacerbated the Italian economy's weak spots (high levels of debt, distorted wage structures, and labor-market rigidities) while undermining its strengths (its capacity for producing high-quality goods for export markets and its artisanal production tradition). Although almost no one expected the post-2007 crisis, Italy was particularly poorly situated to respond to the challenges that it would pose.

Political Sclerosis and Technocratic Temptation: Clientelist Liberalism in the Wake of the Financial Crisis

Like its neighbors, Italy suffered significant economic reversals as a result of the crisis, as growth plummeted to a deeply recessionary low of –5.5 percent in 2009. Unemployment, which had been enjoying slight declines, rose modestly from 6.8 percent in 2006 to 7.8 percent in 2009. The country's budgetary context deteriorated, with annual deficits rising from 2.3 percent of GDP in 2006 to 4.9 percent in 2009 (to decline again to 3.4 percent in 2011) and gross public debt increasing to 117.1 percent of GDP in 2009 (to decline to 108.9 percent by 2011).[69] Although definitely a matter of concern, Italy's economic collapse was not as precipitous as that of many of its neighbors, with its short-term decline in GDP about the same as Germany's and its unemployment rate remaining below French levels. As had long been the case, Italy's public debt remained a significant preoccupation, but as Erik Jones points out, most of Italy's debt has traditionally been held by Italians, with the result that there was little risk that an entity beyond Italians' control would suddenly demand payment.[70] Furthermore, Italy had been running a primary surplus (outside of debt-service obligations, that is) for many years, amounting to about 3.5 percent of GDP in 2007.[71] Italy's current-account deficit, remaining at a modest 3.0 percent of GDP in 2009 and 4.2 percent in 2010, remained far below those of other southern peripheral European states (9.8 percent in Portugal and 11.8 percent in Greece in 2010).[72] Nevertheless, collapses in growth and demand elsewhere in the advanced industrial world constrained markets for critically important Italian exports, prompting fears among some officials.

Although the government did adopt some helpful measures after 2007, this response was "weak"[73] and ultimately inadequate to buffer the country from the effects of the crisis that had engulfed the world and would soon return to Europe in a regionally specific and at least partially self-inflicted guise. The entire stimulus effort amounted to a paltry 0.3 percent of GDP (compared to roughly 4 percent in Germany and 1.75 percent in France).[74] Of this total, 0.2 percent was allocated in 2009, with the remainder appropriated in 2010. To a significant extent, the Italian "stimulus" consisted of "essentially letting the automatic stabilizers operate."[75] The predictable result was continued deterioration of the Italian economy, labor markets, and fiscal balance: by 2012/13, unemployment climbed to 12.2 percent, real wages had declined by 2.5 percent, and public debt remained over 100 percent of GDP.[76] To make matters worse, Italian automatic stabilizers were weak, with total spending of 2.1 percent of GDP over the period 2008–10, less than the corresponding French (2.3 percent) or German (3.8 percent) figures.[77]

A robust fiscal response to the post-2007 crisis was important in Italy for two separate but related reasons. First, although the collapse in economic growth was not significantly greater than in many of its neighbors (including Germany), Italy's debt burden and its decades-long history of stagnation and sluggish growth placed it in a significantly weaker position, making the stimulation of domestic demand in the face of slack export markets more important. Second, unlike the cases of France and Germany, bond markets were quite nervous about Italy's debt load and creditworthiness, with spikes in yields threatening to create a self-reinforcing vicious circle of declining market confidence, increasing debt-service costs, and constraints on credit.[78] Italy's pivotal position within the euro, its history of indebtedness, and its shrinking domestic economy suggested the necessity of a significant fiscal stimulus focused on efforts (such as investments in infrastructure) to spur consumption and demand, combined with targeted labor-market deregulation and expanded income-support policies. Instead, Berlusconi's political fecklessness and his weakening political position led to his reluctant acceptance of an austerity budget in 2010, which Giulio Tremonti, his economics minister, lamely defended by declaring that "austerity has become the new ideology of Europe."[79]

In July 2011, spurred into action by spikes in Italian bond yields and generalizing fears that Italy would be the next domino in the spreading European debt crisis, the government took some small additional steps to stimulate growth and reduce labor-market protections, particularly those of public-sector workers. The first law included modest initiatives to promote investment, research, and employment in the *Mezzogiorno*, as well as reforms designed to simplify the public-procurement process as well as business taxes and regulations.[80] The second measure, which focused on "stabilization," froze salaries in the public sector (thereby further depressing demand) and imposed some restrictions on public-sector benefits and modest cuts in payrolls.[81] Inadequate and incoherent in equal measure, these two laws neither addressed the collapse in domestic demand nor accomplished meaningful labor-market reform that might have spurred private-sector hiring and put Italy on the road to economic recovery.

Italy's essential inaction in the face of crisis stemmed from the same dysfunctions of the clientelist-liberal model that had undermined Italian economic performance since the 1970s and protected insiders conspiring with elites to preserve the status quo, as outsiders—particularly the growing segment of long-term unemployed—struggled to break into the fossilized labor market and system of public administration. As neoliberals such as Alberto Alesina and Silvia Ardagna continued to argue that fiscal contraction could have positive effects on growth and that Italy's main problem was public debt and the clientelism that underpinned it,[82] the Italian government adopted a strategy that produced none of the positive effects that either a strategy of "structural adjustment" or one of robust fiscal expansion might have produced. Instead, held captive by entrenched interest groups (including public-sector employees eager to preserve their jobs and privileges, SMEs unwilling to accept a rationalization of a porous taxation system, and private-sector workers who benefited from strict job protections), the Italian government closed ranks and opted for inaction.[83] As Vito Tanzi, a former undersecretary for economy and finance, put it, "there was simply little understanding of the need for reform."[84]

If the financial crisis and recession failed to spur the government either to move to stimulate demand or to impose budgetary cuts on entrenched interests, renewed spikes in Italian bond yields and pressure from European officials increasingly concerned about speculative contagion and the fragility of the euro prompted action, though in the guise of a series of counterproductive budget cuts that further undermined domestic demand and Italy's potential for growth. In May 2010 the government adopted a budget that contained €24 billion in spending cuts after several years of claiming that the crisis had not seriously affected Italy and that the country was doing better than many of its neighbors. This measure, designed almost exclusively to calm bond markets and to save Italy from becoming the next Greece, centered on a four-year freeze in public-sector salaries and a significant cut in transfers to regional and local governments. Significantly, the measure avoided tax increases on the wealthy and small businesses, core pieces of Berlusconi's political coalition. According to Tito Boeri, an economics professor at Bocconi University, even the cut in transfers was less than met the eye, since "without strict controls on local-authority borrowing, the budget may just shift the generation of new debt from the centre to the periphery."[85] Furthermore, few of the cuts did anything to increase competitiveness or to boost the economy's productive potential, since doing so "would have meant defying the vested producer interests that give Mr. Berlusconi much of his support."[86] At the same time, the fact that the unexpected cuts ran against long-standing assurances that Italy had been spared the worst effects of the crisis, combined with the fact that many of the cuts targeted public-sector workers, imbued them with a symbolic significance suggesting that Italy had abandoned its responsibilities. Over the next year, voter anger led to significant declines in the government's approval ratings and, by mid-2011, mounting protests by public-sector workers, culminating in a demonstration of three million people across several cities in September 2011 in response to €45 billion in proposed budget cuts.[87] Such protests reflected both prevailing economic exigencies and deep distrust of the state that had been exacerbated by more than a decade of Berlusconi's rule.[88]

In November 2011, following his government's loss of a procedural vote in parliament and with his popularity plummeting, Berlusconi resigned. His resignation was met with jubilant demonstrations in the street by Italians angered by his government's turn to austerity and the increasing embarrassment of a man that a growing number of Italians viewed as an ineffectual buffoon.[89] Berlusconi was replaced by a caretaker government of technocrats led by Mario Monti, which was to govern until the next elections (slated for early 2013) and assigned the task of breaking the clientelistic logjam that, under previous administrations, had prevented the kind of deep spending cuts demanded by bond traders and international agents of neoclassical orthodoxy. According to Jonathan Hopkin, "the Monti government . . . represented a doomed attempt by the Troika[90] to impose its preferred policies by legislative fiat, bypassing the normal democratic channel of interparty competition for power."[91] No one could better have embodied either the prevailing European austerity-based orthodoxy or the dynamics of Italian clientelistic liberalism than Monti. An economics professor, president of Bocconi University, and an adviser to Goldman Sachs,[92] Monti was as strongly supported by the international financial community as he was mistrusted by most Italians. His embrace of neoliberalism and his promises to attack many of the privileges that Italians held dear were both encouraged and made possible by the fact that he remained outside the established political system.

In December 2011 the Monti government adopted a more radical austerity package than any considered by previous administrations of either Left or Right. It represented a broadly based attack on many sacred Italian cows, targeting privileged groups in a way that no democratically elected government operating within existing Italian political institutions could plausibly have done. Assuming the roles of prime minister and minister of finance, Monti pushed through the package by emergency decree, meaning that it would take effect before parliament could vote on it. It proposed raising the standard retirement age from sixty to sixty-two for women and from sixty-five to sixty-six for men, with financial incentives to encourage people to continue working until age seventy. It also raised the rate of VAT from 21 to 23 percent, reintroduced a property tax abolished by Berlusconi in 2008, and focused €12–13 billion in spending cuts on regional authorities, long a conduit for corruption and patronage. In an effort to combat tax evasion, something of an Italian national pastime, the measure prohibited cash transactions of more than €1,000.[93] Supported by the center-left Democratic Party (PD)[94] as a regrettable necessity, the package was portrayed as a crisis-driven effort to "save Italy," which continued to confront rising bond yields and a growing fear among its European partners that a full-blown crisis in Italy could become the proverbial straw that broke the euro's back.[95] In the face of such broadly based (if ultimately thin) interparty consensus, the protests of Italy's trade unions, led by the Confederazione Generale Italiana del Lavoro (CGIL), were voices in the wilderness. According to an Italian Treasury official who had previously worked for the IMF, such front-loaded and aggressive austerity measures proved counterproductive and were largely responsible for driving Italy into a recession that increased both economic precariousness and national debt as a percentage of GDP.[96] After modest growth in 2011, Italian GDP shrank by 2.4 percent in 2012 and 1.9 percent in 2013, despite an accelerating international economic recovery. Unemployment spiked from 8.4 percent in 2011 to 12.2 percent in 2012 and 12.6 percent in 2013, and net public debt soared to 127 percent of GDP in 2012 and a record 130.4 percent in 2013.[97]

Monti's technocratic strategy reflected a miscalculation, leading to the government's failure to accomplish much of the substance of his planned reforms while alienating large segments of the Italian public and undermining the parliamentary support on which the effectiveness and legitimacy of any technocratic government crucially depends.[98] Following Monti's defeat in 2013, largely as a result of backlash against his government's austerity agenda, a potential alternative emerged in the form of Matteo Renzi, the charismatic former mayor of Florence whom many saw as a potential savior capable of providing a way out of Italy's clientelistic morass. In the 2013 elections the PD, which had moved from support for the Monti administration to acting as its primary parliamentary opponent in the run-up to the vote, failed to win an overall majority, forcing it to cobble together a center-left coalition to form a government.[99] Renzi, the leader of the party's moderate wing, however, used this disappointing result to launch an internal coup, taking over the party's leadership and ultimately the office of prime minister and leading the party to an improved showing of 40 percent of votes cast in the 2014 European Parliamentary elections.[100] Hearkening back to the center-left administrations of Romano Prodi in the 1990s and 2000s, Renzi's government began to take on many of the sacred cows of the

Left, accomplishing significant reforms of labor-market policy over the strong objections of unions and public-sector workers. Despite the government's leftist hue, financial markets expressed the same real, if tentative, hopes of many in the Italian public, as Moody's boosted Italy's sovereign credit rating and Italian bond yields fell to their lowest level in eight years after Renzi was asked to form a government.[101]

Less than a month after his government assumed power, Renzi launched a number of initiatives that suggested that he was cast from a somewhat different mold than traditional elites. Renzi was viewed as a young, untainted outsider able "to shake up Italy's sclerotic system and overcome entrenched interests, including in his own center-left Democratic Party and the powerful labor unions that have long been a base of support."[102] Even as he promised to take on vested economic interests, Renzi adopted a rhetoric that suggested he was willing to challenge European austerity orthodoxy, although he faced the same structural constraints faced by his predecessors. In October 2014 Renzi announced €18 billion in tax cuts and €4.7 billion in extra spending and, in late 2015, announced a plan to invest €24 billion in infrastructure and €15 billion in local and regional government administration, aimed at fostering growth in Italy's troubled South.[103] Facing mounting pressure from European officials and a level of public debt that by 2015 had ballooned to 158 percent of GDP,[104] the government nevertheless continued to work to boost growth with a 2016 budget that contained almost €33 billion in tax cuts (on primary property taxes, municipal services, and tax credits for companies buying new machinery). In October 2016 the proposed Italian budget for 2017 included some spending cuts, but also increases in pensions for low-income beneficiaries (less than €1,000 a month), a corporate tax cut, and an increased deficit target of 2.4 percent of GDP, which drew the ire of the European Commission.[105] Ultimately the 2017 budget adopted a deficit goal of 2.3 percent of GDP (up from the 1.8 percent previously agreed upon). Following Renzi's resignation in December 2016, however, after the defeat of a referendum on parliamentary reform on which he had staked his political career, efforts to bolster growth came to seem unlikely, even if growing populist backlash offered some hope for renewed fiscal activism.

Sacred Cows and Sisyphean Tasks: Reforming the Italian Labor Market

In the aftermath of *Mani Pulite* and the advent of the Maastricht Treaty, Italian authorities struggled to reform Italy's notoriously sclerotic labor market, in which high non-wage labor costs and strict rules on layoffs for all but the smallest companies had impeded job growth and led to one of the highest unemployment rates in western Europe.[106] Faced with the restrictions on fiscal expansion deriving from EMU's Stability and Growth Pact, Italian governments of both Left and Right during the 1990s worked to loosen job protections and collective-bargaining rules, increase worker productivity, and reduce non-wage labor costs in the hopes of addressing an unemployment rate that by 1995 exceeded 11 percent.[107] Following the abandonment of the *Scala mobile* in the 1980s, new collective-bargaining rules limited wage increases in national contracts (which predominantly affected public-sector workers and state-dominated large concerns such as Fiat) to maintaining workers' purchasing power, with the distribution of the proceeds from productivity increases left to individual firms on a non-compulsory basis.[108] In liberalizing and decentralizing labor relations in this way, policymakers hoped to reduce impediments to job creation and to lessen inflationary pressures by dampening wage growth while also increasing the use of such flexible labor agreements as fixed- and part-time contracts.[109]

They clearly had their work cut out for them. Despite the export-based success of the Third Italy of northern industrial districts, the broader Italian labor market suffered from a number of structural weaknesses that were growing worse over time.[110] Rising unemployment reflected the country's low rate of labor-market participation, about 10 percent below the EU average. This problem was magnified by equally poor productivity growth, which in some years was close to zero and limited firms' incentives to hire additional workers.[111] Underlying these macro-level problems were a number of structural dysfunctions, including a labor-market participation rate for women that was even lower than for men, and rigidities, including restrictions on economically motivated layoffs,[112] which made firms reluctant to hire younger workers and led to one of the lowest participation rates in the EU for workers aged fifteen to twenty-four.[113] Stark regional discrepancies meant that these problems were much worse in the southern half of the country, negating positive trends of participation and productivity in parts of the more developed North. The Italian labor market thus suffered from a vicious circle of low productivity, low labor-market participation rates, slack demand, and slowing economic growth, problems much exacerbated by the anti-growth strictures of the Maastricht Treaty.

Remedies for these dysfunctions were elusive, given an endemic pattern of slowing growth since the 1980s[114] and the mutually reinforcing negative effects of slow productivity growth and stagnant wages, employment, and aggregate demand.[115] This dynamic meant in practice that both workers and firms focused on defending past gains rather than negotiating mutually acceptable reforms, with sharp divisions between the relatively sheltered public sector and private-sector firms more exposed to international competition but struggling under multiple layers of regulations. As one former Treasury official described the imprint, the prevailing view of the labor market since the 1970s has been "dualism" between employees in large, mostly public concerns, who "depend on the state for support," and those in the private sector, "who want mostly to be left alone."[116] In such a climate the cooperation between firms and workers required for effective labor-market adjustment is elusive. A former IMF official and undersecretary for economy and finance was more blunt: "Italy has no real labor market, as economists define that market."[117]

These structural weaknesses were both symptoms and reinforcing causes of the clientelist character of Italian liberalism. Historical patterns of distrust between workers and employers and between both groups and the state had fostered a climate in which reform battles were viewed as zero-sum contests over protecting vested interests rather than opportunities for mutually beneficial compromise. In contrast to Germany in the late 1990s, where the state clearly supported favored insiders and imposed costs on unincorporated outsiders, in Italy the toxic legacies of the Hot Autumn and the dysfunctional policy responses to it had led both employers and workers and their organized representatives to place protecting their *droits acquis* above all else. Operating within this analytical framework, workers feared that any meaningful reform would end their protected status and lead to their becoming labor-market outsiders. Firms were reluctant to invest in innovation and expansion, given slack aggregate demand and weak state support for innovation that might help convert firm investments into productivity and profits.[118] As a result, liberalization of labor-market rules tended to lead to modest increases in precarious employment, such as part- and fixed-time contracts, rather than to the creation of permanent positions, while slow growth and slack demand dampened the potential contributions of these trends to reducing the overall unemployment rate, which by 1995 had reached 11.2 percent.[119]

Beginning in the mid-1990s, a series of Italian governments introduced a series of reforms designed to address these structural weakness of the labor market and associated dysfunctions in the system of social protection. In 1995, for example, the caretaker government of Lamberto Dini introduced a modest reform of the pension system designed to reduce non-wage labor costs and spur job creation, which passed largely due to the shared desire by both Left and Right to rejoin the EMS. Despite the political perils of pension reform, a rock on which previous governments had continually run aground, this measure, passed in the shadow of estimates that Italy's pension obligations amounted to up to six times GDP, or twice the EU average, replaced an entirely income-based system with a contributory system, though one that was still operated on a pay-as-you-go basis.[120] It reconciled some of the differences in rules between the public and private systems, tightened conditions for so-called seniority pensions (paid to workers reaching a certain age irrespective of length of contributions), and created a link between a worker's total contributions and the size of his or her benefit.[121] This reform established a sounder actuarial basis for the system and promised to reduce the long-term ratio of obligations to GDP,[122] despite stiff resistance from unions that forced the government to implement the measure over a longer time horizon. Following its adoption Dini observed laconically that it was "the maximum we could exact from this country at this time."[123] In a pattern that would be repeated in the subsequent decade, technocratic outsiders with few clientelistic links to established interests used their independence to push through a modest and isolated reform of cherished benefits.

A more significant measure was passed by the government of the Olive Tree coalition of Romano Prodi in 1997, in response to the failure of previous reforms to achieve a significant decrease in unemployment, which remained well above the EU average, with long-term joblessness topping 65 percent of total unemployment.[124] Prodi's goal was to reduce joblessness by altering the rules for labor-market entry and fostering the development of flexible labor-market contracts. Much like his counterpart Gerhard Schröder in Germany a few years later, Prodi hoped to use his credibility with unions and public-sector workers to liberalize the Italian labor market and reduce strains on an already overburdened Italian fisc in ways that the political Right might well have been unable to achieve. Unlike Schröder, however, Prodi confronted a much less productive labor market (Italian labor productivity rates were among the lowest among major European economies)[125] and an employment system dominated by unions much less willing than their German counterparts to countenance any meaningful change in labor-market rules or to negotiate with the government in the hope of mutually beneficial outcomes. As a result, the government was reluctant to attempt any ambitious changes to the rules governing traditional labor contracts held by public-sector workers and employees in large industrial concerns, focusing instead on loosening rules for atypical employment and bolstering active labor-market policies aimed at traditionally disadvantaged groups such as younger workers. Dubbed the Treu Package (formally, Measures for the Promotion of Employment), the law introduced "temporary agency work" contracts and liberalized some of the rules on atypical employment, expanded active labor-market policies aimed at the reinsertion of younger workers, and allowed the creation of private temporary-work agencies to coexist with the formerly monopolistic public agencies.[126] These modest measures were extended by the second Olive Tree coalition elected in October 1998, under the leadership of Prime Minister Massimo D'Alema, which hashed out a bargain with major industrialists and trade unions that produced a budget that cut taxes and social security contributions paid by firms, pledged over $900 million to stepped-up job-training schemes, and reduced some bureaucratic burdens on firms.[127] In this instance, a government of the Left was able to secure support for reform by its core labor constituency only by softening the impact of the reform through bolstering job training and only under the threat of failing to meet requirements for joining EMU, which both labor and capital broadly favored.

Berlusconi's mixed record in reforming Italian employment relations following his return to power in 2001 did little to address the deep structural dysfunctions of the Italian labor market. At the same time, his government's measures threw into stark relief the deep divisions in Italian politics and society that would become even more formidable impediments to reform as Berlusconi's power and political credibility waned over the coming decade. In March 2002 the government proposed a measure aiming to liberalize laws that made dismissing workers in any but the smallest firms very difficult, in the hope of encouraging firms to create new jobs. This law, more ambitious than those of the government's leftist predecessors, envisioned opening regular (as opposed to temporary) job-placement services to private firms, proposed new forms of short-term and flexible job contracts, liberalized rules on outsourcing and part time work, and reformed training services so as to make them more responsive to shifts in labor-market demand.[128] The proposal elicited massive protests by trade unions and their supporters, bringing over a million people into the streets in Rome amid claims by protestors that Berlusconi was attempting to "cut every right of workers" and shift Italy to a low-road competitive strategy. The reform, named the Biagi Law after an assassinated Labor Ministry official who had drafted it, was signed into law in July over the continued strong objections of the unions.[129]

In the same deregulatory vein, the government sought to decentralize collective bargaining to the firm level and introduce some modest reforms of the Italian pension system. Berlusconi saw the first measure through by dividing the Left, obtaining the reluctant support of centrist unions Unione Italiana del Lavoro (UIL) and Confederazione Italiana Sindacati Lavoratori (CSIL) despite the strong objections of the left-wing CGIL. Confindustria, the largest employers' association, agreed to support the measure, in large part due to a 2001 change in leadership that replaced a representative of large industrial concerns with one representing SMEs, which were less politically connected and more supportive of decentralized industrial relations.[130] In October 2003, despite campaign promises to the contrary, Berlusconi floated the idea of raising the required pension contribution period from thirty-five to forty years, revisiting the issue that had helped to bring down his government in 1994, in the hope of reducing the 14 percent of GDP that the country spent on pensions (this idea was eventually shelved in the face of massive strikes).[131] In its place, in 2004, the government adopted a more modest measure (the so-called *scalone*, or "big step") that gradually increased the retirement age to sixty and required thirty-five years of contributions for full benefits, though it delayed implementation until 2008, well after the 2006 election, in order to secure parliamentary approval.[132] Such moves seemed to confirm Berlusconi's stated commitment to breathe new life into the Italian economy by confronting Italy's clientelist landscape, which was "a wild forest of little privileges, rents and enclosures" in which "each has its own lobby group," which "together . . . conspire to make reform close to impossible."[133] At the same time, even a reformist administration of the political Right was forced to limit the scope of its reforms, which were quite modest in comparison to measures in other advanced countries and represented at best halting and uneven progress that did little to remedy the structural dysfunctions of the Italian labor market.

The modesty of the reforms under the Olive Tree governments of the 1990s and Berlusconi's post-2001 administration and the political challenges that underlay them were reflected in continued poor macroeconomic and labor-market performance in the first half of the 2000s. In the hope of preserving social peace, strategies of wage moderation, previously agreed to by the social partners, were relaxed significantly, further undermining Italian competitiveness and exacerbating the problematic legacies of the Hot Autumn of 1969. Berlusconi had cooperated with industrialists in decentralizing collective bargaining in key industries, a move which however undermined small firms' ability to resist wage increases in line with productivity gains.[134] Even as wage pressures undermined competitiveness and profitability, net increases in population (largely the result of immigration), combined with near stagnation in an economy that grew by a yearly average of just 0.25 percent in the early-to-mid-2000s, meant that per-capita income and real wages actually shrank (placing Italy at a rank of 167 out of 179 countries in GDP per capita for the first decade of the twenty-first century).[135] Partly as a result, by 2003 Italian economic growth was a barely measurable 0.2 percent and unemployment remained stubbornly high at 8.9 percent.[136] Though the subsequent worldwide economic recovery was reflected in improving growth and jobless numbers in the following few years (GDP growth rose to 2 percent in 2006, and unemployment bottomed out at a bit over 6 percent in the same year),[137] such progress would be uneven and often short lived.

A qualified departure from the pattern of Italian clientelistic stagnation in labor-market policy came in 2007 with a measure introduced by the resuscitated center-left Olive Tree coalition under Prodi. As Lucio Baccaro explains, this reform of pensions and fiscal incentives for firms was made possible by a social pact among the government and union and business leaders that entailed significant trade-offs between capital and labor and succeeded only as a result of a massive mobilizational effort by union elites in exchange for major concessions, leading to a referendum that "proved a powerful legitimating force for the three [union] confederations."[138] Concessions to the Left included the abolition of the *scalone* from the 2004 reform and the reform of the Biagi Law, involving limits on fixed-term contracts, among other measures favored by the unions, along with a strengthening of unemployment insurance. Major business interests, in particular Confindustria, achieved a long-demanded decontribution of overtime. This "mix of retrenchment and expansion" represented a partial exception to the clientelist-liberal pattern of zero-sum competition among interests and internecine battles between the state and interest groups, but it was achieved only through lengthy and cautious (and separate) negotiations both with the social partners and among the members of the governing coalition. Initially opposed by the union rank and file and leftist members of the governing coalition, the reform's success was partially attributable to its reframing as one that would secure the pension system's future solvency and reduce the precariousness of the jobs on which pension eligibility was based and as an outgrowth of a robust democratic process that fully consulted unions' rank and file. This framing shifted an estimated 14 percent of union votes from opposition to support in the referendum and led to its ultimate adoption by the government.[139] At the same time, the trade-offs involved in the pact's negotiation represented at best partial liberalization and, in some areas, an actual increase in labor-market rigidities.

The labor-market reform undertaken by Monti's technocratic government in 2012 bore the same neoliberal, technocratic imprint as his fiscal-policy initiatives and met with similarly disappointing results. In March, with the backing of the country's three largest parliamentary groups, the government entered into negotiations with employers' associations and unions over a slate of proposed reforms, including measures that would make it easier for firms with more than fifteen employees (the previous strict threshold) to dismiss workers for economic reasons (albeit with twenty-seven months' severance pay); the introduction of a more broadly based, less strictly contributory unemployment benefit; and moves to encourage more apprenticeships for younger workers. It also proposed a significant pension reform, the so-called Fornero Reform (named after the then-labor minister), which modestly increased both the retirement age and required contribution periods for some workers. Completely unconsulted on the measure, unions objected strongly to the liberalization of job protections and changes to the pension system, while employers resisted the apprenticeship measures, which were designed in part to discourage the use of temporary contracts. Met with resistance by unions and employers alike, Monti simply abandoned negotiations and vowed to press ahead over the social partners' objections.[140]

After months of wrangling, in June, parliament passed a much-watered down measure that scaled back the reform of employment protections while making firms' recourse to temporary workers more costly. This made no one happy, as unions lamented the loosening of job rules while employers argued that the reform did little to make hiring and firing easier. In the words of one official in Confindustria, "There is no evidence that companies are firing more under the new rules. It just isn't happening."[141] Monti's attempt to break Italy's clientelistic blockade not only failed to accomplish its goals; it ultimately led to the defection of the PD from his parliamentary majority and the collapse of his electoral support in the spring 2013 elections, in which Monti's so-called centrist coalition won a scant 10.5 percent of the vote.

From Savior to Scapegoat: Matteo Renzi and the Failed Promise of the Jobs Act

The voters' repudiation of technocratic administration, which was undemocratic and ineffective in equal measure, opened up "a political space for alternative political forces opposed to both the austerity measures and to entrenched political elites."[142] For many, Matteo Renzi seemed to represent just such an alternative force, and it was both appropriate and symbolically significant that his government made reforming the labor market a central plank of its agenda. The most controversial measure—and the one that suggested he was willing to take on the same entrenched interests that had undermined the initiatives of previous governments of both Left and Right—was the so-called Jobs Act. Consisting of a number of separate proposals, the act aimed to loosen job protections in the hope of spurring the hiring of younger workers, 43 percent of whom were without jobs, while those that were employed usually had part-time or temporary contracts with few if any benefits, in contrast to the ample salaries and generous pensions of protected insiders.[143] The law also created a new standard for open-ended contracts—the so-called *Contratto a tutele crescenti*, which altered Article 18 of the Italian labor statute, adopted in 1970 in the aftermath of the Hot Autumn. That article allowed workers laid off for economic reasons recourse to the courts to win their jobs back and served as a strong disincentive for firms to dismiss them. Under Renzi's proposal, which aimed to narrow the divide between older workers with traditional jobs and their younger counterparts who enjoyed few protections against dismissal, workers fired for economic reasons could seek financial compensation but would lose the right to regain their jobs absent proof that their dismissal had resulted from discrimination. The measure also allowed for the electronic monitoring of workers in the workplace, ended the previous right to permanent employment if the term of a temporary contract was exceeded, and, in a connected provision in the 2015 budget, introduced an exemption of €8,060 per year in firms' social security contributions for each new permanent job.[144]

The measure elicited strong protests by workers and unions throughout 2014, with one CGIL leader claiming that Renzi "has chosen to represent entrepreneurs, and the employers, not the workers."[145] This statement reflected widespread resentment, particularly among public-sector union members, of the reduction in employers' charges alone and fears that regulatory changes governing dismissals would create widespread labor-market precariousness among workers that had long enjoyed some of the strongest protections in Europe.[146] Renzi achieved the passage of one of the most ambitious labor-market reforms since *Mani Pulite,* not by securing a broad societal coalition in support of it, but rather through a clever, *ad hoc,* and multi-dimensional strategy that successfully accounted for many of the political perils endemic to Italy's clientelistic landscape, supported by idiosyncratic factors unique to the existing political context. First, he focused on younger workers, effectively dividing the Left and portraying older, established employees as parasitic and parochial. Tommaso Giuntella, president of the PD's office in Rome, encapsulated this tack: "There is a huge conflict between generations. Renzi knows it and started being the face of the new generation, the generation of the sons. We cannot permit the son to pay for the privileges of the father."[147] Second, Renzi's youth (at forty-one, he was the youngest Italian prime minister in history) and status as a relative novice (his highest position prior to assuming the premiership was mayor of Florence) allowed him plausibly to position himself as an outsider in a way that Berlusconi and even Prodi could not, a posture of particular symbolic importance in the context of efforts to reform Italy's heavily dualistic labor market. Third and crucially, he vocally resisted the European austerity orthodoxy, positioning himself as a business-friendly pragmatist who rejected austerity on the very practical grounds that it did not work rather than as an ideological reflex. This position, which he assumed even as he nimbly cultivated the friendship of Italianophile Angela Merkel, gave him credibility on the Left that a technocrat like Monti never enjoyed. In this vein Renzi worked to redefine the Italian Left, distancing it from its clientelistic history and using his opposition to the austerity prescribed by Germany and the ECB as a cure-all for Europe's economic ills, as an effective foil. In an interview, Renzi was explicit about both the employment focus and the generational logic of his legislative agenda: "What is the identity in Italy of the left? It is to give more rights to young people, give possibilities to a new generation. We had, in Italy, a work apartheid. The Jobs Act is the most leftist thing I've done."[148] In language redolent of the clientelist-liberal tradition's conception of politics as a zero-sum competition between entrenched groups, one senior official of the CGIL union had a much darker take on the reform: "[Renzi] has chosen to represent entrepreneurs and the employers, not the workers. He has broken with the traditions of the Democratic left."[149] Though constituting a clear departure from previous trends of stagnation and uneven progress in Italian labor-market policy, the results of the Jobs Act have been mixed and reflect continued impediments to job creation and unresolved dysfunctions in the Italian labor market. As discussed, the two long-standing central problems in the Italian employment landscape have been low productivity growth and low rates of labor-market participation against a backdrop of slack aggregate demand and slow growth. During the 1990s and early 2000s, these interconnected problems led to the expansion of various forms of precarious employment rather than the sustained creation of permanent positions. Though the recent passage of the Jobs Act means that any evaluation of its effects must remain tentative, the data so far suggest that these problems continue to undermine Italian labor-market performance. According to data from the Italian National Statistics Institute and the Ministry of Labor, in the first six months of 2015 only 20 percent of new hires were permanent, and most of those involved the conversion of previously temporary contracts rather than the creation of new positions. Moreover, even among new permanent contracts, 65 percent were for part-time work, and new hires under the new open-ended contract are earning somewhat lower wages than their traditional counterparts. Finally, about 90 percent of new permanent contracts created resulted from the Budgetary Law's provision that defrayed firms' social security contributions rather than the new-contract provisions themselves. As a result, Italy continues to suffer from rates of transition from joblessness to employment that are well below the EU average.[150] Perhaps the most fundamental and visible indicator of the act's limited effects is the endurance of high rates of unemployment, which remained at 11.7 percent in September 2016, barely a point lower than the rate in December 2014 (12.9 percent), just before the law took effect. In May 2017, it remained at 11.3 percent.[151]

Even Renzi's modest success clearly represents the exception rather than the rule for Italian labor-market reform over the past two decades. Since the mid-1990s, policymakers of both Left and Right have struggled to revitalize the labor market in ways that would produce durable reductions in unemployment and increase rates of labor-market participation. These goals have proven elusive, in large measure because few reforms have successfully tackled the fundamental dysfunctions of the Italian employment landscape that the legacies of the clientelist-liberal tradition have produced. Very low productivity growth, tight restrictions on labor-market mobility, sluggish economic growth, and major regional discrepancies in levels of economic development have been both symptoms and reinforcing causes of a labor market that is quite effective in protecting the positions of labor-market insiders but very poor at creating jobs, particularly for outsider groups such as women and the young. The historical dominance of public-sector workers and their union representatives, coupled with the state's deep involvement in the Italian economy's industrial core, has produced a dynamic whereby any significant attempt at reform has been fiercely resisted by Italian workers, who fear the erosion of their privileges and relegation to the status of unprotected outsiders, a status from which it is very difficult to escape. With so much at stake there is little room for compromise or negotiated solutions, with the result that reform proposals are generally interpreted as existential threats to workers' status, in contrast to the German unions' and employers' agreement to wage moderation in exchange for the protection of skilled positions. This zero-sum climate, in which acquired rights are viewed as sacred cows, has often precluded meaningful reform or resulted in the significant dilution of proposals prior to passage. The few episodes of successful reform, such as Prodi's 2007 measures and Renzi's Jobs Act, have required deft navigation of a perilous political landscape. Moreover, even relatively ambitious reforms like the Jobs Act have failed to address many of the labor market's structural problems, a task that would require systematic recalibrations of the rules and incentives governing traditional, full-time positions. All of this has been exacerbated by a climate of elective austerity within the Eurozone and the deflationary economic climate that it has produced, as well as deep dysfunctions in the Italian financial system, which is the subject of the next section.

Public Banks, Private Goods: Clientelist Liberalism and Instability in Italian Finance

Supported by the Italian state's deep involvement during the post-*Risorgimento* period, the Italian banking system acted as a handmaiden to Italian economic development. The system was modeled after Germany's three-pillared framework, with an important division between commercial and cooperative banks.[152] In the late nineteenth century and under Mussolini, who nationalized many major Italian banks (many of which remained in state hands until the 1990s), the state operated in Gerschenkronian fashion by directly providing finance to large, strategically important industrial concerns like Fiat, Pirelli, and Olivetti through conglomerates like the IRI. This meant that "the ordinary run of Italian business . . . was hard put to it to lay hands on the risk capital that it needed for expansion. It became heavily dependent on the goodwill of the banks, and the banks in turn, operating on too narrow a base of financial resources, looked for support to the public authorities."[153] Both the clientelistic structure of Italian finance and the state's deep involvement in the financial sector thus had their roots in the uneven pattern of late industrialization.

The structure of the Italian financial system reflects the subordination of banks' autonomy to national developmental imperatives. The cooperative banking sector has traditionally been subdivided between the smaller Banche di Credito Cooperativo (BCCs) and the larger Banche Popolari (BPs), with a further subdivision between public long-term (Istituti di Credito Speciale) and short-term credit institutions (Istituti di Credito Ordinario). The system also traditionally featured a number of regional development banks owned at least in part by the state.[154] More or less analogous to American credit unions, BCCs have a mandate to extend credit primarily to their own members within a geographically defined area, with a relatively limited imprint on the Italian economy. The Popolari, by contrast, like German Landesbanken, have long played an instrumental role in supporting industrialization and economic development, particularly through their instrumental role in providing finance to SMEs. Furthermore, although BPs are required to reserve only 10 percent of their profits, as opposed to 70 percent for BCCs, the Popolari have maintained a much more conservative approach to banking than their German counterparts. As with public banks in Germany, however, reforms of these institutions must confront long-standing and powerful vested interests, stemming from their deep connections to regionally concentrated and politically powerful SMEs and a national perception of cooperative banks as economically strategic institutions.

As a result of its clientelistic linkages with SMEs, the banking system in Italy has long been characterized by low profitability and high fragmentation, features that are particularly characteristic of the nation's cooperative banks, in which high costs and low profits stem from robust competition among a large number of branches. Given the large number of banking institutions in Italy, interest rates for deposits must be high to maintain customers' business; these high interest rates are then passed on to borrowers. Taxes and labor regulations discourage Italian firms from becoming large, so that local and regional banks serve their interests better than large commercial banks.[155] Further reinforcing this link between firms and the financial system is the presence of underdeveloped stock and corporate-bond markets, which have historically made SMEs all the more reliant on non-commercial banks for financing. In short, the Italian banking system reflects a high degree of fragmentation and deep local connections to Italian firms even as it has somewhat paradoxically developed as an instrument of state support of a long-standing pattern of regionally concentrated development of SMEs.

In the early 1990s, as EMU loomed and Italian authorities sought to make the financial system competitive with those of its European counterparts, officials introduced a number of measures designed to reduce the number of branches, whose proliferation served domestic businesses at the expense of profitability. In the 1990s, Italian governments sought to foster a series of mergers and programs of banking consolidation. After the passage of the 1988 Exchange Control Act, which significantly liberalized rules on foreign exchange in anticipation of EMU, capital movements steadily increased in Italian financial institutions.[156] The impetus for Italian policymakers to pursue reforms lay primarily with concerns over the ability of Italy's highly regulated financial system to compete in an increasingly integrated Europe. At the same time, the financial crises of the early 1990s, particularly Italy's temporary ejection from the EMS, demonstrated the need for a more competitive banking sector as well as the vulnerability of the Italian financial system to exchange rate fluctuations.

Beginning with the 1990 Amato Law, officials began a long series of efforts to modify the highly clientelistic and regionally focused Italian banking system in ways that would enable it to adjust to EMU and the completion of the single European market. The law began the process of privatization by changing public credit institutions into joint-stock companies.[157] Previously, Italian savings banks functioned to serve the public at the expense of efficiency and profits, with a conflation of the objectives of serving the public interest and profit seeking. This reform separated these roles by forcing the savings banks to create a private foundation to pursue their public interests while maintaining a separate entity for traditional lending practices.[158] By the end of 1992, the eighty-three savings banks that had altered their structure in this way were nominally privatized, albeit with the preservation of important levers of state influence. Nonetheless, many of the newly created foundations maintained shareholder power over the savings banks in ways that preserved historic linkages between regional firms and the financial institutions that served them.

The 1990s witnessed further attempts, prompted by the Maastricht Treaty, to systematize Italian financial regulation and to limit the inefficiencies deriving from continued state dominance. In 1993, in the immediate aftermath of the *Mani Pulite* scandal, the government passed the Consolidated Law on Banking, which ended all forms of banking specialization and paved the way for universal banking.[159] In 1998 the so-called Ciampi Law mandated the sale of all private-law foundations by June 2003 in the hopes of breaking the linkages between private foundations (established by the Amato Law) and bank companies. Despite policymakers' evident ambitions to rationalize the Italian financial system, the results of such measures were modest at best. Between 1990 and 1998, privatization largely occurred in only technical terms, impeded by continued interference on the part of officials seeking to preserve linkages between the state and finance in the furtherance of both developmental and clientelistic imperatives. The Ciampi Law did result in some progress, limiting the foundations' control over the savings banks and encouraging further privatization and consolidation.[160] In other cases, however, the link between public savings banks and private foundations was preserved through sale of the banks to subsidiaries or holding companies controlled by the banks themselves.

Following these reforms, the late 1990s and early 2000s witnessed a number of mergers and acquisitions involving major banking groups, supported by renewed state initiatives designed to harmonize the Italian and European financial systems in the run-up to EMU. The most important merger involved the combination of fifteen banks into the titans of UniCredito and Intesa. Additionally, the Bank of Italy was granted increasing supervisory power by the Consolidated Law on Finance (1998), which built upon the powers granted by the 1993 Consolidated Law. Once again, however, the effectiveness of such measures was limited by political imperatives, in particular authorities' desire to maintain their leverage over the financial system in order to preserve employment and solvency within economically strategic firms and sectors. The result was a limited degree of integration with the European financial system[161] and the perpetuation of a system of small and local banks that display "politicized governance features that blurred commercial incentives."[162]

Somewhat perversely, it was the very clientelistic, hidebound character of the Italian financial system that buffered it from some of the worst effects of the post-2007 financial crisis. Italian banks had traditionally existed to provide finance to favored firms, and as a result of a system of financial regulations designed to perpetuate these arrangements, they had neither the means nor the motive to participate significantly in the investment-banking activities that left their German, British, and American counterparts so exposed to the subprime lending crisis. As a result, with the exception of Unicredito—a commercial bank properly so called—Italian banks participated very little in investment banking in the 1990s and 2000s, focusing instead on traditional retail practices and maintaining relationships with local and regional firms.[163] That said, the collapse in global credit markets as well as preexisting debt loads, along with sluggish economic growth that undermined debtors' capacity to repay loans, ultimately made Italian banks vulnerable to global financial instability. Furthermore, the expansion of several Italian banks after the 1990s into eastern European countries that were more exposed threatened Italy's financial sector, albeit indirectly.[164]

Although Italian banks initially escaped the worst of the global financial turmoil, the structure of the Italian economy and its heavy reliance on a large number of small banks prompted officials to act to shore up the Italian financial system as the crisis worsened. Given the reliance of large numbers of strategically important SMEs on bank financing, the potential reduction in lending resulting from post-2007 constraints in global credit markets served as a powerful motivation for state intervention, despite the absence of the systemic risk suffered by some other Eurozone nations. Although Italy's banks weathered the financial crisis relatively well, characteristically conservative banking practices and low profits also made efforts for recapitalization particularly difficult. Passed soon after the bankruptcy of Lehman, on October 9, 2008, Law Decree no. 155 aimed to recapitalize Italian banks with public funds, support operations to address the liquidity shortage, and guarantee deposits by the state. These measures were expanded with Law Decree no. 157, which granted the Ministry for the Economy and Finance the power to offer state guarantees for banks' bonds and to underwrite capital increases.[165] In February 2009 the state approved a €15.3 billion bank bailout, which was small by international comparison, with all the funds dedicated to recapitalization rather than the mix of recapitalization and guarantees used in most countries.[166] In typical fashion, Italian policymakers deployed the power of the state in a modest fashion to shelter established interests rather than to undertake the politically dangerous task of restructuring the financial sector.

Such timidity soon became unaffordable, however, as the financial crisis gave way in 2010/11 to the Eurozone crisis, which exposed and exacerbated underlying weaknesses in the Italian financial system that decades of clientelism had helped create. One weakness was the "addiction of Italian manufacturers to cheap and available credit," reflected in the deterioration of Italy's competitive position and growing spreads between Italian and German bonds. The second was the increasing (though still comparatively small) share of Italian sovereign debt held by foreign entities, which had more than tripled as a share of GDP since the early 1990s and meant that the growing wave of international insolvency posed a real threat to Italy's financial stability.[167] In 2011 this concomitance of codependence between Italian manufacturing and finance on the one hand and growing exposure to global instability on the other led to a flight of liquidity as foreign banks acted to limit their exposure. This development led in turn to a shrinking of credit markets for bank-reliant Italian SMEs and a spike in bond yields, which increased the cost of borrowing for the state.[168] If Italy had long lived by the sword of clientelist finance, it seemed that it could just as easily die by it in an era of instability and contagion.

Since the mounting Eurozone crisis helped drive Berlusconi from office in 2011, the structural dysfunctions of the euro and long-standing weaknesses in the Italian financial system have combined to exert growing pressures on Italian finance. As credit continued to contract, the ratio of non-performing loans (NPLs) in Italian financial institutions tripled between 2008 and 2012. The growing share of NPLs in Italian banks has been particularly problematic in view of the structure of their balance sheets. While large banks hold the majority of the so-called *sofferenze* (NPLs), ratios are high across all types of Italian financial institutions, and 75 percent of NPLs are loans originating at less than €75,000—illustrating the tight relationship with SMEs.[169] Finally, while NPLs are prevalent throughout Italy, central and southern Italy are disproportionately affected, with NPL ratios roughly double that of the North by 2014.[170]

By 2015, repeated failures during EU stress tests and banks' inability to shed significant shares of NPLs once again forced the state's hand. In March, Italy passed a reform that transformed the shareholder voting structure (previously one person, one vote) within the ten largest Popolari, forcing them to become joint-stock corporations or else to reduce their total assets to a level below €8 billion. This effort to shore up the Italian banking sector, fiercely contested by the Populari, which saw the reform as a threat to their long-nurtured linkages to local and regional firms, paved the way for consolidation, an elusive goal in a country that still has the highest number of bank branches per capita of any OECD nation.[171] An August decree helped banks offload NPLs through better debt enforcement and improvements in the tax code for loss deductions.[172] Such measures did little, however, to address the core problem of toxic balance sheets and the proliferation of uncollectable loans, which are largely collateralized by real estate in a country where a sclerotic judicial system makes foreclosure difficult. Despite EU legislation, adopted in 2012, on the orderly liquidation of failing banks, Italian officials refused to pull the trigger by forcing banks to buy back risky securities, which often constituted banks' own shares and debt sold to their clients. This "massive failure of public policy"[173] is hardly surprising in a system whose prime historical imperative has been protecting political clients rather than rationalizing and stabilizing the allocation of finance and in which "regional lenders are bound up in local politics."[174] With few alternatives, in November 2015 the government approved a bailout of four small banks, establishing a so-called bad bank to which to shift €8.5 billion in toxic assets from their balance sheets and using €3.6 billion provided by three relatively healthy banks (UniCredito, Intesa SanPaolo, and UBI Banca). In February 2016 the government passed a reform of small mutual banks to strengthen the local banking sector and, in April, orchestrated the creation of Atlante—essentially a bad bank set up to remove NPLs from bank balance sheets.

The ongoing (and emblematic) saga of Banca monte dei paschi di Siena (MPS) shows that the deep dysfunctions of the Italian financial system continue to pose systemic risks. Founded in 1472, MPS is considered the world's oldest bank and one of the few Italian banks viewed as having systemic importance. As a result of both its venerable age and its outsized imprint, MPS has long benefited from state support, despite its increasingly parlous financial status.[175] A series of acquisitions in the run-up to the financial crisis increased the number of MPS branches by 50 percent, and many observers and regulators feared it had drastically overpaid for them, particularly for Antonveneta, a Spanish bank acquired from Banco Santander of Spain.[176] The beneficiary of a €1.9 billion bailout in February 2009, MPS required another €4 billion in 2013, a particularly unpopular move given efforts, which MPS had hidden from both its own auditors and the Bank of Italy, to disguise losses through derivative contracts with Deutsche Bank.[177]

Despite these two bailouts in four short years, made necessary by its reckless expansion and comparatively high exposure to Italian sovereign debt, the perpetuation of clientelist linkages has precluded the state from abandoning MPS to its fate. With 49 percent of its shares owned by the public Fondazione Monte dei Paschi di Siena and employing an astonishing 31,000 staff, the bank, locally referred to as Daddy Monte, is deeply intertwined with public affairs.[178] Further complicating matters is that Italian households own around €200 billion in bank bonds, many of which are issued by MPS; under a new EU mandate, Italians would therefore foot the considerable bill for any bail-in of MPS, a method that had been used in November 2015 to rescue four small banks at the cost of €4 billion and to great public outcry.[179] As a planned €5 billion recapitalization for MPS lost traction in late 2016, the bank attempted to raise capital privately through a share sale and debt-for-equity swaps. At the time of this writing, yet another bailout seemed inevitable, a move whose cost the ECB has calculated at an eye-popping €8.8 billion, a figure that, at nearly double the size of the initial recapitalization plan, strained Italian finances can ill afford.[180] With past once again as prologue, the Italian state finds itself enmeshed in a clientelistic web that it can neither unravel nor escape.

As in the cases of fiscal and labor-market policy, the legacies of the clientelist liberal tradition have thus helped to undermine adjustment in the Italian financial system. Drawing on antecedents from the late nineteenth century and the Fascist period, the postwar financial system became financially embedded with the country's small and medium-sized enterprises and politically embedded with local and regional authorities. As the state-driven campaign of industrialization and development though large, state-owned and -managed enterprises faltered for both economic and political reasons in the 1970s, Italy's growing dependence on SMEs reinforced the importance of the bank-centered financial model. This interconnection between political and economic imperatives has frustrated efforts to rationalize the Italian financial system in the post-Maastricht era, preserving the system's illiberal characteristics and perpetuating a framework that is ill suited to contemporary economic challenges. Though these features buffered Italy from the investment-banking-centered excesses occurring in the United States and UK, they also rendered the system quite resistant to reform, posing difficult challenges to authorities attempting to manage the effects of the Eurozone crisis after 2010. The effects of these failures have not been limited to the financial system, moreover, as "weak Italian banks have been the culprits, not just victims, of economic sluggishness," since Italian "banking system fragility results in credit misallocation and a severe drag on economic activity."[181] Therefore, unlike France and Germany, where the postwar period witnessed the synthesis of national liberal traditions with competing developmental models, in Italy the failure of such a synthesis has undermined both needed reform and economic performance, a negative outcome for which the failures of the Italian financial system bear important responsibility.

Conclusion: The Failed Synthesis of Clientelist Liberalism

The clientelist-liberal tradition that emerged in Italy in the late nineteenth century represented a distinctive national response to the challenges of late industrialization and the fraught character of national unification in 1860. As discussed in Chapter 1, the bargain underlying the *Risorgimento* entailed an exchange between northern and southern elites that cemented the respective privileges of prominent political and economic groups—chiefly northern industrialists and latifundian landowners in the South—thereby buying a fragile political stability for the fledgling state at the cost of economic and social stagnation. Rejected as illegitimate by northern manual workers, southern peasants, and the Catholic Church, all losers from the *Risorgimento* in distinctive ways, the unified Italian state struggled to consolidate and project its authority—a dilemma which the economic failures arising from the reactionary and clientelist character of national unification served to exacerbate. Even as they rejected the classical liberal nostrums that had become dominant in England, Italian liberals in the nineteenth and early twentieth centuries struggled to synthesize liberal notions of limits on state power and the substantive vision of how and on whose behalf such power should operate. Reinforced by the long interregnum of Fascism, this dilemma helped to inform a liberal tradition that defined both the limits and purposes of state power in terms of the vested interests of powerful social and economic groups and the regional and local authorities who supported them.

After World War II, the result of this lineage was a liberal tradition that informed a prevailing elite understanding of groups as both the chief constituents of state action and the principal obstacles to successful adjustment, in marked contrast to their adaptive role as partners of state initiatives in Germany. Whereas the architects of the Social Market Economy successfully synthesized older liberal ideas and notions of group privilege with the neocorporatist institutional order and postwar economic realities, their Italian counterparts failed to achieve such a synthesis. This failure yielded a state that came to dominate the Italian economy even as it grew increasingly defensive in the face of challenges by social and economic groups, seeking to buy social peace through clientelistic means that undermined liberal elements in the postwar Italian political economy. In the aftermath of the Hot Autumn of 1969 and declining economic performance in the 1970s, the state increasingly became a patronage machine rather than an agent of economic adjustment, leading to its characterization as a "party state" in the service of the dominant Christian Democrats. Increasingly vocal criticism by a domestic neoliberal elite centered in the Bocconi school was an important symptom of the failed synthesis of Italian liberalism. In contrast to France and Germany, where nationally distinctive lineages of liberal thought informed their political-economic models, in Italy the system's increasingly illiberal character relegated liberals to the role of external critics with the luxury of doctrinal purity that comes from the absence of the need to govern.

Like its French and German analogs, Italian liberalism rejected and evolved in opposition to the gathering neoliberal orthodoxy of the 1980s and 1990s, though in ways that informed a series of maladaptive policy developments across a range of domains. In fiscal policy, authorities struggled to reduce the state's enormous and growing debt burden (itself the legacy of decades of clientelism) by cutting public spending and seeking out new sources of revenue, even as the fiscal strictures of the Maastricht Treaty undermined their ability to foster the economic growth that might have made a return to fiscal balance achievable. Their failure in this regard reflected both the depth of clientelist linkages between privileged groups and the state and the political dilemmas to which attempts to strike sustainable bargains among these groups in a climate of economic austerity give rise. In labor-market policy, officials of both Left and Right have worked to liberalize Italy's notoriously strict workplace regulations and foster job creation in the hopes of reducing the country's stubbornly high jobless rate and the fiscal strains that it produces. Although there have been some limited successes in efforts to liberalize the labor market, most recently and dramatically with the Jobs Act of Matteo Renzi, political resistance has relegated such accomplishments to the margins of the Italian employment market, driving the expansion of low-wage, temporary, and precarious employment rather than achieving the hoped-for recalibration of contract terms of core industrial workers that could lead to the creation for significant numbers of permanent positions. Finally, in the realm of financial regulation, Italian governments have failed to modernize and rationalize the highly fragmented and politically embedded financial system, which they have sought to preserve as a lever of economic policy while adapting it to the realities of an increasingly integrated European financial market, two goals that have worked at cross purposes. The result has been inadequate responses to financial crises in the early 1990s and 2007–9 period, punctuated by a series of expensive, embarrassing, and ultimately futile efforts to shore up important financial clients, most recently the benighted Banca Monte dei Paschi di Siena. In all three policy areas the failed synthesis of Italian liberalism has undermined economic performance, as well as the state's legitimacy, as it has failed to provide effective and feasible recipes for economic adjustment.

Since its consolidation in the 1970s, the Italian clientelist-liberal tradition has informed an elite analytical frame fraught with apparently insoluble tensions and has helped to produce an enduring pattern of economic stagnation, political sclerosis, and deepening public cynicism and alienation from the state. Like the French and German traditions explored in previous chapters, Italian liberalism has rejected neoliberal solutions, seeking instead to develop alternative strategies that fostered economic growth and facilitated the adjustment of workers and firms to a more market-based economic order. As Marco Simoni, a former adviser to Renzi, put it in an interview in the *New Yorker*, "We are definitely free market. But unlike Mrs. Thatcher . . . we want growth *and* social justice."[182] The limited success of such efforts derives in large part from their failure to dislodge entrenched interest groups that for decades have sacrificed the national welfare on the twin altars of stability and self-protection. Though reform has been significant in some areas, it has retreated in others, and such reforms as have proven possible have relied upon short-term, situational coalitions held together with side payments and concentrated but isolated elite efforts to marshal support. The occasional turn to technocratic administrations has likewise done little to place Italy on a more positive long-term economic trajectory and has indeed often, as in the case of the Monti administration, merely confirmed the public's impression of a political class that perceives itself to be beyond the realm of democratic accountability.

As in the French and German cases, then, Italy's variant of liberalism has shaped policy and institutional outcomes across political, economic, and partisan contexts, even if its influence has been largely maladaptive. Italy has long been and remains a society divided between "camps" of Left and Right, which share a deeply cynical view of politics and of the state as merely a font of resources to be captured and a means whereby to undermine the economic interests of their political opponents. In this context, groups have acted as impediments to reform and effective governance, infected by a zero-sum conception of politics that makes adaptive reform and meaningful, sustained economic adjustment very difficult, indeed. Time and again, across partisan and policy contexts, the clientelist-liberal tradition and the political-economic model that it has helped to foster have undermined political coalitions among competing economic interests in an age of austerity and slowed growth, rendering unavailable the kinds of distributional bargains that the similarly group-focused German tradition has managed to sustain.[183] According to one Italian Treasury official with long experience in economic policymaking circles, the conception of liberalism informed by this worldview is one of deep dualities, a paradoxical combination of dependence on and distrust of the state, and a context in which "you always know that you are constrained" by the power of entrenched interest groups.[184] Such a perspective is hardly new in Italy and indeed represents strong continuities with the prewar era. As Jane Kramer, speaking of the "infrastructure" of clientelism that emerged from the nineteenth century, puts it, "'[I]nfrastructure' meant the family, the Church, the party, and in much of the south, the mafias—umbrellas of support, protection, and, of course, jobs, under different names. You took care of your own, bought into the swamp, and ignored the indicators of collapse. The perimeters of a good life depended on the umbrella under which you sheltered."[185] In such a context, the failure of liberal ideas to win out over clientelistic linkages, combined with the failed synthesis of Italian liberalism with Italy's institutional landscape, is perhaps unsurprising, though it does augur ill for Italy's future capacity to confront and address increasingly challenging political and economic realities.

Conclusion

The Contested Politics of Economic Change in a Neoliberal Age

This book has analyzed how national liberalisms have shaped the dynamics of political-economic adjustment in France, Germany, and Italy in the neoliberal era. In continental Europe, as elsewhere across the advanced industrial world, this period has been marked by the liberalization and renegotiation of postwar bargains and social contracts, which have come under powerful and sustained challenges both economic and political. Economically, the policy and institutional foundations of continental Europe's political economies confronted slowed economic growth, the exhaustion of postwar Fordism and resultant deindustrialization, and rising unemployment, all of which have undermined their fiscal and economic foundations. The political challenges, fueled by both declining economic performance and the resultant erosion of the legitimacy of postwar political elites and institutions, have been no less severe. Beginning in the late 1970s, the emergence of a powerful and coherent neoliberal vision of hegemonic markets, denuded states, and what Jamie Peck has aptly termed "politically assisted market rule"[1] called into question both inherited arrangements and the vision of "embedded liberalism"[2] and socially embedded capitalism that underlay them. The ascendant neoliberal vision came to dominate the political discourse across the advanced industrial world with a set of claims about the centrality to human society of market-based relationships and the ostensibly dysfunctional effects of state involvement in the economy, premises that mounting economic challenges lent the same prestige and authority that had accrued to Keynesianism during the postwar boom. For the ensuing three decades, variants of the neoliberal narrative would largely set the terms of debate about the necessary and desirable character of economic policies in an era characterized by significant economic constraints.

For all its power, however, this book has shown that, at least in continental Europe, the hegemony of neoliberalism cannot be assumed, nor are the outcomes of these debates foreordained. In all three countries under study here, national liberal traditions, much older than neoliberalism and offering a much more embedded understanding of state, society, and economy, have challenged neoliberalism's dominance and shaped trajectories of reform that depart in important ways from its standard prescriptions. As discussed in the Introduction, this fact is hardly surprising, given the highly abstract and negative character of the neoliberal agenda and the necessity for any process of liberalization to be negotiated within existing national political institutions in ways that account for the embedded character of politically and economically viable capitalist orders. What is perhaps surprising, however, is the extent to which these alternative national liberalisms—hybrids between neoliberalism's privileging of markets and the social and political realities of institutionalized national capitalisms—have exerted sustained and consistent influence across policy, institutional, and partisan contexts. This book has argued that liberalism in illiberal states yields distinctive understandings of the structure of society and the identification and privileging of particular kinds of political constituencies, the desirable extent and character of state involvement in the economy, and the attendant direction and character of political responsibility, all of which stand in sharp contrast to neoliberalism's assumptions about the desirability of hegemonic market rule and its atomized vision of social order. In so doing, they have, in an era of economic austerity, furnished distinctive templates for economic adjustment that accept liberal notions of the need for limits on state power and the salutary effects of markets, even as they insist on the need to complement and sustain markets through non-market arrangements such as robust social-protection systems and meaningful collective-bargaining frameworks. In the process they have charted their own distinctive paths of economic adjustment, paths that embrace certain liberal imperatives while diverging from neoliberal recipes in significant ways.

Born in the nineteenth century, these national liberal traditions have evolved in response to shifting political and economic challenges, mediating the process of postwar reconstruction and the reinvention of national capitalisms and undergoing a process of consolidation as alternatives to neoliberalism after the 1970s. Though they entail rich and complex ideational lineages, with sometimes contradictory commitments and premises, these traditions have nonetheless provided a coherent, if far from static, set of ideas on which policymakers have drawn during periods of upheaval and uncertainty. As Peter Gourevitch reminds us, it is during precisely such periods that inherited institutions and arrangements are likely to find the limits of their usefulness: "In prosperous times it is easy to forget the importance of power in the making of policy. Social systems appear stable, and the economy works with sufficient regularity that its rules can be modeled as if they functioned without social referent. In difficult economic times . . . patterns unravel, economic models come into conflict, and policy prescriptions diverge."[3] At such moments, established prescriptions, ideologies, and political-economic models, including both those inherited from earlier eras and those imposed from without, are likely to be of limited help for understanding and confronting new social and economic challenges distinct from those that established models were originally built to manage. Though perhaps seductive in their simplicity and rigidity, abstract, disembedded visions like that offered by neoliberalism are thus unlikely to provide politically feasible and economically viable templates for reform.

In their quest to manage the process of adjustment to a more austere and liberalized economic context, policymakers in France, Germany, and Italy have turned to venerable and deeply rooted sets of ideas—widely shared in their essential components if perhaps not in their detailed policy implications—which grew up alongside national capitalist economies and came both to reflect and to reinforce many of their institutional manifestations. In the process, these traditions have acted as conceptual reservoirs and resultant menus of options for policymakers confronting periods of heightened economic uncertainty, even as they have evolved through a process of continual reinterpretation by elites. Another way of thinking about the influence and enduring power of national liberalisms in illiberal states is by analogy to what Peter Haas, borrowing from and modifying a term coined by his father Ernest Haas, labels "epistemic communities," which he defines as networks "of professionals with recognized expertise and competence in a particular domain and an authoritative claim to policy-relevant knowledge within that domain or issue area." Though Haas uses the term in a different context—applying it to communities of policy experts in international relations—his characterization of these communities as sharing sets of "normative and principled beliefs," "causal beliefs," "notions of validity," and "policy enterprises" echoes my understanding of the power of national liberal traditions.[4] Activated during periods of economic uncertainty and sustained challenge to inherited policy and institutional frameworks, these liberal traditions provide elites with shared sets of assumptions and a common language about the structure of society, the dynamics of the economy, and the character of state responsibility within the context of which political decisions about economic reform are made. They have done so, moreover, in ways that reject the abstract, disembedded neoliberal vision in favor of historically rooted and organically evolving notions about the relationship among state, society, and the economy. In this way, they provide economically and politically feasible templates for adjustment, which stand in sharp contrast to neoliberalism's impracticable vision.

Illiberal States in a Neoliberal Era: National Traditions and Economic Change in Embedded Markets

Though their influence has been much broader, the national liberal traditions described here have been particularly influential in fiscal policy, labor-market policy, and financial policy, three areas that both define the contours of national capitalist economies and have come under sustained challenge since the early 1990s. With the end of the postwar boom and the shared experience of slowing growth after the 1970s, authorities across the advanced industrial world were forced to rethink standard assumptions inherited from a time of generalizing prosperity. In place of budget surpluses and expanding economic resources, officials instead confronted rising debt and deficits and tightening constraints on public spending, limitations made all the more problematic by the fiscal strictures of EMU. Instead of full employment, they encountered rising unemployment and increasing long-term joblessness, challenges deriving from the exhaustion of postwar Fordism and attendant deindustrialization, and high non-wage labor costs stemming from social-protection systems designed for periods of prosperity and the more equitable sharing of economic burdens between capital and labor that they helped to inform. In financial policy, the constraints of European institutions and the eventual surrender of monetary-policy autonomy to the ECB with the advent of EMU, coupled with financial internationalization, forced policymakers to relinquish, or at least to loosen their grip on, financial systems that in many cases had been key instruments of the state-directed process of postwar industrialization and in others had been handmaidens to state strategies of economic growth and renewal. Even as they were forced to confront new economic realities, however, French, German, and Italian officials did so in ways that rejected standard neoliberal nostrums, retaining and recalibrating the long-standing and socially embedded relationships between public authority and the market. In so doing, they have overseen a two-decade process of reform in these three policy areas informed by historically rooted and nationally specific understandings of their respective political and economic orders.

In France, the tradition of statist liberalism has informed policy responses centered on macroeconomically oriented strategies designed to bolster economic growth and employment, financial liberalization coupled with continued state support for the financial sector, and the expansion of citizenship-based income-support policies. This tradition, which reflected a republican emphasis on individual equality before the law and a distrust of social and economic groups, encouraged policies that validated the primacy of individuals as the building blocks of society, and preserved a commitment to macroeconomically oriented measures designed to support economic growth and sustain aggregate demand. Such strategies preserved an important role for the state in the economy, though one turned to much different missions than those of the postwar dirigiste era.[5] Having signed on to the Maastricht Treaty's vision of an austere and deflationary euro, French officials pinned their hopes on their ability to shape European economic policy in ways that would enable them to achieve the sort of expansionary strategy that they could no longer pursue unilaterally following the demise of dirigisme. In this way, authorities preserved a robust role for the state, which worked to foster market-based adjustment supported by an expansive network of citizenship-based social protection designed to buffer workers from market vagaries, preserve political support for economic liberalization, and support economic growth. In fiscal policy, French officials slashed public spending on traditional instruments, such as sectoral industrial policies and subsidies for "national champions," even as they expanded it in other areas, such as social protection. In labor-market policy, they limited recourse to traditional instruments of passive subsidization of the unemployed while bolstering job creation through employer subsidies and working to sustain demand through a more equitable distribution of employment. Finally, in financial policy, authorities privatized and liberalized the financial sector while preserving political connections to economically strategic large banks and bailing them out in times of crisis. In all three policy areas, the statist liberal tradition informed and validated a successful synthesis between the state's continued prominence in the economy and a process of liberalization sustained by constrained macroeconomic support and the expansion of citizenship-based social protection. Clearly liberal in comparison with earlier periods, these strategies nonetheless repudiated neoliberal strategies of messianic and disembedded market making.

In Germany, likewise, governments of both Left and Right have fostered political-economic adjustment in ways that have departed from standard neoliberal recipes. There, the tradition of "corporate liberalism" has informed strategies that privilege the political and economic roles of core groups with a policy orientation that combines macro- and microeconomic elements. Evolving out of the ideas of Ordoliberalism as reshaped by postwar circumstances, this tradition both reflected the Ordoliberal and neocorporatist privileging of groups and validated a more active role for the state than either would have countenanced, creating spaces for robust state intervention and aggressive reform in response to economic uncertainty.[6] Whereas their French counterparts sought to bolster growth and support adjustment through macroeconomic stimulus and the expansion of citizenship-based income support, German officials after the early 1990s focused on subsidizing and sheltering key groups, notably skilled industrial workers and firms in export-intensive sectors and the famed *Mittelstand* of internationally competitive SMEs, in the hope of bolstering economic growth and preserving their export-based economic model. If French authorities subordinated microeconomic imperatives (such as targeted labor-market activation) to macroeconomic ones, in Germany the prevailing orientation was "mesoeconomic," with positive macroeconomic outcomes viewed as desirable effects of a group- and sectorally focused strategy of support. In fiscal policy, both after German reunification and during the post-2007 Great Recession, this strategy entailed targeted fiscal expansion and investment within a broader long-term effort to restore fiscal balance and economic-stimulus efforts focused largely on tax cuts for key groups rather than direct spending. In labor-market policy, the corporate-liberal tradition informed the development of instruments, such as the *Kurzarbeit* program, designed to shelter core workers from the costs of adjustment, which were largely borne by a low-wage service sector that expanded in the wake of the Hartz IV and Agenda 2010 reforms of SPD Chancellor Gerhard Schröder. As in labor-market policy, finally, German financial policy has been marked by constrained liberalization coupled with targeted support for key players, in particular the public-savings banks and Landesbanken that have long supplied financial resources to strategically important export firms. As in France, furthermore, this process of buttressed liberalization was accompanied by the preservation and selective expansion of social-protection instruments designed to help workers adjust to a more liberal era.

If France and Germany negotiated relatively successful syntheses of their respective liberal traditions with their political-economic institutions and the exigencies of an era of liberalization and austerity, in Italy the decades since the mid-1990s have been characterized by a failure to do so. The clientelist liberal tradition that emerged after the late 1960s provided an ideational reservoir that reflected the core arrangements of the postwar Christian Democratic party state but also represented possible, albeit largely negative and dysfunctional, alternatives to it. Like its German analog, the Italian liberal tradition viewed groups as the central components of the social order but understood their role in largely negative terms. If groups acted as supported partners in post-1990 German strategies of adjustment, in Italy, following the *Mani Pulite* scandal and the advent of Maastricht-derived fiscal constraints, they served as obstacles to reform, engaging in a zero-sum game whereby one group's loss represented another's gain. Emerging from the *Risorgimento*'s troubled legacy of a weak state acting on behalf of a sectorally and regionally delimited clientele, Italian officials failed to reconcile their liberal commitment to a limited state with strategies of adjustment that groups viewed as a threat to their privileges rather than an opportunity for economic modernization. As a result, the Italian political universe became increasingly divided into warring camps composed of entrenched interest groups supported by their party-political patrons (particularly powerful public-sector unions and managers of public-sector enterprises on the Left and SMEs and white-collar independents on the Right). This prevailing reality undermined the efforts of reform-minded governments like Romano Prodi's center-Left Olive Tree coalitions to achieve meaningful reform. When reform did occur, it eventuated only through episodic, ad hoc coalitions and was often partially reversed or diluted after the fact, or else it was achieved through reliance on short-term technocratic caretaker governments with little political legitimacy. In fiscal policy, the legacies of this state of affairs were mounting public debt that limited officials' room for maneuver and undermined efforts to stimulate the economy during economic downturns. In employment policy, meaningful reform took place at the margins of the labor market, increasing precarious employment but doing little to liberalize and rationalize job-dampening employment regulations in core industrial sectors. Finally, in finance, Italian officials whistled past the proverbial graveyard represented by their overleveraged and underregulated financial system, with few good options for managing such an inevitable crisis as the slow-motion implosion of Banca monte dei paschi di Siena. The Italian case clearly shows that unsuccessful alternatives to neoliberalism are possible, even likely, in countries in which a toxic environment undermines necessary political and economic trade-offs and associated mechanisms of political legitimation.

In all three countries, these nationally distinctive sets of liberal ideas have informed policy trajectories over the past three decades in ways that display surprising degrees of continuity and consistency across economic and partisan contexts. In all three cases, these trajectories have departed significantly from those that characterized the postwar boom, when the central task of national political economies was to administer generalizing prosperity rather than to manage economic constraints. As postwar national models failed to manage new challenges, authorities were forced to rethink inherited assumptions about the role of the state, its relationship to the market and to society, and the nature of their social and political constituencies. As they did so, they sought guidance from liberal traditions that had evolved in important ways since the nineteenth century, ideas that offered conceptual touchstones that they could reinterpret in light of new economic circumstances. In each instance, sensitivity and receptiveness to these traditions led policymakers to eschew neoliberal strategies of expansive market making and attacks on non-market arrangements such as social-protection systems, even as they were forced to rethink the relationship between state and market and renegotiate trade-offs among social and political constituencies, as they understood them. The events described here thus remind us that liberalism, far from being the exclusive province of post-1970s neoliberals, actually represents a much older and richer set of political traditions that reflect commitments not just to limits on state power but also to economic rights, with nationally distinctive conceptions of how society is structured and related conceptions of the constituents of state initiatives that continue to shape elites' understandings of their economic context and the array of meaningful and feasible responses available to them. The enduring power and influence of national liberal traditions reminds one of the wisdom of Faulkner's dictum, expressed by a character in his *Requiem for a Nun*, that "the past is never dead. It isn't even past."

The Power of Economic Ideas in Advanced Capitalist Societies

Though focused empirically on continental Europe, this book's analysis of economic adjustment in illiberal states suggests important lessons for the study of policy and institutional change in advanced industrial democracies and for comparative political economy more broadly. Departing from conventional historical-institutional approaches that privilege formal institutions and stable constellations of interest-group preferences, this book shows that a focus on the power of ideas is essential to any account that aims to capture broad national patterns of adjustment over time. By providing frames of reference on which policymakers draw in times of uncertainty and upheaval, when established institutional frameworks and the distributions of authority that they embody prove maladaptive, constellations of politically operative ideas allow officials both to interpret the character of prevailing challenges and to arrive at sets of politically feasible and, potentially, economically effective responses. In the cases under examination here, political authorities rejected a neoliberal template that was foreign (even anathema) to their prevailing political discourse and instead sought answers within their own distinctive liberal traditions. These traditions had grown up with the emergence and consolidation of national capitalisms in the nineteenth and early twentieth centuries and were continually reinterpreted, first during the postwar boom and then once again after the slowdown beginning in the 1970s. Just as these traditions evolved in opposition to classical liberalism in the nineteenth century, as discussed in Chapter 1, they have departed from the disembedded vision of neoliberalism in the contemporary era, drawing on older sets of assumptions and premises about the structure of society and the scope and character of the state's economic responsibilities. Ideas thus offered the conceptual building blocks of new solutions that often departed in important ways from patterns of adjustment and political norms that had grown up in an era defined by different challenges and imperatives. As these experiences show, ideas cannot be reduced to mere analogs of existing institutional models, which after all represent only one possible set of arrangements that such ideational frames imply.

In privileging the political role of ideas in shaping trajectories of adjustment in illiberal states, this book has highlighted the limitations of strands of scholarship that focus on formal institutions as the principal drivers of political and economic change. One of the most important contributions of post-1970s historical-institutionalist scholarship, which built on the insights of Andrew Shonfield and others in the 1970s and 1980s, was its focused attention on national variations in state capacity and the structure of constellations of interest groups, a strength which likewise characterized the subsequent (and now quasi-canonical) work on Varieties of Capitalism.[7] This literature taught the crucial lesson that capitalism is not of a piece, nor is it destined to converge on a single, Anglo-American variant of sharply constrained states, arm's-length relationships between capital and finance, and an atomized and highly individualistic conception of social organization. Instead, this literature demonstrated that capitalism is in fact a broad economic framework with myriad historically informed and nationally specific variations on central themes of private ownership of capital, limits on state authority, and competition and entrepreneurship. Providing a lesson no less important today than it was during the postwar boom, this work cast a jaundiced eye on conventional wisdoms, themselves the product of postwar modernization theory and its intellectual successors, that predicted convergence across capitalist systems on a narrow range of policy and institutional arrangements epitomized by the more neoliberal American capitalist model. Just as such work helpfully pointed to the great diversity of capitalist political economies in the postwar era, its insights continue to offer important lessons in a neoliberal era in which many observers, scholarly and popular alike, contend that convergence on a neoliberal model is once again inevitable.[8]

Although such neoinstitutionalist approaches have provided important insights into the institutional sources of capitalist diversity, they also suffer from important limitations that this book's focus on ideas aims to redress. Though institutions remain important shapers of policy trajectories, the evidence presented here suggests that their influence cannot be understood apart from the processes of elite interpretation of both the character of prevailing challenges and the appropriate and feasible menu of policy responses to them. Though this interpretive process takes place within a broad set of institutionalized constraints and levers of influence, the conclusions to which it leads often depart from established precedents with respect to both the contours of policy and operative political dynamics. There is, in other words, no mechanistic and predictable relationship between the distributions of political authority that institutional frameworks embody and the policy outcomes that they produce. Within the constraints represented by a given institutional context, ideas and national traditions offer a range of possibilities for responses that are deemed economically appropriate and politically feasible by members of relevant policy communities. These considerations must be continually revisited in the light of economic challenges whose character is often starkly different from those that the institutions themselves were originally designed to address. The concomitance of institutional stability and policy discontinuity, in other words, is not only possible; it is inevitable, given the shifting character of political and economic challenges and the continual process of elite interpretation to which they invariably give rise. Far from epiphenomenal to institutions' effects on policy, in other words, ideas are actually constitutive of them. As Mark Blyth reminds us, "structures do not come with an instruction sheet."[9] Instead, in ways to which historical-institutionalist accounts have remained relatively insensitive, political and economic interests are shaped dynamically by processes of interpretation, which in turn mediate the power and influence of political institutions themselves.[10]

A focus on the power of ideas, exemplified here as historically rooted conceptions of liberalism, helps to explain policy outcomes that diverge from those that established neoinstitutionalist perspectives would tend to predict, at moments when the prevailing economic circumstances are quite different from those that surrounded and informed these frameworks' postwar genesis. The national economic models that grew up during the postwar boom both reflected and helped to reinforce the contemporaneous climate of rapid economic growth, full employment, and broadly (if not universally) shared political and social consensus. Beginning in the late 1960s, however, these models' implicit assumptions about the nature of advanced capitalism proved increasingly out of sync with the challenges posed by the post-1960s period of economic decline. Even as earlier variants of national liberalisms had helped to inform the development of these countries' postwar models, then, subsequent versions have served as reservoirs of alternatives to them that were foregone during earlier periods marked by different sets of economic, social, and political challenges. These remaining possibilities, analogous to items on a menu left unchosen, have provided authorities with new possibilities at moments when inherited arrangements seem maladaptive, as in the era of liberalization and economic austerity since the early 1990s.[11] As postwar arrangements experienced pressures for reform after the 1970s, political authorities sought new templates for policy and institutional adjustment to a more liberal era, even as they repudiated neoliberal prescriptions as both economically ineffective and politically infeasible. Although scholarship on national models helpfully highlighted the diversity of advanced capitalisms, its emphasis on institutionalized allocations of political authority has limited its ability to explain departures from the standard divisions of political labor among states and organized interests. If institutional frameworks define the distribution of political authority within a given country's political economy, they are often unreliable guides to understanding how such authority is exercised in particular contexts. In order to understand that, we must account for the interpretative processes whereby elites devise solutions to current challenges, a move that in turn requires us to understand the ideas that their respective traditions make available. Context, in other words, matters a great deal.

Careful attention to the political power of ideas enables us to devise a richer and more robust account of policy and institutional change across economic, political, and partisan contexts than would otherwise be possible. In the French case, for example, the literature on postwar dirigisme highlighted the strong, centralized French state, which dominated policymaking for more than three decades. This literature has proven less well equipped, however, to explain French policymaking in a post-dirigiste context, when a liberalizing and marketizing state finds itself bereft of many of its traditional tools.[12] During the past two decades, the state has continued to favor macroeconomic strategies focused on broad notions of economic citizenship, preserving and expanding income support that helps workers adjust to a more liberal era in ways that postwar accounts of labor-exclusionary policy are poorly equipped to capture. That said, limits on its ability to project its power, deriving from both the structure of post-dirigiste institutions and the constraints on fiscal and monetary policy stemming from EMU, have led the state to adopt new strategies, such as supporting aggregate demand through labor-market reform, seeking new allies in the business community, and expanding and relying upon robust automatic stabilizers to support demand and foster social peace and economic adjustment and inclusion. In Germany, likewise, standard notions, first, of the "semi-sovereign" state[13] reluctant to intervene in the economy and limited by a paucity of interventionist tools and, relatedly, of consensual, neocorporatist bargaining are poorly equipped to explain either the significant projection of state power following German reunification and during the period of rapid labor-market reform during the late 1990s and early 2000s or the surprisingly robust Keynesian response to the post-2007 downturn.[14] In such episodes, the corporate liberal tradition supported a more robust role for the state and efforts to subsidize and protect key groups, rather than workers at large, in the French fashion. Finally, in Italy a focus on the relatively centralized Italian state would leave us incapable of explaining the clientelist deadlock that emerged after the *Mani Pulite* scandal in the early 1990s or the qualified successes in those few labor-market policy episodes where authorities were able to account for the limitations of a political environment beset by partisan recrimination and a zero-sum conception of politics. In this context, the clientelist liberal tradition informed responses that focused on (often unproductive) attempts to wrest inherited benefits from entrenched interest groups rather than on devising elusive compromise solutions that would represent politically acceptable trade-offs.

Just as established neoinstitutionalist accounts are poorly equipped to explain departures from past practice in a context of formal institutional continuity, interest-based approaches, which constitute a subset of the broader neoinstitutionalist tradition, likewise fail to provide the conceptual tools required for explaining patterns of adjustment in illiberal states.[15] For example, work on German neocorporatism that emphasizes the robust role of organized labor helpfully highlights unions' institutionalized authority within collective-bargaining frameworks, social-policy administration, and shop-floor organization.[16] In so doing, it offers a potential means whereby to explain reforms that benefit labor, such as reliance on *Kurzarbeit* programs of wage subsidization after reunification and once again after 2007. That said, it is less able to explain significant departures from such policy patterns, such as Gerhard Schröder's attack on the interests of his traditional labor allies in the Hartz IV and Agenda 2010 reforms in the early 2000s and his decision to deepen the divide between labor-market insiders and outsiders. Nor can it well explain officials' decision to rely disproportionately on tax cuts as a mechanism of economic stimulus after 2007, a move that dampened the package's job-creating effects, or their decision to focus their support for the financial system on Landesbanken and public-savings banks rather than the industrial banks that had been the centerpieces of the postwar growth strategy. In the French case, scholarship on the postwar marginalization of labor contributed to scholarly accounts of the state's labor-exclusionary strategy under dirigisme and its prioritization of growth and profits for strategically important industrial concerns over improving wages and workers' purchasing power.[17] Such work struggles, however, to explain both key policy outcomes since the 1970s that have favored labor, such as the sustained expansion of the French welfare state and income support since the mid-1980s, or policies, such as the Aubry Laws on the thirty-five-hour workweek, that were designed to bolster job creation through demand stimulus rather than subsidize key sectors in the German fashion. In Italy, finally, traditional work on the Italian Christian Democratic party state and the privileged role of public-sector unions and state-owned enterprises can account for the inflationary wage bargains and expansion of industrial subsidies in the decade following the 1969 Hot Autumn of industrial unrest, but struggles to explain subsequent attacks on the interests of such groups, including Romano Prodi's embrace of modified fiscal austerity in the 1990s and Berlusconi's repeated attacks on labor's social benefits. While interest-based accounts, like those that focus on formal distributions of authority, can explain some such episodes, moreover, they cannot well account for broad patterns of adjustment across policy domains, which often entail important trade-offs among the interests of competing groups or are driven by other imperatives, such as macroeconomic stability or influence and status within international fora like the EU.

With respect to all three countries, this book argues that sensitivity to the power of national liberal traditions helps to explain outcomes that reflect enduring tensions among competing elements of the liberalizing agenda, for which straightforward institutionalist and interest-based analyses cannot account.[18] These traditions informed German support for particular elements of organized labor, business, and finance over others, the French synthesis of liberalization and citizenship-based income support despite a history of labor exclusion, and Italian distrust of the state and understanding of economic policy as a zero-sum game aiming at state capture rather than classically clientelist distributions of political and economic resources. Although interest-based explanations dovetail with the approach adopted here in some respects, such as the privileged role of insider labor interests in Germany, my approach treats ideas as exerting a broader influence on wider and sometimes apparently contradictory policy trajectories across time. This book contends that ideas help shape both the analytical context within which elites operate and the menu of policy responses that they deem appropriate and feasible. Furthermore, even to the considerable extent that institutional arrangements, devised and consolidated during the postwar period, have shaped policy outcomes, this book has shown that they themselves are artifacts of the same ideational lineages that have continued to exert political influence, quite independently of institutional effects and indeed often in contravention of them. To the extent that institutional arrangements remain stable, they do so because, to a significant extent, they reflect the premises and commitments of the traditions that gave rise to them. In this respect, the book treats ideas as *preceding* institutions and organized interests both analytically and empirically and as informing and constraining their evolution in response to evolving political-economic challenges. Understanding the political force of ideas in this more dynamic way helps to highlight the limitations of analyses that focus on established and relatively stable ideological packages, such as Keynesianism or neoliberalism. Such approaches cannot explain national variation in these packages' application, as with the adoption of Keynesian policies after 2007, and still less policy and institutional trajectories in countries to which such intellectual frameworks are largely foreign, as in the case of neoliberalism in continental Europe.[19]

Taking ideas seriously in this way does not mean treating them uncritically or, still less, falling prey to the tendency to use them as post hoc explanations for overdetermined outcomes. But it does mean viewing them as powerful causal factors in their own right, capable of shaping the terms of policy debates as well as the menu of options that policymakers consider. This book has shown that such an approach provides powerful analytical tools for explaining policy responses to moments of heightened political and economic instability, when established practices and patterns of adjustment break down and alternative political and economic possibilities are likely to be unearthed. These possibilities stem from the same conceptual reservoirs on which officials had drawn in earlier periods to craft one—but far from the only—possible set of arrangements and institutions consistent with their core premises. These conceptual reservoirs and frames of reference intimate multiple, though constrained, possible futures for capitalist societies and serve as anchors for policy trajectories that grow out of successive moments of decision making in times of uncertainty. It is at such times, which provide moments of openness that periods of prosperity do not, that officials are likely to return to the intellectual well, Prufrock-like, "for decisions and revisions" to established ways of doing things. By highlighting how shared liberal commitments to limits on state power and the protection of a social sphere beyond its writ evolve in nationally specific ways, the study of how national traditions shape adjustment provides a powerful means of accounting for the development of contemporary capitalism in all its diversity.

Of course, the national liberalisms analyzed in this book do not exist in a vacuum; rather, they coexist and often overlap and dovetail with other political-economic traditions. As discussed in the Introduction, the coexistence and co-evolution of national liberalisms with these traditions, such as republicanism in France, neocorporatism in Germany, and social Catholicism in France and Italy, recall Rogers Smith's thesis of multiple traditions in the United States, whose political culture and discourse have been shaped by both liberalism and (a point of perhaps even greater relevance since 2016) anti-liberal, exclusionary traditions in fraught and often contradictory ways.[20] Though multiple traditions exist in every country, some are more relevant to prevailing challenges than others. During the past two decades, the context in continental Europe has been defined centrally by the economic challenges of slowed growth and (largely self-imposed) economic austerity and the ideological challenge posed by transnational neoliberalism. The resulting combination of economic and ideological uncertainty has activated national liberalisms, as authorities have sought politically viable and economically sustainable responses, much as the corporatist elements of German and the statist components of French liberalism were activated in the postwar era, as officials sought recipes that could reconcile economic growth and political stability in the war's aftermath.

The interaction of national liberalisms with other, related traditions in Germany, France, and Italy both shaped the character of the three countries' postwar orders and informed prevailing understandings of subsequent economic and ideological challenges to them. In Germany, for example, the neocorporatism that became an institutional anchor of the postwar Social Market Economy was informed by many of the same conceptual commitments inherent to corporatist liberalism, particularly the emphasis on groups as the building blocks of the social and economic order. At the same time, however, this tradition also offered a broader array of ideas that the institutional contours of the postwar system reflected, ones that would inform policy responses to challenging economic circumstances in subsequent periods. In France, likewise, the statist liberal tradition that emerged after the 1970s both reflected and departed from many of the institutional commitments and structures of the postwar French dirigiste model, and economic success during the postwar boom validated and stabilized these institutional arrangements. After the late 1960s, however, deteriorating economic circumstances and mounting social unrest and political instability encouraged successive French administrations to develop new interpretations of and responses to prevailing circumstances, including the expansion of citizen-based social protection, which departed from both postwar Bismarckian welfare-state institutions and France's labor-exclusionary postwar growth strategy.[21] Finally, in Italy the clientelist liberal tradition both shaped the state's postwar growth strategy of state-dominated industrialization that used favored clients as institutional levers for economic modernization and informed the abandonment of this strategy in favor of anti-liberal and increasingly dysfunctional clientelism in the wake of the post-1960s era of social unrest and slowed growth. The result was two decades of relative policy and institutional sclerosis and an inability successfully to confront periods of economic stress and uncertainty, even when, as during the Eurozone crisis, the very survival of the European order—of which Italy is a central component—seemed at stake. Whereas national liberalisms offered relatively adaptive alternatives to established modes of adjustment in the French and German cases, the Italian variant fostered cynicism, self-protection, and passivity. Though some national responses were clearly more adaptive than others, then, they each bore the hallmarks of their respective liberalism's understandings of state, society, and economy in ways that worked to reconcile the exigencies of a more liberal economic era, in politically meaningful ways, with the predicates of their socially embedded economic orders. In all three cases, these liberalisms shaped how national policymaking elites viewed the world, their country's place within it, and the distinctive character of their respective political and economic communities.

Capitalism and Challenges to Democracy in a Neoliberal Age

The national traditions and patterns of economic adjustment analyzed in this book suggest important lessons for students and practitioners of contemporary politics and policymaking beyond continental Europe. Despite neoliberalism's reach and durability as a dominant paradigm, its failure to recognize and account for the socially embedded character of market economies has undermined its effectiveness as a template for adjustment in both the advanced industrial and developing worlds. As has been argued, this failure seems almost inevitable, given its highly abstract and negative orientation and its resultant inability to account for or adjust to nationally specific arrangements, which provide the social and political foundations that allow the economy to function. The cases described here suggest that, far from offering a universally applicable recipe for capitalist adjustment and growth, neoliberalism actually generates pressures for strategies that contravene many of its premises. This book argues that liberal alternatives to neoliberalism are not only possible but necessary, accounting as they do for the embedded character of national economies and for nationally specific understandings of the proper character and scope of the state's role. A cursory glance at the myriad failures of neoliberal economic policies—from failed structural-adjustment policies imposed on developing countries by the International Monetary Fund (IMF) to the reckless investment practices encouraged by expansive financial deregulation in the run-up to the post-2007 financial crisis to the destructive and counterproductive insistence by Germany and other northern European countries on economic austerity for the European periphery (though, as this book has shown in the German case, not for themselves) during the Eurozone crisis—provides ample evidence for the paradigm's economic limitations.[22]

Perhaps even more worrying than neoliberalism's flaws as an economic paradigm are its political consequences, many of which have been unforeseen by its acolytes. At a time when populist, antiestablishment parties, many on the ethnonationalist fringes of the Far Right, are enjoying a resurgence that threatens political stability and even democratic capitalism itself, we are reminded of the inextricable connections between economic prosperity and the often fragile political legitimacy enjoyed by the parties and institutions charged with delivering it. Although a systematic explanation of this resurgence is beyond the scope of this book, it is clear that economic grievances and discontent with the effects of neoliberal policies are important parts of the mix.[23] The destruction of manufacturing jobs resulting from financial deregulation and from trade deals adopted without mechanisms to help workers adjust,[24] the manufactured poverty and Depression-level rates of unemployment heedlessly (and almost certainly fruitlessly) imposed on southern Europe by dominant Eurozone countries, and the exploding levels of inequality stemming from real-wage stagnation and, as Thomas Piketty has described, the long-term discrepancy between wages and returns to capital,[25] have all provided ample grist for the Far Right populist mill. The French Front National, the Alternative für Deutschland in Germany, and the Lega Nord in Italy, not to mention more explicitly neofascist parties like the Golden Dawn in Greece, Fidesz in Hungary, and the Law and Justice Party in Poland (the latter two of which are currently in power) all draw strength from voters' economic grievances and related desires to redraw political and economic communities in exclusionary ways. Concerns about resurgent right-wing populism became even more acute in the wake of the European refugee crisis since 2015, which has further undermined faith in European political elites and heightened voters' concerns about both physical and economic security in ways that nationalist and semi-authoritarian parties have eagerly exploited.[26] Not only does neoliberalism's abstract and negative character leave it bereft of substantive answers to such challenges, attempts to impose its prescriptions without accounting for nationally specific social structures and understandings of economic community fuel generalizing senses of economic exclusion that have left Europe in a position in which the stability of democracy itself suddenly seems at stake.[27] The final lesson is one that will be familiar to students of nineteenth-century history but that is often forgotten by contemporary observers—that political and economic liberalism are not of a piece. Decades of reassuring nostrums about the ostensible inevitability of what came to be known as "liberal democracy"[28] obscured economic liberals' historical ambivalence about, even hostility to, political democracy, as well as the implications of this ambivalence for efforts to reconcile the two. In the nineteenth century, many classical liberals feared that universal suffrage would lead to mob rule and the destruction of nascent market economies by demagogues bent on wresting economic fruits from the emerging middle classes and distributing them to the masses as a means of generating political support.[29] These concerns point to a deeper tension in the relationship between capitalism and democracy: that economic prosperity and political legitimacy are inextricably intertwined and that systems that fail to deliver the former—as those dominated by neoliberal economic policies have so often done—struggle to produce the latter, at least in the longer term. Simply put, as an abstract ideological project necessarily divorced from complex national social and economic contexts, neoliberalism lacks the mechanisms of its own political legitimation. It is thus no accident that some of the purest examples of neoliberal systems have been implemented by authoritarian regimes untroubled by their electoral prospects, such as Augusto Pinochet's Chile and the People's Action Party in Singapore, as an extensive literature on "authoritarian liberalism" attests.[30] As demonstrated by the election of Donald Trump as president of the United States in 2016, the administration's authoritarian tendencies, and the dominance of doctrinaire neoliberals within it, moreover, an alternative scenario features, in past-as-prologue fashion, the demagoguery feared by nineteenth-century liberals but with a twist. Substituting grand, empty promises of restored working-class prosperity for the real thing, demagogues like Trump engage in a classic bait-and-switch strategy, drawing support from working-class economic grievances even as they place the economy in the hands of people whose preferences are hostile to the kinds of policies that might allow such grievances meaningfully to be addressed.[31]

Whether in totalitarian or formally democratic guise, however, the authoritarian bent of such regimes offers cautionary tales for elites wishing to impose a neoliberal agenda within what often turn out to be surprisingly fragile political democracies. For the first time since the aftermath of World War II, a number of countries are confronting the necessity of reconfiguring, or devising anew, social and institutional buffers that alone can make capitalism politically viable and economically sustainable. In the process, they might well look to countries like those analyzed in this book, where neoliberalism has limited political currency and policy and institutional legacies have informed quite different adjustment strategies, although, to be sure, the Continent has its own political and economic struggles, and the Italian case shows that not all such strategies are equally successful. That said, the contrast between the (so far) relatively successful continental European resistance to populist and anti-systemic pressures (at least beyond the former Soviet bloc) and the recent experience of the Anglo-American world is striking. There, where neoliberalism finds more fertile soil, rising inequality, deindustrialization, and the economic marginalization of the working class have helped to fuel a politics of resentment that has destabilized existing political arrangements and contributed to clearly self-injurious collective decisions like Brexit and Trump's election. In this respect, despite long-standing neoliberal narratives of continental European sclerosis and decline, then, perhaps the Anglo-American world has something to learn from the European experience after all.

NOTES

Preface

1. Peter A. Hall, "Systematic Process Analysis: When and How to Use It," *European Management Review* 3 (2006): 28.
2. Theda Skocpol and Margaret Somers, "The Uses of Comparative History in Macrosocial Inquiry," *Comparative Studies in Society and History* 22, no. 2 (April 1980): 178.

Introduction

1. The quasi-hegemony of contemporary neoliberalism and nostrums about postwar "liberal democracy" also make it easy to forget that democracy and economic liberalism have historically been antagonists rather than allies. The 2016 election of Donald Trump as president of the United States and the dominance of neoliberal market fundamentalists within his administration; the decision by Britain, traditionally the strongest European advocate of neoliberal economic policies, to leave the European Union on the strength of anti-immigrant animus and working-class economic anxiety; and the so-far constrained but nonetheless significant resurgence of authoritarian nationalism in parts of continental Europe bring home this point with renewed force. For a cogent recent analysis of the relationship between economic liberalism and political illiberalism, see Pankaj Mishra, "Welcome to the Age of Anger," *Guardian*, December 8, 2016, https://www.theguardian.com/politics/2016/dec/08/welcome-age-anger-brexit-trump?INTCMP=sfl.
2. Such triumphalism was most famously, but far from exclusively, advanced in Francis Fukuyama, *The End of History and the Last Man* (New York: Free Press, 1992).
3. Coined by John Williamson in his *Latin American Adjustment: How Much Has Happened?* (Washington, DC: Institute for International Economics, 1990), this term entailed core policy proposals for market-based economic reform in the developing world.
4. Karl Polanyi, *The Great Transformation: The Political and Economic Origins of Our Time* (Boston: Beacon Press, 2001 [1944]).
5. I owe this formulation to Robert Adcock.
6. As John Gray has pointed out, this vagueness in the substantive definition of liberalism has contributed to millenarian claims about its hegemonic status. See Gray, "The Liberal Delusion," *Prospect*, October 2014, 38–45.
7. For a sophisticated treatment of neoliberalism and national convergence that focuses on national systems of industrial relations, see Lucio Baccaro and Chris Howell, *Trajectories of Neoliberal Transformation: European Industrial Relations since the 1970s* (Cambridge: Cambridge University Press, 2017).

8. Most recently, such an understanding of liberalism as neoliberalism can be found in *Resilient Liberalism in Europe's Political Economy*, ed. Mark Thatcher and Vivien Schmidt (Cambridge: Cambridge University Press, 2013). For a more subtle treatment of the relationship between liberalism and neoliberalism, see Philip G. Cerny, *Rethinking World Politics: A Theory of Transnational Neopluralism* (New York: Oxford University Press, 2010), ch. 7. For an analysis of the limits of the concept of neoliberalism applied to urban planning and governance, see Patrick Le Galès, "Neoliberalism and Urban Change: Stretching a Good Idea Too Far?" *Territory, Politics, Governance* 4, no. 2 (2016): 154–72.
9. David Harvey, *A Brief History of Neoliberalism* (Oxford: Oxford University Press, 2005), 2–3.
10. Jamie Peck, *Constructions of Neoliberal Reason* (Oxford: Oxford University Press, 2010), 15–16.
11. As Michael Freeden puts it in his discussion of the reverential adoption of neoliberal economic prescriptions in postcommunist central and eastern Europe, "[N]eo-liberal economics . . . was an emaciated liberalism artificially detached from many of the values and ends it needed to promote," such as a substantive notion of individual dignity and autonomy and a concern for robust human agency. See Freeden, "European Liberalisms: An Essay in Comparative Political Thought," *European Journal of Political Theory* 7, no. 1 (2008): 24.
12. As Peck points out, the contemporary equation of neoliberalism with advocacy of a homogeneous, messianic project of market making stems from the Chicago School's ascendancy in the 1970s at the expense of competing "neoliberal" variants, such as German Ordoliberalism, which recognized to a far greater extent the need for projects of economic reform to be socially embedded and institutionalized. Peck, *Constructions of Neoliberal Reason*, 18.
13. In Gamble's words, neoliberals viewed the state as a tool whereby to "reshape the institutional framework of the free economy. Citizens have to be forced to be free and enterprising, otherwise there is no guarantee they will be so." Gamble, *The Free Economy and the Strong State: The Politics of Thatcherism*, 2nd ed. (Houndmills: Macmillan, 1994 [1988]), 42.
14. I borrow this formulation from Mark Granovetter (484), whose eloquent and pathbreaking analysis of capitalism's social embeddedness remains a touchstone for contemporary critiques of neoliberalism. See Granovetter, "Economic Action and Social Structure: The Problem of Embeddedness," *American Journal of Sociology* 91, no. 3 (1985): 481–510.
15. Adam Smith's *Wealth of Nations*, more often cited than read, constituted just such an effort in the context of the small-scale, highly localized nascent capitalism of eighteenth-century Britain. Unfortunately, the specific context of Smith's work, and his relatively embedded understanding of society and his support for a significant role for the state, is either forgotten or deliberately ignored by those who cite him, most inappropriately, as the intellectual wellspring of neoliberalism.
16. As Peck also points out, such rejections of transnational neoliberalism and the emergence of nationally embedded forms of liberalism in its place might usefully be understood as an ideational analog to Karl Polanyi's notion of the "double movement," whereby the extension of state authority to create a market produces social demands for protection against market vagaries that must ultimately be politically negotiated. See Peck, *Constructions of Neoliberal Reason*, 27–28.
17. In the same vein, Cerny also argues that the historical reliance of capitalist markets on state intervention for their creation and viability reflects the fact that "the conditions for market efficiency do not arise spontaneously from human (or social) interaction." Philip G. Cerny, "In the Shadow of Ordoliberalism: The Paradox of Neoliberalism in the 21st Century," *European Review of International Studies* 3, no. 1 (2016): 81, 83–84.
18. Smith's argument about American political traditions is analogous to my own in important respects. Smith argues persuasively that prevailing claims about the hegemony of the liberal democratic tradition and principle of equality in the United States obscure the powerful influence of competing ascriptive and exclusionary traditions, such as "rival norms" relating to African Americans' inferiority to whites and the ostensibly "natural" subordination of women to men (558). In contrast to prevailing narratives of an essentially liberal, inclusive America, Smith argues for a "multiple traditions thesis [that] holds that the definitive feature of American political culture has been . . . [a] more complex pattern of apparently inconsistent combinations of the traditions, accompanied by recurring conflicts." Smith's analysis provides significant explanatory power in the service of arguments about the dynamic character of

national traditions and their interaction with others with which they might or might not be wholly consistent. In the context of the national cases analyzed in this book, such multiple traditions include Ordoliberalism, neocorporatism, and social democracy in Germany; statism, bourgeois commercialism, and Republicanism in France; and anti-statism and clientelism in Italy. Smith, "Beyond Tocqueville, Myrdal, and Hartz: The Multiple Traditions in America," *American Political Science Review* 87, no. 3 (September 1993): 549–66.

19. The literature on democratic corporatism in western Europe is venerable and vast. For two representative treatments of the German variant, see Wolfgang Streeck, "Neo-Corporatist Industrial Relations and the Economic Crisis in West Germany," in *Order and Conflict in Contemporary Capitalism*, ed. John H. Goldthorpe (Oxford: Clarendon Press, 1984), 291–314; and Andrei S. Markovits, *The Politics of West German Trade Unions: Strategies of Class and Interest Representation in Growth and Crisis* (Cambridge: Cambridge University Press, 1986).
20. As is always the case with the imprecise concept of "liberalism," moreover, each country's variant has been defined as much by its enemies as by its substantive policy agenda. In France, these enemies have been represented by ostensibly parochial, self-serving interest groups, in Germany by the predations of an overly powerful state, and in Italy by a state captured by competing interest groups and the clientelist system that serves them.
21. It is important to emphasize that I do not use "illiberal" here in its political sense. Indeed, as I argue in the Conclusion, there is ample reason to believe that states that have eschewed neoliberalism's messianic market-making agenda, such as those in continental Europe, might well be more resistant to the predations of political illiberalism than their more neoliberal counterparts.
22. *Britannica Online Encyclopaedia*, s.v. "Liberalism," by Kenneth Minogue et al., accessed January 4, 2016, http://academic.eb.com.libproxy.tulane.edu:2048/levels/collegiate/article/117288. In this context, it is worth emphasizing that Britain's postwar welfare state, crafted by William Beveridge in order to combat such "impediments to freedom," was very much consistent with the tenor of British liberalism.
23. Jacob Hacker and Paul Pierson argue that Teddy Roosevelt and FDR should be thought of as "bookending a long Progressive era" in American politics, with the former focused on regulation and breaking up the monopolies of the Gilded Age and the latter emphasizing social and economic policy that "inserted government deeply into previously untouched areas of the U.S. political economy." In this way, they both represented the culmination of American liberalism in an edifice far removed from the tenets of classical liberalism. See Hacker and Pierson, "Making America Great Again," *Foreign Affairs*, May/June 2016, 80–81.
24. *Britannica Online Encyclopaedia*, "Liberalism."
25. L. T. Hobhouse, *Liberalism* (London: Oxford University Press, 1942 [1911]), 86.
26. Ibid., 128, 158.
27. For a fully developed analysis of this argument, see Steven K. Vogel, *Marketcraft: How Governments Make Markets Work* (New York: Oxford University Press, 2018). For an earlier formulation of Vogel's central point about the relationships between markets and government regulation, see his *Freer Markets, More Rules: Regulatory Reform in Advanced Industrial Countries* (Ithaca, NY: Cornell University Press, 1998).
28. Peck, *Constructions of Neoliberal Reason*, 7. Original italics.
29. Duncan Bell, "What Is Liberalism?" *Political Theory* 42, no. 6 (2014): 686. Debates among political theorists about the concept of "traditions" are extensive and have tended to divide those, like the antirationalist Michael Oakeshott, who view traditions as deeply embedded, socially and historically constituted habits of mind and behavior, from those who adopt a more rationalistic view of traditions as menus of concepts and commitments from which individuals can choose. My conception of traditions lies in sympathy with Bell's and Oakeshott's understanding, which is consistent with the notion of social and economic embeddedness advanced by Karl Polanyi and the historical work of E. P. Thompson. For a brief treatment of this debate, see Mark Bevir, "On Tradition," *Humanitas* 13, no. 2 (2000): 28–53; and Bruce Frohnen, "Tradition, Habit, and Social Interaction: A Response to Mark Bevir," *Humanitas* 14, no. 1 (2001): 108–16. For Oakeshott's view of tradition, which he variously also terms "practical knowledge, "concrete activity," and "idiom of activity," see his "Rationalism in Politics" (6–42) and "Rational Conduct" (99–131), both in *Rationalism in Politics and Other Essays* (London: Methuen, 1962). I am indebted to Martyn Thompson for these references.

30. Naomi Choi defines "interpretive theory" as an "orientation, approach, or method in political studies that arose in opposition to various positivistic, empiricist . . . outlooks within the human sciences. . . . Interpretive approaches offer narrative accounts of social and political life and emphasize the meaning-laden and even contingent nature of [their] subject matter. . . . Although interpretivists do not, in principle, reject the use of statistics and quantitative measurements, they see their interpretive analysis as necessarily and appropriately extending beyond the data supplied by empirical inquiry." Although my approach is more empiricist than the body of work described by Choi, it shares with such scholarship an emphasis on the importance of ideas, interpretation, and meaning as drivers of political and economic change. See Choi, "Interpretive Theory," in *Encyclopedia of Political Theory*, vol. 2, ed. Mark Bevir (Los Angeles: Sage, 2010), 707–10.
31. Alan Finlayson, "The Interpretive Approach in Political Science: A Symposium–Introduction," *British Journal of Politics and International Relations* 6, no. 2 (2004): 154. Quoted in Mark Bevir, Oliver Daddow, and Pauline Schnapper, "Introduction: Interpreting British European Policy," special issue, *Journal of Common Market Studies* 53, no. 1 (2015): 6. In like fashion, in an excellent recent dissertation on the historical development of banking regulation in Canada, the United States, and Spain, Kimberly Pernell argues that national practices emerged from distinctive "frames of regulatory order" that reflect multiple "meanings within institutions." Pernell, "The Causes of the Divergent Development of Banking Regulation in the U.S., Canada, and Spain" (PhD diss., Harvard University, 2016), 4, 35, and passim.
32. Mark Bevir, *Democratic Governance* (Princeton, NJ: Princeton University Press, 2010), 10.
33. For a discussion, see Hobhouse, *Liberalism*, 8–18, esp. 11–13.
34. One important example of this pattern in the German case was Bismarck's pioneering creation of a welfare state in the first decade following German unification, by which he aimed to neutralize a large and rapidly growing German working class during the process of industrialization. Here, too, state action was conceived in response to group identity, as the "organizational structure of the new social insurance built upon existing forms of collective self-help and self-administration." Philip Manow, "Welfare State Building and Coordinated Capitalism in Japan and Germany," in *The Origins of Nonliberal Capitalism: Germany and Japan in Comparison*, ed. Wolfgang Streeck and Kōzō Yamamura (Ithaca, NY: Cornell University Press, 2001), 111.
35. Alexis de Tocqueville, *L'ancien régime et la révolution*, nouvelle éd. (Paris: Lévy, 1887).
36. For a discussion, see Georges Lefebvre, *The French Revolution*, vol. I: *From Its Origins to 1793*, trans. Elizabeth Moss Evanson (New York: Columbia University Press, 1962), 165–66, 176.
37. The anarcho-syndicalist tradition in French labor organization, in which groups were weak, ideologically oriented, and fragmented and which emphasized direct action, broad social solidarity, and the general strike rather than social and political incorporation and integration, was one outgrowth of this antigroup and individualistic ethos.
38. Hobhouse, *Liberalism*, 11.
39. In Jacob Levy's formulation, "Liberalism is a doctrine both arising in and centrally about the modern state. But it grows in part out of earlier-modern skepticism of that state." Jacob Levy, "From Liberal Constitutionalism to Pluralism," in *Modern Pluralism*, ed. Mark Bevir, 25.
40. In important respects, this book thus parallels the separately developed work of Cornel Ban, which analyzes the "translation" of neoliberalism into domestic political-economic debates in Spain and central and eastern European countries since the 1970s. Though I attribute more importance to organic national traditions and focus on different national cases, our books share an emphasis on national variations in the interpretation and application of liberal precepts. See Ban, *Ruling Ideas: How Global Neoliberalism Goes Local* (Oxford: Oxford University Press, 2016).
41. For a discussion of the origins of early capitalism as a constraint on the arbitrary power of absolutist states, see Albert O. Hirschman, *The Passions and the Interests: Political Arguments for Capitalism before Its Triumph* (Princeton, NJ: Princeton University Press, 1997 [1977]).
42. John Ruggie, "International Regimes, Transactions, and Change: Embedded Liberalism in the Postwar Era," *International Organization* 36, no. 2 (Spring 1982): 379–415. Borrowing from Polanyi's notion of social and economic "embeddedness," Ruggie contends that fears of a repetition of the twin calamities of war and fascism informed a pattern of multilateral political-economic governance sustained by state interventions in both the domestic

economy and international relations. The establishment of robust institutional frameworks designed to buffer and channel market forces in postwar continental Europe and their endurance in the post-1970s neoliberal era both reflect and help to explain the marginal status of neoliberalism in Continental political discourses.

43. In a sense, this book aims to flesh out the substance of Berlin's contrasting notion of "positive freedom" as it is understood in three national traditions and applied to specific instances of economic crisis and austerity. See Berlin, "Two Concepts of Liberty," in *The Proper Study of Mankind: An Anthology of Essays—Isaiah Berlin*, ed. Henry Hardy and Roger Hausheer (London: Chatto and Windus, 1997), 191–242.
44. Polanyi, *The Great Transformation.*
45. Elements of what would come to be construed as "neoliberalism" (quite distinct from how that term came to be used after the 1970s) emerged in each of these three countries during the inter- and postwar periods. However, associated notions of the primacy of the market as the organizing force for healthy economic development and of the state as inimical to such development remained marginal and were often subsumed into subtler and richer conceptions of the proper relationship of the state, society, and the economy. For discussions of the place of market liberalism in postwar French and German economic thought, see the chapters by Denord (45–67) and Ptak (98–138) in *The Road from Mont Pèlerin: The Making of the Neoliberal Thought Collective*, ed. Dieter Plehwe and Philip Mirowski (Cambridge, MA: Harvard University Press, 2009).
46. Gourevitch eloquently captures this logic: "In prosperous times it is easy to forget the importance of power in the making of policy. Social systems appear stable, and the economy works with sufficient regularity that its rules can be modeled as if they functioned without social referent. In difficult economic times . . . patterns unravel, economic models come into conflict, and policy prescriptions diverge." Gourevitch, *Politics in Hard Times: Comparative Responses to International Economic Crises* (Ithaca, NY: Cornell University Press, 1986), 17.
47. Mark Blyth, *Great Transformations: Economic Ideas and Institutional Change in the Twentieth Century* (New York: Cambridge University Press, 2002), 22–23. Blyth develops this argument in his discussion of important historical-institutionalist work, notably Peter Hall's influential study of the adoption of Keynesianism in national political systems. See Peter A. Hall, ed., *The Political Power of Economic Ideas: Keynesianism across Nations* (Princeton, NJ: Princeton University Press, 1989).
48. Important examples of work that calls into question strongly empiricist approaches include Erik Albæk, "Between Knowledge and Power: Utilization of Social Science in Public Policy Making," *Policy Sciences* 28 (1995): 79–100; and Brian Fay, *Contemporary Philosophy of Social Science: A Multicultural Approach* (Oxford: Blackwell, 1996).
49. As Jamie Peck points out, however, even neoliberalism, as it developed in the interwar period, represented a much richer, more affirmative, and more dynamic vision of how society and the economy should be constructed than that advanced by the denuded, essentially negative one represented by contemporary usage. See Peck, *Constructions of Neoliberal Reason*, 30.
50. Marion Fourcade, *Economists and Societies: Discipline and Profession in the United States, Britain, and France, 1890s to 1990s* (Princeton, NJ: Princeton University Press, 2009), 3.
51. In this respect, Ban's work dovetails with my own, albeit with a distinctive understanding of the extent to which national liberalisms can usefully be construed as "neoliberal." For his discussion of the distinctiveness of his approach from that of Fourcade, see Ban, *Ruling Ideas*, ch.1, esp. 22–23.
52. See, e.g., Jeffry Frieden and Ronald Rogowski, "The Impact of the International Economy on National Policies: An Analytical Overview," in *Internationalization and Domestic Politics*, ed. Robert Keohane and Helen Milner (Cambridge: Cambridge University Press, 1996), 21–47.
53. Andrew Shonfield, *Modern Capitalism: The Changing Balance of Public and Private Power* (London: Oxford University Press, 1969 [1965]).
54. Peter Hall, *Governing the Economy: The Politics of State Intervention in Britain and France* (Cambridge: Polity Press, 1986).
55. Suzanne Berger, ed., *Organizing Interests in Western Europe: Pluralism, Corporatism, and the Transformation of Politics* (Cambridge: Cambridge University Press, 1981). An excellent recent volume builds on and extends Berger's insights but adopts an approach that places

greater emphasis on elites' dynamic interpretations of interests. One of its core arguments is that "interests invariably emerge from processes of interpretation, whereby the relevant political actors make determinations among their priorities and weigh the costs and benefits of particular courses of action, often in light of limited information about the effects of those courses of action" (6). This perspective shares certain elements with the approach that I employ here. See Peter A. Hall et al., eds., *The Politics of Representation in the Global Age: Identification, Mobilization, and Adjudication* (New York: Cambridge University Press, 2014).

56. John Zysman, *Governments, Markets, and Growth: Financial Systems and the Politics of Industrial Change* (Ithaca, NY: Cornell University Press, 1983).
57. See, e.g., Hall, *Governing the Economy*; and Jonah D. Levy, *Tocqueville's Revenge: State, Society, and Economy in Contemporary France* (Cambridge, MA: Harvard University Press, 1999).
58. Peter Katzenstein, *Policy and Politics in West Germany: The Growth of a Semisovereign State* (Philadelphia: Temple University Press, 1987). See also Kees van Kersbergen, *Social Capitalism: A Study of Christian Democracy and the Welfare State* (London: Routledge, 1995).
59. Peter A. Hall and David Soskice, "An Introduction to Varieties of Capitalism," in *Varieties of Capitalism: The Institutional Foundations of Comparative Advantage*, ed. Peter A. Hall and David Soskice (Oxford: Oxford University Press, 2001).
60. For excellent formulations of this criticism of the Varieties of Capitalism framework, see Jonah D. Levy, "The State also Rises: The Roots of Contemporary State Activism," in *The State after Statism: New State Activities in the Age of Liberalization*, ed. Jonah D. Levy (Cambridge, MA: Harvard University Press, 2006), esp. 22–24; and Chris Howell, "Varieties of Capitalism: And Then There Was One?" *Comparative Politics* 36, no. 1 (October 2003): 103–24. As Howell takes pains to emphasize, the fact that Hall and Soskice's categories of Liberal and Coordinated Market Economies are essentially abstractions away from the American and German cases, respectively, leaves them poorly equipped to explain political-economic dynamics and trajectories of reform in countries like France and Italy, where the state has long been and remains a central driver of adjustment. For a cogent analysis of the limitations of this approach and the importance of attention to ideas for understanding capitalist diversity in peripheral European countries, see Dorothee Bohle and Béla Greskovits, *Capitalist Diversity on Europe's Periphery* (Ithaca, NY: Cornell University Press, 2012), ch. 1.
61. Chris Howell, *Trade Unions and the State: The Construction of Industrial Relations Institutions in Britain, 1890–2000* (Princeton, NJ: Princeton University Press, 2007), esp. ch. 1. See also Howell, "The State and the Reconstruction of Industrial Relations after Fordism: Britain and France Compared," in *The State after Statism*, ed. Jonah D. Levy, 139–84.
62. Wolfgang Streeck and Kathleen Thelen, "Introduction: Institutional Change in Advanced Political Economies," in *Beyond Continuity: Institutional Change in Advanced Political Economies*, ed. Wolfgang Streeck and Kathleen Thelen (Oxford: Oxford University Press, 2005), 1. Original emphasis.
63. Ibid., 9.
64. Kathleen Thelen, *How Institutions Evolve: The Political Economy of Skills in Germany, Britain, the United States, and Japan* (Cambridge: Cambridge University Press, 2004), 35.
65. Michel Goyer, "Varieties of Institutional Investors and National Models of Capitalism: The Transformation of Corporate Governance in France and Germany," *Politics and Society* 34, no. 3 (September 2006): 402.
66. As Cornel Ban shows convincingly, both in the Spanish and Romanian cases and by extension in other national cases, as well, approaches that focus on interests alone tend significantly to underpredict policy outcomes, a shortcoming that only a focus on ideas can remedy. See Ban, *Ruling Ideas*, chs. 8 and 9. For an analysis that portrays this characteristic limitation of historical-institutionalist scholarship as the result of a frustrated search for a comprehensive account of endogeneity, see Mark Blyth, "The New Ideas Scholarship in the Mirror of Historical Institutionalism: A Case of Old Whines in New Bottles?" *Journal of European Public Policy* 23, no. 3 (2016): 464–71.
67. For a leading example of such an approach to the influence of Keynesianism, as well as one of the seminal examples of ideational analysis in comparative political economy, see Hall, ed., *The Political Power of Economic Ideas*. For work in a similar vein on the transnational

purchase of neoliberalism, see Gamble, *The Free Economy and the Strong State*; and Schmidt and Thatcher, eds., *Resilient Liberalism*.

68. For a list of such core negative tenets of neoliberalism, see Vivien A. Schmidt and Mark Thatcher, "Theorizing Ideational Continuity: The Resilience of Neo-liberal Ideas in Europe," in ibid., 5.
69. For an excellent analysis of the origins of neoliberalism's enduring appeal in its logical circularity, see Damien Cahill, *The End of Laissez-Faire? On the Durability of Embedded Neoliberalism* (Cheltenham: Edward Elgar, 2014), esp. ch. 7.
70. Recent work by Kathleen Thelen investigates patterns of liberalization in Coordinated Market Economies (CMEs) and Liberal Market Economies (LMEs), arguing (against prevailing interpretations) that coordination among firms and producer groups tends to correlate with greater economic and income inequality. Although this work adds needed nuance to broad-brush categories like "neoliberalism," it nevertheless captures only one dimension of national liberalisms. Thelen, "Varieties of Capitalism: Trajectories of Liberalization and the New Politics of Social Solidarity," *Annual Review of Political Science* 15, no. 1 (2012): 137–59; and *Varieties of Liberalization and the New Politics of Social Solidarity* (Cambridge: Cambridge University Press, 2014).
71. This work shares intellectual terrain with the constructivist approach in international relations, as well as with the interpretivist approach discussed above. For a helpful overview of recent work on the political role of ideas, see Sheri Berman, "Ideational Theorizing in the Social Sciences since 'Policy Paradigms, Social Learning, and the State,'" *Governance* 26, no. 2 (2012): 217–37.
72. Blyth, *Great Transformations*, 10, n. 20; 11. For an earlier, concise formulation, see Blyth, "'Any More Bright Ideas?' The Ideational Turn of Comparative Political Economy," *Comparative Politics* 29, no. 2 (January 1997): 229–50.
73. John L. Campbell, *Institutional Change and Globalization* (Princeton, NJ: Princeton University Press, 2004), 115, 117. See also Campbell, "Ideas, Politics, and Public Policy," *Annual Review of Sociology* 28 (August 2002): 21–38.
74. John L. Campbell and Ove Kaj Pedersen, *The National Origins of Policy Ideas: Knowledge Regimes in the United States, France, Germany, and Denmark* (Princeton, NJ: Princeton University Press, 2014), esp. ch. 1. Although Campbell and Pederson's approach shares elements with my own, my focus is on how such national regimes operate and shape policy rather than on their origins.
75. Daniel Béland, "The Idea of Power and the Role of Ideas," *Political Studies Review* 8, no. 2 (2010): 145–54.
76. Daniel Béland and Robert Henry Cox, "Introduction: Ideas and Politics," in *Ideas and Politics in Social Science Research*, ed. Daniel Béland and Robert Henry Cox (Oxford: Oxford University Press, 2011), 1–20. This piece is the introduction to an excellent collection of contributions by some of the leading voices in this emerging body of work.
77. Craig Parsons, *A Certain Idea of Europe* (Ithaca, NY: Cornell University Press, 2003). Though my work shares certain elements with Parsons's conception of the role of ideas, notably with respect to their role as "filters" between elite understandings and the environment that they face, it differs in its emphasis on *traditions*, as opposed to established ideational "models" ("confederal," "national," or "supranational" in Parsons's case) from which elites choose and one or another of which becomes dominant over time. My approach speaks both to how such "models" evolve over time, along identifiable national trajectories, and how they are then modified and redeployed in response to subsequent and often quite different sets of economic challenges.
78. Schmidt, "Reconciling Ideas and Institutions through Discursive Institutionalism," in *Ideas and Politics in Social Science Research*, ed. Daniel Béland and Robert Henry Cox, 47–64. See also Schmidt, *The Futures of European Capitalism* (Oxford: Oxford University Press, 2002), and "Speaking to the Markets or to the People? A Discursive Institutionalist Analysis of the EU's Sovereign Debt Crisis," *British Journal of Politics & International Relations* 16, no. 1 (2014): 188–209. Schmidt's work calls useful attention to the role of discourse as a contextual variable, but it is unclear at times whether, for her, ideas serve as a constitutive force for, or, rather, a reflection of underlying ideational currents. For a helpful formulation of the fluid

relationship between ideas and interests, centered upon the notion of "constructivist institutionalism," see Colin Hay, "Ideas and the Construction of Interests," in *Ideas and Politics*, ed. Daniel Béland and Robert Henry Cox, 65–82. Though less constructivist in inspiration, Pepper Culpepper's inventive notion of "common knowledge" parallels some aspects of these approaches by showing that changes in prevailing assumptions about politics and the economy can "change both the institutional preference ordering and bargaining leverage of social actors" and "alte[r] socially agreed facts about the character of the economy." See Culpepper, "The Politics of Common Knowledge: Ideas and Institutional Change in Wage Bargaining," *International Organization* 62, no. 1 (January 2008): 2.

79. While Ban focuses on the "translation" of neoliberalism into nationally distinctive hybrids in Spain and Romania, Widmaier analyzes the evolution of economic policy orders in the United States. See Ban, *Ruling Ideas*, and Wesley W. Widmaier, *Economic Ideas in Political Time: The Rise and Fall of Economic Orders from the Progressive Era to the Global Financial Crisis* (Cambridge: Cambridge University Press, 2016).
80. Guido De Ruggiero, *The History of European Liberalism*, trans. R. G. Collingwood (Boston: Beacon Press, 1927 [1959]), 161, 178–79.
81. As David Spector has recently pointed out, this tension between egalitarianism and statism in the French liberal tradition finds echoes in a shared distrust of economic competition and market mechanisms by both the Left and the Right. The result was a common embrace of protectionism across the political spectrum in the service of both the established economic order (for the Right) and individual welfare (for the Left). Spector, *La gauche, la droite et le marché: Histoire d'une controversée (XIXe–XXIe siècle)* (Paris: Odile Jacob, 2017), introduction and esp. 20–21.
82. For an overview of Ordoliberalism and its influence on the postwar German Social Market Economy, see Razeen Sally, "Ordoliberalism and the Social Market: Classical Political Economy from Germany," in *L'ordolibéralisme allemand: Aux sources de l'économie sociale de marché*, ed. Patricia Commun (Cergy-Pontoise: CIRAC/CICC, 2003), 31–36; and Ralf Ptak, *Vom Ordoliberalismus zur Sozialen Marktwirtschaft: Stationen des Neoliberalismus in Deutschland* (Opladen: Leske und Budrich, 2004).
83. Spector, *La gauche, la droite et le marché*, 22.
84. It has become commonplace in discussions of the Eurozone crisis to refer to the prevailing German economic perspective as "Ordoliberal." As I show in Chapters 1 and 3, many of the ideas and institutional commitments of the postwar German Social Market Economy departed sharply from traditional Ordoliberal prescriptions. Such reflexive uses of "Ordoliberalism" obscure both the profound evolution of German economic thinking since the 1950s (the last period during which dominant German economic paradigm might justifiably have been described as "Ordoliberal") and the emphasis on groups that long predated the emergence of Ordoliberalism in the interwar period. They also fail to recognize the discrepancies between German prescriptions for peripheral Eurozone economies and for its own, evident in the robust, if disguised, German Keynesian response to the post-2007 economic crisis. For a recent example of such elisions of "Ordoliberalism" and the dominant German policy regime, see "Of Rules and Order," *Economist*, May 9, 2015, 46–47. For an analysis of the "rule consequentialist" character of Ordoliberalism and its relationship to the central ideas of the Social Market Economy, see David M. Woodruff, "Governing by Panic: The Politics of the Eurozone Crisis," *Politics and Society* 44, no. 1 (2016): 81–116.
85. The notion of "mesoeconomics" advanced here echoes earlier work on the concept, most notably Stuart Holland, *The Market Economy: From Micro to Mesoeconomics* (New York: St. Martin's Press, 1987).
86. De Ruggiero, *History of European Liberalism*, 254, 256.
87. Ibid. As I discuss in chapter 2, the importance of "group personality" stemmed from nineteenth-century German historical legal scholarship of figures such as Otto von Gierke. For an overview, see Jacob T. Levy, "From Liberal Constitutionalism to Pluralism," 33–34.
88. Raimondo Cubeddu and Antonio Masala, "Introduction," in *Histoire du libéralisme en Europe*, ed. Philippe Nemo and Jean Petitot, 1st ed. (Paris: Presses universitaires de France, 2006), 559. De Ruggiero argues that three themes in particular, born in the proto-capitalist north and then enshrined in the post-*Risorgimento* national model, became hallmarks of

Italian liberalism: independence, unity, and freedom. De Ruggiero, *History of European Liberalism*, 284.

89. For a trenchant analysis of the corrosive effects of this system on recent Italian political engagement, see Maurizio Viroli, *The Liberty of Servants: Berlusconi's Italy* (Princeton, NJ: Princeton University Press, 2012).

Chapter 1

1. In Eli Heckscher's words, mercantilism was both "the economic system of nationalism" and an ideology underlying a distinctive "system of power." Heckscher, *Mercantilism*, trans. Mendel Shapiro, vol. 2 (London: Allen & Unwin, 1935), 13 and ch. 1, passim.
2. Adam Smith, *The Wealth of Nations*, bk. 1 (London: Penguin, 1986 [1776]), 121.
3. For a discussion, see Harold Laski, *The Rise of European Liberalism: An Essay in Interpretation* (London: Allen & Unwin, 1936), ch. 2.
4. Ibid., 18.
5. Robert L. Heilbroner, *The Worldly Philosophers: The Lives, Times & Ideas of the Great Economic Thinkers*, rev. ed. (New York: Simon and Schuster, 1961 [1953]), 38.
6. Jamie Peck, *Constructions of Neoliberal Reason* (Oxford: Oxford University Press, 2010), 7. As Peck relates, even Milton Friedman recognized in his early writings the problematic character of this negative legacy: "The fundamental error in the foundations of 19th century liberalism [was that it] gave the state hardly any other task than to maintain peace, and to foresee that contracts were kept. It was a naïve ideology." Ibid., 3.
7. See, for example, Mark Thatcher and Vivien Schmidt, eds., *Resilient Liberalism in Europe's Political Economy* (Cambridge: Cambridge University Press, 2013). Even neoliberalism, as it developed in the interwar period, represented a richer vision of how society and the economy should be constructed than suggested by contemporary usage. As Peck notes, "There may . . . be a certain degree of truth in what otherwise might seem to be a sloppy and unprincipled claim, that neoliberalism has become omnipresent, but it is a complex, mediated, and heterogeneous kind of omnipresence, not a state of blanket conformity." Peck, *Constructions of Neoliberal Reason*, 30.
8. As Minogue et al. acknowledge, "[S]ince the late nineteenth century . . . most liberals have insisted that the powers of government can promote as well as protect the freedom of the individual. According to modern liberalism, the chief task of government is to remove obstacles that prevent individuals from living freely or from fully realizing their potential. Such obstacles include poverty, disease, discrimination, and ignorance. *Britannica Online Encyclopaedia*, s.v. "Liberalism," Kenneth Minogue et al., accessed January 4, 2016, http://academic.eb.com.libproxy.tulane.edu:2048/levels/collegiate/article/117288.
9. L. T. Hobhouse, *Liberalism* (London: Oxford University Press, 1942 [1911]), 136.
10. Ibid., 123.
11. Ibid., 128, 191.
12. Such convictions were widely shared among members of Franklin Roosevelt's New Deal administrations, stated perhaps most eloquently by Jerome Frank, an official in the Agricultural Adjustment Administration: "When the community, exercising intelligent choice and acting through the Government, puts a solid material foundation under the individual, it does not intrude on individual freedom and dignity; it makes them possible." Cited in Arthur M. Schlesinger Jr., *The Age of Roosevelt*, vol. II: *The Coming of the New Deal, 1933–1935* (Boston: Houghton Mifflin, 2003 [1958]), 491.
13. For a discussion, see Dieter Plehwe, "Introduction," in *The Road from Mont Pèlerin: The Making of the Neoliberal Thought Collective*, ed. Philip Mirowski and Dieter Plehwe (Cambridge, MA: Harvard University Press, 2009), 1–42.
14. In words that could easily have been taken from the writings of a German Social Democrat at the time, Lippmann wrote that there was a fundamental difference between respecting an individual "as an autonomous person" and "degrad[ing] him to a living instrument." Lippmann, *An Inquiry into the Principles of the Good Society* (Boston: Little, Brown, 1937), 387, quoted in Nicholas Deakin, *Origins of the Welfare State* (London: Routledge, 2000 [1957]), 15.

15. Here we see the intersection of the prevailing European and American uses of the term, more recently buried under distinctive rhetorical and polemical practices on the two continents.
16. See Berlin, "Two Concepts of Liberty," in *The Proper Study of Mankind: An Anthology of Essays, Isaiah Berlin*, ed. Henry Hardy and Roger Hausheer (London: Chatto and Windus, 1997). Michael Freeden emphasizes the potential of totalitarian imposition on individual choice implied by Berlin's understanding of positive freedom. See Freeden, "European Liberalisms: An Essay in Comparative Political Thought," *European Journal of Political Theory* 7, no. 1 (2008): 29, n. 19.
17. Duncan Bell, "What Is Liberalism?" *Political Theory* 42, no. 6 (2014): 682–715.
18. Ibid., 686. As discussed in the introduction, my understanding thus embraces something very much like Oakeshott's view of traditions as deeply embedded, socially and historically constituted habits of mind and behavior, in contradistinction to a more rationalist understanding that views traditions as intellectual tools to be deployed deliberately.
19. Mark Blyth, *Great Transformations: Economic Ideas and Institutional Change in the Twentieth Century* (New York: Cambridge University Press, 2002), 9.
20. Perhaps the most famous and emblematic example of the neoliberal rejection of the concept of society is Margaret Thatcher's quip in a 1987 interview that "there is no such thing as society. There are individual men and women and there are families." Cited in Samuel Brittan, "Thatcher Was Right—There Is No 'Society,'" *Financial Times*, April 18, 2013, https://www.ft.com/content/d1387b70-a5d5-11e2-9b77-00144feabdc0.
21. François Caron views these features as central to the development of the French liberal tradition in the nineteenth century: "The French always mistrusted market mechanisms, considered threats to the ideal of a coherent and balanced society." Caron, "Le développement économique, entre libéralisme et intervention," in *Aux sources du modèle libéral français*, ed. Alain Madelin (Paris: Perrin/Association d'histoire de l'entreprise, 1997), 237. Throughout this chapter and the rest of the book, translations of all non-English passages are the author's, unless otherwise indicated.
22. I derive this term from the Latin *corpus*, or "body," rather than from more contemporary (though etymologically related) notions of "corporations." For an overview of Ordoliberalism and its influence on the postwar German Social Market Economy, see Razeen Sally, "Ordoliberalism and the Social Market: Classical Political Economy from Germany," in *L'ordolibéralisme allemand: Aux sources de l'économie sociale de marché*, ed. Patricia Commun (Cergy-Pontoise: CIRAC/CICC, 2003), 31–36; and Ralf Ptak, *Vom Ordoliberalismus zur sozialen Marktwirtschaft: Stationen des Neoliberalismus in Deutschland* (Opladen: Leske und Budrich, 2004).
23. Loïc Charles, "L'économie politique française et le politique dans la seconde moitié du XVIIIe siècle," in *Histoire du libéralisme en Europe*, ed. Philippe Nemo and Jean Petitot (Paris: Presses universitaires de France, 2006), 287–88.
24. Ibid., 289–90; and Edmund Fawcett, *Liberalism: The Life of an Idea* (Princeton, NJ: Princeton University Press, 2014), 23.
25. At times, as with the work of Étienne Dumont, this focus on individualism resembled Benthamite utilitarianism, which ironically destroyed individualism even as it elevated the individual to the sole meaningful measure of welfare and value. See Cheryl B. Welch, "'Anti-Benthamism': Utilitarianism and the French Liberal Tradition," in *French Liberalism from Montesquieu to the Present Day*, ed. Raf Geenens and Helena Rosenblatt (Cambridge: Cambridge University Press, 2012), 136–45. For detailed discussions of the related conceptions of Say and the "Ideologues," see Alain Laurent, "Lumières et laissez-faire: Turgot, entre les Physiocrates et un 'moment américain'" (313–22) and Philippe Nemo, "Les Idéologues et le libéralisme" (323–67), both in *Histoire du libéralisme*, ed. Philippe Nemo and Jean Petitot.
26. As Albert Hirschman has pointed out, Montesquieu viewed "*doux commerce*" as a force capable of calming the despotic and "barbaric" tendencies of rulers, placing him in a group of preindustrial thinkers who saw economic exchange as an antidote to absolutism. See Hirschman, *The Passions and the Interests: Political Arguments for Capitalism before Its Triumph*, 20th anniversary ed. (Princeton, NJ: Princeton University Press, 1997 [1977]), esp. 59–61 and 70–81.

27. Charles de Secondat Montesquieu, *De l'esprit des lois*, ed. Robert Derathé, vol. 2, bk. XX (Paris: Classiques Garnier, 2011 [1748]), 3. Elsewhere, Montesquieu holds up England as a shining example of a free society whose commercial "spirit" is both constitutive and reflective of freedom, independence, and the rule of law. Ibid., 7; and vol. 1, bk. XI, passim.
28. Thomas L. Pangle, *Montesquieu's Philosophy of Liberalism: A Commentary on the Spirit of the Laws* (Chicago: University of Chicago Press, 1973), 204.
29. In Pangle's words, Montesquieu thus identifies the "irreconcilable tension between virtue and freedom" that continues to inform modern French liberalism. Ibid., 5.
30. Alexis de Tocqueville, *L'ancien régime et la Révolution*, nouvelle éd. (Paris: Lévy, 1887 [1856]), esp. ch. 5. The literature on Tocqueville is encyclopedic, and detailed discussion of his work is beyond the scope of this book's focus on liberalism's economic variant. Nonetheless, as Richard Swedberg indicates, Tocqueville's comparison of the relatively egalitarian American economy with hidebound, aristocratic post-revolutionary France touches on many of the economic themes—particularly the importance of partible inheritance and the erosion of inherited privilege, as well as the emphasis on individual initiative and dignity and the distrust of group parochialism—central to the liberalism of the day. See Swedberg, *Tocqueville's Political Economy* (Princeton, NJ: Princeton University Press, 2009), esp. chs. 1 and 10. For Tocqueville's analysis of inheritance and land reform in the United States and France, see Tocqueville, *Democracy in America*, ed. J. P. Mayer, trans. George Lawrence (New York: Harper Collins, 1988 [1835]), part 1, ch. 3.
31. Guido De Ruggiero, *The History of European Liberalism*, trans. R. G. Collingwood (Boston: Beacon Press, 1927 [1959]), 171–72.
32. This fact informed a shared hostility to economic competition among the bourgeoisie, whose interests lay in protecting the established order, and the nascent Left, for whom the economic status of France's peasants and small artisans was the focus. The result was a shared goal of the "preservation of [an] idealized social equilibrium" and a fear of markets and economic competition as potentially destabilizing forces. For a discussion, see David Spector, *La gauche, la droite et le marché: Histoire d'une controversée (XIXe–XXIe siècle)* (Paris: Odile Jacob, 2017), 28–31.
33. This character was particularly emblematic of the July Monarchy (1830–1848), under which the Orléanist king Louis-Philippe sought to expand the burgeoning power of merchants and industrialists, with whom he coexisted in a somewhat uneasy symbiosis. Though something of a caricature, Interior Minister Guizot's appeal to citizens to "enrich yourselves" ("enrichissez-vous!") was nonetheless broadly consistent with the character of the regime.
34. As De Ruggiero points out, however, the limitation of political rights through such means as limiting suffrage to around 250,000 property holders did not represent a stable equilibrium, despite the accelerating accumulation of wealth by a much broader middle class. Gathering demands for expanded and, ultimately, universal suffrage would fuel discontent and instability and help lead to the collapse of the regime in 1848. See De Ruggiero, *History of European Liberalism*, 177.
35. Ibid., 169. This fact furnishes a clearer reminder than in perhaps any other country's liberal tradition that the linking of liberalism and democracy is a thoroughly contemporary confection with little precedent in pre-twentieth-century history.
36. Aurelian Craiutu, *Liberalism under Siege: The Political Thought of the French Doctrinaires* (Lanham, MD: Lexington Books, 2003), 3, 7.
37. Aurelian Craiutu, "Raymond Aron and the Tradition of Political Moderation in France," in *French Liberalism*, ed. Raf Geenens and Helena Rosenblatt (Cambridge: Cambridge University Press, 2012), 272.
38. Craiutu, *Liberalism under Siege*, 137. Original italics.
39. Lucien Jaume, "Un libéralisme de rupture," *Le Monde*, May 14, 2017, 24.
40. Fawcett, *Liberalism*, 41.
41. For a detailed discussion of Say's work, see Philippe Steiner, "Say et le libéralisme économique," in *Histoire du libéralisme*, ed. Philippe Nemo and Jean Petitot, 381–403.
42. Quoted in *De Ruggiero, History of European Liberalism*, 167.
43. Ibid., 173.

44. For Rousseau, "if groups . . . are formed at the expense of the larger association, the will of each of these groups will become general in relation to its own members and private in relation to the state. . . . [T]here should be no sectional associations in the state, and that every citizen should make up his mind for himself." Jean-Jacques Rousseau, *The Social Contract*, trans. Maurice Cranston (London: Penguin, 1968 [1762]), 73.
45. The Le Chapelier Law banned guilds, trade unions, and other subnational interest groups such as trading monopolies, thereby working to ensure individual equality before the law and to prevent the reconstitution of groups that had been favored clients under the Ancien Régime. The Declaration of the Rights of Man and the Citizen declared the law to be "the expression of the general will." Lucien Jaume, "Two Liberal Traditions," in *French Liberalism*, ed. Raf Geenens and Helena Rosenblatt, 40.
46. In a characteristic passage, Sismondi claimed that he and others who shared his convictions "view the government as the protector of the weak against the strong, the defender of he who cannot defend himself and the representative of the permanent yet quiescent interest of everyone as against the temporary yet passionate interests of each one." Quoted in Alain Laurent, "Le groupe de Coppet: Mythe et réalité. Staël, Constant, Sismondi," in *Histoire du libéralisme*, ed. Philippe Nemo and Jean Petitot, 417.
47. These competing versions of state neutrality echo Michael Freeden's distinction between the "republican communitarianism" of thinkers like Michael Sandel, which "engages civic virtues: 'a sense of belonging, a concern for the whole, a moral bond with the community,' and a 'liberalism that conceives persons as free and independent selves,' manifesting a voluntarism that casts them 'as the authors of the only obligations that constrain,'" Freeden, *Liberal Languages: Ideological Imaginations and Twentieth-Century Progressive Thought* (Princeton, NJ: Princeton University Press, 2005), 42.
48. Richard Bellamy uses the term "neutralist liberalism" to describe Rawls's and Dworkin's vision of a state that is neutral with respect to individuals but "fail[s] to see how the institutions of the market and democracy do not operate according to neutral norms of universal rationality, but reflect the organizational capacities of different corporate and group interests." Though Bellamy identifies this neutralist tradition as central to Anglo-American thought, French Republicanism produced a similar neutralist tradition with respect to individuals but with a more robust role for public authority. Bellamy, *Liberalism and Modern Society* (University Park, PA: Pennsylvania State University Press, 1992), 249.
49. De Ruggiero, *History of European Liberalism*, 178–79.
50. Robert Adcock, "Rethinking Classical Liberalism in the Age of Organized Capitalism: The Divergent Disillusionment of Spencer and Sumner," paper presented at panel "Historicizing Capitalism," Southern Economic Association Conference, Washington, DC, November 19, 2011, 5–11. In this way Comte accepted Montesquieu's identification of commercial society with an individualistic, free society but rejected such a template as inappropriate for industrial society.
51. De Ruggiero, *History of European Liberalism*, 182–83.
52. It is interesting to note the relatively fine line and significant overlap between liberalism and socialism in the French tradition. In ways that echoed both the utopian collectivism of antistatist variants of Socialism, such as Fourier's, and the workerist statism of thinkers like Saint-Simon, as well as twentieth-century debates between French associational socialists and their more Stalinist counterparts, the evolution of French liberalism was long shaped by points of tangency with both radical individualism and neo-mercantilist *étatisme*. This unresolved contradiction would leave a powerful imprint on the post-1958 Fifth Republic.
53. Charles Brook Dupont-White, *L'individu et l'état*, 3rd ed. (Paris: Librairie de Guillaumin, 1865), ix.
54. De Ruggiero, *History of European Liberalism*, 199–200.
55. Jean-Fabien Spitz, "The 'Illiberalism' of French Liberalism: The Individual and the State in the Thought of Blanc, Dupont-White and Durkheim," in *French Liberalism*, ed. Raf Geenens and Helena Rosenblatt, 262–63.
56. Dupont-White, *L'individu et l'état*, lxvi, lxx.
57. De Ruggiero, *History of European Liberalism*, 200.

58. See Eugen Weber, *Peasants into Frenchmen: The Modernization of Rural France, 1870–1914* (Stanford, CA: Stanford University Press, 1976), for a discussion.
59. Stanley Hoffmann, "Paradoxes of the French Political Community," in *In Search of France*, ed. Stanley Hoffmann (New York: Harper and Row, 1963), 17.
60. Spector, *La gauche, la droite et le marché*, 27–28, 127. As Spector points out, competitive market mechanisms that might undermine concentrations of wealth were considered "too socialist for the liberals," but their threat to establish smallholders was considered "too liberal for the socialists." The result was the unavailability of a social-liberal coalition of the kind that would come to mark Hobhousian English liberalism and the "Lib-Lab" parliamentary coalitions around the turn of the twentieth century that it underpinned.
61. William Shirer, *The Collapse of the Third Republic* (New York: Simon and Schuster, 1969), 39. As Shirer describes, the regime's preference for stability above all was far from unchallenged, as anti-democratic enemies of both the Left and the Right attacked it with regularity. The same smug complacency that lent the regime its bourgeois character would eventually undermine its social, political, and economic foundations and eventually help lead to its collapse in 1940.
62. For a discussion of the corrosive effects of the Third Republic's policies on French society, see Eugen Weber, *The Hollow Years: France in the 1930s* (New York: Norton, 1994).
63. The definitive English-language history of the Vichy period is Robert O. Paxton, *Vichy France: Old Guard and New Order* (New York: Columbia University Press, 2001 [1972]).
64. For a concise description of the contours of the French planning process, see Karl Orfeo Fioretos, *Creative Reconstructions: Multilateralism and European Varieties of Capitalism after 1950* (Ithaca, NY: Cornell University Press, 2011), 105–7.
65. Laroque also drew inspiration from the leading example of the postwar British welfare state constructed under the leadership of William Beveridge and its attendant notions of social citizenship. Bruno Palier, *Gouverner la sécurité sociale: Les réformes du système français de protection sociale depuis 1945* (Paris: Presses universitaires de France, 2002), ch. 6. For an excellent history of the early evolution of the postwar French welfare state, see Henry C. Galant, *Histoire politique de la sécurité sociale française, 1945–1952* (Paris: Armand Colin, 1955).
66. Palier, *Gouverner la sécurité sociale*, 73–4.
67. Charles de Gaulle dismissed it as a "regime of mediocrity and chloroform." Quoted in Gordon Wright, *France in Modern Times: From the Enlightenment to the Present*, 5th ed. (New York: Norton, 1995), 411–12.
68. For a detailed discussion, see Peter Baldwin, *The Politics of Social Solidarity: Class Bases of the European Welfare State, 1875–1975* (Cambridge: Cambridge University Press, 1990), 163–86.
69. Jonah D. Levy, *Tocqueville's Revenge: State, Society, and Economy in Contemporary France* (Cambridge, MA: Harvard University Press, 1999), 7, 31.
70. Rousseau, *Social Contract*, 63–64.
71. Peter Hall, *Governing the Economy: The Politics of State Intervention in Britain and France* (Cambridge: Polity Press, 1986), 178–79.
72. For full descriptions of the development of French dirigisme, see Levy, *Tocqueville's Revenge*, esp. introduction and ch. 1; Hall, *Governing the Economy*, esp. chs. 6 and 7; and Richard F. Kuisel, *Capitalism and the State in Modern France: Renovation and Economic Management in the Twentieth Century* (Cambridge: Cambridge University Press, 1981).
73. These powers stood in stark contrast to the much weaker authority of the executive under the Third and Fourth Republics.
74. Andrew Shonfield, *Modern Capitalism: The Changing Balance of Public and Private Power* (London: Oxford University Press, 1965), 131.
75. As Suzanne Berger acknowledged in her 1981 retrospective on French industrial policy under the Fifth Republic, "Liberal and statist doctrines and practices have coexisted from the beginnings of De Gaulle's Republic." My analysis suggests that this coexistence actually stems from a much earlier set of conceptual frameworks. Berger, "Lame Ducks and National Champions: Industrial Policy in the Fifth Republic," in *The Fifth Republic at Twenty*, ed. William G. Andrews and Stanley Hoffmann (Albany: State University of New York Press, 1981), 292.

76. Craiutu, "Raymond Aron and the Tradition of Political Moderation in France," 274–76. Original italics.
77. Shonfield, *Modern Capitalism*, 126.
78. Levy, *Tocqueville's Revenge*, 32.
79. Kuisel, *Capitalism and the State*, 224.
80. Christian Sautter, "France," in *The European Economy: Growth and Crisis*, ed. Andrea Boltho (Oxford: Oxford University Press, 1982), 450, 461. For inflation and unemployment figures, see Richard Layard, Stephen Nickell, and Richard Jackman, *Unemployment: Macroeconomic Performance and the Labour Market* (Oxford: Oxford University Press, 1991), 526–31.
81. Chris Howell, *Regulating Labor: The State and Industrial Relations Reform in Postwar France* (Princeton, NJ: Princeton University Press, 1992), 61–73.
82. The precedent was set in the 1968 Grenelle Accords, which raised the minimum wage by 35 percent, committed to raising wages across the economy, and cut the length of the working week. Sautter, "France," 461–62.
83. Chris Howell, "The State and the Reconstruction of Industrial Relations Institutions after Fordism," in *The State after Statism: New State Activities in the Age of Liberalization*, ed. Jonah D. Levy (Cambridge, MA: Harvard University Press, 2006), 151–53.
84. The most important of these measures was the 1973 Royer Law, which "essentially gave local shopkeepers veto power over all proposed supermarket construction in their communities." For a discussion, see John T. S. Keeler, "Corporatist Decentralization and Commercial Modernization in France: The Royer Law's Impact on Shopkeepers, Supermarkets, and the State," in *Socialism, the State, and Public Policy in France*, ed. Philip Cerny and Martin Schain (London: Frances Pinter, 1985), 265–91.
85. For a description of France's reliance on "national champions" at the expense of efforts to promote the growth of SMEs, see Levy, *Tocqueville's Revenge*, 35–38.
86. For example, a 1975 law gave inspectors from the Ministry of Labor the authority to approve (or, more often, to deny) moves by French firms to lay off more than ten workers. Ibid., 41.
87. Mark I. Vail, *Recasting Welfare Capitalism: Economic Adjustment in Contemporary France and Germany* (Philadelphia: Temple University Press, 2010), ch. 7. See also Palier, *Gouverner la sécurité sociale*, ch. 6.
88. Levy, *Tocqueville's Revenge*, 19, 43–46.
89. Policies included measures that increased the minimum wage (the *Salaire minimum interprofessionel de croissance*, or SMIC) by 15 percent, boosted housing allowances for low-wage workers by 25 percent, and increased the availability of national health insurance to part-time workers and others with uneven contribution histories. Hall, *Governing the Economy*, 194.
90. Levy, *Tocqueville's Revenge*, ch. 1. See also Vail, *Recasting Welfare Capitalism*, ch. 2.
91. Vail, *Recasting Welfare Capitalism.*, chs. 2 and 7.
92. Jonah D. Levy, "France: Directing Adjustment?" in *Welfare and Work in the Open Economy*, vol. II: *Diverse Responses to Common Challenges*, ed. Fritz W. Scharpf and Vivien A. Schmidt (Oxford: Oxford University Press, 2000), 326. Elsewhere, Levy has labelled this a "social anaesthesia" strategy, which "seek[s] to permit French firms to reorganise on a more market-rational basis by pacifying and demobilising the potential victims and opponents of economic liberalisation." Jonah D. Levy, "From the Dirigiste State to the Social Anaesthesia State: French Economic Policy in the Longue Durée," *Modern & Contemporary France* 16, no. 4 (October 2008): 417–35.
93. Jonah D. Levy, Mari Miura, and Gene Park, "Exiting Étatisme? New Directions in State Policy in France and Japan," in *State after Statism*, ed. Jonah D. Levy, 113.
94. Fritz W. Scharpf and Vivien A. Schmidt, "Statistical Appendix," in *Welfare and Work in the Open Economy*, vol. I: *From Vulnerability to Competitiveness*, ed. Fritz W. Scharpf and Vivien A. Schmidt (Oxford: Oxford University Press, 2000), 341.
95. Marc de Montalembert, ed., *La protection sociale en France*, 3rd ed. (Paris: La documentation française, 2001), 146.
96. Other important examples included significant increases in the statutory minimum wage and the 2000 *Couverture maladie universelle* (CMU), which created a universal right to health insurance irrespective of one's contribution history and subject only to an income

ceiling. See Palier, *Gouverner la sécurité sociale*, 252; and Mireille Elbaum, *Économie politique de la protection sociale* (Paris: Presses universitaires de France, 2008), 121.

97. De Ruggiero, *History of European Liberalism*, 212.
98. Patricia Commun, "Introduction: Les libéralismes allemands," in *Histoire du libéralisme*, ed. Philippe Nemo and Jean Petitot, 848–49; and De Ruggiero, *History of European Liberalism*, 220–21.
99. The exception was Prussia, where a powerful, centralized state developed much earlier and existed in symbiosis with a powerful landed aristocracy. For a discussion, see James J. Sheehan, "Conflict and Cohesion among German Elites in the Nineteenth Century," in *Imperial Germany*, ed. James J. Sheehan (New York: Franklin Watts, 1976), 62–84; and Alexander Gerschenkron, *Bread and Democracy in Germany* (Ithaca, NY: Cornell University Press, 1989 [1943]), 19–26.
100. De Ruggiero, *History of European Liberalism*, 223.
101. For a discussion, see Fawcett, *Liberalism*, 296–97.
102. Dietmar Doering, "Wilhelm von Humboldt et les origines du libéralisme allemand," in *Histoire du libéralisme*, ed. Philippe Nemo and Jean Petitot, 861.
103. Ibid., 865–66.
104. De Ruggiero, *History of European Liberalism*, 221–22.
105. Fawcett, *Liberalism*, 34.
106. Wilhelm von Humboldt, *Ideen zu einem Versuch, die Gränzen der Wirksamkeit des Staates zu bestimmen* (Breslau: Verlag von Edouard Treuwendt, 1851), 39, 112.
107. Returning to Berlin as a royal chamberlain after a long interregnum, mostly in Paris, the younger Humboldt despondently observed the reactionary Prussian state, which fostered the self-conception of the incipient middle classes as humanistic islands in a sea of reaction: "The country to which Humboldt had returned was decidedly anti-liberal. With few political rights and a general suppression of liberal ideas, Prussia's middle classes had turned inwards and into the private sphere. Music, literature and art were dominated by expressions of feelings rather than revolutionary sentiment. The spirit of 1789, as Humboldt had called it, had ceased to exist." Andrea Wulf, *The Invention of Nature: Alexander von Humboldt's New World* (New York: Knopf, 2015), 192.
108. James J. Sheehan, *German Liberalism in the Nineteenth Century* (Chicago: University of Chicago Press, 1978), 31–32, 249, 253.
109. Spector, *La gauche, la droite et le marché*, 22.
110. Otto Friedrich von Gierke, *Das deutsche Genossenschaftsrecht*, vol. 1, *Rechtsgeschichte der deutschen genossenschaft* (Berlin: Weidmann, 1868), 14–15. Original italics.
111. Otto Friedrich von Gierke, *Community in Historical Perspective: A Translation of Selections from Das Deutsche Genossenschaftsrecht (The German Law of Fellowship)*, ed. Antony Black (Cambridge: Cambridge University Press, 1990), 14.
112. Gierke, *Deutsche Genossenschaftsrecht*, 220–21.
113. Gierke, *Community in Historical Perspective*, 19.
114. Antony Black, "Editor's Introduction," in ibid., xiv, xvii.
115. See, e.g., Putnam, *Making Democracy Work: Civic Traditions in Modern Italy* (Princeton, NJ: Princeton University Press, 1993).
116. De Ruggiero, *History of European Liberalism*, 253–54. De Ruggiero (253) provides a sketch of the wide influence of this model of state and society: "it is the legal tradition of the whole people, from Thomasius to Kant and Hegel; and in the second half of the nineteenth century it inspired the great scientific constructions of Mohl, Gerber, Gneist, Laband, Meyer, and Jellnick."
117. This dynamic would presage the corrosive role played by groups in postwar Italy, as will be discussed.
118. Ralf Ptak, "Neoliberalism in Germany," in *The Road from Mont Pèlerin*, ed. Mirowski and Plehwe, 108–11. Original emphasis. Others, notably the Nazi sympathizer and statist Carl Schmitt, went further, arguing that the experience of Weimar showed that liberalism and democracy were ultimately incompatible and that only an authoritarian state could preserve the social order that liberal capitalism required. In his emphasis of the need for a strong

state to regulate the market order, Schmitt was in agreement with Ordoliberals like Rüstow and Eucken, though the latter did not extend this analysis to a rejection of democracy. For a discussion, see Renato Cristi, *Carl Schmitt and Authoritarian Liberalism: Strong State, Free Economy* (Cardiff: University of Wales Press, 1998), introduction and 193–95.

119. Peck, *Constructions of Neoliberal Reason*, 17.
120. The semantic isomorphism between this "neoliberalism" and the variant pursued by Margaret Thatcher and Milton Freidman is not coincidental, but unpacking the complex connections of these distinct strands of liberal thought is beyond the scope of this chapter. For a detailed account, see Angus Burgin, *The Great Persuasion: Reinventing Free Markets since the Depression* (Cambridge, MA: Harvard University Press, 2012), esp. chs. 2–5.
121. Quoted in Ptak, "Neoliberalism in Germany," 111.
122. Fawcett, *Liberalism*, 309. As Angus Burgin points out, Röpke's critique of unregulated capitalism highlighted the crucial role of traditional, preindustrial groups and lamented "the decline of traditional modes of agriculture, as signs of the dehumanizing influence of unregulated competition on interpersonal relationships. . . . [H]e extolled 'the social life of the family farm' and observed that it required economic 'units smaller than would otherwise be rational for normal business standards.'" Burgin, *Great Persuasion*, 115.
123. Ptak, "Neoliberalism in Germany," 105. Original italics.
124. Ibid., 105–106.
125. Viktor J. Vanberg, "L'école de Fribourg: Walter Eucken et l'ordolibéralisme," in *Histoire du libéralisme*, ed. Philippe Nemo and Jean Petitot, 921.
126. Ibid., 123.
127. For Erhard, too, the social embedding of the market economy called for by Ordoliberals was dependent upon bridging the class divides that had rent German society in the interwar period and ultimately helped to open the door for the Nazis: "The restructuring of our economic order must thus create conditions such that the purchasing power associated with rapid economic growth can overcome obstacles and finally end the resentment between 'poor' and 'rich.'" Erhard, *Wohlstand für Alle*, ed. Wolfram Langer (Düsseldorf: Econ-Verlag, 1957), 7.
128. Nils Goldschmidt, "Alfred Müller-Armack et Ludwig Erhard: Le libéralisme social de marché," in *Histoire du libéralisme*, ed. Philippe Nemo and Jean Petitot, 976–78.
129. Ptak, "Neoliberalism in Germany," 123.
130. Alfred Müller-Armack, "The Meaning of the Social Market Economy," in *Germany's Social Market Economy*, ed. Peacock and Willgerodt, 84. This piece is an excerpt from "*Sozialmarktwirtschaft*," which Müller-Armack published in 1956 in the *Handwörterbuch der Sozialwissenschaften* and became a sort of manifesto for the Social Market Economy.
131. In contrast to the misleading labeling of Germany's economic-policy stance in the Eurozone crisis as "Ordoliberal," Ordoliberalism never adopted a minimalist, neoliberal conception of the state's role. Rather, for Ordoliberals, the state's "goal was not to weaken the state but to direct its intervention into [*sic*] the . . . market-conforming direction" (380). For a discussion, see Matthias Siems and Gerhard Schnyder, "Ordoliberal Lessons for Economic Stability: Different Kinds of Regulation, Not More Regulation," *Governance* 27, no. 3 (July 2014): 377–96.
132. For the classic description of Germany's postwar model, see Shonfield, *Modern Capitalism*, chs. 11–12.
133. For seminal studies of neocorporatism, see Philippe C. Schmitter and Gerhard Lehmbruch, eds., *Trends towards Corporatist Interest Intermediation* (Beverly Hills, CA: Sage, 1979); Philippe C. Schmitter, "Still the Century of Corporatism?" *Review of Politics* 36, no. 1 (1974): 85–131; and Peter J. Katzenstein's magisterial *Small States in World Markets: Industrial Policy in Europe* (Ithaca, NY: Cornell University Press, 1985). For representative treatments of the German variant, see Katzenstein, *Policy and Politics in West Germany: The Growth of a Semi-Sovereign State* (Philadelphia: Temple University Press, 1987); Wolfgang Streeck, "Neo-Corporatist Industrial Relations and the Economic Crisis in West Germany," in *Order and Conflict in Contemporary Capitalism*, ed. John H. Goldthorpe (Oxford: Clarendon Press, 1984), 291–314; and Andrei S. Markovits, *The Politics of West*

German Trade Unions: Strategies of Class and Interest Representation in Growth and Crisis (Cambridge: Cambridge University Press, 1986).

134. In somewhat functionalistic fashion, this scholarship tended to assume a natural concomitance between divided political authority and political consensus. As a result, it tended both to undertheorize the forces shaping state authorities' understanding of their own policymaking roles and to underestimate the potential for significant departures either from standard corporatist practices or from the prevailing policy consensus. For a discussion see Mark I. Vail, "Rethinking Corporatism and Consensus: The Dilemmas of German Social-Protection Reform," *West European Politics* 26, no. 3 (2003): 41–66.
135. Of course, as Jürgen Kocka has pointed out, such groups can also be brought into being by the state, as in the case of Bismarck's creation of politically powerful white-collar groups in the late nineteenth century. Kocka, "Class Formation, Interest Articulation, and Public Policy: The Origins of the German White-Collar Class in the Late Nineteenth and Early Twentieth Century," in *Organizing Interests: Pluralism, Corporatism, and the Transformation of Politics*, ed. Suzanne Berger (Cambridge: Cambridge University Press, 1981), 63–82.
136. Gerhard Lehmbruch, "The Institutional Embedding of Market Economies: The German 'Model' and Its Impact on Japan," in *The Origins of Nonliberal Capitalism: Germany and Japan in Comparison*, ed. Wolfgang Streeck and Kōzo Yamamura (Ithaca, NY: Cornell University Press, 2001), 84–85. See also Kees van Kersbergen, *Social Capitalism: A Study of Christian Democracy and the Welfare State* (London: Routledge, 2003).
137. Kathleen Thelen, *Union of Parts: Labor Politics in Postwar Germany* (Ithaca, NY: Cornell University Press, 1991).
138. Peter Gourevitch, *Politics in Hard Times: Comparative Responses to International Economic Crises* (Ithaca, NY: Cornell University Press, 1986), 171.
139. Fritz Scharpf, "Economic and Institutional Constraints and Full-Employment Strategies: Sweden, Austria, and Western Germany, 1973–1982," in *Order and Conflict in Contemporary Capitalism*, ed. John H. Goldthorpe, 274–86.
140. Fawcett, *Liberalism*, 362.
141. The most influential formulation of the importance of this kind of coordination is presented in the contributions in *Varieties of Capitalism: The Institutional Foundations of Comparative Advantage*, ed. Peter A. Hall and David Soskice (Oxford: Oxford University Press, 2001).
142. The sole exception was a brief and halfhearted experiment under the SPD-CDU Grand Coalition between 1966 and 1969.
143. Peck, *Constructions of Neoliberal Reason*, 29.
144. Phillip Cerny, "Embedding Neoliberalism: The Evolution of a Hegemonic Paradigm," *Journal of International Trade and Diplomacy* 2, no. 1 (2008): 1–46. Cited in ibid.
145. As Wade Jacoby points out, "while invoking ordoliberalism is popular to explain why German [policy] responses differ from those of other states, this ideology appears to underdetermine outcomes. Ordoliberal principles—never completely worked into a full theory of the economy—are invoked in all parts of the German debate" (8). See Jacoby, "The Politics of the Eurozone Crisis: Two Puzzles behind the German Consensus," *German Politics & Society* 32, no. 2 (June 2014): 70–85.
146. De Ruggiero, *History of European Liberalism*, 275–76.
147. Amintore Fanfani, *Catholicism, Protestantism, and Capitalism*, trans. ed. (New York: Sheed & Ward, 1939), 142.
148. Christopher Duggan, *A Concise History of Italy*, 2nd ed. (Cambridge: Cambridge University Press, 2014), 119.
149. Raimundo Cubeddu and Antonio Masala, "Introduction," in *Histoire du libéralisme*, ed. Philippe Nemo and Jean Petitot, 558–59.
150. Ibid., 559.
151. De Ruggiero, *History of European Liberalism*, 288.
152. Cubeddu and Masala, "Introduction," 560.
153. For this reason, among others, it is more difficult to separate, either empirically or analytically, economic and political liberalism in Italy than it is in either France or Germany.
154. De Ruggiero, *History of European Liberalism*, 294–95.

155. It did so by allowing southern, latifundian elites to preserve their quasi-medieval agrarian system with their semi-enserfed peasantry in exchange for a policy regime that systematically subsidized and developed northern industry.
156. Gramsci himself borrowed the term from French revolutionary syndicalist Georges Sorel and viewed the Italian variant as an instrument of post-*Risorgimento* "hegemony." For a discussion and citation of original source material, see Gwyn A. Williams, "The Concept of '*Egemonia*' in the Thought of Antonio Gramsci: Some Notes on Interpretation," *Journal of the History of Ideas* 21, no. 4 (October–December 1960): 586–99.
157. De Ruggiero, *History of European Liberalism*, 326.
158. Ibid., 327.
159. Quoted in Jan-Werner Müller, *Contesting Democracy: Political Ideas in Twentieth-Century Europe* (New Haven, CT, and London: Yale University Press, 2011), 12.
160. Pareto defined economic equilibria by the fact that any shift would improve the situation of one actor by degrading that of others.
161. Philippe Steiner, "Vilfredo Pareto et la révision du libéralisme économique classique," in *Histoire du libéralisme*, ed. Philippe Nemo and Jean Petitot, 603.
162. Pareto was thus justified in his jaundiced view of the character of the Italian state, which he considered an instrument of "organized despoilment by means of law." Ibid., 605.
163. Duggan, *Concise History of Italy*, 161.
164. Steiner, "Vilfredo Pareto et la révision du libéralisme," 613.
165. De Ruggiero, *History of European Liberalism*, 339. The continued underdevelopment of the Italian welfare state, a product of both enduring distrust of the state and the historic monopoly of the Catholic Church over social assistance, thus both informed and validated liberals' championing of the market rather than the state as the source of meaningful economic welfare. For a detailed discussion, see Josef Hien, "Competing Ideas: The Religious Foundations of the German and Italian Welfare States" (PhD diss., European University Institute, 2012), ch. 7.
166. Vilfredo Pareto, *The Transformation of Democracy*, ed. Charles H. Powers, trans. Renata Girola (London: Transaction Books, 1984), 41.
167. Enzo di Nuoscio, "Le libéralisme de Luigi Einaudi," in *Histoire du libéralisme*, ed. Philippe Nemo and Jean Petitot, 653.
168. Quoted in Duggan, *Concise History of Italy*, 246.
169. Di Nuoscio, "Le libéralisme de Luigi Einaudi," in *Histoire du libéralisme*, ed. Philippe Nemo and Jean Petitot, 661.
170. Elsewhere, Einaudi argued that social legislation should be a central task of the liberal state, which should reflect "the general principle according to which, in a healthy society, man must be able to count on the minimum necessary for survival." Quoted in ibid., 662.
171. Vera Zamagni, *The Economic History of Italy, 1860–1990* (Oxford: Clarendon Press, 1993), 338.
172. Ibid., 37, 40.
173. Duggan, *Concise History of Italy*, 265.
174. Ibid., 656.
175. Hien, "Competing Ideas," 291. In Mark Blyth's words, "Einaudi sought to develop a '*liberalismo economico*'—the economic order adequate to the liberal vision that would augment man's natural drive to work, save, and compete." Blyth, *Austerity: The History of a Dangerous Idea* (Oxford: Oxford University Press, 2013), 166.
176. Nuoscio, "Le libéralisme de Luigi Einaudi," 659–61.
177. Ibid., 663.
178. Duggan, *Concise History of Italy*, 159.
179. Ibid., 161, 165. The contrast with the French case is instructive. During roughly the same period, the French Third Republic successfully stabilized parliamentary democracy and integrated the French political community by investing heavily in a system of free public education and local service provision in ways that won over the peasantry to democracy.
180. Frederic Spotts and Theodor Wieser, *Italy, a Difficult Democracy: A Survey of Italian Politics* (Cambridge: Cambridge University Press, 1986), 2.
181. Ibid., 3.

182. Lorenzo Moretti, "A Tale of Failures: Neoliberalism in the Italian Economy, 1945–2011" (unpublished B.A. thesis, Brown University, 2014), 52–53. Such priorities were also central to the original vision of De Gasperi, the founding father of postwar Italian Christian Democracy, though they were soon sacrificed to the exigencies of coalition building and the perceived necessity to make concessions to the illiberalism of the Catholic Church. Hien, "Competing Ideas," 287–89.
183. Blyth, *Austerity*, 165–67.
184. Interview, September 19, 2014.
185. Maurizio Viroli, *The Liberty of Servants: Berlusconi's Italy* (Princeton, NJ: Princeton University Press, 2012), xxi.
186. Hien, "Competing Ideas," 315.
187. Moretti, "Tale of Failures," 68–72.
188. Duggan, *Concise History of Italy*, 266.
189. Shonfield, *Modern Capitalism*, 184.
190. Zamagni, *Economic History of Italy*, 338.
191. Ibid., 344–45; and Duggan, *Concise History of Italy*, 259–60.
192. Duggan, *Concise History of Italy*, 260–66.
193. Hien, "Competing Ideas," 302–17.
194. The *Economist* marked the IRI's dissolution in 2000 by quoting the agency's chairman at the time, who identified the seeds of its demise as the politicization of its goals in the 1960s and 1970s: "The effect of giving the public sector businesses objectives that were not aimed at profit was like that of a Trojan horse. It let the political parties in." *Economist*, "End of an IRI," June 22, 2000, http://www.economist.com/node/81311.
195. Paul Ginsborg, *A History of Contemporary Italy, 1943–1988* (New York: Palgrave Macmillan, 2003), 166, quoted in Moretti, "Tale of Failures," 72.
196. Moretti, "Tale of Failures," 72–73.
197. Duggan, *Concise History of Italy*, 270.
198. Hien, "Competing Ideas," 315.
199. Duggan, *Concise History of Italy*, 272–76.
200. Such measures included sharp wage increases, efforts to bolster public housing, and increases in the progressive character of the tax system and the generosity of pensions. Ibid., 270–76.
201. Spotts and Wieser, *Italy, a Difficult Democracy*, 200–2.
202. Richard M. Locke, *Remaking the Italian Economy* (Ithaca, NY: Cornell University Press, 1995), 5.
203. Interview, Nicoletta Batini, former IMF official and current Italian Treasury official, October 10, 2014.
204. Nicholas Crafts and Marco Magnani, "The Golden Age and the Second Globalization in Italy," in *The Oxford Handbook of the Italian Economy since Unification*, ed. Gianni Toniolo (Oxford: Oxford University Press, 2013), 75.
205. Locke, *Remaking the Italian Economy*, 6.
206. Guido M. Rey, "Italy," in *The European Economy*, ed. Andrea Boltho, 505.
207. Layard, Nickell, and Jackman, *Unemployment*, 527. Using OECD historical statistics, Locke reports higher unemployment rates during this period, increasing from 6.2 percent in 1972 to 7.4 percent in 1979. The same trend is evident in both data sets, despite the differences.
208. Zamagni, *Economic History of Italy*, 345; and Mario Baldassarri and M. Gabriella Briotti, "The Government Budget and the Italian Economy during the 1970s and 1980s: Causes of the Debt, Strategy for Recovery, and Prospects for Restructuring," in *The Italian Economy: Heaven or Hell?* ed. Mario Baldassarri (Rome: St. Martin's Press, SIPI, 1994), 162.
209. Locke, *Remaking the Italian Economy*, 10, 17.
210. Burgin, *Great Persuasion*, 90–91, 184. In his portrayal of the foundation and evolution of the liberal Mont Pelerin Society, Burgin describes the growing divergence of American neoliberals like Friedman from their Continental counterparts, who held more embedded understandings of society and a less restrictive view of the proper role for the state.

Chapter 2

1. Quoted in Guido De Ruggiero, *The History of European Liberalism*, trans. R. G. Collingwood (Boston: Beacon Press, 1927 [1959]), 167.
2. Ibid, 178–79.
3. Sismondi favored state intervention to support workers and others dispossessed by industrialization. In like fashion, Charles Dupont-White argued that the state is a moral being, a "person that represents society," and that "there is no contradiction between the State and liberty; because the State is the form of authority that . . . is deployed as soon as an abuse of force is foreseeable or needs to be redressed." For both authors, then, the state's responsibility for ensuring workers' access to economic goods implied a notion of individual freedom reliant upon that access. See ibid., 173, and Charles Brook Dupont-White, *L'individu et l'état*, 3rd ed. (Paris: Librairie de Guillaumin, 1865), ix, lxvi, lxx.
4. For a discussion of negative social legacies of the Third Republic's policies, see Eugen Weber, *The Hollow Years: France in the 1930s* (New York: Norton, 1994). For a magisterial chronicle of the Vichy period, see Robert O. Paxton, *Vichy France: Old Guard and New Order* (New York: Columbia University Press, 2001 [1972]).
5. Stanley Hoffmann, "Paradoxes of the French Political Community," in *In Search of France*, ed. Stanley Hoffmann (New York: Harper and Row, 1963).
6. Peter Hall, *Governing the Economy: The Politics of State Intervention in Britain and France* (Cambridge: Polity Press, 1986), chs. 6 and 7.
7. Andrew Shonfield, *Modern Capitalism: The Changing Balance of Public and Private Power* (London: Oxford University Press, 1965), 126–27. Original emphasis.
8. Ibid., 131.
9. John Zysman, *Governments, Markets, and Growth: Financial Systems and the Politics of Industrial Change* (Ithaca, NY: Cornell University Press, 1983), ch. 3.
10. For an overview of French dirigisme, see Jonah D. Levy, *Tocqueville's Revenge: State, Society, and Economy in Contemporary France* (Cambridge, MA: Harvard University Press, 1999), esp. introduction and ch. 1; and Richard F. Kuisel, *Capitalism and the State in Modern France: Renovation and Economic Management in the Twentieth Century* (Cambridge: Cambridge University Press, 1981).
11. Christian Sautter, "France," in *The European Economy: Growth and Crisis*, ed. Andrea Boltho (Oxford: Oxford University Press, 1982), 449.
12. Aurelian Craiutu, "Raymond Aron and the Tradition of Political Moderation in France," in *French Liberalism from Montesquieu to the Present Day*, ed. Raf Geenens and Helena Rosenblatt (Cambridge: Cambridge University Press, 2012), 274–76. Original italics.
13. Chris Howell, *Regulating Labor: The State and Industrial Relations Reform in Postwar France* (Princeton, NJ: Princeton University Press, 1992), 61–73.
14. Sautter, "France," 450, 461; and Richard Layard, Stephen Nickell, and Richard Jackman, *Unemployment: Macroeconomic Performance and the Labour Market* (Oxford: Oxford University Press, 1991), 526–31. For an account of France's strategy of social and economic compensation during this period, see Levy, *Tocqueville's Revenge*, 39–43; and John T. S. Keeler, "Corporatist Decentralization and Commercial Modernization in France: The Royer Law's Impact on Shopkeepers, Supermarkets, and the State," in *Socialism, the State, and Public Policy in France*, ed. Philip Cerny and Martin Schain (London: Frances Pinter, 1985), 265–91.
15. Ben Clift, "Economic Policy," in *Developments in French Politics 4*, ed. Alistair Cole, Patrick Le Galès, and Jonah D. Levy (Houndmills, UK: Palgrave Macmillan, 2008), 185–89. For a discussion of the declining importance of planning, see Hall, *Governing the Economy*, ch. 7.
16. Levy, *Tocqueville's Revenge*, 19, 43–46.
17. Ibid., ch.1.
18. As Levy, Miura, and Park point out, this pattern reflects the logic of the "double movement" of market expansion and societal demands for protection from the state identified by Karl Polanyi in his analysis of the Industrial Revolution in Britain. Jonah D. Levy, Mari Miura, and Gene Park, "Exiting Étatisme? New Directions in State Policy in France and Japan," in *The State after Statism: New State Activities in the Age of Liberalization*, ed. Jonah D. Levy (Cambridge, MA: Harvard University Press, 2006), 108. For Polanyi's account, see Karl

Polanyi, *The Great Transformation: The Political and Economic Origins of Our Time* (Boston: Beacon Press, 1957 [1944]), esp. chs. 7 and 12.

19. Jonah D. Levy, "France: Directing Adjustment?" in *Welfare and Work in the Open Economy*, vol. II: *Diverse Responses to Common Challenges*, ed. Fritz W. Scharpf and Vivien A. Schmidt (Oxford: Oxford University Press, 2000), 326.
20. Marc de Montalembert, ed., *La protection sociale en France*, 3rd ed. (Paris: La documentation française, 2001), 146.
21. World Bank, "World Development Indicators," http://data.worldbank.org/data-catalog/world-development-indicators, accessed March 28, 2015; and Marie-Thérèse Join-Lambert et al., eds., *Politiques sociales*, 2nd ed. (Paris: Presses de Sciences Po et Dalloz, 1997), 198.
22. The so-called Stability and Growth Pact limited annual budget deficits to 3 percent and gross debt to 60 percent of GDP.
23. Crucially, these interests included protecting the country's still-large agricultural sector, which benefitted from enormous subsidies and protection from import competition through the EEC's Common Agricultural Policy (CAP). For a discussion see John T. S. Keeler, "Agricultural Power in the EC: Explaining the Fate of CAP and GATT Negotiations," *Journal of Comparative Politics* 28, no. 2 (January 1996): 127–49.
24. By the late 1970s France exported a full 10 percent of the total manufactures of the world's twelve largest exporting countries. Sautter, "France," 454.
25. Of course, As Jonah Levy has pointed out, Mitterrand's abandonment of reflationary Keynesianism and his subsequent dismantling of dirigisme reflected his implicit choice of European relevance over statist economic policy. The French position on the single currency had thus effectively been cast almost a decade before the conclusion of the Maastricht Treaty, much as French officials would continue to strain against its strictures. See Levy, *Tocqueville's Revenge*, ch. 1.
26. The daunting prospect of German economic dominance of Europe was not lost on either Mitterrand or British Prime Minister Margaret Thatcher, both of whom had significant misgivings about German reunification and the potential for the re-emergence of a "bad" Germany. They feared that "if Chancellor Kohl were to get his way, Germany could win more ground than Hitler ever did and that Europe would have to bear the consequences." For a discussion, see James Blitz, "Mitterrand Feared Emergence of 'Bad' Germans," *Financial Times*, September 9, 2009, https://www.ft.com/content/886192ba-9d7d-11de-9f4a-00144feabdc0.
27. These strategies aimed to stabilize the franc and control inflation in the aftermath of the events of 1981–1982 while also seeking to gain international competitiveness by exporting rates of inflation that were lower than the Germans'. For discussions, see Pepper D. Culpepper, "Capitalism, Coordination, and Economic Change: The French Political Economy since 1985," in *Changing France: The Politics That Markets Make*, ed. Pepper Culpepper, Peter A. Hall, and Bruno Palier (Houndmills, UK: Palgrave Macmillan, 2006), 44; and Clift, "Economic Policy," 197.
28. Nicolas Jabko, *Playing the Market: A Political Strategy for Uniting Europe, 1985–2005* (Ithaca, NY: Cornell University Press, 2006), 156–58.
29. In the run-up to the treaty negotiations in December 1991, Mitterrand made this strategy explicit: "France will grow through Europe. Its voice will be better heard." See Alan Riding, "Shaky but Resolute, France Is Gambling on European Unity," *New York Times*, December 1, 1991, http://www.nytimes.com/1991/12/01/world/shaky-but-resolute-france-is-gambling-on-european-unity.html.
30. In Jabko's apt formulation, "There was a contradiction at the heart of the French embrace of EMS discipline, because French officials never came to terms with the consequences of that choice, which was accepting Germany's superior position within the monetary system." Jabko, *Playing the Market*, 158.
31. Ibid., 155–56. Such assurances were reinforced by policy decisions by both the German government and the Bundesbank. In December 1991, for example, the Bundesbank opted for a very controversial and, elsewhere in Europe, unwelcome increase in interest rates close on the heels of the international economic downturn in 1990–1991, forcing other countries to raise rates in turn to avoid violating the narrow bands of currency fluctuation allowed by EMS. Apparently unconcerned by widespread criticism of the move, the bank's president, Helmut

Schlesinger, ascribed the move to a "*Kultur* of stability in Germany" and then, in a somewhat smug formulation that foreshadowed future debates about the desired character of German economic policy, claimed that "[t]his is what we need in Europe, as well. I doubt whether such a consensus already exists in the EC as a whole." Tom Redburn, "Europeans Chafe at Bundesbank's Yoke," *New York Times*, January 20, 1992, http://www.nytimes.com/1992/01/20/news/20iht-bund_1.html.

32. For a more detailed discussion, see Mark I. Vail, "Europe's Middle Child: France's Statist Liberalism and the Conflicted Politics of the Euro," in *The Future of the Euro*, ed. Mark Blyth and Matthias Matthijs (New York: Oxford University Press, 2015), 136–60.
33. Barry James, "Doubts on Maastricht Grow in France," *New York Times*, August 12, 1992, http://www.nytimes.com/1992/08/12/news/12iht-pari.html.
34. Tom Redburn, "Strident French Campaign Fails to Unnerve Partners: The Maastricht Referendum," *New York Times*, September 3, 1992, http://www.nytimes.com/1992/09/03/news/03iht-mas_.html.
35. Jabko, *Playing the Market*, 173.
36. Ibid.
37. OECD, "Main Economic Indicators" database, doi:10.1787/data-00052-en; and World Bank, "World Development Indicators" database, http://databank.worldbank.org/data/views/reports/tableview.aspx, accessed April 12, 2015.
38. Interview, Stéphane Le Foll, Chef du cabinet du Premier Sécrétaire, Parti Socialiste, Paris, April 11, 2002.
39. In 2000, for example, Jospin's Finance Minister Laurent Fabius enacted a package of tax cuts for businesses, with the vast majority centered in SMEs. "Contradictory France," *Economist*, September 7, 2000, http://www.economist.com/node/359973. Unlike the German case, however, these tax cuts were organized and targeted on the basis of the firms' size, rather than their location in a particular sector. This approach was echoed under succeeding administrations of both the Left and the Right, most recently under Socialist President François Hollande, whose government in 2016 proposed a measure that would reduce tax rates on SMEs to 28 percent by 2020, in line with the EU average. For a discussion, see "France to Make Wave of Tax Cuts (Just in Time for Elections)," *The Local*, September 9, 2016, http://www.thelocal.fr/20160909/france-to-make-wave-of-tax-cuts-just-in-time-for-elections.
40. OECD, "Harmonised Unemployment Rate" database, doi:10.1787/52570002-en, accessed April 12, 2015.
41. Richard Posner, "How I Became a Keynesian: Second Thoughts in the Middle of a Crisis," *New Republic*, September 22, 2009, https://newrepublic.com/article/69601/how-i-became-keynesian.
42. Official, Ministre de Défense, personal communication, January 21, 2017.
43. A condensed analysis of some of the developments described in this section can be found in Mark I. Vail, "Varieties of Liberalism: Keynesian Responses to the Great Recession in France and Germany," *Governance* 27, no. 1 (January 2014): 63–85. Reused by permission.
44. Cécile Cornudet, "Nicolas Sarkozy répond à la crise économique par un effort public massif," *Les Échos*, December 5, 2008, 2.
45. Nelson D. Schwartz, "France, Unlike U.S., Is Deep into Stimulus Projects," *New York Times*, July 7, 2009, B1.
46. Cornudet, "Nicolas Sarkozy répond à la crise économique."
47. "Plan de relance: 's'il faut faire plus, il faudra faire plus', affirme Lagarde," *Le Parisien économie*, December 19, 2008, http://www.leparisien.fr/flash-actualite-economie/plan-de-relance-s-il-faut-faire-plus-il-faudra-faire-plus-affirme-lagarde-19-12-2008-348088.php.
48. Interview, former *Trésor* official, Ministre des Finances, February 16, 2015.
49. Guillaume Delacroix, "10 milliards d'investissements publics accélérés et un Code de marchés public allégé," *Les Échos*, December 5, 2008, 4.
50. Claire Guélaud, Sophie Landrin, and Arnaud Leparmentier, "Rien ne serait pire qu'un changement de cap," *Le Monde*, February 3, 2009, 10. Emphasis added.
51. OECD, "Social Expenditure, Aggregated Data" database, doi: 10.1787/socx-data-en, accessed July 31, 2017.
52. "Vive la Différence," *Economist*, May 9–15, 2009: 28.

53. In this respect, the French strategy was consistent with the character of the French industrial-relations landscape, as French unions have historically been organized by ideology and confessional history rather than by sector, as in Germany.
54. Cécile Cornudet, "Sarkozy veut prendre le temps d'expliquer sa politique anticrise," *Les Échos*, February 2, 2009, 3.
55. Susan Milner, "France: Steering out of Crisis," in *Europe and the Financial Crisis*, ed. Pompeo Della Posta and Leila Simona Talani (Houndmills, UK: Palgrave Macmillan, 2011), 189–90.
56. Eswar Prasad and Isaac Sorkin, "Assessing the G-20 Stimulus Plans: A Deeper Look," Brookings Institution Working Paper, December 14, 2009.
57. Guillaume Delacroix, "10 milliards d'investissements publics accélérés."
58. In 2005 France spent 1.2 percent of GDP on non-contributory income support, compared to 0.6 percent in Germany. ILO, *World Social Security Report: Providing Coverage in Times of Crisis and Beyond, 2010–2011* (Geneva: ILO, 2010), 264.
59. The package's limited size was related to its scope, since direct spending tends to have a greater stimulative effect than tax cuts by a ratio of about 1.6:1. Veena Jha, "The Effects of Fiscal Stimulus Packages on Employment," ILO Working Paper no. 34, 2009, 1.
60. This modest response was particularly surprising given France's relatively dire economic situation: in 2009, French GDP shrank by 2.5 percent, and by the end of the year, unemployment had climbed to 9.5 percent, compared to 7.8 percent in Germany. OECD, *OECD Economic Outlook, Interim Report* (Paris: OECD, 2009).
61. Interview, former *Trésor* official, February 16, 2015.
62. Quoted in Jonah Levy, "The Return of the State? French Economic Policy under Nicolas Sarkozy," paper presented at the annual meeting of the American Political Science Association, Washington, DC, September 2–5, 2010.
63. Unlike its German counterpart, Sarkozy's administration adopted very limited budget cuts in the aftermath of the euro crisis, limiting cuts in 2009 and 2010 to a dubious freeze on new spending and the token sale of a few government buildings. See Matthew Campbell Paris, "Sarkozy Gets Twitchy as French Rise Up against Austerity," *Sunday Times* (London), June 13, 2010, 30; and "How Buoyant Is France?" *Economist*, June 19–25, 2010, 51–52.
64. Interviews with a wide range of officials, including members of the Labor and Finance Ministries, trade union officials, and academic economists, suggest that the goal of reinstituting Keynesian demand management and industrial policy on the European level was a central preoccupation of French governments of both the Left and the Right after the 1980s.
65. A *New York Times* columnist provided at the time an apt formulation of the divergence between France's and Germany's European vision: "In Berlin, it is a common belief that the Eurozone would be just fine if it could somehow turn itself into a large version of Germany: respectful of rules, wary of deficits, cautious of over expenditure. As for the French, they never love Europe so much as when they think it is like France: brilliant rhetoric, lots of rules and a capacity to go around them." Christine Okrent, "Can 'Merkozy' Save the Day?" *New York Times*, December 8, 2011, http://www.nytimes.com/2011/12/09/opinion/can-merkozy-save-the-day.html. For a discussion of the evolution of the Franco-German relationship during the Eurozone crisis, see Vail, "Europe's Middle Child."
66. Interview, former Elysée official, February 16, 2015.
67. OECD, "OECD Country Statistical Profile: France 2011–2012" (Paris: OECD, 2012).
68. Philipp Wittrock, "Can Merkel Teach Hollande Austerity?" *Der Spiegel*, May 7, 2012, http://www.spiegel.de/international/europe/chancellor-merkel-wants-to-teach-president-hollande-merits-of-austerity-a-831845.html.
69. Alan Cowell and Nicholas Kulish, "Austerity Faces Sharper Debate after European Elections," *New York Times*, May 7, 2012, http://www.nytimes.com/2012/05/08/world/europe/francois-hollandes-victory-sharpens-european-austerity-debate.html.
70. OECD, "Main Economic Indicators" database, doi:10.1787/data-00052-en, accessed April 12, 2014.
71. World Bank, "World Development Indicators database," http://databank.worldbank.org/data/views/reports/tableview.aspx, accessed April 14, 2014.
72. Hugh Carnegy, "France Misses 2012 Deficit Target," *Financial Times*, March 29, 2013, https://www.ft.com/content/7d3ae0f8-984c-11e2-a853-00144feabdc0.

73. However unrealistic such pledges were, they also flew in the face of Hollande's increasingly reflationary rhetoric, such as his proclamation on his first visit as president to Greece (of all places) that he "reject[s] a Europe that condemns countries to austerity without end." Hugh Carnegy, "Hollande Wrestles with Austerity Demands," *Financial Times*, February 18, 2013, https://www.ft.com/content/0bdd9f80-79d0-11e2-9015-00144feabdc0.
74. By October 2013 Hollande's domestic approval rating had plummeted to 26 percent, the lowest figure for any French president under the Fifth Republic. Angelique Chrisafis, "François Hollande Becomes Most Unpopular French President Ever," *Guardian*, October 29, 2013, https://www.theguardian.com/world/2013/oct/29/francois-hollande-most-unpopular-president.
75. The campaign pledge by Hollande to increase the tax rate on the wealthiest French citizens to 75 percent was included in his first budget but swiftly struck down as unconstitutional in January of 2013. See "À bas les riches!," *Economist*, January 5, 2013, http://www.economist.com/news/europe/21569068-fran%C3%A7ois-hollande-remains-intent-introducing-punishing-top-income-tax-%C3%A0-bas-les-riches.
76. Hugh Carnegy and Adam Thompson, "François Hollande Purges Government after Leftwing Revolt," *Financial Times*, August 25, 2014, https://www.ft.com/content/31abc3a2-2c2d-11e4-8eda-00144feabdc0.
77. Cited in Hugh Carnegy, "Hollande Replaces Firebrand Economy Minister with Former Banker," *Financial Times*, August 26, 2014, https://www.ft.com/content/31664b6a-2d09-11e4-911b-00144feabdc0.
78. "France Unlikely to Achieve 2017 Deficit Target: Fiscal Watchdog," Reuters, September 27, 2016, http://www.reuters.com/article/us-france-budget-idUSKCN11X15I.
79. Anne-Sylvaine Chassany, "Emmanuel Macron Proposes Nordic Economic Model for France," *Financial Times*, February 23, 2017, https://www.ft.com/content/3691a448-fa1d-11e6-9516-2d969e0d3b65.
80. Jaume elaborates on this central claim by highlighting the tensions between the visions of Guizot, which embodied the "unitary and antipluralist" "Republican spirit" under the Third Republic, and of Constant, which "advocated confidence in the individual and the guarantee of liberty by the Constitution and the judge." Lucien Jaume, "Un libéralisme de rupture," *Le Monde*, May 14, 2017, 24. For a discussion of Constant's ideas and their differences with respect to the statist strand of nineteenth-century French liberalism, see Ch. 1.
81. La documentation française, *Vingt ans de transformations de l'économie française*, Cahiers français, 311 (Paris: La documentation française, 2002), 48.
82. For a discussion see Mark I. Vail, "The Better Part of Valour: The Politics of French Welfare Reform," *Journal of European Social Policy* 9, no. 4 (November 1999): 311–29.
83. Jonah D. Levy, Alistair Cole, and Patrick Le Galès, "From Chirac to Sarkozy: A New France?" in *Developments in French Politics 4*, ed. Cole, Le Galès, and Levy, 5–6.
84. Here the contrast with the German approach, which focused on subsidizing and protecting *insider* groups rather than supporting the incomes of excluded, outsider groups is indicative of the differences between the two countries' strategies.
85. Here again, French authorities' approach represents a contrast to the German strategy, which involved imposing the costs of adjustment on the less skilled with little in the way of support for workers' incomes or skill development.
86. Levy, Miura, and Park, "Exiting Étatisme?" 114.
87. Catherine Bruno and Sandrine Cazes, "French Youth Unemployment: An Overview," ILO Employment and Training Paper no. 32 (Geneva: ILO, 1998), 11.
88. Contracts lasted for five years, offering recipients the kind of positions most likely to lead to permanent full-time employment.
89. Levy, *Tocqueville's Revenge*, 256.
90. Agence France Presse wire service, October 14, 1997.
91. Interviews, Gilbert Cette, Banque de France, Paris June 20, 2008, and Pierre-Alain de Malleray, Ministre du travail, des relations sociales et de la solidarité, Paris, July 1, 2008.
92. These subsidies were to decline by €152 per year until they reached €762 in 2002.
93. Employers of 90 percent of private-sector workers failed to reach an accord by the beginning of 2000. Culpepper, "Capitalism, Coordination, and Economic Change,"39.

94. Vail, *Recasting Welfare Capitalism*, ch. 5. In July 2000 these exemptions averaged FFr 21,500 (€3,278) for workers earning the minimum wage, declining as wages increased to FFr 4,000 (€610) at the ceiling of 1.8 times the minimum wage. Direction de l'Animation de la Recherche, des Études, et des Statistiques (DARES), "Le passage à 35 heures vu par les employeurs," *Premières Synthèses*, April 2002, 10.
95. Interview, Xavier Lacoste, (Altédia), Paris, July 17, 2008.
96. According to one Labor Ministry official, Gandois had met secretly with government officials before the law was made public and had assumed that his demands for substantive negotiations between the government and social partners would be reflected in the laws' ultimate provisions. Interview, Dominique Libault, Chef de Service adjoint au Directeur, Direction de la sécurité sociale, Ministère de l'emploi et de la solidarité, Paris, February 7, 2002.
97. In addition to influencing public debates, the campaign reflected MEDEF's attempt to reclaim the initiative in the face of what both employers and unions viewed as the government's growing intrusion into the purview of the social partners. In the words of Ernest-Antoine Seillière, MEDEF's president at the time, "Of course, the State has social responsibilities, but that does not mean that it should carry them out in an authoritarian way, with sole regard to its own initiative." Ernest-Antoine Seillière, "Indispensable et fragile refondation sociale," *Le Monde*, December 6, 2000, 16.
98. Interview, Denis Kessler, president, Fédération française des sociétés d'assurances, Paris, May 15, 2002.
99. According to one Labor Ministry official familiar with behind-the-scenes negotiations, the discrepancy between MEDEF's public condemnation of the law and its sub rosa support for its provisions reflected "bad faith." Interview, Chargée de mission, Délégation générale à l'emploi et à la formation professionnelle, Département synthèses, Ministère de l'emploi et de la solidarité, Paris, March 21, 2002.
100. Marc de Montalembert, ed., *La protection sociale en France*, 4th ed. (Paris: La documentation française, 2004), 53.
101. Etienne Lefebvre, "Heures supplémentaires: Vers un régime avantageux avec garde-fous," *Les Échos*, June 4, 2007, 3.
102. In 2009, the ANPE merged with the Union nationale interprofessionnelle pour l'emploi dans l'industrie et le commerce (UNEDIC), the agency that managed the unemployment-benefit system, to form the so-called *Pôle emploi*.
103. In a claim that was echoed by several other officials and observers, one Labor Ministry official at the time stated that the core of Sarkozy's strategy for reform was to advance a set of policy reforms aggressively, encouraging the social partners to agree and threatening to impose reforms if they did not. Interview, Pierre-Alain de Malleray, Conseillier, Ministère du travail, des relations sociales et de la solidarité, Paris, July 1, 2008. The contrast with the German case is striking. As I discuss in the next chapter, even under the relatively impositional government of SPD Chancellor Gerhard Schröder, officials took seriously the economic interests of powerful insider groups such as skilled industrial workers and their employers, even as they imposed reform without systematically consulting their representatives among the leadership of trade unions and employers' associations.
104. In this respect, Sarkozy's strategy echoed that of his center–left predecessor Jospin in the latter's promulgation and enactment of the Aubry Laws.
105. The law defined a "reasonable job offer" as one that paid 95 percent of a worker's most recent salary after three months of unemployment benefits, 85 percent after six months, and the level of unemployment insurance after a year. For a detailed discussion, see Mireille Elbaum, *Économie politique de la protection sociale* (Paris: Presses universitaires de France, 2008), 128–29.
106. Interview, official, Ministre des Finances, Paris, July 10, 2015.
107. See Liz Alderman, "In France, New Review of 35-Hour Workweek," *New York Times*, November 26, 2014, http://www.nytimes.com/2014/11/27/business/international/france-has-second-thoughts-on-its-35-hour-workweek.html.
108. Interview, Paris, July 18, 2008. This sentiment was echoed by a highly placed official in the Defense Ministry, who attributed the fact to the effects of the elite educational system and its

propagation of a shared vision of the economy that transcends partisan differences. Personal communication, January 21, 2017.

109. Interview, official, Ministre des Finances, Paris, July 10, 2015.
110. IMF, "France: Selected Issues," July 24, 2016.
111. Mehreen Khan, "French Unemployment Rate Hits Five-Year Low," *Financial Times*, May 18, 2017, https://www.ft.com/content/83e1c85c-3b97-11e7-821a-6027b8a20f23.
112. For a discussion, see Zysman, *Governments, Markets, and Growth*, ch. 3.
113. Suzanne Berger, "Lame Ducks and National Champions: Industrial Policy in the Fifth Republic," in *The Fifth Republic at Twenty*, ed. William G. Andrews and Stanley Hoffmann (Albany: State University of New York Press, 1981), 295.
114. Zysman, *Governments, Markets and Growth*, 121, quoted in Levy, *Tocqueville's Revenge*, 259.
115. Levy, *Tocqueville's Revenge*, 259–60.
116. Ibid.
117. Andrew Shonfield describes the banks' relationship to major firms as "tutelary," averring in an illustrative contrast between the French and German cases that "what the great public and semi-public institutions are to the French economy, the big banks are to Germany." Shonfield, *Modern Capitalism*, 247.
118. Most of the major French industrial banks, including Société Générale, Crédit Lyonnais, and what would later become the Banque Nationale de Paris (BNP), were either entirely or partially taken over by the state in the first few postwar years.
119. The sordid story of Crédit Lyonnais's demise reflects stark differences between the French and German financial sectors. In the early 1990s, under the direction of new CEO Jean-Yves Haberer, the bank sought to become the "Deutsche Bank of France," with close ties to French industry and a powerful role in shaping France's course of economic development. The effort, undermined by the unavailability of German-style institutional linkages between the bank and firms and by starkly different industrial landscapes, resulted in a series of disastrous loans and increasing indebtedness in an unpropitious deregulatory environment. For details, see Levy, *Tocqueville's Revenge*, 273–76.
120. In Levy's apt formulation, this failure was the predictable result of conflicting imperatives within the French program of bank privatization, the goal of which "was not to replicate a foreign model of capitalism but to transfer the core of French finance and industry to a coterie of Gaullist allies at relatively low cost." Ibid., 265.
121. Jonathan Story and Ingo Walter, *Political Economy of Financial Integration in Europe: The Battle of the Systems* (Cambridge, MA: MIT Press, 1997), 194 and 197.
122. As late as 2009, 72 percent of French firm financing came from banks rather than from equity markets. Cornelia Woll, "Bank Rescue Schemes in Continental Europe: The Power of Collective Inaction," *Government and Opposition* 49, no. 3 (2014), 431.
123. Cornelia Woll, *The Power of Inaction: Bank Bailouts in Comparison* (Ithaca, NY: Cornell University Press, 2014), 112–13.
124. They also point out that this cozy relationship between the state and finance reflects a rejection of the "liberal economic doctrine of strict separation between the public and private spheres." Jabko and Massoc, "French Capitalism under Stress: How Nicolas Sarkozy Rescued the Banks," *Review of International Political Economy* 19, no. 4 (June 2012), 565–66.
125. The movement towards consolidation paralleled similar trends among the largest commercial banks in the late 1990s, such as Société Générale's 1999 bid to absorb Paribas, which resulted in the politically contentions acquisition of Paribas by BNP, with significant state involvement. Gregory W. Fuller, *The Great Debt Transformation: Households, Financialization, and Policy Responses* (New York: Palgrave Macmillan, 2016), 140.
126. Ibid., 136.
127. As Gregory Fuller notes, "France liberalized the financial sector without fully liberalizing how French citizens and businesses interact with it." Ibid., 143.
128. Jack Hayward, "*Moins d'État* or *Mieux d'État*: The French Response to the Neo-Liberal Challenge," in *The Mitterrand Years: Legacy and Evaluation*, ed. Mairi Maclean (New York: St. Martin's Press, 1998), 26.
129. For details, see http://www.tresor.economie.gouv.fr/AMF.
130. Interview, Paris, July 10, 2015.

131. In 2008, six institutions accounted for roughly 80 percent of banking activity in France. Woll, *Power of Inaction*, 113.
132. Jabko and Massoc, "French Capitalism under Stress," 566.
133. Guillaume Delacroix, "Nicolas Sarkozy présente un plan de 360 milliards d'euros pour aider les banques," *Les Échos*, October 14, 2008, 2.
134. Emiliano Grossman and Cornelia Woll, "Saving the Banks: The Political Economy of Bailouts," paper presented at the Nineteenth International Conference of Europeanists, Council for European Studies, Boston, March 22–24, 2012, 14, 23.
135. For a detailed overview of these two entities, see Cour des Comptes, "Le plan de soutien aux banques: Un bilan financier encore provisoire, un encadrement des rémunérations à compléter," *Rapport publique annuel 2013*, February 2013.
136. Woll, *Power of Inaction*, 117.
137. Ibid., 121–23.
138. Scheherazade Daneshkhu, "Merger Shakes Up French Mutuals," *Financial Times*, July 13, 2009, https://www.ft.com/content/f30f33e4-6fdb-11de-b835-00144feabdc0. This episode is illustrative of both the strong tradition of retail banking in France and the effects of French financial liberalization after the 1980s. Prior to the merger of Banque Populaire and Caisse d'Epargne, both institutions had served middle- and working-class clients without losses since World War II, and, in the case of Caisse d'Epargne, in its entire two-hundred-year existence.
139. "France: New Law on Banking and Financial Regulation," Law Library of Congress, December 2010.
140. Scheherazade Daneshkhu and Hugh Carnegy, "France Unveils Bank Reforms," *Financial Times*, December 19, 2012, http://www.ft.com/cms/s/0/1463dd2249d811e2a7b-100144feab49a.html#axzz4DtDfe68O.
141. For all of its liberalization since the 1980s, France continues to adhere to a liberal model that reserves a central, even dominant, role for the state. In the words of one official in the French Ministry of Finance under the center–left administration of François Hollande (hardly where one would expect to find reflexive criticisms of state dominance), the central concept of this model is the "protector state" responsible for the welfare of individual citizens, who are equal before the law. In his words, "as soon as there is a problem, people turn to the state." Interview, Paris, July 10, 2015.
142. As Samuel Moyn argues, both post-revolutionary French liberalism and French strands of nineteenth-century Marxism were powerfully informed by the ethos of individualism. Such motifs can be found, for example, in the twentieth-century writings of Pierre Rosanvallon, Claude Lefort, and Marcel Gauchet, as well as in the nineteenth-century liberalism of de Tocqueville. See Moyn, "The Politics of Individual Rights: Marcel Gauchet and Claude Lefort," in *French Liberalism from Montesquieu to the Present Day*, ed. Raf Geenens and Helena Rosenblatt (Cambridge: Cambridge University Press, 2012), 300 and passim.
143. De Ruggiero, *History of European Liberalism*, 245.
144. The term is Peter Katzenstein's, from his *Policy and Politics in West Germany: The Growth of a Semi-Sovereign State* (Philadelphia: Temple University Press, 1987).

Chapter 3

1. For a discussion of the antecedents of core elements of neoliberalism in Hume's and Locke's writings, see Mark Blyth, *Austerity: The History of a Dangerous Idea* (Oxford: Oxford University Press, 2013), 104–8.
2. Jamie Peck, *Constructions of Neoliberal Reason* (Oxford: Oxford University Press, 2010), 17.
3. Ralf Ptak, "Neoliberalism in Germany," in *The Road from Mont Pèlerin: The Making of the Neoliberal Thought Collective*, ed. Philip Mirowski and Dieter Plehwe (Cambridge, MA: Harvard University Press, 2009), 101.
4. Ibid., 102.
5. Indeed, adherents of variants of the Ordoliberal vision, including Ludwig Erhard, Economics Minister under CDU Chancellor Konrad Adenauer in the 1950s and a future Bundeskanzler, viewed the framework as a way to avoid recourse to economic planning in the French style. I am indebted to Wade Jacoby for this point.

6. Hans Willgerodt and Alan Peacock, "German Liberalism and Economic Revival," in *Germany's Social Market Economy: Origins and Evolution*, ed. Alan Peacock and Hans Willgerodt (Houndmills, UK: Macmillan, 1989), 8.
7. Blyth, *Austerity*, 136–37.
8. Ralph Raico, "Le libéralisme allemand authentique du XIXe siècle," in *Histoire du libéralisme en Europe*, ed. Philippe Nemo and Jean Petitot, 1st ed. (Paris: Presses universitaires de France, 2006), 929. Translation by the author.
9. Franz Böhm, "Rule of Law in a Market Economy," in *Germany's Social Market Economy*, ed. Peacock and Willgerodt, 51.
10. Ptak, "Neoliberalism in Germany," 123.
11. Ibid., 104, quoted in Blyth, *Austerity*, 138.
12. Jan-Werner Müller, *Contesting Democracy: Political Ideas in Twentieth-Century Europe* (New Haven, CT: Yale University Press, 2011), 153.
13. Ibid., 153–54.
14. In Blyth's formulation, "[A]lthough the ordoliberals really did not want the economic constitution to be tied to a welfare state, circumstances and politics dictated otherwise: the market economy had to become social." Blyth, *Austerity*, 138.
15. Andrew Glyn et al., "The Rise and Fall of the Golden Age," in *The Golden Age of Capitalism: Reinterpreting the Postwar Experience*, ed. Stephen A. Marglin and Juliet B. Schor (Oxford: Clarendon Press, 1990), 47.
16. Ibid., 43, 47.
17. Gerald A. Epstein and Juliet B. Schor, "Macropolicy in the Rise and Fall of the Golden Age," in *Golden Age*, ed. Marglin and Schor, 136.
18. Although Germany performed better than most of its peers in the 1970s, slowing growth and modestly rising unemployment and inflation showed that the postwar boom was over. Between 1973 and 1980 unemployment averaged 2.9 percent (up from 0.8 percent over the previous seven-year period), average annual inflation had jumped to around 4.6 percent, and average annual growth rates had declined to 2.4 percent. See Andrea Boltho, "Growth," in *The European Economy: Growth and Crisis*, ed. Andrea Boltho (Oxford: Oxford University Press, 1982), 34; Christopher Alsopp, "Inflation," in ibid., 79; and Barry J. Eichengreen, *The European Economy since 1945: Coordinated Capitalism and Beyond* (Princeton, NJ: Princeton University Press, 2007), 264.
19. Following on the distinction already laid out, I mean here the neoliberalism that emerged in the 1970s, championed by Milton Friedman and similar economists and their political handmaidens, like Margaret Thatcher, rather than the neoliberalism that emerged in the interwar period and furnished many of the foundational principles of Ordoliberalism. Although beyond the scope of this discussion, the coincidence of the two terms to refer to distinct bodies of thought reflects the attempts of two separate groups, at different times, to move beyond the self-contradictory and impracticable character of laissez-faire and nineteenth-century classical liberalism in an increasingly complex set of economic and social circumstances.
20. For an admirable discussion of the intellectual foundations of neoliberalism, see Andrew Gamble, *The Free Economy and the Strong State: The Politics of Thatcherism* (Houndmills, UK: Macmillan, 1988), esp. ch. 2.
21. Vivien A. Schmidt and Mark Thatcher, "Theorizing Ideational Continuity: The Resilience of Neo-liberal Ideas in Europe," in *Resilient Liberalism in Europe's Political Economy*, ed. Vivien Schmidt and Mark Thatcher (Cambridge: Cambridge University Press, 2013), 11.
22. Such efforts to chart a "third way" between socialism and unfettered capitalism were hardly new. Indeed, they had informed the earliest debates out of which Ordoliberalism emerged in the 1930s, particularly marking the writings of Wilhelm Röpke. For a discussion, see Angus Burgin, *The Great Persuasion: Reinventing Free Markets since the Depression* (Cambridge, MA: Harvard University Press, 2012), 78–85.
23. Jamie Peck, *Constructions of Neoliberal Reason* (Oxford: Oxford University Press, 2010), xii–xiii.
24. James J. Sheehan, *German Liberalism in the Nineteenth Century* (Chicago: University of Chicago Press, 1978), 31–32, 249–50.

25. In some respects my analysis of the German case echoes insights from the extensive literature on the German "insider-outsider" dilemma and "dualism." Unlike such work, which focuses largely on the effects of institutional structures in the labor market and the welfare state, however, I argue that those institutional arrangements are themselves products of broader and older liberal ideas that exert consistent kinds of influence across a wide array of political-economic domains. For classic treatments of the insider-outsider dilemma in continental Europe, see Gøsta Esping-Andersen, "Welfare States without Work: The Impasse of Labour Shedding and Familialism in Continental European Social Policy," in *Welfare States in Transition: National Adaptations in a Global Economy*, ed. Gøsta Esping-Andersen (Thousand Oaks, CA: Sage, 1996), 66–87. See also Anton Hemerijck and Phillip Manow, "The Experience of Negotiated Reform in the Dutch and German Welfare States," in *Comparing Welfare Capitalism: Social Policy and Political Economy in Europe, Japan and the USA*, ed. Bernhard Ebbinghaus and Phillip Manow (London: Routledge, 2001), 217–38. For an analysis that applies this rubric to both France and Germany, see Bruno Palier and Kathleen Thelen, "Institutionalizing Dualism: Complementarities and Change in France and Germany," *Politics & Society* 38, no. 1 (March 2010): 119–48.
26. OECD, "Labour Market Statistics," Main Economic Indicators database, doi:10.1787/data-00046-en, accessed May 6, 2014.
27. Fritz Scharpf, "Economic and Institutional Constraints of Full-Employment Strategies: Sweden, Austria, and West Germany, 1973–1982," in *Order and Conflict in Contemporary Capitalism*, ed. John H. Goldthorpe (Oxford: Clarendon Press, 1984), 258. Although rising inflation and slowing growth reflected the effects of the 1973 OPEC oil shock and the global economic slowdown of the 1970s, the decline in economic performance was nonetheless striking. Here and elsewhere I use "Germany" to refer to West Germany prior to 1990 and to unified Germany thereafter.
28. Fritz W. Scharpf and Vivien A. Schmidt, "Statistical Appendix," in *Welfare and Work in the Open Economy*, vol. 1: *From Vulnerability to Competitiveness*, ed. Fritz W. Scharpf and Vivien A. Schmidt (Oxford: Oxford University Press, 2000), 341.
29. These arguments were presented in Michel Albert, *Capitalisme contre capitalisme* (Paris: Editions du Seuil, 1991), an influential volume that celebrated the virtues of the German model to which its French analog was invidiously compared.
30. Peter J. Katzenstein, *Policy and Politics in West Germany: The Growth of a Semi-Sovereign State* (Philadelphia: Temple University Press, 1987).
31. Mario Baldassarri and M. Gabriella Briotti, "The Government Budget and the Italian Economy during the 1970s and 1980s: Causes of the Debt, Strategies for Recovery, and Prospects for Restructuring," in *The Italian Economy: Heaven or Hell?* ed. Mario Baldassarri (London: St. Martin's Press, 1994), 157–217.
32. *Encyclopedia Britannica Online*, s.v. "J. B. Say," http://academic.eb.com/levels/collegiate/article/65984, accessed October 11, 2016.
33. Such an approach was all the more likely given the increasingly hegemonic status of neoliberal economic thought and the so-called Washington Consensus to which it had helped to give rise. For an outline of just such a blueprint proposed for the Polish case, see Jeffrey Sachs, "Poland and Eastern Europe: What Is to Be Done?" in *Foreign Economic Liberalization: Transformations in Socialist and Market Economies*, ed. András Koves and Paul Marer (Boulder, CO: Westview, 1991), 235–46.
34. See, e.g., Hans-Werner Sinn, *Can Germany Be Saved? The Malaise of the World's First Welfare State* (Cambridge, MA: MIT Press, 2007), ch. 5.
35. Wade Jacoby, *Imitation and Politics: Redesigning Modern Germany* (Ithaca, NY: Cornell University Press, 2000).
36. Jürgen A. K. Thomaneck, "From Euphoria to Reality: Social Problems of Post-Unification," in *The New Germany: Social, Political and Cultural Challenges of Unification*, ed. Derek Lewis and John R. P. McKenzie (Exeter: University of Exeter Press, 1995), 8.
37. The best full-length scholarly study of reunification in English is Charles S. Maier, *Dissolution: The Crisis of Communism and the End of East Germany* (Princeton, NJ: Princeton University Press, 1997).

38. Gerhard Ritter, *Der Preis der deutschen Einheit: Die Wiedervereinigung und die Krise des Sozialstaats* (München: Beck, 2006), 12. This and all subsequent translations from German are the author's.
39. The scope of the privatization effort, headed by the so-called *Treuhandanstalt*, was breathtaking, with more than 20,000 small firms and 3,400 industrial concerns sold off by the end of 1991. Dennis L. Bark and David R. Gress, *A History of West Germany*, 2nd ed., vol. 2: *Democracy and Its Discontents* (Oxford: Blackwell, 1993), 756.
40. The revamping of the postal and telecommunications systems, for example, each cost DM 100 billion (or around €51 billion) over the 1990s. Christopher Flockton, "Policy Agendas and the Economy in Germany and Europe," in *The New Germany in the East: Policy Agendas and Social Developments since Unification*, ed. Christopher Flockton, Eva Kolinsky, and Rosalind Pritchard (London: Frank Cass, 2000), 65.
41. Matthias Knuth, "Active Labor Market Policy and German Unification: The Role of Employment and Training Companies," in *Negotiating the New Germany: Can Social Partnership Survive?* ed. Lowell Turner (Ithaca, NY: Cornell University Press, 1997), 69.
42. The other component of this strategy, which I discuss in the subsequent section, entailed the targeted expansion of social protection and subsidies for skilled industrial labor designed to help this key group adjust to new economic realities.
43. Kenneth Dyson, "The Economic Order—Still *Modell Deutschland*?" in *Developments in German Politics* 2, ed. Gordon Smith, William E. Paterson, and Stephen Padgett (Durham, NC: Duke University Press, 1996), 204–5; and Karl Koch, "The German Economy: Decline or Stability?" in *New Germany*, ed. Lewis and McKenzie, 136–37.
44. Christopher Flockton, "Economic Management and the Challenge of Reunification," in *Developments in German Politics*, ed. Smith, Paterson, and Padgett, 2, 216.
45. Ibid., 219. In 1993, officials projected that reunification would entail a total transfer of about 7 percent of GNP to the eastern Länder over the subsequent decade. Fritz Stern, *Five Germanys That I Have Known* (New York: Farrar, Straus and Giroux, 2006), 478.
46. Ritter, *Preis der deutschen Einheit*, 13.
47. The terms of the treaty limited prospective members of EMU to annual budget deficits of 3 percent and gross public debt of no more than 60 percent of GDP, except in extraordinary circumstances.
48. Craig Parsons, *A Certain Idea of Europe* (Ithaca, NY: Cornell University Press, 2003), 213.
49. Nicolas Jabko, *Playing the Market: A Political Strategy for Uniting Europe, 1985–2005* (Ithaca, NY: Cornell University Press, 2006). Although relinquishing control over the ECB's policymaking process was difficult for many of Germany's European partners to swallow (this was particularly true for the French), a combination of technocratic consensus among central bankers in favor of a strong anti-inflationary and anti-Keynesian stance and the need to assuage Germany's economic concerns for the sake of the larger political goal of economic and monetary union converged to create a euro with an independent central bank modeled on the Bundesbank at its core.
50. The same double standard would be applied in the aftermath of the post-2007 financial and economic crisis, as will be discussed.
51. By 1992 total public-sector deficits amounted to DM 92 billion (€47 billion) (DM 40 billion for the federal government, DM 18 billion borne by western Länder, DM 10 billion by eastern Länder, and DM 24 billion by the Fund for German Unity). Maier, *Dissolution*.
52. Ibid.
53. Flockton, "Economic Management," 225. Between 1991 and 1996, DM 18.15 billion (€9.3 billion) was furnished to eastern industry through this program. Flockton, "Policy Agendas," 67.
54. That said, the government also undertook a number of efforts to promote the growth of SMEs, which, it was hoped, would be able to take advantage of lower eastern labor costs and hire many unemployed industrial workers. A prime example was the Kreditanstalt für Wiederaufbau (KfW), an agency which offered low-interest loans to SMEs. Ibid., 65, 69.
55. At nearly 30 percent of eastern GDP in 1990, manufacturing output plummeted to less than 15 percent by 1993. Henning Klodt, "Public Transfers and Industrial Restructuring in Eastern

Germany," in *Ten Years of German Unification: Transfer, Transformation, Incorporation?* ed. Jörn Leonhard and Lothar Funk (Birmingham: Birmingham University Press, 2002), 217.

56. Gary Herrigel, "The Limits of German Manufacturing Flexibility," in *Negotiating the New Germany*, ed. Lowell Turner, 186. Elsewhere, Herrigel shows that this collapse accelerated a broader decline in the German machine-tool industry that had begun in the 1980s. Herrigel, *Industrial Constructions: The Sources of German Industrial Power* (Cambridge: Cambridge University Press, 1996), 194–99.
57. World Development Indicators, World Bank, http://data.worldbank.org/data-catalog/world-development-indicators, accessed May 2015.
58. Deutsche Welle online, "VAT Increase Puts Germany Closer to EU Average," 19 May 2006, http://www.dw.com/en/vat-increase-puts-germany-closer-to-eu-average/a-2026126.
59. World Bank, World Development Indicators. Washington, DC, http://databank.worldbank.org/data/views/reports/tableview.aspx, accessed November 12, 2016.
60. OECD, "Main Economic Indicators" database, doi:10.1787/data-00052-en; and Eurostat, "Unemployment Rate by Sex and Age Groups" database, http://appsso.eurostat.ec.europa.eu/nui/show.do?dataset=une_rt_a&lang=en, accessed November 12, 2016.
61. For canonical discussions of German market coordination and the economic strategy of "Diversified Quality Production" that underpinned it, see Wolfgang Streeck, "On the Institutional Conditions of Diversified Quality Production," in *Beyond Keynesianism. The Socio-Economics of Production and Employment*, ed. Egon Matzner and Wolfgang Streeck (London: Edward Elgar, 1991), 21–61; and Peter A. Hall and David Soskice, eds., *Varieties of Capitalism: The Institutional Foundations of Comparative Advantage* (Oxford: Oxford University Press, 2001).
62. See Richard Posner, "How I Became a Keynesian: Second Thoughts in the Middle of a Crisis," *New Republic*, September 22, 2009, https://newrepublic.com/article/69601/how-i-became-keynesian.
63. A critical perspective shared by disturbingly few of his colleagues, even with the crisis itself offering a fount of evidence for the validity of many of Krugman's claims. See Paul Krugman, "How Did Economists Get It So Wrong?," *New York Times Magazine*, September 6, 2009, 36–43.
64. Statistisches Bundesamt database, https://www.destatis.de/EN/FactsFigures/NationalEconomyEnvironment/ForeignTrade/TradingPartners/Current.html, accessed November 1, 2016.
65. Interview, Hans-Jürgen Völz, Bundesvereinigung der Deutschen Arbeitgeberverbände (BDA), Berlin, June 22, 2011.
66. Interviews, Roland Lang-Neyjahr, Bundesministerium für Arbeit und Soziales (BMAS), Berlin, June 23, 2011; and official, Bundesvereinigung der Deutschen Arbeitgeberverbände (BDA), Berlin, June 22, 2011.
67. A condensed analysis of some of these developments is presented in Mark I. Vail, "Varieties of Liberalism: Keynesian Responses to the Great Recession in France and Germany," *Governance* 27, no. 1 (January 2014): 63–85. Reused by permission.
68. Interview, official, Bundesverband der Deutschen Industrie (BDI), Berlin, June 30, 2011.
69. In part this hesitation stemmed less from a lack of consensus about the necessary policy direction and more from concerns about appearing overly impositional. Interview, official, Bundesministerium für Arbeit und Soziales, Berlin, July 20, 2015.
70. *Frankfurter Rundschau*, "CSU dreht am Steuerrad: Niedrige Sätze und ein Konjunkturpaket sind in Berlin noch kein Thema," January 30, 2008, 3.
71. "How Very Stimulating," *Economist*, January 17–23, 2009, 52.
72. "A Little Stimulus," *Economist*, November 15–21, 2008, 62.
73. Stefan von Borstel, "Milliarden gegen die Rezession," *Die Welt*, November 6, 2008, 13.
74. OECD, "Main Economic Indicators" database, doi:10.1787/data-00052-en, accessed November 12, 2016.
75. Interview, official, Bundesverband der Deutschen Industrie (BDI), Berlin, June 30, 2011.
76. This characterization is based upon data drawn from the following interviews: official, Bundesministerium für Arbeit und Soziales (BMAS), Berlin, June 23, 2011; Hans-Jürgen

Volz, Bundesverband der Deutschen Arbeitgeber (BDA), Berlin, June 22, 2011; and official, Deutscher Gewerkschaftsbund, Berlin, June 21, 2011.

77. This conflict revolved around the Labor Ministry's push for a robust response designed to protect jobs and shore up Germany's export sectors, in contrast to the position of the Finance Ministry, which was much more skeptical and wanted to rely instead on Germany's automatic stabilizers. Interviews, official, Bundesministerium für Arbeit und Soziales, Berlin, July 20, 2015; officials, Bundesministerium für Arbeit und Soziales (BMAS), Berlin, June 14 and 23, 2011.
78. Interview, Jan Brahmst, SPD Parteivorstand, Berlin, May 31, 2011.
79. Interview, official, Deutsche Gewerkschaftsbund (DGB), Berlin, June 21, 2011.
80. "Regierung beschließt Rekordverschuldung: 50 Milliarden Euro für Konjunkturpaket II," *Berliner Morgenpost*, January 28, 2009, 2.
81. "Zweites Konjunkturpaket nimmt konkrete Formen an," Agence France Presse wire service (German), January 9, 2009.
82. Arne Leifels, Stefan Moog, and Bernd Raffelhüschen, "Auswirkungen der Konjunkturpakete auf die öffentlichen Haushalte in 2009 und 2010," Working Paper, Albert-Ludwigs-Universität Freiburg, March 2009, 9.
83. This emphasis on tax cuts, which colored both the first stimulus package and subsequent measures implemented by the succeeding CDU-FDP coalition (as will be discussed), was consistent with traditional German beliefs that "the state is not the best director of the economy" and that sound economic strategy involves "leaving more money in the pockets of the private sector." Interview, official, Bundesministerium der Finanzen, July 30, 2015.
84. Interview, Gerd Heyer, Bundesministerium für Arbeit und Soziales (BMAS), Berlin, June 14, 2011.
85. "German MP Says Economic Stimulus Package Will Have Only Minor Effect," BBC Worldwide Monitoring, December 27, 2008, http://www.bbc.co.uk/monitoring.
86. Interview, official, Bundesverband der Deutschen Industrie (BDI), Berlin, June 30, 2011.
87. Interview, official, Deutsche Gewerkschaftsbund (DGB), Berlin, June 21, 2011.
88. Child benefits were one of the three central components of the first German stimulus package. See Gary Becker, "Germany vs. US: Two Different Approaches to the Recession," Becker-Posner Blog, August 9, 2010, at http://www.becker-posner-blog.com/2010/08/germany-vs-us-two-different-approaches-to-the-recession-becker.html.
89. Interview, Roland Lang-Neyjahr, Bundesministerium für Arbeit und Soziales (BMAS), Berlin, June 23, 2011.
90. "Versuch einer Irreführung," *Der Spiegel* 51 (December 14, 2009), 29.
91. "Angela's New Team Claims Its Seats," *Economist*, October 31–November 6, 2009, 61. Such views were confirmed in interviews with officials in trade unions and employers' associations.
92. This claim was echoed in interviews with other officials, e.g., Gerd Heyer, Bundesministerium für Arbeit und Soziales (BMAS), Berlin, June 14, 2011.
93. "Versuch einer Irreführung."
94. Iain Hardie and David Howarth, "Die Krise but Not La Crise? The Financial Crisis and the Transformation of German and French Banking Systems," *Journal of Common Market Studies* 47, no. 5 (November 1, 2009): 1017–39.
95. Veena Jha, "The Effects of Fiscal Stimulus Packages on Employment," ILO Working Paper no. 34, 2009, 3.
96. Eswar Prasad and Isaac Sorkin, "Assessing the G-20 Stimulus Plans: A Deeper Look," Brookings Institution Working Paper, December 14, 2009.
97. ILO, *World Social Security Report: Providing Coverage in Times of Crisis and Beyond, 2010–2011* (Geneva: ILO, 2010), 33.
98. Prasad and Sorkin, "Assessing the G-20 Stimulus Plans," 5. In both cases, of course, there is a connection between the size and the scope of stimulus spending: because tax cuts are less effective than direct spending at boosting demand, they must be larger to have an effect of a similar magnitude, all else equal.
99. Though my findings are thus partially consistent with Palier and Thelen's portrait of German "institutionalized dualism" between protected insiders and increasingly exposed outsiders, this image cannot explain either the strong German preference for tax cuts or the benefits accruing to other core groups, such as families and the Mittelstand. Palier and Thelen, "Institutionalized Dualism."

100. "Slash and Bounce," *Economist*, June 12–18, 2010: 56–57.
101. Roger Boyes, "Merkel Faces Budget Trouble over £66bn 'List of Horrors,'" *Times* (London), June 8, 2010, 31.
102. Germany's unemployment rate dipped to a post-reunification low of 6.3 percent in November 2015. Alessandro Speciale and Alexander Kell, "Germany's Unemployment Rate Falls to Record Low on Domestic Demand," Bloomberg, December 1, 2015, http://www.bloomberg.com/news/articles/2015-12-01/german-unemployment-rate-falls-to-record-low-on-domestic-demand.
103. For details see Deutsche Bundesbank, "The Debt Brake in Germany: Key Aspects and Implementation," Working Paper, October 2011.
104. This characterization of Germany's obsession with balancing the budget first appears in *Der Spiegel* and was later echoed by French Economy Minister Emmanuel Macron: "The risk facing Germany is a new form of conservatism, which is balanced-budget fetishism." See Stacy Meichtry, "Germany Risks Balanced-Budget 'Fetishism,' French Minister Says," *Wall Street Journal*, January 29, 2015, http://www.wsj.com/articles/french-minister-calls-on-germany-to-relax-tight-public-spending-1422531828.
105. Ben Clift and Magnus Ryner, "Joined at the Hip, but Pulling Apart? Franco-German Relations, the Eurozone Crisis and the Politics of Austerity," *French Politics* 12, no. 2 (June 2014): 142.
106. The passage of the TSCG meant that structural deficits could no longer exceed 0.5 percent of GDP for most states.
107. IMF, "Germany: Selected Issues," IMF Country Report No. 14/217 (July 2014).
108. For a discussion of the features of the Christian Democratic, or "Conservative" welfare state, of which Germany serves as an exemplar, see Gøsta Esping-Andersen, *The Three Worlds of Welfare Capitalism* (Princeton, NJ: Princeton University Press, 1990).
109. Ritter, *Preis der deutschen Einheit*, 14.
110. Lowell Turner, *Fighting for Partnership: Labor and Politics in Unified Germany* (Ithaca, NY: Cornell University Press, 1998), 2.
111. Jacoby, *Imitation and Politics*, 145.
112. Although this process was generally successful, it did entail a number of innovations and alterations in the face of East German circumstances. For example, many eastern wage agreements contained so-called *Öffnungsklauseln*, or "opening clauses," which allowed employers to petition for exemptions from certain contract provisions, including temporary reductions in pay rates. Other alterations include firm-specific renegotiations of work time, such as a deal between IG Metall and Volkswagen in 1993 that reduced the work week to four days in order to allow the struggling company to reorganize. Kirsten S. Wever, "Renegotiating the German Model: Labor-Management Relations in the New Germany," in *Negotiating the New Germany*, ed. Lowell Turner, 217–18. See also Wolfgang Streeck, *Re-Forming Capitalism: Institutional Change in the German Political Economy* (Oxford: Oxford University Press, 2009), ch. 2. This trend became more pronounced over time; by 1997, only about a quarter of eastern firms were covered by nationwide sectoral contracts. It was also reproduced with growing frequency in western Germany. Kathleen Thelen and Ikuo Kume, "The Effects of Globalization on Labor Revisited: Lessons from Germany and Japan," *Politics & Society* 27, no. 4 (December 1999): 480.
113. Ritter, *Preis der deutschen Einheit*.
114. This process was a key element of the overall financial support for reunification, 23 percent of which was accounted for by unemployment insurance and pension expenditures. See ibid., 360–61.
115. Maier, *Dissolution*.
116. Philip Manow and Eric Seils, "Adjusting Badly: The German Welfare State, Structural Change, and the Open Economy," in *Welfare and Work in the Open Economy*, vol. 2: *Diverse Responses to Common Challenges*, ed. Fritz W. Scharpf and Vivien A. Schmidt (Oxford: Oxford University Press, 2000), 293; and Knuth, "Active Labor Market Policy," 72.
117. Dominique Taddei, ed., *Retraites choisies et progressives*, Rapport du Conseil d'Analyse Economique (Paris: La documentation française, 2000), 213.
118. By 1997 the number of workers in the new Länder participating in such schemes had declined to around 362,000. OECD, *OECD Economic Surveys, 1997–1998: Germany* (Paris: OECD, 1998), 100, 102.

119. Knuth, "Active Labor Market Policy and German Unification," 71, 75.
120. The difference between registered and effective unemployment (including participants in job-creation and retraining schemes) can be considerable. In 1996, for example, the registered unemployment rate in the East was 15.1 percent, while the estimated total of both official and "hidden" unemployment was 28.9 percent. OECD, *OECD Economic Surveys, 1997–1998: Germany*, 100.
121. In 1991 an estimated 18.5 percent of employed eastern workers were receiving this benefit. Alan B. Krueger and Jörn-Steffen Pischke, "A Comparative Analysis of East and West German Labor Markets: Before and after Unification," NBER Working Paper 4154 (Cambridge, MA: NBER, August 1992), 26.
122. Knuth, "Active Labor Market Policy," 72; OECD, *OECD Economic Surveys, 1997–1998: Germany*, 100; and OECD, *OECD Economic Surveys, 2000–2001: Germany* (Paris: OECD, 2001), 115.
123. Despite the government's selective and targeted approach, the result was repeated short-term violations of the Maastricht criteria on fiscal policy.
124. OECD, *OECD Employment Outlook* (Paris: OECD, June 2001), 24.
125. Mary Daly, "Globalization and Bismarckian Welfare States," in *Globalization and European Welfare States: Challenges and Changes*, ed. Robert Sykes, Bruno Palier, and Pauline M. Prior (Houndmills, UK: Palgrave, 2001), 95.
126. Although prompted by the challenges of reunification, this response was not limited to the East, as many of the benefits and subsidies offered to eastern workers were subsequently extended to the entire German labor market, as with the deployment of *Kurzarbeitergeld* schemes in the German automobile sector in the early-to-mid-1990s. Andreas Crimmann, Frank Wießner, and Lutz Bellman, "The German Work-sharing Scheme: An Instrument for the Crisis," Working Paper, Institute for Employment Research, Bundesagentur für Arbeit (Geneva: ILO, 2010), 17. Herbert Kitschelt and Wolfgang Streeck characterize the German pattern during this period as one of "austerity plus selective expansion." Even as German budget deficits ballooned during the period, reaching 4.4 percent of GDP in 1993, authorities continued to expand targeted benefits, including the stepping up of child benefits and child tax credits in the mid-1990s. Kitschelt and Streeck, *Germany: Beyond the Stable State* (London: Frank Cass, 2004), 210–11.
127. OECD, "Labour Market Statistics," "Main Economic Indicators" database, doi:10.1787/data-00046-en, accessed May 6, 2014.
128. This period witnessed the appearance of a number of analyses of Europe's syndrome of "welfare without work," of which Germany was cited as a prime example. For the classic treatment of the "welfare-without-work" syndrome, see Esping-Andersen, "Welfare States without Work." Others, like Wolfgang Streeck, expressed concern about the model's long-term survival. See Streeck, "German Capitalism: Does It Exist? Can It Survive?" *New Political Economy* 2, no. 2 (1997): 237–56.
129. Wolfgang Streeck, "Endgame? The Fiscal Crisis of the German State," Max-Planck-Institut für Gesellschaftsforschung Discussion Paper 07/7 (Köln: MPIfG, 2007), 15–16.
130. OECD, "Labour Market Statistics," "Main Economic Indicators" database, doi:10.1787/data-00046-en, accessed May 6, 2014.
131. For a discussion of labor-market institutions in the German Social Market Economy, see Kathleen Thelen, *Union of Parts: Labor Politics in Postwar Germany* (Ithaca, NY: Cornell University Press, 1991).
132. Mark I. Vail, *Recasting Welfare Capitalism: Economic Adjustment in Contemporary France and Germany* (Philadelphia: Temple University Press, 2010).
133. The Bündnis had been initiated by the administration of Schröder's CDU predecessor Chancellor Helmut Kohl in the hopes of facilitating job creation through sustained peak-level negotiations between unions and employers, particularly in the export-intensive sectors in which neocorporatist bargaining had long dominated.
134. The Schröder administration hoped to use the Bündnis as a means to spread blame for unemployment, but neither unions nor employers were prepared to make major concessions. This account is supported by an expert who participated in the closed negotiations of the Bündnis. The government finally allowed it to dissolve in 2003.

135. This discrepancy between the process and substance of reform helps to explain why the unions continue to view Schröder as a traitor to the interests of the Left, even as the substance of his labor-market reforms left their membership relatively unscathed. In the words of Michael Guggemos, an official with IG Metall, unions and the SPD continue to have a "love-hate relationship" that shows that "no one can fight like siblings." Interview, Berlin, July 23, 2007.
136. Konstantin von Hammerstein and Michael Sauga, "Das System ist faul," *Der Spiegel* 21 (May 21, 2001), 96–97.
137. Perceptions to this effect on the left wing of the SPD led to widespread accusations that Schröder had sold out to the interests of business. Such recrimination ultimately helped to spur the emergence of Die Linke, an electorally viable far left party composed of former East German Communists and disaffected western Social Democrats. For a full discussion, see Mark I. Vail, "Left of Eden: The Changing Politics of Economic Inequality in Contemporary Germany," *German Politics* 18, no. 4 (December 2009): 559–76.
138. "Reasonableness" was defined with respect to positions' physical proximity to a worker's residence and their wage levels compared to his or her employment history.
139. SPD und Bündnis 90/Die Grünen Bundestagsfraktionen, "Zur Reform der Arbeitsförderung: Eckpunkte der Fraktionen SPD und Bündnis 90/Die Grünen vom 3. Juli 2001 für ein Job-Aktivierien, Qualifizieren, Trainieren, Investieren, Vermitteln-Gesetz," July 2001.
140. For details, see Bundesanstalt für Arbeit, "Sofortprogramm zum Abbau der Jugendarbeitslosigkeit: Zwischenergebnisse aus der Begleitforschung," Informationen für die Beratungs- und Vermittlungsdieste der Bundesanstalt für Arbeit, 20/00, May 17, 2000.
141. This scandal, in which the BA was found to have inflated job-placement statistics, led to the resignation of BA President Bernhard Jagoda and to major reforms of the agency's administrative structure. For a discussion, see "Bundesanstalt gerät immer stärker ins Kreuzfeuer der Kritik," *Frankfurter Allgemeine Zeitung*, February 6, 2002, 13; and "Jagoda weist Rücktrittsforderungen zurück," *Frankfurter Allgemeine Zeitung*, February 7, 2002, 13.
142. For details, see Hartz Commission, "Moderne Dienstleistungen am Arbeitsmarkt: Vorschläge der Kommission zum Abbau der Arbeitslosigkeit und zur Umstrukturierung der Bundesanstalt für Arbeit," August 2002. The commission was named after its leader, Peter Hartz, the personnel director at Volkswagen and Schröder's former business associate.
143. The other elements of Agenda 2010 involved liberalizing protections against layoffs in some of Germany's smallest firms, loosening the country's strict shop-opening laws, reducing health-insurance contributions, and cutting some taxes.
144. The reform sparked massive protests in which tens of thousands of Germans participated over a period of several weeks in 2004; it ultimately led to the SPD's defeat in the 2005 elections, which forced the SPD to share power in a "grand coalition" with the CDU-CSU. It also resulted in a flood of court challenges, leading to a decision in early 2008 by the Federal Constitutional Court that eligibility restrictions for some groups must be loosened. See "Der Nebel über Hartz IV lichtet sich: Bundesrichter haben viele Grundsatzentscheidungen zur Arbeitsmarktreform gefällt," *Frankfurter Allgemeine Zeitung*, January 29, 2008, 14.
145. One trade union official expressed this logic in stark terms, claiming that Schröder pushed through reforms without *any* consultation of the unions, having decided "that he didn't need them" politically. Interview, official, Deutsche Gewerkschaftsbund (DGB), Berlin, July 9, 2007.
146. Interview, Günther Horzetsky, Bundesministerium für Arbeit und Soziales (BMAS), Berlin, June 10, 2009.
147. It also was consistent with the "lifetime learning" initiatives undertaken by unions during this period to expand training opportunities as a means of both attracting new members and supporting the skills and productivity of existing ones. Interview, Michael Guggemos, IG Metall, Berlin, January 19, 2001.
148. Interview, Johannes Jakob, Deutscher Gewerkschaftsbund (DGB), Berlin, December 4, 2000.
149. Wolfgang Streeck referred to the labor-employer nexus in the BA as the "Nürnberg Complex," after the city where the BA headquarters is located. Personal conversation, Köln, January 29, 2001.

150. Interview, Jan Brahmst, SPD Parteivorstand, Berlin, May 31, 2011.
151. See, e.g., Alexander Reisenbichler and Kimberly J. Morgan, "From 'Sick Man' to 'Miracle': Explaining the Robustness of the German Labor Market during and after the Financial Crisis 2008–2009," *Politics and Society* 40, no. 4 (2012): 549–79.
152. For a full discussion of the rise of Die Linke and its connections to rising economic inequality, see Benjamin T. Bowyer and Mark I. Vail, "Economic Insecurity, the Social Market Economy, and Support for the German Left," *West European Politics* 34, no. 4 (2011): 683–705.
153. An intervening coalition between the CDU and liberal FDP was in power from 2009–2013.
154. Judy Dempsey, "Merkel Says Worst Still Ahead in Germany," *International Herald Tribune*, November 11, 2009, 13.
155. Matthew Saltmarsh, "Europe Gets Creative in Limiting Job Losses," *International Herald Tribune*, June 17, 2009, Finance section, 14.
156. "Industrie klagt über Kosten der Kurzarbeit," *Der Tagesspiegel*, July 22, 2009, 13.
157. Barbara Schwengler and Veronika Loibl, "Aufschwung und Krise wirken regional unterschiedlich," IAB Kurzbericht 1 (Nürnberg: IAB, 2010), 6.
158. Between September 2008 and June 2009, the increase in the number of workers benefitting from the program in former western Länder soared from 32,000 to 1.23 million, while in the former DDR it increased much more modestly, from 7,000 to 174,000. Ibid., 4, 6.
159. The program's expansion in July 2010 increased workers' eligibility from eighteen to twenty-four months and exempted participating firms from social contributions.
160. OECD, *OECD Employment Outlook, 2010* (Paris: OECD, 2010), 71, 74; and Bundesagentur für Arbeit, Statistical Database, https://statistik.arbeitsagentur.de/, accessed November 12, 2016.
161. Interview, official, Deutsche Gewerkschaftsbund, Berlin, June 21, 2011.
162. Vail, "Left of Eden," 569.
163. Interview, Günther Horzetzky, Bundesministerium für Arbeit und Soziales (BMAS), Berlin, July 23, 2007.
164. Vail, "Left of Eden," 571; and interview, Michael Guggemos, IG Metall, Berlin, July 23, 2007.
165. Frank Bandau and Kathrin Dümig, "Administering the Inherited 'Employment Miracle': The Labor Market Policy of the Second Merkel Government," *German Politics* 23, no. 4 (2014): 345.
166. Stefan Wagstyl, "Germany Closer to Adopting Minimum Wage," *Financial Times* online, July 3, 2014, https://www.ft.com/content/68a7a822-02ce-11e4-a68d-00144feab7de, accessed November 16, 2016.
167. Ibid.
168. Alexander Gerschenkron argues that the consolidation of German industrial banking emerged concomitantly with the strategic cartelization of the German industrial landscape in the nineteenth century. In Gerschenkron's words, "the banks refused to tolerate fratricidal struggles among their children (15)." The collusive relationships among the state, industry, and finance were thus established in the earliest period of German industrial development. Alexander Gerschenkron, "Economic Backwardness in Historical Perspective," in *Economic Backwardness in Historical Perspective, a Book of Essays* (Cambridge, MA: Harvard University Press, 1962), 5–30.
169. Shonfield, *Modern Capitalism*, 246–48.
170. John Zysman, *Governments, Markets, and Growth: Financial Systems and the Politics of Industrial Change* (Ithaca, NY: Cornell University Press, 1983), 260.
171. *Economist*, "Lost a Fortune, Seeking a Role," January 10, 2015, http://www.economist.com/news/finance-and-economics/21638143-seven-german-landesbanken-survived-financial-crisis-are-still. Since the 1960s, the Landesbanken and Sparkassen had used their economically important positions to justify significant subsidies and protection from the state, including favorable tax treatment and explicit state backing of their debt. Gregory W. Fuller, *The Great Debt Transformation: Households, Financialization, and Policy Responses* (Houndmills, UK: Palgrave Macmillan, 2016), 173.

172. Cornelia Woll, *The Power of Inaction: Bank Bailouts in Comparison* (Ithaca, NY: Cornell University Press, 2014), 113.
173. Daniel Detzer and Hansjörg Herr, "Financial Regulation in Germany," Financialisation, Economy, Society and Sustainable Development Department (FESSUD), European Union, Working Paper, no. 55 (September 2014), 11–12.
174. Ibid., 11.
175. Jack Ewing, "In Germany, Little Appetite to Change Struggling Banks," *New York Times*, August 9, 2013, http://www.nytimes.com/2013/08/10/business/global/in-germany-little-appetite-to-change-troubled-banking-system.html.
176. Andreas Busch, *Banking Regulation and Globalization* (Oxford: Oxford University Press, 2009), 98.
177. Woll, *Power of Inaction*, 113.
178. Richard Deeg, "The Comeback of *Modell Deutschland*? The New German Political Economy in the EU," *German Politics* 14, no. 3 (2005): 332–53; cited in Iain Harding and Huw Macartney, "EU Ring-Fencing and the Defense of Too-Big-to-Fail Banks," *West European Politics* 39, no. 3 (2016), 505.
179. Maximilian Hall, *The International Handbook on Financial Reform* (Cheltenham, UK: Edward Elgar, 2003), 95.
180. Detzer and Herr, "Financial Regulation in Germany," 13. Both the industrial banks and Landesbanken responded to the increasingly competitive environment through a series of mergers, the most notable of which was the 2008 buyout of Dresdner Bank by Commerzbank.
181. Woll, *Power of Inaction*, 113.
182. Harding and Macartney, "EU Ring-Fencing," 504–5.
183. Collectively, the Landesbanken accrued so many toxic assets that the ultimate cost of their post-2007 bailout ran to an astonishing €70 billion. Markus Fischer et al., "Government Guarantees and Bank Risk Taking Incentives," SSRN Paper (Rochester: Social Science Research Network), August 2014.
184. J. Lawrence Broz, "Partisan Financial Cycles," in *Politics in the New Hard Times: The Great Recession in Comparative Perspective*, ed. Miles Kahler and David A. Lake (Ithaca, NY: Cornell University Press, 2013), 96.
185. Nina Eichacker, "German Financialization, the Global Financial Crisis, and the Eurozone Crisis," Working Paper, Political Economy Research Institute, University of Massachusetts, Amherst, October 2015, 17.
186. Klaus J. Hopt, Christoph Kumpan, and Felix Steffeck, "Preventing Bank Insolvencies in the Financial Crisis: The German Financial Market Stabilization Acts," *European Business Organization Law Review* 10 (2009), 519.
187. Woll, *Power of Inaction*, 119.
188. For an excellent discussion of the relationship between this guarantee and public support for the governing coalition, see Achim Goerres and Stefanie Walter, "The Political Consequences of National Crisis Management: Micro-Level Evidence from German Voters during the 2008/09 Global Economic Crisis," *German Politics* 25, no. 1 (March 2016): 131–51.
189. OECD, "The Federal Agency for Financial Market Stabilization in Germany: From Rescuing to Restructuring," in *OECD Journal: Financial Market Trends*, no. 2 (Paris: OECD, 2011), 3.
190. Hopt, Kumpan, and Steffeck, "Preventing Bank Insolvencies," 542.
191. Andres Kröner, "German Landesbanks Relieve Merger Pressure through Cooperation," Reuters, March 22, 2015, http://www.reuters.com/article/germany-banks-landesbanks-idUSL6N0WL4AU20150322.
192. This debate echoes elements of the debate in the US over restoring the Glass-Steagall Act, which separated these two spheres of activity and was abolished in the 1990s.
193. Harding and Macartney, "EU Ring-Fencing," 513.
194. For a detailed discussion, see "Deutsche Bank: Bundesregierung bereitet Notfallplan für Deutsche Bank vor," *Die Zeit*, September 28, 2016, http://www.zeit.de/wirtschaft/2016-09/deutsche-bank-rettungsplan-finanzaufsichtsbehoerde.

195. One prominent French economist, formerly employed by Société Générale, recently characterized this longstanding policy posture as a "highly protectionist niche strategy." Interview, Paris, June 29, 2017.
196. Interview, Berlin, July 30, 2015.

Chapter 4

1. Such symbiotic relationships between managers and party elites have traditionally been particularly pronounced in the public sector, which Jonathan Hopkin describes (in Italy as elsewhere in southern Europe) as dominated by "partisan political interference with clientelistic patterns of recruitment, corrupt allocation of public contracts, and weak accountability." Jonathan Hopkin, "The Troubled Southern Periphery: The Euro Experience in Italy and Spain," in *The Future of the Euro*, ed. Mark Blyth and Matthias Matthijs (Oxford: Oxford University Press, 2015), 169–70.
2. Andrea Boltho, "Italy, Germany, Japan: From Economic Miracles to Virtual Stagnation," Economic History Working Paper no. 14, presented at the Conference "Italy and the World Economy 1861–2011," Rome, Banca d'Italia, October 12–15, 2011, 7–8.
3. Giulia Sandri, Mario Telò, and Luca Tomini, "Political System, Civil Society and Institutions in Italy: The Quality of Democracy," *Comparative European Politics* 11, no. 3 (May 2013): 265.
4. Enzo di Nuoscio, "Le libéralisme de Luigi Einaudi," in *Histoire du libéralisme en Europe*, ed. Philippe Nemo and Jean Petitot (Paris: Presses universitaires de France, 2006), 653ff.
5. Andrew Shonfield, *Modern Capitalism: The Changing Balance of Public and Private Power* (London: Oxford University Press, 1965), 179–83.
6. Vera Zamagni, *The Economic History of Italy, 1860–1990* (Oxford: Clarendon Press, 1993), 37, 40.
7. Shonfield, *Modern Capitalism*, 178.
8. The state resources involved in sustaining the postwar clientelist web ranged from contracts for public infrastructure projects to state subsidies for new factories and commercial services to public-sector jobs of often dubious merit. Tony Judt, *Postwar: A History of Europe since 1945* (New York: Penguin, 2005), 258.
9. Christopher Duggan, *A Concise History of Italy*, 2nd ed. (Cambridge: Cambridge University Press, 2014), 161.
10. Guido M. Rey, "Italy," in *The European Economy: Growth and Crisis*, ed. Andrea Boltho (Oxford: Oxford University Press), 512–15.
11. Judt, *Postwar*, 556.
12. Richard M. Locke, *Remaking the Italian Economy* (Ithaca, NY: Cornell University Press, 1995), 10, 17.
13. Ibid., ch. 1; and Zamagni, *Economic History of Italy*, 365.
14. Boltho, "Italy, Germany, Japan," 15.
15. Charles S. Maier, "Conti e racconti: Interpretazioni della performance dell'economia italiana dal dopoguerra a oggi," in *Storia economica d'Italia*, vol. I: *Interpretazioni*, ed. Pierluigi Ciocca and Gianni Toniolo (Bari: Laterza, 1999), 281. Quoted in ibid.
16. The EMS involved an Exchange Rate Mechanism (ERM), a system of fixed but adjustable exchange rates that limited fluctuations to a band of ±2.25 percent.
17. Daniel Gros, "The EMS Crisis of the 1990s: Parallels with the Current Crisis?" CEPS Working Document no. 393 (Brussels: Centre for European Policy Studies, March 2014), 2–3.
18. Paul de Grauwe, "European Monetary System," *Oxford Encyclopedia of Economic History*, vol. 1 (Oxford: Oxford University Press, 2003), 240–41.
19. William Drozdiak, "A 'Government of Necessity' Challenges Italy's Sacred Cows," *Washington Post*, October 3, 1992, A16.
20. This calculus echoed and was reinforced by the vocal but dubious claims of the European Commission that EMU was the only way to preserve national sovereignty and dilute the de facto dominance of the Bundesbank. For a discussion, see Nicolas Jabko, *Playing the Market: A Political Strategy for Uniting Europe, 1985–2005* (Ithaca, NY: Cornell University Press, 2006), 154–58.
21. Ibid.

22. Alan Cowell, "Italian Premier Backs Off His Austerity Measures," *New York Times*, October 17, 1992, http://www.nytimes.com/1992/10/17/world/italian-premier-backs-off-his-austerity-measures.html.
23. This would be the first in a series of periodic technocratic, so-called caretaker governments in the 1990s and 2000s, which were designed to break the clientelistic logjam but generally ended up as "emergency measures to secure short-term objectives." Hopkin, "Troubled Southern Periphery," 179.
24. John Tagliabues, "Italy's Spending Cuts Are Facing Labor Obstacles," *New York Times*, September 26, 1993, 10.
25. Duggan, *Concise History of Italy*, 293.
26. Michael E. Shin and John A. Agnew, *Berlusconi's Italy: Mapping Contemporary Italian Politics* (Philadelphia: Temple University Press, 2008), 48.
27. Duggan, *Concise History of Italy*, 293.
28. Elisabetta Gualmini and Jonathan Hopkin, "Liberalization within Diversity: Welfare and Labor Market Reforms in Italy and the UK," *Spanish Labour Law and Employment Relations Journal* 1, nos. 1–2 (2012): 74.
29. I am indebted to Michael Jones for this formulation.
30. The party drew on football imagery, including the name of the party, which translates roughly as "Go Italy!"
31. Steffano Fella and Carolo Ruzza, "Populism and the Fall of the Centre-Right in Italy: The End of the Berlusconi Model or a New Beginning?" *Journal of Contemporary European Studies* 21, no. 1 (2013): 39–40.
32. Duggan, *Concise History of Italy*, 297.
33. Gianni Toniolo, "An Overview of Italy's Economic Growth," in *The Oxford Handbook of the Italian Economy since Unification*, ed. Gianni Toniolo (Oxford: Oxford University Press, 2013), 23–26. By 1995, Italy's gross public debt had grown to 121 percent of GDP. OECD, "General Government Debt" database, doi:10.1787/a0528cc2-en, accessed November 15, 2016.
34. Fella and Ruzza, "Populism and the Fall of the Centre-Right," 41.
35. Interview, September 19, 2014.
36. Duggan, *Concise History of Italy*, 297.
37. Fella and Ruzza, "Populism and the Fall of the Center-Right," 40.
38. Shin and Agnew, *Berlusconi's Italy*, 72–74.
39. Ibid., 74.
40. Duggan, *Concise History of Italy*, 297.
41. Ibid., 298.
42. "Italy: Forza Dini," *Economist*, August 12, 1995: 43; World Bank, World Development Indicators Database, http://data.worldbank.org/data-catalog/world-development-indicators, accessed December 29, 2015.
43. Duggan, *Concise History of Italy*, 299.
44. John Rossant, "Italy's Prodi May Be Derailed before His Reforms Get on Track," *Bloomberg Businessweek*, December 8, 1996.
45. Duggan, *Concise History of Italy*, 299. As adopted, the tax represented a "watered down" version of the large tax increases initially threatened by Prodi. For a discussion see Nicholas Bray and Maria Sturani, "Surprise! Italy's 'Euro Tax' Provides for Give-Backs," *Wall Street Journal*, November 20, 1996, http://www.wsj.com/articles/SB848443423358366500.
46. Rossant, "Italy's Prodi May Be Derailed."
47. World Bank, "World Development Indicators database," http://data.worldbank.org/data-catalog/world-development-indicators, accessed September 15, 2016.
48. It also "finessed away" Italy's continuing heavy debt burden, which remained larger than the Italian economy. Hopkin, "Troubled Southern Periphery," 163.
49. As David Marsh once observed, "To release themselves from the grip of the D-Mark, the French and the Italians were ready to promise almost anything." Marsh, *The Bundesbank: The Bank That Rules Europe* (London: Heinemann, 1992), 215, quoted in Jabko, *Playing the Market*, 165, n. 51.
50. Duggan, *Concise History of Italy*, 301.

51. Shin and Agnew, *Berlusconi's Italy*, 11–12.
52. World Bank, "World Development Indicators database," http://data.worldbank.org/data-catalog/world-development-indicators, accessed May 24, 2014. Italy's longstanding and endemic problem of tax evasion, particularly by those in upper income brackets who can afford the requisite attorneys and accountants, further undermines its fiscal situation.
53. Interview, September 19, 2014.
54. Hopkin, "Troubled Southern Periphery," 172.
55. Bill Emmott, *Good Italy, Bad Italy: Why Italy Must Conquer Its Demons to Face the Future* (New Haven, CT: Yale University Press, 2012), 37–39.
56. Duggan, *Concise History of Italy*, 303.
57. Sergio Fabbrini, "The Rise and Fall of Silvio Berlusconi: Personalization of Politics and Its Limits," *Comparative European Politics* 11, no. 2 (March 2013): 153–71. This trend was exacerbated by Berlusconi's 2005 electoral reform, which introduced a modified system of proportional representation that made MPs even more dependent upon their parties. Sandri, Telò, and Tomini, "Political System, Civil Society and Institutions in Italy," 275–76.
58. Ibid.
59. Vito Tanzi, *Dollars, Euros, and Debt: How We Got into the Fiscal Crisis and How We Get out of It* (Houndmills, UK: Palgrave Macmillan, 2013), 56.
60. Jabko, *Playing the Market*, 174, n. 82.
61. Elisabetta Gualmini and Vivien A. Schmidt, "State Transformation in Italy and France: Technocratic versus Political Leadership on the Road from Non-Liberalism to Neo-Liberalism," in *Resilient Liberalism in Europe's Political Economy*, ed. Vivien A. Schmidt and Mark Thatcher (Cambridge: Cambridge University Press, 2013), 354.
62. Mediaset, a large Italian media conglomerate in which Berlusconi's holding company Fininvest held a more than 35 percent interest, was accused of having acted as a tax shelter and fiscal curtain behind which massive amounts of money were moved to fictitious foreign companies in ways that allowed participants to book fictive losses even as gains were paid out as foreign profits not subject to Italian income tax.
63. Viroli, *Liberty of Servants*, 72.
64. Emmott, *Good Italy, Bad Italy*, 38.
65. World Bank, "World Development Indicators" database, http://data.worldbank.org/data-catalog/world-development-indicators, accessed May 6, 2014.
66. Ibid.
67. Stephen N. Broadberry, Claire Giordano, and Francesco Zollino, "Productivity," in *Oxford Handbook of the Italian Economy*, ed. Gianni Toniolo, 208.
68. Emmott, *Good Italy, Bad Italy*, 190–91. For the classic formulation of the virtues of the Third Italy, see Michael J. Piore and Charles F. Sabel, *The Second Industrial Divide: Possibilities for Prosperity* (New York: Basic Books, 1984), esp. ch. 10.
69. World Bank, "World Development Indicators" database, http://data.worldbank.org/data-catalog/world-development-indicators, accessed May 6, 2015.
70. Erik Jones, "Italy's Sovereign Debt Crisis," *Survival* 54, no. 1 (February–March 2012), 87.
71. Erik Jones, "The Forgotten Financial Union: How You Can Have a Euro Crisis without a Euro," in *Future of the Euro*, ed. Blyth and Matthijs, 55.
72. Jones, "Italy's Sovereign Debt Crisis," 88.
73. Gualmini and Schmidt, "State Transformation," 356.
74. Veena Jha, "The Effects of Fiscal Stimulus Packages on Employment," ILO Working Paper no. 34 (2009), 23.
75. Ricardo Rovelli, "Economic Policy in a Global Crisis: Did Italy Get It Right?" *Italian Politics* 25 (2009), 226.
76. Hopkin, "Troubled Southern Periphery," 176; and Mark Blyth, *Austerity: The History of a Dangerous Idea* (New York: Oxford University Press, 2013), 47. According to one Italian Treasury official, Economics Minister Giulio Tremonti was "merely following the austerity line," which drove Italy into another recession. Interview, October 10, 2014.
77. Mark Horton and Anna Ivanova, "The Size of the Fiscal Expansion: An Analysis for the Largest Countries," IMF Working Paper (Washington, DC: IMF, February 2009), 1–2.

78. By mid-2001 yield spreads on long-dated Italian bonds relative to German debt were around 300 basis points (reaching about 5 percent on the ten-year Italian bond) and climbing. Jones, "Italy's Sovereign Debt Crisis," 91; Blyth, *Austerity*, 80.
79. This budget included €24.9 billion in cuts focused on transfers to subnational governments, disability pensions, and the abolition of wage increases for public-sector workers. Vivien Schmidt and Elisabetta Gualmini, "The Political Sources of Italy's Economic Problems: Between Opportunistic Political Leadership and Pragmatic, Technocratic Leadership," *Comparative European Politics* 11, no. 3 (2013): 376.
80. Jones, "Italy's Sovereign Debt Crisis," 90.
81. Ibid.
82. See Alberto Alesina, Dorian Carloni, and Giampaolo Lecce, "The Electoral Consequences of Large Fiscal Adjustments," in *Fiscal Policy after the Financial Crisis*, ed. Alberto Alesina and Francesco Giavazzi (Chicago: University of Chicago Press, 2013), 531–70; and Alberto Alesina and Silvia Ardagna, "Large Changes in Fiscal Policy: Taxes versus Spending," in *Tax Policy and Economy*, vol. 24, 2010, ed. Jeffrey R. Brown, cited in Tanzi, *Dollars, Euros, and Debt*, 19.
83. Officials were also increasingly distracted by Berlusconi's cascade of lurid legal problems, including charges that he had had sex with underage prostitutes.
84. Interview, October 20, 2014.
85. "Slash and Burn: Italy's Fiscal Austerity," *Economist*, May 29, 2010, http://www.economist.com/node/16218360.
86. Ibid.
87. Nick Pisa, "Italy Grinds to a Halt as Three Million Strike over €45 billion (£39.5 billion) Austerity Package," *Daily Mail*, September 7, 2011, http://www.dailymail.co.uk/news/article-2034352/Italy-strike-THREE-million-protest-austerity-package.html.
88. In 2011, Eurobarometer data showed that a mere 12 percent of those polled trusted the government, the lowest level among all EU member states besides Greece (at 8 percent) and 12 percentage points lower than the EU 27 mean. Data cited in Sandri, Telò, and Tomini, "Political System, Civil Society, and Institutions," 271.
89. Stacey Meichtry and Alessandra Galloni, "Berlusconi Bows Out; Austerity Lies Ahead," *Wall Street Journal*, November 13, 2011, http://www.wsj.com/articles/SB10001424052970204358004577033703085619754.
90. This infelicitous term came to be used to refer to the consortium of the ECB, IMF, and European Commission, whose self-appointed role it became to monitor peripheral European countries' adherence to austerity conditions and the terms of bailouts during the Eurozone crisis.
91. Hopkin, "Troubled Southern Periphery," 179.
92. Meichtry and Galloni, "Berlusconi Bows Out."
93. Rachel Donadio, "Emergency Decree Puts in Place More Cuts in Italy," *New York Times*, December 4, 2011, http://www.nytimes.com/2011/12/05/world/europe/mario-monti-of-italy-calls-cabinet-to-consider-austerity-measures.html.
94. The PD was formed in 2007 through a union of former members of Prodi's "Olive Tree" coalition, notably the Democratici di sinistra (DS), an heir to the PCI, and the more centrist Daisy (Margherita) Party. It would come to be the major center–left party in a system that was becoming ever more polarized, as centrist coalitions like the Olive Tree and Freedom Pole proved no longer feasible.
95. According to one former French Treasury official who was a close advisor to President Nicolas Sarkozy at the time, the widespread fear among French and German officials was that "if this [contagion] happens to Spain or Italy, we're all dead." Interview, February 16, 2015.
96. Interview, Nicoletta Batini, October 10, 2014. About three-fourths of the increased Italian debt load during the Eurozone crisis resulted from the negative effects on GDP of Monti's reforms rather than from increases in spending.
97. Data at http://www.economywatch.com/economic-statistics/country/Italy; and Andrew Davis and Lorenzo Totaro, "Italy's Debt to Rise to Record in 2013 as Recession Lingers," Bloomberg.com, April 10, 2013, https://www.bloomberg.com/news/articles/2013-04-10/italy-s-debt-to-rise-to-record-this-year-as-recession-lingers.

98. Monti's high-handedness was both a symptom and a reinforcing cause of his technocratic view of the economy. According to a former Italian IMF official, he was encouraged in this attitude by his friendship with Angela Merkel as well as his desire to be perceived as an "intellectual savior" of the country. Interview, October 10, 2014.
99. In a reflection of widespread cynicism and frustration with the Italian political system, the party receiving the most votes in the election was the vaguely anti-establishment and farcical Five Stars Movement led by comedian Beppe Grillo, which won an astonishing 8.7 million votes. For complete results see Laura Sajik, "The 2013 Italian National Elections: A Commentary," *Social Policy* (Spring 2013): 15–17.
100. Hopkin, "Troubled Southern Periphery," 180.
101. Guy Dinmore and Giulia Segreti, "Matteo Renzi Sets Out Plans for First 100 Days," *Financial Times*, February 17, 2014, https://www.ft.com/content/d4939144-97cc-11e3-ab60-00144feab7de.
102. Elisabetta Povoledo, "In Test for Premier, Italians Rally against Plan to Relax Labor Rules," *New York Times*, November 18, 2014, https://www.nytimes.com/2014/11/19/world/europe/in-italy-jobs-law-ignites-protests-before-it-is-even-written.html.
103. Richard Blackden, "Italy Lays Out €160 Billion Industrial Investment Plan," *Financial Times*, December 18, 2015, https://www.ft.com/content/ffc8cc85-8cca-3f1b-b033-59c4670dcd9d.
104. OECD, "General Government Debt" database, doi:10.1787/a0528cc2-en, accessed November 15, 2016.
105. Giada Zampano, "Italy Unveils 2017 Budget Plan," *Wall Street Journal*, October 15, 2016, http://www.wsj.com/articles/italy-unveils-2017-budget-plan-1476558935.
106. On Italy's rigid labor laws, see "Waiting for a Job," *Economist*, Survey of Italy, November 8, 1997, 5–7.
107. OECD "Harmonised Unemployment Rate" database, doi:10.1787/52570002-en, accessed November 15, 2016.
108. Federico Lucidi and Alfred Kleinknecht, "Little Innovation, Many Jobs: An Econometric Analysis of the Italian Labour Productivity Crisis," *Cambridge Journal of Economics* 34 (2010): 526–27.
109. Ibid., 527.
110. Even the vaunted export leaders of the "Third Italy" were limited in their ability to lead a labor-market revival. Forced to compete with producers in emerging markets with lower labor costs and constrained by their small size in their ability to delocalize (unlike their German counterparts, who did so with great enthusiasm in eastern Europe in the 1990s), such firms enjoy limited opportunities for expansion. Given that SMEs account for a larger share of manufacturing employment in Italy than in Germany (38.9 percent versus 20.5 percent in 1991), the effects on the labor market are pronounced. Boltho, "Italy, Germany, Japan," 18, 31.
111. Marta Fana, Dario Guarascio, and Valeria Cirillo, "Labour Market Reforms in Italy: Evaluating the Effects of the Jobs Act," Working Paper 5/2015, ISI Growth, December 2015, 8.
112. One of the most controversial of such provisions is laid out in Article 18 of Italy's so-called workers' statute of 1970, which requires firms with at least fifteen employees to rehire workers found to have been wrongfully dismissed. In practice this law prohibits economically motivated dismissals given the lengthy process of litigating such cases in labor courts and the threat of automatic reinstatement. Changing this provision would become one of the central priorities of Renzi's Jobs Act. For a discussion see "Italy: The Jobs Act 2015 Introduces Labor Law Reforms," Willis Towers Watson Global News Brief, February 6, 2015, https://www.towerswatson.com/en/Insights/Newsletters/Global/global-news-briefs/2015/02/italy-the-jobs-act-2015-introduces-labor-law-reforms.
113. In 1995 this rate was 26 percent, compared to an EU average of 37 percent. Fana, Guarascio, and Cirillo, "Labour Market Reforms," 10.
114. Between 1973 and 1995, average annual GDP growth was 2.3 percent, compared to 1.8 percent for the rest of the OECD. By 1996, growth had slowed to a mere 1.29 percent and, with the exception of 2000 and 2006, would never again exceed 2 percent, usually hovering at between 0.5 percent and 1.5 percent. Boltho, "Italy, Germany, Japan," 27; and OECD,

"Harmonised Unemployment Rate" database, doi:10.1787/52570002-en, accessed November 15, 2016.

115. Lucidi and Kleinknecht, "Little Innovation, Many Jobs," 531–32.
116. Interview, October 10, 2014.
117. Interview, Vito Tanzi, October 20, 2014.
118. Italian expenditure on R&D had long been stagnant in both the public and private sectors, remaining relatively stable at around 1 percent of GDP, compared with between 2 and 3 percent for Germany and Japan. Fana, Guarascio, and Cirillo, "Labour Market Reforms," 14–15; and Boltho, "Italy, Germany, Japan," 37.
119. OECD, "Harmonised Unemployment Rate" database, doi:10.1787/52570002-en, accessed November 15, 2016.
120. For a full discussion, see A. Javier Hamann, "The Reform of the Pension System in Italy," IMF Working Paper 97/18 (February 1997).
121. "An Age-Old Problem," in *Economist,* A Survey of Italy, November 8–14, 1997, 25.
122. Hamann, "Reform of the Pension System," 22.
123. "Italy: Forza Dini."
124. Matteo Jessoula, Paolo R. Grazziano, and Ilaria Madama, "Selective Flexicurity in Segmented Labour Markets: The Case of Italian 'Mid-Siders,'" *Journal of Social Policy* 39, no. 4 (2010): 569.
125. Lucidi and Kleinknecht, "Little Innovation, Many Jobs," 526.
126. Jessoula, Grazziano, and Madama, "Selective Flexicurity," 570–71.
127. For a full discussion, see Deborah Ball, "Italy's D'Alema Wins One for Economy—Jobless Rise Underscores Need for Stimulus Pact with Industry, Unions," *Wall Street Journal,* December 23, 1998, A12.
128. Maurizio Ferrera and Elisabetta Gualmini, *Rescued by Europe? Social and Labour Market Reforms in Italy from Maastricht to Berlusconi* (Amsterdam: Amsterdam University Press, 2004), 160. See also Schmidt and Gualmini, "Political Sources," 367.
129. Gillian Hargreaves, "Analysis: Italy's Labour Dilemma," BBC News online, March 24, 2002, http://news.bbc.co.uk/2/hi/europe/1890313.stm. In an event that highlighted the stakes of this reform and depth of opposition to it, Marco Biagi, a professor of labor law and Labor Ministry advisor in charge of drafting the measure, was assassinated three days before the protest by the Red Brigades, who cited the proposal as the reason.
130. Hopkin, "Troubled Southern Periphery," 167.
131. Tony Barber, "Italians Braced for Clash over Pension Reform," *Financial Times,* October 24, 2003, 8.
132. Baccaro, "Discursive Democracy," 36.
133. John Prideaux, "Oh for a New Risorgimento," Special Report on Italy, *Economist,* June 11, 2001, cited in Emmott, *Good Italy, Bad Italy,* 101.
134. Hopkin, "Troubled Southern Periphery," 163–64, 167.
135. Emmott, *Good Italy, Bad Italy,* 79.
136. World Bank, "World Development Indicators" database, http://data.worldbank.org/data-catalog/world-development-indicators, accessed May 24, 2015.
137. OECD, "Harmonised Unemployment Rate" database, doi:10.1787/52570002-en, accessed November 15, 2016.
138. Lucio Baccaro, "Discursive Democracy and the Construction of Interests: Lessons from Italian Pension Reform," in *The Politics of Representation in the Global Age: Identification, Mobilization, and Adjudication,* ed. Peter A. Hall et al. (Cambridge: Cambridge University Press, 2014), 37.
139. Ibid., 36, 45.
140. "Monti's Labour-Law Tangle," *Economist,* March 24–30, 2012, 51.
141. Gavin Jones, "Analysis: Six Months On, Monti's Labor Reform Has Changed Little," Reuters, January 2, 2013, http://www.reuters.com/article/us-italy-labour-idUSBRE90105Q20130102.
142. Hopkin, "Troubled Southern Periphery," 179–80.
143. Ibid. For a piece that encapsulates the generational aspects of Italy's insider-outsider divide, see Beppe Severgnini, "Italy: The Nation That Crushes Its Young," *New York Times,* October 30, 2013, http://www.nytimes.com/2013/10/31/opinion/severgnini-italians-on-the-run.

html. The results of some recent efforts to liberalize labor laws to the benefit of younger workers have been "illusory," undermined by the same clientelistic patterns and deep cleavages between insiders and outsiders that have characterized the Italian labor market since the 1960s. For a discussion, see Julia Lynch, "The Italian Welfare State after the Financial Crisis," *Journal of Modern Italian Studies* 19, no. 4 (2014): passim and 385–86.

144. Fana, Guarascio, and Cirillo, "Labour Market Reforms in Italy," 15–16. See also "Italy's Renzi Clears Hurdle in Parliament on Labor Law," Reuters, November 25, 2014, http://www.reuters.com/article/us-italy-politics-idUSKCN0J923B20141125.
145. Jim Yardley, "In Italy, Matteo Renzi Aims to Upend the Old World Order," *New York Times*, March 31, 2015, http://www.nytimes.com/2015/04/01/world/europe/in-italy-matteo-renzi-aims-to-upend-the-old-world-order.html.
146. Patrik Vesan, "Young Workers and the Labor Market Policies of Renzi's Government," in *Italian Politics: Governing under Constraint*, ed. Maurizio Carbone and Simona Piattoni (New York: Berghahn, 2016), 194.
147. Cited in ibid.
148. Ibid.
149. Ibid.
150. Fana, Guarascio, and Cirillo, "Labour Market Reforms," 17–19.
151. "Economic and Financial Indicators," *Economist*, February 7–13, 2015, 84; December 3–9, 2016; 78, and July 29–August 4, 2017, 76.
152. For more on the establishment of the Popolari in Italy and their direct modeling after the German system, see G. François, "People's Banks in Italy," *Journal of Political Economy* 7, no. 4 (1899): 456–67.
153. Shonfield, *Modern Capitalism*, 178–79.
154. Ibid., 180.
155. "The Italian Job," *Economist*, January 30, 2016, http://www.economist.com/news/finance-and-economics/21689630-reviving-italys-economy-will-require-sacrifices-not-just-italians-also.
156. Giampaolo Gabbi, Massimo Matthias, and Pietro Vozzella, "Financial Regulation in Italy," in *Financial Regulation in the European Union*, ed. Rainer Kattel, Jan Kregel, and Mario Tonveronachi (London: Routledge, 2016), 80.
157. Ibid., 82–4.
158. These foundations are explicitly described as philanthropic organizations.
159. Domenico Siclari, "Context, Specific Features and Potential Evolution of the Italian Banking and Financial Law," in *Italian Banking and Financial Law: Supervisory Authorities and Supervision*, ed. Domenico Siclari (London: Palgrave Macmillan, 2015), 3–42.
160. For more background on Italian bank foundations, see Chiara Leardini et al., "Outlining Italian Bank Foundations," in *Board Governance in Bank Foundations*, ed. Chiara Leardini, Gina Ross, and Sara Moggi (Berlin: Springer, 2014), 9–28.
161. Prior to the advent of EMU, the Italian financial sector was almost entirely devoid of foreign banks, and even after the EU endorsed a plan to open Italy's financial sector to international institutions, the governor of the Bank of Italy acted to protect Italian owners.
162. Nicolas Véron, "ECB Finally Addressing Italian Bank Woes," *The Hill*, December 15, 2016, http://thehill.com/blogs/pundits-blog/international-affairs/310545-ecb-finally-addressing-italian-bank-woes.
163. Whereas large German firms needed industrial banks in the postwar era, in Italy banks and smaller firms existed in what might best be described as a codependent relationship.
164. Roberto Di Quirico, "Italy and the Global Economic Crisis," *Bulletin of Italian Politics* 2, no 3 (2010): 6–7.
165. Lucia Quaglia, "The Response to the Global Financial Turmoil in Italy: 'A Financial System that Does Not Speak English,'" *South European Society and Politics* 14, no. 1 (March 2009): 14–15.
166. Cornelia Woll, *The Power of Inaction: Bank Bailouts in Comparison* (Ithaca, NY: Cornell University Press, 2014), 36–7.
167. Jones, "Forgotten Financial Union," 55–56.
168. Ibid., 56.

169. José Garrido, Emanuel Kopp, and Anke Weber, "Cleaning-up Bank Balance Sheets: Economic, Legal, and Supervisory Measures for Italy," IMF Working Paper 135 (July 2016), 6.
170. Ibid.
171. Manuela Moschella, "A New Governance for Banks: The Short- and Long-Term Drivers of the Italian Financial Sector Reform," in *Italian Politics: Governing under Constraint*, ed. Carbone and Piattoni, 175–6. Predictably, the reform was opposed by local banking unions as well as by the Catholic Church.
172. Garrido, Kopp, and Weber, "Cleaning-up Bank Balance Sheets," 13.
173. Véron, "ECB Finally Addressing Italian Bank Woes."
174. "The Italian Job," *Economist*, July 9–15, 2016, 9.
175. In July 2016 it was worth less than 10 percent of its book value and required an estimated €2–6 billion of fresh capital to survive. Ibid.; also, "Crisis and Opportunity," *Economist*, July 9–15, 2016, 59.
176. Adrian Michaels and Leslie Crawford, "MPS Shares Slump after Antonveneta Deal," *Financial Times*, November 9, 2007, https://www.ft.com/content/c123e1aa-8e04-11dc-8591-0000779fd2ac.
177. In 2014 MPS failed an EU stress test, leading to forced closures and mergers. It continued to fail these tests, most recently in summer 2016.
178. The foundation pumped over €2 billion into the bank between 1996 and 2010—on everything from horse training for Siena's famous Palio races to a biotech facility.
179. "Crisis and Opportunity." This extremely unpopular maneuver cost many Italians thousands of euros, resulted in widespread protests, and prompted the suicide of one man whom the bail-in had cost his entire €100,000 investment.
180. James Politi, "Italian Finance Minister Attacks 'Rigid' European Central Bank," *Financial Times*, https://www.ft.com/content/c517cafa-cdc0-11e6-864f-20dcb35cede2. This estimate prompted criticism from the Italian Finance Minister, who decried the ECB's accounting methods as "rigid" and argued that the package would result in an "excessively capitalised bank."
181. Véron, "ECB Finally Addressing Italian Bank Woes."
182. Jane Kramer, "The Demolition Man," *New Yorker*, June 29, 2015, 44.
183. In this way, unlike Germany, Italy has repeatedly fallen prey to the predations of sectionalism, which, as Michael Freeden reminds us, is an ever-present threat to the basic bargain between state and citizen that lies at the heart of all liberal traditions. Freeden, *Liberal Languages: Ideological Imaginations and Twentieth-Century Progressive Thought* (Princeton, NJ: Princeton University Press, 2005), 59.
184. Interview, October 10, 2014.
185. Kramer, "Demolition Man," 47.

Conclusion

1. Jamie Peck, *Constructions of Neoliberal Reason* (Oxford: Oxford University Press, 2010), xii.
2. John Ruggie, "International Regimes, Transactions, and Change: Embedded Liberalism in the Postwar Economic Order," *International Organization* 36, no. 2 (1982): 379–415.
3. Peter Gourevitch, *Politics in Hard Times: Comparative Responses to International Economic Crises* (Ithaca, NY: Cornell University Press, 1986), 17.
4. Peter M. Haas, "Introduction: Epistemic Communities and International Policy Coordination," *International Organization* 46, no. 1 (Winter 1992): 3. For an excellent study of how such epistemic frames have shaped banking regulation in Canada, the United States, and Spain, see Kimberly Pernell, "The Causes of the Divergent Development of Banking Regulation in the U.S., Canada, and Spain" (PhD diss., Harvard University, 2016).
5. For an excellent analysis of the evolving missions of the French state after the demise of dirigisme, see Jonah D. Levy, Mari Miura, and Gene Park, "Exiting Étatisme? New Directions in State Policy in France and Japan," in *The State after Statism: New State Activities in the Age of Liberalization*, ed. Jonah D. Levy (Cambridge, MA: Harvard University Press, 2006), 93–136.

6. For excellent accounts of the growing discrepancies between postwar German economic thinking and standard Ordoliberal recipes, see Ch. 1; Wade Jacoby, "The Politics of the Eurozone Crisis: Two Puzzles behind the German Consensus," *German Politics & Society* 32, no. 2 (June 2014): 70–85; and Philip G. Cerny, "In the Shadow of Ordoliberalism: The Paradox of Neoliberalism in the 21st Century," *European Review of International Studies* 3, no. 1 (2016): 78–91.
7. Prominent examples of the literature on national models of capitalism include Andrew Shonfield, *Modern Capitalism: The Changing Balance of Public and Private Power* (London: Oxford University Press, 1965); Peter A. Hall, *Governing the Economy: The Politics of State Intervention in Britain and France* (Cambridge: Polity Press, 1986); and John Zysman, *Governments, Markets, and Growth: Financial Systems and the Politics of Industrial Change* (Ithaca, NY: Cornell University Press, 1983). The classic statement of the "Varieties of Capitalism" approach is Peter A. Hall and David Soskice, "An Introduction to Varieties of Capitalism," in *Varieties of Capitalism: The Institutional Foundations of Comparative Advantage*, ed. Peter A. Hall and David Soskice (Oxford: Oxford University Press, 2001), 1–70.
8. The parallels between postwar modernization theory and the neoliberalism of the contemporary era are difficult to ignore. One important difference is the neoliberal reliance on assumptions about economic rationality rather than upon an inexorable (and logically circular and mechanism-free) process of "modernization" among postwar modernization theorists. Though products of different ideological and geopolitical environments, however, both perspectives share a profound disregard for the importance of politics and therefore suffer from a similar analytical poverty.
9. Mark Blyth, "Structures Do Not Come with an Instruction Sheet: Interests, Ideas, and Progress in Political Science," *Perspectives on Politics* 1, no. 4 (2003): 695–706.
10. As discussed in the Introduction, more recent work in this vein on institutional change does little to address the analytical limitations deriving from a relatively formal conception of institutions and a materialist understanding of interests. For examples, see Wolfgang Streeck and Kathleen Thelen, eds., *Beyond Continuity: Institutional Change in Advanced Political Economies* (Oxford: Oxford University Press, 2005); and Kathleen Thelen, *How Institutions Evolve: The Political Economy of Skills in Germany, Britain, the United States, and Japan* (Cambridge: Cambridge University Press, 2004).
11. As Blyth argues, "economic ideas provide agents with an interpretive framework" that "allow[s] agents to . . . propose a particular solution to a moment of crisis." Blyth, *Great Transformations: Economic Ideas and Institutional Change in the Twentieth Century* (New York: Cambridge University Press, 2002), 10, n. 20; 11.
12. For the classic analysis of the dismantling of French dirigisme and France's search for a post-dirigiste identity, see Jonah D. Levy, *Tocqueville's Revenge: State, Society, and Economy in Contemporary France* (Cambridge, MA: Harvard University Press, 1999).
13. The notion of the postwar German "semi-sovereign state" is Peter Katzenstein's, from his *Policy and Politics in West Germany: The Growth of a Semisovereign State* (Philadelphia: Temple University Press, 1987).
14. The more recent incarnation of this scholarly tradition in the influential Varieties of Capitalism literature emphasizes the stability of distinctive types of coordination among firms as the source of capitalist diversity. This paradigmatic assumption of policy and institutional stability both neglects the state's role in shaping trajectories of adjustment and undermines the approach's ability to explain departures from past policy practice or shifting elite conceptions of economic crises and appropriate responses to them. While such approaches can explain elements of the liberal trajectories, therefore, none can successfully explain the distinctive national syntheses of policy form, content, and scope analyzed here.
15. The classic in this scholarly vein is Suzanne Berger, ed., *Organizing Interests in Western Europe: Pluralism, Corporatism, and the Transformation of Politics* (Cambridge: Cambridge University Press, 1981).
16. For seminal descriptions of postwar German neocorporatism, see Andrei S. Markovits, *The Political Economy of West Germany*: Modell Deutschland (New York: Praeger, 1982); Katzenstein, *Policy and Politics*; and Kathleen Thelen, *Union of Parts: Labor Politics in Postwar Germany* (Ithaca, NY: Cornell University Press, 1991).

17. In addition to the foundational neoinstitutionalist scholarship of Shonfield and his intellectual heirs, the dynamics of France's labor-exclusionary model are admirably analyzed in Chris Howell, *Regulating Labor: The State and Industrial Relations Reform in Postwar France* (Princeton, NJ: Princeton University Press, 1992); and Anthony Daley, *Steel, State, and Labor: Mobilization and Adjustment in France* (Pittsburgh: University of Pittsburgh Press, 1996).
18. Nor can an emphasis on partisanship do so. Such an approach would be unable to explain the isomorphism of French labor-market reforms in the 1990s and 2000s under governments of the Left and the Right or Schröder's embrace of aggressive labor-market reforms that nonetheless sheltered key economic groups, to pick just a couple of examples.
19. For this reason, recent work on the transnational influence of neoliberalism enjoys limited analytical purchase over variations in policy outcomes in continental Europe. See, e.g., Mark Thatcher and Vivien Schmidt, eds., *Resilient Liberalism in Europe's Political Economy* (Cambridge: Cambridge University Press, 2013). For a treatment that is more sensitive to the variation of neoliberal ideas, see Philip G. Cerny, *Rethinking World Politics: A Theory of Transnational Neopluralism* (New York: Oxford University Press, 2010).
20. Rogers Smith, "Beyond Tocqueville, Myrdal, and Hartz: The Multiple Traditions in America," *American Political Science Review* 87, no. 3 (September 1993): 549–66.
21. Attention to the French liberal tradition thus suggests an alternative interpretation of the "dualization" of France's welfare state, involving a turn away from employment-based, contributory social insurance to universalistic, citizenship-based forms of social protection such as guaranteed income support and universal health insurance. For a description of this pattern, see Bruno Palier, "The Dualizations of the French Welfare System," in *A Long Goodbye to Bismarck? The Politics of Welfare Reforms in Continental Europe*, ed. Bruno Palier (Amsterdam: University of Amsterdam Press, 2010). See also Bruno Palier and Kathleen Thelen, "Institutionalizing Dualism: Complementarities and Change in France and Germany," *Politics & Society* 38, no. 1 (March 2010): 119–48.
22. Even the IMF, long the avatar of neoliberal orthodoxy and an enforcer of its precepts, has begun to question the wisdom of rigid adherence to its standard prescriptions. In a report published in May 2016 in its flagship magazine, the IMF acknowledged that both capital-account liberalization and economic austerity—central elements of standard neoliberal prescriptions—had both undermined economic growth and exacerbated economic inequality in many countries. For a discussion, see Shawn Donnan, "IMF Economists Put 'Neoliberalism' under the Spotlight," *Financial Times*, May 26, 2016, https://www.ft.com/content/4b98c052-238a-11e6-9d4d-c11776a5124d.
23. On the centrality of appeals to workers' sense of economic grievance to the political strategy of the French Front National, see Susan Dominus, "The National Front's Post–Charlie Hebdo Moment," *New York Times Magazine*, February 18, 2015, https://www.nytimes.com/2015/02/22/magazine/the-national-fronts-post-charlie-hebdo-moment.html.
24. For a succinct discussion of how financial globalization and the resultant fragmentation of vertically integrated companies have undermined successful manufacturing sectors, see Suzanne Berger, "How Finance Gutted Manufacturing," *Boston Review*, April 1, 2014, http://bostonreview.net/forum/suzanne-berger-how-finance-gutted-manufacturing.
25. Thomas Piketty, *Capital in the Twenty-First Century* (Cambridge, MA: Harvard University Press, 2014).
26. Despite the loss of the Front National's Marine Le Pen to centrist Emmanuel Macron in the second round of the French presidential election in May 2017, her ability to garner an unprecedented 33.9 percent of the vote reflects many voters' deep and unresolved sense of economic exclusion and political marginalization at the hands of an opaque and unresponsive elite, channeled in part through anti-immigrant animus. In keeping with the contours of statist liberalism, Macron's economic proposals (at the time of this writing) combine targeted cuts in public spending with expansions of income support; for example, extending eligibility for unemployment insurance to entrepreneurs and the self-employed. For detailed results of the election, see *Le Monde*, "Les résultats en graphes du second tour de l'élection présidentielle 2017," http://www.lemonde.fr/les-decodeurs/article/2017/05/07/les-resultats-du-second-tour-de-l-election-presidentielle-2017_5123789_4355770.html. For an overview

of Macron's economic-policy proposals, see Anne-Sylvaine Chassany, "Emmanuel Macron Proposes Nordic Economic Model for France," *Financial Times*, February 23, 2017, https://www.ft.com/content/3691a448-fa1d-11e6-9516-2d969e0d3b65.

27. Mark Blyth has recently argued that the rise of anti-systemic, populist movements of both Left and Right in Europe and the United States stem from a revolt of debtors against the creditors and financial elites that the post-1970s neoliberal economic regime made ascendant. See Blyth, "Global Trumpism: Why Trump's Victory Was 30 Years in the Making and Why It Won't Stop Here," *Foreign Affairs* online, November 2016, https://www.foreignaffairs.com/articles/2016-11-15/global-trumpism. For a dark recent analysis of the corrosive effects of stagnant wages, growing economic inequality, and the erosion of middle-class incomes on political democracy, see Edward Luce, *The Retreat of Western Liberalism* (London: Little, Brown, 2017).
28. See, e.g., Francis Fukuyama, *The End of History and the Last Man* (New York: Free Press, 1992).
29. For a compelling study of such tensions in the crucible of nineteenth-century American capitalism, see Charles Sellers, *The Market Revolution: Jacksonian America, 1815–1846* (Oxford: Oxford University Press, 1994).
30. In Chile, neoliberalism was intimately bound up with "a far-reaching programme of social transformation" that aimed to "obliterate" the fractious political factions and civil-society organizations that had led to social and political instability in the 1960s and early 1970s. Much as in Thatcher's Britain, though cast in a much darker hue, Chilean neoliberalism was inseparable from a campaign to disembed the economy from its social foundations. Marcus Taylor, *From Pinochet to the 'Third Way': Neoliberalism and Social Transformation in Chile* (London: Pluto Press, 2006), 7. For a discussion of the Singaporean case, see Garry Rodan, "Neo-liberalism and Transparency: Political versus Economic Liberalism," in *The Neo-Liberal Revolution: Forging the Market State*, ed. Richard Robson (Houndmills, UK: Palgrave Macmillan, 2006), 201–11.
31. In an incisive recent article, Mark Blyth and Matthias Matthijs argue convincingly that the increasingly fraught combination of economic neoliberalism and semi-authoritarian economic populism are symptomatic of the exhaustion of the neoliberal "macroeconomic regime" that has prevailed since the 1980s. See Blyth and Matthijs, "Black Swans, Lame Ducks, and the Mystery of IPE's Missing Macroeconomy," *Review of International Political Economy* 24, no. 2 (2017): 203–31.

INDEX

Tables are indicated by "t" following the page numbers.